Constructing Digital Cultures

Constructing Digital Cultures

Tweets, Trends, Race, and Gender

Judith E. Rosenbaum

LEXINGTON BOOKS
Lanham • Boulder • New York • London

Published by Lexington Books
An imprint of The Rowman & Littlefield Publishing Group, Inc.
4501 Forbes Boulevard, Suite 200, Lanham, Maryland 20706
www.rowman.com

Unit A, Whitacre Mews, 26-34 Stannary Street, London SE11 4AB

British Library Cataloguing in Publication Information Available

Library of Congress Cataloging-in-Publication Data Available

ISBN: 978-1-4985-4690-4 (cloth : alk. paper)
ISBN: 978-1-4985-4691-1 (electronic)

∞™ The paper used in this publication meets the minimum requirements of American National Standard for Information Sciences—Permanence of Paper for Printed Library Materials, ANSI/NISO Z39.48-1992.

Printed in the United States of America

Contents

Acknowledgments vii

1 Introduction 1

What We Tweet: Reconstructing Race and Gender in Entertainment

2 Constructing #Cookie: Analyzing Collaborative Interpretations of African American Femininity and Masculinity 27

3 #NotMiAbuela and Tuco Salamanca: Exploring Latinx Masculinity and Femininity 63

4 #AsianProblems: Constructing Cultural Understandings of Asian Americans 99

Tweeting with a Passion: Twitter, Politics, and Social Justice

5 From #PantSuitNation to #AllLivesMatter: Understanding User-Driven Social Media Movements 137

6 #MAGA, #ImWithHer, and #Snowflake: Politics and Twitter 173

Who Tells the Story: Analyzing Twitter Users

7 Is It #WorthSaying? Twitter, Marketing Campaigns, and Controlling the Narrative 211

8 I Tweet, You Tweet: Examining How Ethnic Minority Groups Use Social Media 249

Conclusion 277
Notes 295
References 297
Index 327
About the Author 335

Acknowledgments

This idea for this book grew out of a series of class discussions held during my time at Albany State University. Whenever my students and I talked about how the media portrayed certain events or people, but especially ethnic minorities, my students, most of whom were young African American adults, would often bring up the responses they had seen on Twitter. They talked about how some tweets added to their enjoyment of a show, others shaped their opinion, how conversations on Twitter made them feel included and empowered, and how Twitter gave them a voice. As an avid Twitter user myself, this piqued my interest. I started to take a closer look at how my students, and young African Americans in general, used Twitter to speak out. These class discussions and my ensuing observations led to the book that you have in your hands today. Without my students, this book may not have happened at all.

There are a number of other people whose assistance was instrumental to this project as well. I would be remiss to not mention them.

To all of my colleagues, both near and far, who encouraged me, gave me advice, helped me untangle some of the concepts and ideas described in this book, told me to get to work, brought me coffee, and kept me sane: Thank you.

Melissa Gosdin, Benjamin "Mr. Ben" Johnson, Scott Pierce, thank you for your friendship, support, practical advice, valuable feedback, and the well-timed sharing of funny news stories or videos. Without the three of you, I might have never gotten past chapter 1. Johanna Slot, thank you for your ideas and advice regarding chapter 7, they were very much appreciated. Thank you to those who reviewed (parts of) the manuscript, giving me much-needed feedback: Gwen Bouvier, Anedith Clark, Thuc-Nhi Nguyen, and Aydrea Walden.

I want to also thank all of my students at Albany State University. Your curiosity, tenacity, and critical attitude has truly been inspirational. To those students who gave feedback on some of my analyses, you are very much appreciated: Amber, Tiana, Imani, Darais, and Krista—thank you for bringing the material to life.

Thank you, Albany State University, for encouraging me to pursue my research interests and write the book.

Thanks also to the Department of Communication and Journalism at the University of Maine for the confidence in my abilities and the space and time to finish the final tweaks.

To the folks at Lexington Books; Nicolette, Jimmy, and Jessica who guided me through this project with a lot of encouragement and fielded all of my questions (and there were many): thank you.

My friends, Kelly, Wietse, Marije, Eva, and Andrea, I don't know where I would be without you. Without a smile, a working computer, coffee, socks, and a cover, most likely. Thank you for your love and support.

Dennis, you taught me to skin the cat my own way and then reminded me to write down that no cats were harmed during the writing of this book. Thank you for that and for so much more. And yes, I got the fish.

1

Introduction

It's tempting to wonder what would have happened had Twitter been around in 1973 when then President Richard Nixon uttered the now famous words, "I am not a crook." Would #IAmNotACrook have become a trending topic immediately, complete with memes and gifs drawn from popular culture? Would the Twitter response have fueled public discontent, leading to protests and petitions that would have forced the 37th president of the United States to resign in the weeks after the speech? Or would his remarks have gone unnoticed on Twitter until a year later, when Nixon resigned from office?

Obviously, events ran their course in 1973, and we will never know what the fallout from the Watergate scandal would have been like had Twitter been around. Today, however, Twitter and other social media platforms play an inexorable role in writing and recording history. Scholars may disagree on how much Twitter and other platforms influence politics, culture, and life in general, but the fact that Twitter has become the thermometer for the country's mood is undeniable. A quick glance at the list of trending topics will tell anyone, journalists and politicians alike, what the tweeting public is thinking. Political faux pas, unexpected developments in popular television shows, breaking news—nothing goes unnoticed in the Twittersphere, and Twitter has become an important platform for people to make sense of the world around them. More importantly, Twitter provides a space for people to broadcast their ideas, connect with others, and collaborate to negotiate cultural understandings. As such, Twitter has become a space to be reckoned with when considering current social, political, and cultural trends and changes.

This book aims to explore the (re)negotiation of cultural meanings on Twitter in more detail. In particular, it investigates how Twitter contributes to cultural constructions of race and gender by examining Twitter's content as well as the people using it. In doing so, *Constructing Digital Cultures* provides insight into the extent to which Twitter functions as a virtual public sphere as well as the digital cultures produced by that sphere. In a world where social media has become an inescapable part of many people's lives, especially among marginalized groups, understanding the role Twitter plays in the construction of meaning and subsequent cultural and social changes is paramount.

A growing body of research has started to examine this online meaning-making on Twitter and has looked into Twitter's potential as a virtual public sphere and a platform for the production of digital culture. This research (which will be discussed below and in later chapters) has focused on a variety of specific cases where Twitter has played a pivotal role in making sense of issues related to race and/or gender, including #BlackLivesMatter, femininst hashtags, advertising campaigns such as #RaceTogether, and Black Twitter. Scholars have also considered the role played by Twitter in politics and some of the recent social movements, such as Occupy Wall Street and the Arab Spring. The contributions this research has made to our understanding of Twitter as a space for (counter)cultural meaning making are invaluable, yet they are tailored to the individual cases under study. As a result, it has been difficult to make any generalized statements about how Twitter is used to (re)produce cultural understandings of race and gender and the type of digital culture that is produced on the platform. In addition, research into Twitter tends to be divided into two camps. While some investigations are of a very celebratory nature, heralding all forms of Web 2.0 as a new era of participation and collaboration, other research is much more skeptical, discarding any ideas about social media use as an agent of change as technological determinism. This book aims to tie these diverse approaches and exploratory investigations together by providing a comprehensive view of how people use Twitter to create shared understandings of gender and race across a wide variety of topics.

In this chapter, I start by explaining the book's focus on Twitter. I explain how this social media platform is different from other social networking sites currently in use, and warrants research. Next, I discuss extant research on collaborative meaning making on Twitter. This discussion includes a consideration of the different dimensions of Twitter's potential as a virtual public sphere and/or a counterpublic identified in previous research. Finally, I provide a more detailed discussion of the purpose of the research presented in the book, outline the layout of the coming chapters, and discuss the methodology.

SOCIAL MEDIA: A USER-DRIVEN REVOLUTION

It is hard to imagine a world without social media, yet the oldest and most popular social media platform still in use today, Facebook, is only thirteen years old. Although it is still the undefeated champion at the time of publication, many social networking sites have since joined the social media giant: Twitter, Instagram, Snapchat, Pinterest, and LinkedIn are some examples, and these will have undoubtedly been joined by several other ones by the time you read this chapter. To claim that social media platforms are popular among people from all backgrounds and ages does not begin to cover the extent to which social media have become woven into the fabric of daily life. Research puts the number of American adults who regularly use social media platforms as high as 68 percent (Greenwood, Perrin, & Duggan, 2016), and the uses that people have for social media far extend the uses that have been commonly attributed to the traditional media (TV, radio, film) to include socialization, surveillance, self-promotion, and identity formation (e.g., Whiting & Williams, 2013).

While most social media platforms have been at the center of investigations into how users experience and make sense of the world around them, this book focuses specifically on Twitter. Founded in 2006, Twitter has approximately 313 million active monthly users and has gained ground as one of the most popular social media platforms (Milestones, 2016; Twitter, 2016). While Twitter was initially seen as a space where users could share their everyday, mundane experiences, it quickly grew into a medium people use to find and share newsworthy information, express their thoughts and feelings, and connect with others to debate everything from the latest sporting event to social issues, politics, and the most recent episode of their favorite show. Twitter has been described as "event driven" (Murthy, 2012, p. 1064). Expressions and conversations on the platform are organized around ongoing events, and as such the platform can be seen as more democratic than other social media, as it allows regular individuals and major corporations to interact side by side and contribute to the narratives used to describe ongoing events (see also Rogers, 2014). Recognizing the importance of Twitter in people's daily lives, major corporations, news organizations, and politicians have also taken to Twitter in record numbers to gather information, win public approval, and gain consumers (e.g., Lee, Hutton, & Shu, 2015; Loader, Vromen, & Xenos, 2016). More than any other social media platform in use today, Twitter is characterized by multilayered connectivity and extensive opportunities for participation, rendering it a particularly interesting site for the study of the construction of meaning and the creation of digital cultures.

Connectivity on Twitter

One important factor to consider is connectivity. Twitter is fairly unique in the world of social media as it allows people to connect on three different levels: a community-wide or macrolevel, through personal networks, i.e., a mesolevel, and on a micro-, or interpersonal level (Bruns & Moe, 2014).

The hashtag (#) has become Twitter's most famous technological affordance and is solely responsible for the macro level connections created on the platform. Copied by other social networking sites, the hashtag has become an integral part of social networking life. Marking one's tweets using a hashtag allows users to provide a semiotic frame for their tweets, i.e., to specify the meaning they want others to attach to their tweet, and it lets people connect their posts to others. Looking at the trending topics on Twitter, this is one of Twitter's most defining and successful technological affordances. Twitter users will "jump in" on trending topics with great enthusiasm, sharing ideas and responding to others using the same hashtag. Subsequently, people create ad hoc communities surrounding specific topics or networked publics (Boyd, 2011), i.e., online communities where people connect, deliberate, and construct meaning. Using a hashtag thus means active participation in the building of a community and the subsequent creation of social capital. These communities can reach well outside of someone's network of followers and evolve as the discussion grows and changes, leaving Twitter users with the feeling that they are actively involved with a real-life community (e.g., Brown, Hendrickson, & Littau, 2014; Bruns & Burgess, 2012; Bruns & Moe, 2014).

Unlike other social media, Twitter also allows for the creation of unilateral relationships, where following someone does not require reciprocity. On Twitter, an individual can follow anyone without their permission, providing they have a public account, allowing each Twitter user to create their "own" Twitter timeline filled with tweets from people they are interested in but don't necessarily know in real life. Twitter users can choose to connect outside their normal social circle and form communities around shared interests, as opposed to shared backgrounds. The meso-connections created as a result of this technological affordance can thus be more diverse than one's normal social circle and include people from a wide variety of cultural backgrounds (e.g., Acosta, 2014; Halavais, 2014).

Connectivity on Twitter is further facilitated through the use of "@" symbol, which enables users to address specific people, even those outside their network of followers. This particular affordance was adopted by Twitter users to create a more interpersonal, or microlevel, method of communication (Halavais, 2014). While the use of the @ symbol allows Twitter users to directly address one another, the tweets are still visible to all users. This means that a one-on-one conversation can easily turn into a multiuser discussion, moving a microlevel discussion to a meso- or even macrolevel. The possibility of retweeting adds another layer of connectivity as it allows for one-on-one conversations to move across communities, again expanding people's reach (Bruns & Burgess, 2012; Bruns & Moe, 2014; Bonilla & Rosa, 2015).

Twitter's ability to move conversations from the interpersonal to the public is one of the platform's defining features. Of all social media platforms, Twitter has best combined interpersonal with mass communication, by allowing for the broadcasting of ideas as well as personal interaction and collaboration (Honeycutt & Herring, 2009; Sharma, 2013). This collapse of the public with the private has led to the creation of personal publics, a space where people can share personal ideas in a very conversational manner with highly public audiences (Schmidt, 2014). The context collapse that characterizes social media is thus especially pronounced on Twitter where users perform before an audience that is a combination of all of their social networks, one that can be both very personal as well as very public (Marwick & Boyd, 2011a). In addition, the medium is unmoderated, the default profile option is public, and the majority of Twitter users have a public account, suggesting that people's voices can be heard far beyond their personal networks (Brickner, 2016; Zimmer & Proferes, 2014). Even if a user has a private account, it is possible for their tweets to become public if other users share the content of their tweet with their followers. In other words, what anyone says on Twitter could technically be seen by everyone online. At the same time, people can and do experience connections made on Twitter as intimate (Lin, Levordashka, & Utz, 2016), implying that people potentially reveal more than they would were they aware of the number of strangers who could be reading their tweets. This means that people whose voices would normally not reach outside their circle of friends and family are now able, intentionally and by accident, to contribute to discussions in a much wider arena (e.g., Halavais, 2014; Harrington, Highfield, & Bruns, 2013).

Twitter and User Participation

In addition to providing new ways of connecting, Twitter also provides its users with extended opportunities for engagement and participation in culture and politics (Cummings & Gotshall, 2014). Twitter's technological affordances allow users to actively engage in the creation of interpretations and meaning.

Twitter has structurally altered our understanding of audience participation. Media users have always been able to negotiate their understanding of a media text and interpret content to suit their needs. But until the past few decades, these interpretations never made it outside the physical boundaries of the user's own social circle. Social media platforms, and Twitter in particular, provide an excellent opportunity for television users to "talk back" to their television sets on a public platform that broadcasts their responses among a much wider audience. Not only that, but Twitter provides users with the ability to connect with others, creating a shared viewing experience (Harrington, et al., 2013; Gallardo-Camacho, Lavín, & Fernández-Garcia, 2016). Twitter thus affords strangers the opportunity to connect over a shared experience, and they have been doing just that in record-breaking numbers. Television users commonly use Twitter as a "second screen," and this ability has increased engagement among television users, especially among ethnic minority groups and younger viewers (Nielsen, 2013, 2014). Television producers have become aware of this trend and capitalize on it, using strategies such as promoting hashtags for specific shows or televised events in the hopes of increasing viewer engagement (Gallardo-Camacho, et al., 2016). Some television shows have actors live-tweet with fans during the broadcasting of an episode (e.g., *Black-ish, Fresh Off the Boat*), encouraging the use of the platform as a second screen and increasing audience involvement with a media text.

Due to the platform's fast-paced nature, many people now turn to Twitter for breaking events and developing stories, as well as real-time insight into those ideas that currently dominate public consciousness (Lin, Keegan, Margolin, & Lazer, 2014; Sharma, 2013). As a result, many use Twitter as a way to gather information outside of traditional media sources such as radio and television, circumventing these sources' interpretations of events. While this poses the risk of people accepting unverified, and possibly incorrect, information as fact, it does allow individuals to bypass the hegemonic frames often adopted by the mainstream media. In addition to gathering information, Twitter affords users the ability to critically discuss ongoing events, challenge others' interpretations (Lin, et al., 2014), and create their own frames for understanding (e.g., Burch, Frederick, & Pegoraro, 2015). Research has shown that the interpretations created by Twitter users can run counter to the ideas that dominate mainstream media and can shape how other Twitter users and even the mainstream media make sense of that event (cf. Conway, Kenski, & Wang, 2013, Hamdy & Gomaa, 2012). For the first time in the history of the mass media, the broadcasting abilities usually only afforded to the mainstream media have been extended to those individual voices active on social media platforms (see also Tufekci, 2017). While major corporations, celebrities, and other public figures are still more likely to influence discourse on Twitter than individual users, the latter do have the opportunity to interact and express themselves in the same public space, potentially contributing to the public discourse surrounding current events.

In other words, while all social networking sites allow for the quick and easy (re)production of meaning (Lewis, Pea, & Rosen, 2010), it would appear that Twitter, with its speed and user base that is connected on more than one level, is the ideal space for such activities. As such, Twitter users are generally seen as able to more actively participate in public life (Cummings & Gottshall, 2014) and have unprecedented abilities to create cultural and social changes (Cross, 2011).

TWITTER: A PLATFORM WITH DEMOCRATIZING POTENTIAL

The rise of user-driven social media sites has led to an ongoing debate about the power of these online spaces to provide users with a platform where they can be heard across communities and play an active role in the creation of public opinion and digital culture. In other words, the birth of Web 2.0 has led to a revitalization of the debate surrounding the conceptualization of the public sphere and its political and cultural impact. In considering how people use Twitter to express and negotiate their understanding of issues relevant to society at large, this book will join this debate and address the feasibility of a virtual public sphere and the subsequent production of a more inclusive digital culture. In effect, I will consider whether Twitter forms what Dahlgren (2013, p. 3) dubbed an "alternative democracy" where people connect and deliberate to construct meanings and create culture, or if Twitter is a virtual public space where parallel publics may resist hegemonic narratives, but never interact to maintain and strengthen democracy, thus falling short of becoming a true virtual public sphere (Papacharissi, 2002, 2010).

When Habermas first coined his ideas about the public sphere, he viewed it as an inclusive, public space where rational, reflexive debate between equal participants helped form the public opinion that guided democracy (cf. Dahlberg, 2001, 2007; cf. Habermas, 1989; 2006). In order for the Habermasian public sphere to function, it needs to include a diverse set of voices that help create shared understandings that reflect all of society (e.g., P. Shaw, 2014). Until recently, the mass media controlled the communicative aspect of the public sphere and thus public meaning making and the subsequent culture formation (Gere, 2008). As widely documented, the media have failed in providing diverse and equal representation, creating a public sphere that is exclusive and nonrepresentative. Groups that were excluded from the traditional public sphere formed subaltern counterpublics where they could connect and create counterhegemonic discourses (e.g., Fraser, 1992; Papacharissi, 2002, 2009). These counterpublics, however, were never part of the mainstream public sphere, their contributions to society hard-won and usually incidental.

With the arrival of the Internet, and especially with the birth of Web 2.0, the belief in a virtual public sphere that is truly democratic and all-inclusive grew exponentially (cf. Papacharissi, 2002). Scholars argue that now individuals can produce and disseminate their own information almost as quickly and as widely as the mainstream media, gaining the visibility and voice usually reserved for the major culture industries (Castells, 2015; Dahlgren, 2013). Social media in general, and Twitter in particular, are especially popular among marginalized groups and minority Internet users (Acosta, 2014; Brown, et al., 2014; Duggan, Ellison, Lampe, Lenhart, & Madden, 2015; Nielsen, 2015a). These platforms thus afford a voice to populations that often go unheard, creating the potential for a more inclusive virtual public sphere (cf. Tufekci, 2017).

Many scholars have heralded this inclusion as a sign that social media platforms in particular, but especially Twitter, are the ideal public spaces for the formation of a virtual public sphere. Twitter allows for personalized, oppositional, user-driven creation of cultural understandings (e.g., Eriksson, 2016; Hoskins, 2013) and is the perfect platform for subaltern counterpublics to form and grow (e.g., Jackson & Foucault Welles, 2015), providing one public space that could connect all segments of society. This enthusiasm about social media, however, is not without its detractors, and the debate surrounding social's media potential to democratize society focuses on the levels of interactivity, the shift in control over meaning-making processes, and the space for cultural citizenship. These three ideas form the foundation for the questions that drive the research conducted in this book, and will be discussed in more detail next.

Interactivity and the Construction of Meaning

Twitter's ability to afford users connectivity and interaction with people outside their normal social circle, including authorities, is an important factor in the consideration of Twitter as a virtual public sphere. Implicit in Habermas's conceptualization of the public sphere is the notion that it is accessible to all, allowing interactions between actors from all walks of life and levels of political involvement. While most scholars agree that universal accessibility of the public sphere as well as the Internet are both a long way off, they do actively debate the level of interactivity afforded to and used by those people who are active on platforms such as Twitter.

Some researchers, who have been labeled as techno-optimists (e.g., Fuchs, 2012), argue that even though social media are owned by large corporations, they lack official gatekeepers, thus allowing for more inclusive participation, the creation of a wider understanding of social issues, as well as the formation of countercultural opinions (e.g., Bessant, 2014; Brickner, 2016; Hoskins, 2013). In addition, the argument goes, social media allow individuals to interact with people in power directly. Before the arrival of Web 2.0, direct interaction between politicians and individuals was difficult if not impossible, and often mediated by Dahlgren's (2013) second tier of public sphere, the mainstream media. Today, these scholars argue, individual citizens can directly engage with their elected representatives through Twitter. However, research findings temper this enthusiasm, for even though many Twitter users communicate with (or rather at) politicians on a daily basis, politicians themselves rarely use Twitter to engage in conversation, instead relying on the platform to broadcast their ideas, as one would on television or the radio (e.g., Parmalee & Bichard, 2011; Small, 2014; Zamora Medina & Zurutuza Munõz, 2014).

According to the techno-optimist approach, social media have also made it easier for individuals to collaborate; people produce and make sense of cultural productions online and these interactions have the potential to help them create a shared sense of understanding (Balance, 2012; Guo & Lee, 2013; Mazali, 2011). In fact, social media in general have facilitated the interactive and collaborative activities that, before the arrival of Web 2.0, characterized only fan communities that had to put a lot of effort into interacting and collaborating with other fans. Nowadays, the act of turning "static content into a participatory activity" (Coppa, 2014, p. 85), a staple of fan communities, is available to all social media users who can use existing popular cultural expressions and alter them to meet their own needs. This collaboration has led to the creation of "knowledge communities" (Jenkins, 2006, p. 27) where people connect to discuss mainstream media productions, sharing ideas and knowledge about a show or movie, creating a fan-based culture that could potentially alter the dominant culture supported by mainstream media productions (cf. Evans, 2014).

The extent to which Twitter and other social media have been used to build the kinds of communities needed to create alternative interpretations has been questioned, though. Rossi and Giglietto's (2016) study did not show any sort of community among Twitter users who were live-tweeting about a television show, and instead found that behavior on Twitter involved low reciprocity, with users interacting a lot less than what one would expect. When looking at the actual content of the tweets, Rossi and Giglietto realized that many of them were no different from the "Hey, did you see that?" comments that often occur in shared viewing situations, and users did not seem to be looking for actual interaction. Lewis et al. (2010) agreed and posited that the level of collaboration between users and subsequently the level of collective meaning making is highly overrated: Most social media platforms are focused on unidirectional expressions or comments and are not geared toward the back and forth required for true collaboration. During major events, it is in fact quite common for social media users to turn to well-known reporters, politicians, or other authorities for information, instead of turning to other users (see also Lin, et al., 2014). Not in the least, social media users' tendency toward "self-promotion and meaningless disembodied interaction" (Gere, 2008, p. 221) means that any dialogue that does take place may not contribute to the creation of a participatory culture at all. If online discussions do involve some back and forth, there are often few if any attempts to bridge divides. Instead, participants appear to dig in their heels and engage in "negative identification" (Al-Tahmazi, 2015, p. 177), whereby they create clear and impenetrable boundaries between their own group and what they perceive to be "the other."

Twitter's technological affordances (i.e., the retweet and the hashtag) have been heralded as an important factor in the platform's potential to serve as a virtual public sphere as well. These functions facilitate conversations, creating the "interactive social agents" (Carney, 2016, p. 183) that are required for a well-functioning public sphere. These functions not only allow like-minded people to connect, they have also turned the platform into a site of discursive struggle. Different groups take to Twitter to combat what they perceive as incorrect perceptions about their group by using the platform to rewrite their story, as was the case with hashtags like #IfTheyGunnedMeDown or #Deplorables. Sometimes, these stories clash, as shown by studies into #BlackLivesMatter and #Ferguson. These investigations revealed how Twitter can become a space for people to contest dominant interpretations and share these ideas with audiences composed of supporters and detractors (e.g., Carney, 2016; Chaudhry, 2016). In other words, in the eyes of these scholars, the media user has transformed from a mere consumer of popular culture to an active player in the virtual public sphere who participates in the creation and dissemination of digital culture.

Techno-skeptics, however, have questioned the extent to which social media are actually used for democracy-building conversations. Among the detractors of the power of Twitter is Gerbaudo (2012), who argues that when it comes to social movements, Twitter merely facilitates the communication between people with shared ideas that would have taken place without the platform too. Some researchers have affirmed his belief and shown that people, in online spaces as in real life, tend to associate mainly with people who share their political ideas (e.g., Conway, et al., 2013; Farrell, 2012; Parmalee & Bichard, 2011). This implies that most people's social media sites become an echo chamber, i.e., a space where they are only confronted with variations of their own opinion (Colleoni, Rozza, & Arvidsson, 2014). While the internet in general, and social media in particular do allow for the creation of counterpublics where marginalized groups can connect and create a common identity, this fragmentation implies that there is little inter-group dialogue, preventing the cross-political, critical debate that characterizes the public sphere (Papacharissi, 2002, 2010).

Several studies into political discussions on social media also call into the question the nature of the interactions on social media platforms, arguing that reciprocity is the exception instead of the rule (cf. Morozov, 2013). Social media users often make statements addressing a person or a group and then leave the discussion, never to engage with the other again (e.g., Bouvier, 2015). Numerous investigations into, among other things, social media responses to a Greek TV panel, Facebook discussions about Iraqi politics, and YouTube comments left for Turkish anti-government pop videos that showed that online conversations are often far from the interactive, constructive discussion that techno-optimists describe (Al-Tahmazi, 2015; Georgakopoulou, 2014; Lindgren, 2011; Poell, 2009; Way, 2015). Often, these studies show, online discussions are dominated by a few voices, and the interaction is far for democratic or constructive, serving instead as a space for people to express their opinions without looking to engage with others (Georgakopoulou, 2014; Papacharissi, 2002; Lindgren, 2011; Way, 2015). As Bouvier (2015) explains, online spaces do not encourage constructive interactions, with the majority of participants lurking, and many of those who do actively engage do so in a combative, inflammatory manner characterized by personal attacks (see also Georgakopoulou, 2014; Lindgren, 2011).

However, the fact that online discussions are often characterized by heated, profanity-laden, provocative statements does not necessarily have to be viewed as evidence that these spaces do not function as an extension of or an alternative to the public sphere. First of all, when assessing political discourse as "useful" or "not useful," it is tempting to see any discussion that does not reflect the style of debate and argumentation used by the political elite as not constructive or contributing to democracy. But, as Poell (2009) points out, this style of interaction is foreign to many of the groups excluded from the mainstream political discussion. So, the inflammatory, combative dialogue often seen on social media could in fact be interpreted as a way for people who are usually not part of the political arena to contribute. Second, the argument has been made that the Habermasian ideal dialogue, one that is rational, calm, and geared toward increasing mutual understanding does not adequately capture how political discussion are carried out today. Mouffe (1999) posits that contemporary democracy is characterized by agonistic dialogue, i.e., interactions that are passionate and argumentative. She reasons that this kind of discussion may not be the interaction that Habermas had in mind, but that it is in fact useful and helpful in supporting democracy. However, not all heated debates qualify as constructive; antagonistic dialogue, whereby participants are out to destroy their opponents, does not contribute to democracy. In other words, while not all heated, combative interactions are constructive, some can be. This will be further explored in chapter 6.

Online dialogue can also be thwarted by the presence of major corporations. Jenkins (2006) points out that while digital culture centers on the interaction between individuals, media corporations are players in these conversations too, and they have much more power at their disposal to ensure that their ideas are heard by as many people as possible. Virality, a term often invoked to showcase the democratizing potential of social media, has been argued to be the result of PR efforts and corporate interference more than it is the outcome of regular individuals spreading a message (Morozov, 2013). When it comes to Twitter, Dean (2010) questions whether the sentiments made visible on this platform are truly a reflection of a wider public or merely reflect a few "super users and a bunch of automated zombies" (p. 98). Even without the influence of corporate power, however, research has shown that after a while, discussions on social media sites begin to circle back to the same ideas and perspectives, marginalizing opinions that were voiced earlier in the conversation (Georgakopoulou, 2014; Poell, 2009). It would appear, thus, that while social media in general, and Twitter in particular, offer a platform for those members of society who are active online to equally participate in political debates, the main players of those debates don't necessarily use the space to its fullest potential.

Part of the analysis presented in this book thus considers the level of interactivity between users. I will, among other things, look at the extent to which users interact when constructing their interpretations of current events and popular culture, with whom they interact if they do, and what these interactions look like.

Power and Social Media

The concept of influence, or power, is central to any discussion surrounding the notion of the public sphere. Power in this case refers to who creates the dominant culture, i.e., who controls the process of meaning making (Castells, 2015). Until recently, this power was mainly in the hands of the mainstream media, whose discourses often reflect visions and narratives that reproduce existing power structures (e.g., Dahlberg, 2005, 2007; Dahlgren, 2013; Tufekci, 2017). The mainstream media tend to marginalize or even censor voices that do not reflect this ideology, and the voices that are heard generally engage in superficial, ineffective dialogue, effectively rendering it a "pseudo public sphere" (McGuigan, 2005, p. 429). While, as mentioned above, in the past individuals were able to engage in the production of participatory culture through counterpublics, the power these groups had over the production of meaning was limited to their own physical sphere of influence. As a result, the circulation of these ideas was often a cumbersome and lengthy process. With the advent of social media, this seems to have changed, and scholars have begun to examine and debate the potential of these platforms to afford users the ability to construct and broadcast personalized understandings of mainstream culture.

Techno-optimists have pointed to social media as affording people the ability to create their own cultural understandings, using elements from hegemonic as well as their own vernacular discourses, and circulate them across communities (Cloete, 2015; Eriksson, 2016; Gere, 2008; Guo & Lee, 2013; Mazali, 2011). Twitter especially, with its collapse of the public with the private, is seen as a platform that allows users to render the private public, create personal publics, and broadcast their personal ideas to a global audience with the click of a button (Schmidt, 2014). Subsequently, Twitter expands who and what can influence culture, taking the town hall discussions and middle school performances out to the world. Discussions between friends or neighbors can now take place in a public forum where others can follow or join in, and where ideas and creations can easily transfer from a small, private audience, to a large, society-wide network. Moreover, thanks to Twitter, the physical boundaries between communities have dissipated. Individuals can connect with other people without having to go through traditional cultural and political institutions. These connections can be based on needs or interests, not location, and allow for collaboration on meaning making and sharing of ideas across society (Cloete, 2015; Iosifidis & Wheeler, 2015).

However, the idea of social media granting everyone equal opportunities to contribute to meaning making, subsequently creating an inclusive and egalitarian public space, is not without its detractors. One of the concerns centers on the issue of the digital divide. While in the past, the digital divide was mainly associated with access inequalities, contemporary researchers are more concerned about the "second-level digital divide," i.e., the fact that even in societies where most people have access to the Internet, not everyone knows how to use digital technologies to their fullest potential (Hargittai, 2002). This divide, which is commonly associated with socioeconomic status, education level, and age, refers to people only using digital technologies for entertainment as opposed to information seeking, and shying away from the active creation of digital content (e.g.,

Schradie, 2011; Van Deursen & Van Dijk, 2014; Wei & Hindman, 2011). This means that participation in the virtual sphere created by social media platforms is potentially reduced to the same middle-class voices that are most visible in mainstream media.

Questions have also been raised about the influence of corporate ownership of social media sites, with scholars such as Fuchs (2014) arguing that social media's public sphere potential is undermined by the fact that social media are owned and controlled by for-profit corporations with their own agenda. These companies reinforce the same hegemonic views presented in the mainstream media and generally approach users as consumers, not citizens, reducing critical dialogue and the subsequent participatory culture, to conversations that support consumerist capitalism (cf. Dahlberg, 2005, 2007). The same technological affordances that give people a voice also render some voices louder than others, especially those owned by powerful corporations or individuals (through the use of bots, for instance) (Lin et al., 2014; Loader & Mercea, 2011). In other words, the technologies that are used to publicize these previously unheard voices also play an important role in determining how much each voice is heard and the impact they have on the culture created (Langlois, 2011).

Concerns about access and corporate influence aside, social media such as YouTube and Twitter have been heralded as providing marginalized groups with unique opportunities to renegotiate their ethnic identity and place in society with a wider audience (e.g., Balance, 2012; Nakamura, 2008). Groups that are generally ignored or sidelined by the mainstream media are afforded a space to connect and share experiences, creating their own stories without the moderating influence of the official gatekeepers associated with major media corporations (e.g., F. Shaw, 2012). Twitter and other platforms are seen as the ideal spaces for the creation of counternarratives, especially for marginalized groups, turning the subaltern counterpublics that were previously restricted to small, localized groups into networked counterpublics that can span across the globe (e.g., Eriksson, 2016; Fraser, 1992; Keller, 2012). An excellent example of a networked subaltern counterpublic is "Black Twitter," the space created by African Americans to connect and discuss issues relevant to the Black community and create shared cultural understandings that are not part of mainstream discourses (e.g., Brock, 2012; Florini, 2014; see chapter 2 for a more in-depth discussion).

Twitter's potential to serve as a subaltern counterpublic moves beyond Black Twitter though. A 2015 investigation by Bonilla and Rosa into the use of Twitter during and after the Michael Brown shooting in Ferguson showed that Twitter gives users the space to "collectively construct counternarratives" (p. 6). Similar results were reported for studies that looked into domestic violence, police brutality, Twitter user responses to documentaries on colorism, and protests against misogynist media content. Here, too, people used Twitter to express their rejection of mainstream interpretations of these issues and construct alternate understandings (e.g., Freelon, McIlwain, & Clark, 2016; Dragiewicz & Burgess, 2016; Horeck, 2014; Huntemann, 2015; Jackson & Foucault Welles, 2015; Maragh, 2016). This means that groups that have traditionally been under- or misrepresented in the mainstream media now have a space where their voices can be mobilized en masse. A space where they, along with everyone else, can actively participate in the creation of public opinion and cultural understandings that are more inclusive, more democratic, and better reflect society (Creeber & Martin, 2009; Jenkins, 2006; Reed, 2014; Shifman, 2014).

The idea of active and critical citizens taking to Twitter or other social media to voice their opinion has been questioned, however. While research discussed above shows that people use Twitter to counter dominant narratives, investigations have also demonstrated that in many cases, only a few of the people active online pursue serious conversations. Most people participate in Web 2.0 for entertainment purposes, eschewing anything too serious (e.g., Papacharissi, 2002; Poell, 2009). Dean (2010) in fact makes the argument that social media move so quickly, people don't have to commit to any one position or idea, and that even though these online discourses might be critical or skeptical, the participants, in an effort to stay entertained, will jump from topic to topic, issue to issue, ensuring that no real change ever comes from their online behavior.

Extant research has also cast doubts on whether social media users truly create counternarratives that reflect their cultural identity and political position. While Web 2.0 may offer previously unseen levels of participation and interaction, the digital cultures that are produced and sustained by this user engagement have not really challenged the "continued dominance of the main cultural industries" (Reed, 2014, p. 44), instead reproducing the white, patriarchal discourse that still dominates much of the conversation in these platforms (see also Iosifidis & Wheeler, 2015). Several investigations into the nature of videos created by ethnic minorities and posted on YouTube underscored his belief. These studies found that many of these videos contained racial stereotypes, showing that user-generated does not necessarily equal oppositional. So, while YouTube does give ordinary media users a space to be heard, their voices replicate rather than challenge existing racial beliefs (Balance, 2012; Guo & Harlow, 2014; Guo & Lee, 2013). Ironically, the people who use platforms like YouTube and Twitter to create their own cultural productions often do so in the hopes of getting picked up by a record label or production company. Their aim is for their productions to go viral, which can only be achieved by touching on common ground with as many audiences as possible (Balance, 2012). This, coupled with an unawareness of the stereotypes they reproduce, may go some way toward explaining the lack of resistance to hegemonic interpretations in their productions. In fact, investigations into the nature of online discussions in the comments section of YouTube videos, on public forums, and on Facebook show that these often re-create a populist or even an extremist discourse, one that centers on proving one's patriotism and nationalism, and are a far cry from resisting hegemonic discourses (Poell, 2009; Way, 2015).

Studies into Twitter cast similar aspersions on the narratives to come out of this platform. Cisneros and Nakayam's 2015 investigation into Twitter's response to the crowning of an Indian American woman as Miss America showed that many of the tweets reflected outright racism. The tweets that attempted to counter this racism did so utilizing a color-blind ideology, which embodies ideas that are equally racist, albeit less directly. A study into Twitter discussions about the police shooting of Michael Brown in Ferguson in 2014 showed that even though the platform provided African Americans with the space to express their views on the case and reflect on the structural racism that caused it, Twitter also provided room for racist discourses to challenge these ideas (Chaudhry, 2016). In other words, while Twitter does allow for occasional "democratic moments" (Cummings & Gottshall, 2014, p. 621), it could equally merely amplify existing public discourse about events and people. In that sense, while Twitter encourages citizen participation, it is equally capable of simply promoting the status quo and echoing dominant narratives.

To provide insight into these opposing claims, I consider the different discourses that characterize people's meaning making, as well as assess the extent to which these discourses reflect or counter dominant cultural ideas.

Cultural Citizenship and Twitter

A final theme to consider is the kind of deliberation that constitutes the public sphere. Habermas originally envisioned the public sphere as centering on political dialogue. Some scholars have taken his beliefs, looked at young people's discussions on social media about the latest iteration of *Real Housewives* or *Scandal*, and concluded that social media do little to promote the kinds of discussions relevant to the public sphere. Discarding these kinds of conversations as politically irrelevant however, ignores the contemporary reality of political dialogue (e.g., Harris, 2008). The phrase "cultural citizenship" is often used to describe how arenas other than the political are also relevant to people's formations of political opinion. Popular culture and everyday life are often used to address social issues and construct political opinion, especially by marginalized groups. Any domain where people consider their place in society is part of a larger political dialogue, warranting an extension of how we understand the public sphere (Burgess, Foth, & Klaebe, 2006; Hermes & Stello, 2000; McGuigan, 2005; Papacharissi, 2010).

Social media have become a prime location for this kind of cultural citizenship. Because these platforms, as discussed above, collapse the distinction between private and public, they make it much easier to blend personal discussions with political opinions. The line that used to demarcate the distinction between serious, political debate, and discussions about one's favorite movie or most inspiring quote has faded away as people do both in the same space and can, within a single conversation or even a single tweet, touch on both personal and political issues (e.g., Loader, et al., 2016; Murthy, 2012; Papacharissi, 2010). Platforms such as Twitter afford people the space to perform their cultural citizenship, whether it is by relating discussions on racism to *Black-ish* or jumping in on a trending topic about Hillary Clinton's "Just like your abuela" advertisement to discuss Latinx identity.[1] Political opinions are made visible though a much wider range of expressions as well, including the more playful modalities common to social media such as memes. Social media have thus facilitated people's tendency to mix the personal with the political, allowing "the spheres for democratic engagement" to include elements of individuals' private lives (Loader & Mercea, 2011, p. 761).

When considering dialogue outside of politics as part of the public sphere, however, one of the dangers is the encroachment of consumerist ideology. As mentioned above, social media are owned by for-profit corporations that could, in an effort to increase their bottom line, create situations whereby certain discourses are promoted over others (e.g., Dahlberg, 2005; Jenkins, 2006). Not only that, but corporations will use social media to advance their business, addressing social media users as consumers and encouraging those discourses that increase profits. A television show, for instance, will have its actors live-tweet during a show's broadcast not because they want to increase discussion about the social issues on their show, but because they want to increase viewership. The actors themselves have something to lose or gain, and will probably favor tweets (or other expressions) that help their show's popularity. The same applies to companies who design hashtags to promote a cause. Even though Dove's #BeautyBias campaign might be aimed at increasing women's self-esteem for example, the company is ultimately concerned about its bottom line and promoting expressions that support that. As such then, cultural citizenship has become infused with consumerist discourse, and consumption has been inexorably intertwined with civic activities (Papacharissi, 2010).

To understand how and if Twitter functions as a virtual public sphere, I thus also examine how people use popular culture to construct race and gender. Moreover, this book explores how people handle corporate interference on Twitter to see to what extent consumerist ideology shapes political deliberation.

CONSTRUCTING DIGITAL CULTURES: TWEETS, TRENDS, RACE, AND GENDER

In short, while Twitter could conceivably function as a more egalitarian, inclusive virtual public sphere, providing the space to create a more diverse digital culture, the jury is still out on whether the social media platform lives up to this potential. This book attempts to shed light on this issue by conducting an in-depth exploration of how people use Twitter to collaboratively (re)negotiate cultural beliefs, specifically those centered on race and gender.

Narratives surrounding race and gender are some of the most contested areas in contemporary culture. Mainstream media often create hegemonic presentations of issues related to race and gender, and with Twitter's popularity among marginalized groups as well as its unprecedented opportunities for connectivity and participation, it has become the ideal space to debate these issues. This is reflected in the many trending topics that center on race and gender (e.g., Carney, 2016; Rightler-McDaniels & Hendrickson, 2014; Thrift, 2014). As such, these hashtags make excellent case studies for examining the process of meaning making on this platform. Examining race and gender will reveal if and how users collaborate to create meaning, i.e., what their dialogue looks like, thus shedding light on whether and how Twitter functions as a virtual public sphere. Moreover, focusing on these two specific constructs provides insight into the nature of the digital culture produced by Twitter users and the extent to which it reflects or counters mainstream culture.

Popular Culture, Politics, and Users

This book has been divided into three sections, with each section addressing a different aspect of meaning making on Twitter.

The first section addresses how users collaborate to make sense of representations of race and gender in popular culture. As discussed above, cultural citizenship means that a considerable part of people's political opinions is formed through their dealings with the popular culture to come out of entertainment media. In recent years, the representation of African Americans, Latinx, and Asian Americans on television has increased, providing viewers with more opportunities to view and reflect on the nature of this representation. Twitter has become a prime location for people to discuss this portrayal. Research has shown that hashtags such as #Empire and #Scandal frequently dominate Twitter on the nights these shows are on television, while discussions about the Salamanca family from *Breaking Bad* as well as #FreshOffTheBoat have also attracted a fair amount of attention (e.g., Hautman, 2016; Jurgensen, 2014; King Collier, 2015; Lee, 2015). These three chapters examine how people make sense of this portrayal, whether they see it as perpetuating existing stereotypes or not, and how these interpretations figure into their understanding of African American, Latinx, or Asian American culture. Besides using Twitter to negotiate mediated constructions of race and gender, the popularity of hashtags such as #NotMiAbuela, #StarringJohnCho, and #AskRachel, indicates that people frequently use Twitter to debate the meaning and position of race and gender in American society as a whole. The three chapters in this section also address what this meaning making looks like on Twitter. Each chapter focuses on shows and trending topics that center on a specific ethnic minority. Chapter 2 looks at tweets about African American culture, chapter 3 analyzes expressions about Latinx culture, and chapter 4 examines how Twitter addresses aspects of Asian American culture. Analysis focuses on how these tweets negotiate shared understandings of ethnic and gender identity. In the analysis, I examine how the patterns that are distilled from the tweets reflect, renegotiate, or counter existing stereotypes and dominant discourses. This aims to shed light on the kinds of networked publics Twitter is used to create, as well as the nature of the digital culture produced by these publics.

In the second section, I explore how people use Twitter to make sense of political developments and social movements. In the past few years, Twitter has become a major political battleground, with politicians, activists, and ordinary citizens alike using the platform as a space for vigorous debate. The two chapters in this section take a closer look at this debate, in particular how political discussion and social justice movements use Twitter to negotiate race and gender. Chapter 5 looks at on online social movements and analyzes the discourse of those movements focused on race and gender. It investigates a select number of these movements, revealing how tweets negotiate the meaning of each movement and how these expressions make sense of dominant narratives about race and gender. The investigation examines the interaction between Twitter users and how this interaction contributes to the creation of networked publics and subaltern counterpublics. Chapter 6 explores how supporters and opponents of the presidential candidates during the 2016 election season utilized Twitter to negotiate the meanings attached to their platforms, with a specific focus on issues related to race and gender. This chapter examines if and how these negotiations reflect the deliberative dialogue that is deemed the foundation for a public sphere.

The third and final section of the book takes a closer look at the Twitter user. Chapter 7 looks at the interaction between consumers and large organizations. Using social media marketing campaigns to improve a company's profits has become second nature to most corporations. But social media platforms such as Twitter provide users with the opportunity to create their own interpretation of the corporate narrative. This chapter focuses on a select number of campaigns that incorporated either race or gender in their message and examine how users made sense of these campaigns and the constructs presented in the narrative. The analysis provides insight into who tells the story on Twitter when it comes to marketing companies: Do the corporations who start the campaigns run the narrative, or do users find and exploit spaces in the offered narratives to tell their own story, usurping the original message? Finally, chapter 8 sheds light on the users themselves. In this chapter, I present findings from focus groups, personal interviews, and surveys carried out among social media users from ethnic minority groups. This chapter explores how Twitter users from ethnic minority groups utilize the platform, and how they view the role that Twitter plays in their lives and in society at large.

Analyzing the Construction of Meaning

Constructing Digital Cultures explores how Twitter users collaboratively (re)construct existing beliefs about race and gender by examining Tweets and Twitter users' opinions using a qualitative methodology. Qualitative research is mainly interpretive in nature and focuses on exploring, describing, and understanding how meaning is created (Creswell, 2003; Finlay, 2011; Kohlbacher 2006; Lindoff, 1991). This project aims to understand how people use Twitter to reproduce, recreate, and counter dominant cultural understanding and is thus best served by a qualitative research method. Using this type of analysis also answers the call for a more in-depth, qualitative examination of Twitter content (Bruns & Burgess, 2011; Harrington, et al., 2013).

The research method used in this book can best be described as interpretive content analysis. The term "content analysis" is generally associated with a systematic, most often quantitative analysis of manifest, or denotative, characteristics (Ahuvia, 2001; Kohlbacher, 2006). Interpretive content analysis, however, is a type of qualitative analysis that focuses on understanding the construction of meaning as evidenced in textual material using an inductive, comparative approach akin to grounded theory. Interpretive qualitative content analysis can be hermeneutic, i.e., focused on capturing and describing latent meanings of a text. Additionally, interpretive content analysis can be ethnographic in nature, with some researchers calling it "ethnographic content analysis." In this case, it is focused on analyzing cultural phenomena and understanding "the communication of meaning" (Altheide, 1987, p. 68; Hijmans, 1996; Neuendorf & Kumar, 2015). With its focus on understanding how cultural meanings are constructed on Twitter, as well as the nature of the digital culture produced on the platform, the analysis carried out in this book encompasses both the hermeneutic and the ethnographic dimensions of interpretive content analysis.

The analysis applies interpretive content analysis to tweets and feedback from Twitter users through focus groups, interviews, and open-ended surveys with Twitter users. In combining the study of online content with an examination of the producers of this content, the book adheres to the triangulation of methods proposed by Gerodimos and Ward (2007). They argue that understanding engagement with online materials is only possible through a triangulation of content-driven analysis and research among users of that content. In relying on this triangulation, this book aims to provide a more complete picture of how meaning making takes place through Twitter and hopefully overcomes any limitations posed by any one of the methods.

In line with interpretive content analysis, the data for this project was collected through theoretical, or purposive, sampling. This means that tweets and respondents were selected based on their applicability to the research problem identified above (Hijmans, 1996; Wester, Pleijter, & Renckstorf, 2004; White & Marsh, 2006). The respondents interviewed for this book were selected through a combination of purposive and snowball sampling; the details for the process can be found in chapter 8. The process through which the tweets were collected varied per chapter, but in general, I sampled the most popular trending topics regarding that chapter's topic. Collecting tweets from those topics that created the most discussion provides the most detailed information about the kinds of ideas that Twitter users expressed and contested. Identifying the hashtags that were sampled occurred in several ways. Trending topics were identified through the interviews held with Twitter users from ethnic minority backgrounds for chapter 8; Twitter's own list of top trending topics; and using websites such as Trend24, which provide information about currently trending topics. Popular trending topics were also identified by looking at which hashtags were mentioned in the news, or appeared as a compilation lists created by mainstream media outlets over the past two years. In order for a hashtag to be noticed by the mainstream media and "cross over" into the official public sphere, it has to attract a great deal of participation and cover an especially poignant topic, making it an excellent case study for this investigation. Finally, the analysis would, at times, reveal the use of other hashtags in conjunction with the one under investigation. When such hashtags were uncovered, they were investigated, and if deemed relevant to the investigation, included in the data collection. Data collection for chapters 2, 3, and 4 also included tweets from television shows that featured African Americans, Asian Americans, and Latinx as their main characters. Tweets were sampled from the 24-hour period following each show's latest premiere and finale. The specific topics that were included are identified in each chapter.

Once identified, a minimum of 800 tweets per topic were included in the sample. In most cases, this meant sampling the 24-hour period after the topic started trending, but in some cases this entailed collecting tweets from the week after the hashtag started trending. Data collection occurred simultaneously with the analysis, and the collection of tweets with a specific hashtag ended when theoretical saturation had been reached. This will be discussed in more detail below.

Data collection took place using Twitter's advanced search function. Because Twitter's API only shows tweets from the previous week, publicly available tweets were collected using an html-based web scraper. In addition, if tweets were part of a public conversation that had not been sampled during initial data collection, these tweets were including in the analysis. As the tweets that were collected and analyzed are public, meaning they are visible to anyone with an internet connection, their inclusion in the analysis was deemed ethical (cf. Markham & Buchanan, 2012). During the analysis, periodic random checks were carried out to ensure users had not deleted their tweets. If tweets had been deleted, these were removed from the analysis. Data collection and analysis took place between February 2016 and March 2017. While every attempt was made to only include tweets that remained online, especially those used as examples in the following chapters, it is possible that some were deleted after the analysis and write-up was completed. No information regarding the user's ethnic background was collected or included in the analysis. However, in the case of the tweets associated with hashtags focused on discussion about African American (chapter 2), Latinx (chapter 3), and Asian American (chapter 4) culture, the use of pronouns such as "I" and "my" in the majority of the tweets using these hashtags was taken to imply that these tweets came from members of these ethnic groups. Subsequently, these hashtags are, when appropriate, used to surmise how the respective ethnic group uses Twitter to construct their own racial identity. While it is always possible, due to the anonymity of Twitter, that a user is posing as someone else, the use of a large corpus of tweets to induce codes and subsequent categories prevents any one, or even a couple of users, from skewing the overall findings.

In line with interpretive content analysis, which leans heavily on grounded theory, data analysis for *Constructing Digital Cultures* began with sensitizing concepts. Sensitizing concepts have been called "interpretive devices" (Bowen, 2006, p. 14), i.e., ideas that reference existing theory or acknowledge "the life world of the people involved" (Wester, et al., 2004, p. 500) and help guide analysis. While interpretive content analysis is very much inductive, these sensitizing concepts allow the researcher to create a theoretical/social frame through which to view the data. Numerous sensitizing concepts were used in this investigation. Theories about identity formation, human interaction, and hegemonic beliefs about race, gender, and beauty played a large role in guiding the analysis. Chapters 2, 3, and 4 relied in particular on stereotypes of ethnic minorities, while the analysis for chapters 5, 6, and 7 was mainly guided by the notions of identity, interaction, and dominant ideologies pertaining to gender and race.

Interpretive content analysis puts the text under analysis at the center of the research. While research can be informed by existing theory, the analysis itself is inductive and reflexive. Researchers use close reading to identify patterns in the text and then, through an iterative process involving the constant comparative technique, formulate increasingly complex themes that shed light on the issue under investigation (e.g., Ahuvia, 2001; Altheide, 1987; Hijmans, 1996; White & Marsh, 2006). The tweets in this investigation were analyzed using the constant comparative technique (Corbin & Strauss, 1990; Glaser, 1965). This means that each tweet was subjected to a close reading and coded for the manifest themes it addressed (e.g., "women defeating expectations" and "women as driven"—chapter 2). I also considered what kind of extra-textual information the tweet included (e.g., a picture, a link, a gif). Langlois (2011) called this the "technocultural dimension of meaning" (p. 1), arguing that to understand the meaning created on social media platforms, one needs to not only look at the content of the different messages but also the technologies used to create these messages. Once I coded the first 200 tweets for each hashtag, the codes were subjected to a close reading, and grouped into categories that captured the latent meanings of the codes (e.g., "the strong African American woman"). The categories were refined through a reiterative process, whereby the coded tweets in a category were analyzed for similarities and differences, and yet unanalyzed tweets were coded and used to elaborate on existing or create new categories. This process (also called a "hermeneutic circle" (Krippendorf, 2004, p. 89) continued until the unanalyzed tweets could only be coded using codes already in use, and added nothing new to the developed categories, in other words, until theoretical saturation had been reached. To ensure that the findings adequately captured the perspectives under investigation, the analysis also relied on sensitivity readers and member checks. The data collection and analysis carried out for chapter 8 is founded on the same principles used for the analysis of the tweets, and discussed in more detail in that chapter.

When discussing the findings from the analysis, I adhere the principle of public justifiability identified by Ahuvia (2001). Public justifiability replaces intercoder reliability as a way to assess the quality of coding and entails presenting the themes distilled from the text and examples of the text to justify the analysis. In the remainder of this book, I will discuss the results and present a typical tweet or excerpt from an interview of focus group to underscore the findings.

Constructing Digital Cultures

With the birth of each new medium, scholars have anxiously debated the potential of the new platform. This is no different for Twitter, with some viewing it as the solution to the current cultural and political inequalities, and others seeing it as a new way to dress up the same problems. *Constructing Digital Cultures* explores the reality of the new virtual public sphere both heralded and critiqued by many, provides insight into the nature of the digital culture to come out of Twitter, and, most importantly, answers the question if #IAmNotACrook would have indeed become a trending topic back in 1973.

WHAT WE TWEET

Reconstructing Race and Gender in Entertainment

2

Constructing #Cookie

Analyzing Collaborative Interpretations of African American Femininity and Masculinity[2]

> We're beautiful queens, we're intelligent, everything about us is magical #BeingABlackGirlIsLit
>
> @melanin_queen

"First the broom and then the palm . . . #cookie does not play" is one of the tens of thousands of tweets about Cookie, the lead character from the hit show *Empire*. The show's initial popularity among viewers was easily surpassed by the discussion it generated on Twitter. #Empire dominated Twitter's top trending topic lists for its first two seasons. Each new episode generated thousands of tweets debating the storylines, quoting favorite lines, and relating the characters' antics to personal experiences.

The television portrayal of African Americans has come a long way since *Amos 'n' Andy*, the downtrodden Florida Evans in *Good Times*, or even the impossibly perfect Huxtable family on *The Cosby Show*. *Empire* is only one of the many recent shows centered on African Americans. In the past years, the number of shows focused on African Americans in general and women in particular, has increased exponentially, from the aforementioned *Empire* to *Scandal* and shows like *Black-ish*. The popularity of these shows is reflected by the flurry of activity on Twitter that accompanies each new episode.

Besides using Twitter to discuss shows featuring African Americans, Twitter has also become a space for African Americans to connect and debate their racial identity (Wortham, 2016). Coupled with the popularity of Twitter among African Americans (Smith, 2014), it appears that Twitter has become a space where people gather to collaboratively (re)construct their understandings of African American men, women, and culture. In this chapter, I examine what meanings people construct when discussing popular cultural understandings of African Americans, and how these meanings reflect and/or contest dominant cultural beliefs about Black femininity and masculinity.

REPRESENTING AFRICAN AMERICANS

The portrayal of African Americans in the media has been intensely debated and contested in the past fifty years. While the blatant stereotyping that came out of slavery and Reconstruction (e.g., the Uncle Tom, the mammy, and the brute) has long been recognized as inappropriate, mainstream media still represent African Americans as economically disadvantaged, criminal, and a threat to society (Gilens, 1996; Guo & Lee, 2013; Gray, 1989).

One of the most persistent stereotypes of African American men is the violent, criminal, and aggressive brute. He is also shown as overtly sexualized or a "hustler" who would rather live off others than work himself. Conversely, the African American male is also portrayed as the deferential, loyal, and nice "Black buddy," or the "sissy," the effeminate, often gay, comedic sidekick (Cicchirillo, 2015; Hill Collins, 2004, p. 167, 171). Finally, African American men are also often portrayed as the comic relief, or the "coon," a self-deprecating character who ridicules his own ethnic group (Hoon Park, Gabbadon, & Chernin, 2006, p. 159).

For decades, if not longer, African American women were represented as the overtly sexualized Jezebel, the nurturing and asexual mammy, the angry Sapphire, or the tragic mulatto (e.g., Bogle, 2007; West, 1995). Today's media representations frame African American women slightly differently but with the same basic characteristics; they are still seen as hostile, rebellious, and excessively sexual (Thomas, Witherspoon, & Speight, 2004). The mammy has been resurrected as the "Black Lady" (Hill Collins, 2004, p. 141) who portrays African American women as respectable and successful, and, in line with the mammy trope, nurturing, loyal, and hard working. The Black Lady, or modern mammy, will always put her family before her career, and thus is often portrayed only at home (with storylines only hinting at her career), or is presented as a career-woman without a family. The "Black Bitch" (Hill Collins, 2004, p. 145), or evil Black woman, is a successful woman who is in charge of her own sexuality, and who will do what it takes to attain success. She is sexualized like the Jezebel and angry like the Sapphire (Hill Collins, 2004). The diva is described as a talented, neurotic, unpredictable, and demanding woman (Mowatt, French, & Malebranche, 2013; Springer, 2007).

BLACK TWITTER: AFRICAN AMERICAN RESISTANCE AND SOCIAL MEDIA

Much has been written about how African Americans have used social media, and in particular Twitter, to connect, express, and contest racial identity, and, in some cases, resist hegemonic narratives (e.g., Brock, 2012; Sharma, 2013; Vega, 2014). The ad hoc community of African American Twitter users that will form around hashtags that focus on issues relevant to African Americans is generally known as Black Twitter. It has been widely recognized by mainstream media and scholars alike as a source of empowerment and influence, although recent research has shown that not all the hashtags associated with Black Twitter resist dominant cultural understandings (e.g., Esco, 2011; Florini, 2014; Rightler-McDaniels & Hendrickson, 2014; Wortham, 2016).

One of the reasons Twitter has become the platform for African Americans to engage with each other and the world at large is its ability to afford users the space for *signifyin'*. This practice refers to a series of verbal tactics used by African Americans to resist hegemonic narratives in the past and which relies on the collaboration that Twitter so easily affords its users (Florini, 2014). Using signifyin' when tweeting provides African American Twitter users with the discursive space needed to resist dominant narratives. This is especially evident during hashtags where users will "dis" others, both people and institutions, or collaborate to re-create spoofs of existing movies, shows, or music (Brock, 2012; Florini, 2014). A recent example of signifyin' is the #AskRachel hashtag that trended in 2015. In this hashtag, African American Twitter users created quizzes about being African American that, so the assumption went, only African Americans could answer. This hashtag was used to express disdain for Rachel Dolezal's assumption that looking African American was sufficient to assume an African American identity. At the same time, hashtag became a space for African Americans to assert their own identity and collaborate with others in creating examples that captured what it means to be African American.

Twitter's use of hashtags was essential in the formation of Black Twitter. Hashtags allow users to find tweets that match their interests, and by responding, increase the impact of that hashtag. Many of the hashtags (or *Blacktags*; Sharma, 2013) that come out of Black Twitter challenge the mainstream narrative surrounding African Americans, the most famous of which is of course #BlackLivesMatter (see chapter 5 for a more in-depth discussion). But other hashtags had similar intentions, such as #IfTheyGunnedMeDown and #BlackGirls and #LightGirls, which aimed to challenge the dominant narrative about the African American males getting shot by police and colorism as experienced by African American women (Vega, 2014; Maragh, 2016). While not all tweets associated with these hashtags were able to counter dominant constructions of these issues (see below and chapter 5 for a more detailed discussion), Black Twitter has thus come to play a pivotal role in the creation of African American virtual discourse (McElroy, 2015, p. 16).

CONSTRUCTING AFRICAN AMERICAN CULTURE ON TWITTER

Recently, researchers have started to investigate if and how minorities utilize social media platforms to construct counterhegemonic presentations of themselves. Guo and Lee (2013) examined user-produced videos uploaded to YouTube and discovered that the vast majority of the videos that featured African Americans perpetuated stereotypes. While this suggests that social media users are perhaps not as eager to counter dominant narratives as some scholars had anticipated, Guo and Lee did address the possibility that viewers could undermine these stereotypes in their discussions of the videos in the comments left on the site.

Examining Twitter, with its short messages and subsequent ability to serve as a site for live-commenting on current events, television shows, and other ongoing developments, is a logical next step. Research carried out to date is not unequivocal in its findings. Black feminist scholars have pointed at the power of hashtag activism, i.e., the use of hashtags to attract public attention to instances of violence against women and to activate large groups of people (Williams, 2015). Similarly, Bonilla and Rosa's (2015) investigation of Twitter's response to the shooting of Michael Brown revealed that people use Twitter to construct their own interpretations of an event, resist the mainstream media's construction of Michael Brown's shooting, and create a call to action. However, a closer look at Africans Americans' use of Twitter revealed that not all hashtags lead to counternarratives. An examination of African Americans' use of the #BecauseOfHoes hashtag showed that in this hashtag, Twitter was used to construct a shared code of conduct that reflected a hegemonic, patriarchal discourse that degrades women (Rightler-McDaniels & Hendrickson, 2014).

Twitter thus affords African Americans a space where they can be heard, discuss issues relevant to them and society at large, and reproduce, discuss, mock, and counter dominant narratives, from the very serious (#IfTheyGunnedMeDown, #BlackLivesMatter) to the whimsical

(#AskRachel). Participation in Twitter also allows African Americans to create their own narratives, ones that run parallel to or counter to those disseminated through the traditional media, and that, in some cases, influence the media and the public agenda (Acosta, 2014; Freelon et al., 2016). In this chapter, I examine how people use Twitter to construct their understanding of African Americans. The analysis investigates how people comment on the portrayal of African Americans in popular culture and examines hashtags that focus on issues related to African American culture, masculinity, and femininity.

When examining tweets about popular culture, this chapter focuses specifically on the shows *Empire, How to Get Away with Murder (HTGAWM), Scandal,* and *Black-ish*. With their explosive popularity in terms of viewers, but especially when it comes to activity on Twitter, these shows make excellent case studies for examining how people use Twitter to construct and contest cultural understandings of African American culture. Hashtags like #Empire, #Cookie, #Scandal, #Gladiators, #Blackish, and #HTGAWM frequently dominate the top trending lists during the broadcasting of the respective shows. Episodes commonly produce hundreds of thousands of tweets per episode while some finales and premieres have produced over two million tweets each (Hamedy, 2015; Hautman, 2016; Hughes, 2014; King Collier, 2015; Prince, 2014). The popularity of these hashtags indicates that people are not only invested in these shows but also eager to divulge their own views and collaborate on shared interpretations of the show and its characters. While there are a number of other shows that feature African Americans (e.g., *Quantico, Orange is the New Black*), many of these are ensemble shows where the lead character is not African American (as is the case in *HTGAWM*), and none of them have created the kind of Twitter response that the four shows discussed in this chapter have. In addition, what makes the four shows under consideration particularly interesting is their focus on the African American female who is traditionally underrepresented and stereotyped in the media. The data for the analysis conducted in this chapter was collected from public tweets bearing the hashtags #Empire, #Cookie, #Scandal, #Blackish, and #HTGAWM. The data was collected during the 24-hour period that included and followed the season premiere and midseason finale of *Empire, Scandal,* and *How to Get Away with Murder* in September and December 2015. The data for *Black-ish* was collected during the 24-hour period including and following the 2016 season premiere in September and midseason finale in December.

To consider the influence and importance of Black Twitter in shaping digital culture, I also considered top trending hashtags from 2015 and 2016 that focused specifically on African American culture, masculinity, and femininity. The hashtags considered included #OscarsSoWhite (also considered in chapter 4), which trended in January and February of 2015 after the Oscar nominations failed to reflect the diversity seen on the big screen (Ryan, 2016). I also included #AskRachel, which trended in June of 2015 when it became public knowledge that Rachel Dolezal, head of a local NAACP chapter had been lying about her ethnic background, and #ThanksgivingWithBlackFamilies, which trended on Thanksgiving in 2015 (and then resurfaced in 2016) (Barksdale, 2015; Walker, 2015). Furthermore, I examined #GrowingUpBlack which trended in July 2015 and was about African Americans sharing childhood experiences (Finley, 2015), #HowItFeelsToBeABlackGirl, created by Jada Mosley in June 2015 (Grant, 2015), as well as #BeingABlackGirlIsLit, which trended early in 2016 and then again during the 2016 Olympics (R. Davis, 2016; Samuel, 2016). While numerous other hashtags centered on African Americans trended during this time period, some of which attracted far more attention than the ones mentioned above (e.g., #SayHerName, #BlackLivesMatter, and #BernieMadeMeWhite), these and others will be discussed in more detail in chapters 5 and 6. A total of 5,410 Tweets were analyzed.

CONSTRUCTING THE AFRICAN AMERICAN FEMALE

Tweets that addressed the African American female appeared to specifically focus on the trope of the strong African American female. African American women as mothers was also a recurring theme in the tweets analyzed for this chapter, as was the angry Black woman trope, and the tragic mulatto trope. Finally, Twitter users also reflected on African American women's sexuality and the African American women as educated.

The Black Superwoman

While tweets address different facets of femininity (which will be discussed below), they all view African American women through the frame of the all-capable, all-power woman. African American women, whether they are angry, a mother, or a sexual being, should somehow be capable of doing it all. Cookie, Olivia, Annalise, Bow, as well as the other African American minor characters are all seen as women who should be self-sufficient and resilient, and tweets either confirm that they are, or clearly comment on how they are not, implying that the ability to do it all is the norm for these women.

In many cases, tweets applaud the female characters for being strong, unmovable, and successful. Viewers of *Scandal,* for instance, really seemed to enjoy pointing out similarities between Olivia Pope and the then-First Lady, Michelle Obama. They especially used imagery to emphasize the overlap between the show and the current first family. *Empire* viewers celebrate whenever female characters they admire show strength and courage. They talk about Becky's (a minor character from *Empire*) ability to handle business and praise Cookie's support of her husband:

> Y'all don't sleep on Becky she was handling business last night!
>
> @dupi07

> The difference between a black woman & every other woman is she will pull u up when the chips r down. #Cookie #Empire She had Luscious back
>
> @ExpertBizness

This view is reminiscent of the Black superwoman trope that Springer (2007) described as one of the main premises of postfeminist, post–civil rights movement, which views African American women as in charge and in control. Yet in spite of having to ensure everything runs smoothly, they are also expected to always be their best self. The Black superwoman is not only expected to take care of everything and everyone and do so well, but also "maintain a sense of self" (Springer, 2007, p. 252). As a result, African American women have learned to appear resilient, tough, and strong regardless of how insecure of afraid they might feel (Thomas, et al., 2004). This trope has been readily embraced by the African American community, which became especially evident through trending topics such as #BeingABlackGirlIsLit:

> #BeingABlackGirlIsLit because we excel, even when they doubt our abilities and intelligence
>
> @karamel_ky

The narrative that African American women are successful, even in the face of adversity has become a badge of honor for women who participated in this trend.

At the same time, women acknowledge that the Black superwoman trope is also a burden:

> #HowItFeelsToBeABlackGirl to know that you have to be strong for yourself no matter the adversity.
>
> @thaishamsmith

> "You can't be suicidal, you can't have depression/anxiety/bipolarII, you can't self harm" because you're black! #HowItFeelsToBeABlackGirl
>
> @JloAndSelena

These tweets and others like it touch on the contradiction inherent to this trope that goes unrecognized in media portrayals: African American women have to hold it all together, regardless of their own feelings, and that subsequently, this discourse forces African American women to forego the self-care and vulnerability that is allotted to women from other racial backgrounds (cf. West, 1995).

Interestingly, when characters on these shows let their guards down, revealing their weakness, viewers respond in a way that indicates that that behavior is not what they expected from these women:

> Lmaooooo why does cookie look scared of Jamal #Empire
>
> @_CallMeTeQuila

> Liv, really? It's not like you to hide from ANYBODY. Wth is this? #Scandal
>
> @well_2bHonest

It is clear that behavior that indicates a weakness (in this case, Olivia was hiding from an opponent) is seen as outside the norm. African American women are, as Springer (2007) pointed out, expected to "handle her business," and anything less than that is seen as a violation of the "strongblackwoman discourse" (p. 252).

Numerous tweets address specific facets of femininity, all of which still comfortably fit into the post-civil right, postfeminist discourse that Springer (2007) and Thomas et al. (2004) discussed, which I shall discuss below.

Women as Mothers

This theme is especially prevalent among fans of *Empire*, where Cookie's role as a mother to three sons, Andre, Jamal, and Hakeem, is a pivotal part of the show's narrative development. The show presents numerous scenes where Cookie takes her anger out on her sons through what could be classified as verbal and physical abuse, and yet on Twitter, these scenes are praised, laughed at, and serve as a ground for interaction about the appropriateness of her responses:

> Lol I felt them both bruh! "@ILoveMathuli: Those Slaps . . . LMAO" @MsKhanyaG: Absolutely loveeee #Empire"
>
> @_khanyaa_

Twitter users express similar emotions when on *Black-ish* Dre threatens a Disney employee with a whooping from his mother, indicating appreciation and recognition of the particular scene:

> "Do you really wanna get Molly-wopped by my momma?!" I just died. #Blackish
>
> @TheBGates

Even though research has shown that African American families are no more likely to engage in corporal punishment than families from other ethnic groups, the myth of the tough African American mother who will beat her children persists in society and is thus reflected in the media and apparently accepted by viewers (Hattery & Smith, 2012). Twitter users actually use these scenes to discuss how these parenting styles remind them of their parents, indicating that they are comfortable reproducing the Black matriarchal discourse that portrays the African American mother as hardworking, emasculating, and controlling (Woodard & Mastin, 2005).

While the argument could be made that Cookie's antics are so over the top that they are meant to be a critique of the overbearing, tough African American mother, none of the tweets about the show suggest that viewers see her character in that way. Instead, viewers celebrate her abusive behavior, their interpretations straddling the stereotypes of the modern mammy (the nurturing but successful Black mother figure) and the Black Bitch (the hostile, pushy, but successful African American woman) (Hill Collins, 2004). According to the modern mammy trope, African American women are allowed to be aggressive, but only if this aggression is utilized to benefit others—in this case, Cookie's children.

Interestingly, the tendency to look at African American women as mothers is extended to Annalise Keating in *HTGAWM*. While she does not have any children, the five law students she has taken in as interns often serve as surrogates, as evidenced by the remark made by the following Twitter user:

> Always call on mom for help #HTGAWM
>
> @DineroBaby_

So, even though Annalise is a successful lawyer and mentor, viewers still interpret her coaching of her students as maternal above everything else. However, there are cracks in these interpretations, which come from Annalise's sexuality. This is particularly obvious in Twitter users' discussions about Wes, the one African American student in Annalise's crew, and her odd relationship with him:

> I'll protect you. Always. Gah. I can't decide if Annelise wants to bone Wes or she gave birth to him. Or both! #HTGAWM
>
> @badnecklace

It would appear that Annalise's sexuality makes it impossible for viewers to comfortably fit her into the modern mammy trope. In short, viewers appear to faithfully reproduce the ideologies surrounding Black motherhood without any real questions or critique.

Tweeting about Bad Girls: Deconstructing the "Black Bitch"

African American women are often presented as aggressive, loud, and unafraid to speak up for what they want: Springer's (2007) evil Black woman is very much a part of stereotypes about African American women. This theme returns in a large number of tweets, with users renegotiating what this means to them.

On the one hand, scores of African American women take to Twitter to describe how the evil woman stereotype affects them personally. They express frustration at people who interpret their emotions as something negative, leaving them little room to fight the systematic oppression that created the angry Black woman trope in the first place:

> White women talk about sexism & they're assertive. I talk about racism & I'm angry black woman. #HowItFeelsToBeABlackGirl
>
> @tenspeaks

> #HowItFeelsToBeABlackGirl every time I'm upset about something I have to have a "attitude"
>
> @lemondropmeela

These tweets reflect the "hypervisibility" of the African American woman as the angry Black woman (Mowatt, et al., 2013, p. 645). In other words, when African American women speak up about issues important to them, they are quickly labeled as an angry Sapphire, even, or especially, when their concerns are legitimate. By affixing a stereotypical label, society renders whatever African American women had to say as irrelevant, effectively silencing them.

On the other hand, some tweets reflect a pride in the label. This is exemplified through tweets that use the #BeingABlackGirlIsLit to applaud the designation of African American women as no-nonsense:

> #BeingABlackGirlIsLit we don't take no shit!
>
> @CAUTION_bbw

> Why are #BlackGirls lit? We are different shades, body types, hair textures and a whole lot of attitude. #BeingABlackGirlIsLit
>
> @ByTierraSmith

This attitude appears to be an attempt to undermine the label that is meant to define African American women who are smart and outspoken as evil and "bitchy," by seeing it as a source of pride. In a sense, then, viewers reject the dominant (white) femininity that forced them to remain silent and invisible (Fordham, 1993).

Twitter users also revel in the tough, bitchy African American women the small screen gives them. All leading characters in the shows under analysis are viewed as tough and short-tempered. Tweets often describe them as "badass" or "spirit animals," with Twitter users claiming the characters as their inspiration. Ruby, the fast-talking no-nonsense grandmother from *Black-ish,* is portrayed as the short-tempered emasculating matriarch with little patience for either Dre or Bow, and viewers appear to embrace this stereotypical portrayal. They celebrate how Ruby always outwits Bo, reproducing the stereotypical difficult mother-in-law trope. Twitter users quote Ruby's funniest and rudest sayings, e.g., "Bo, are you good at anything" and comment on the high level of "family shade" (@justmediaworks) in *Black-ish,* generally constructing this portrayal as a source of merriment. They take the same approach when talking about Diane, the family's youngest daughter who never misses an opportunity to put down her brothers.

On occasion, the actors from *Black-ish* will live-tweet during an episode, and in one case, Jenifer Lewis (who plays Ruby) interacted with a fan about Ruby's antisocial behavior:

> Can't take Ruby nowhere! #Blackish
>
> @AuthorCrissyDee

> No, you certainly cannot. #Blackish "@AuthorCrissyDee: Can't take Ruby nowhere! #Blackish"
>
> @JeniferLewis

In this case, Jenifer Lewis affirms the dominant interpretation of Ruby as rude and without a filter, i.e., the stereotypical angry Black woman. Hostile behaviors like Ruby's lie at the foundation of the humor found in situation comedies (Mastro & Tropp, 2004). While the use of comedy creates the possibility for audiences to subvert the racial ideology that has created them, this ultimately hinges on the audience's interpretation (e.g., King, 2002). The tweets analyzed for this chapter appear to confirm previous research findings that viewers' enjoyment of these exchanges indicates an acceptance of the racial prejudice that underpins the stereotypes (Hoon Park, et al., 2006; Mastro & Tropp, 2004).

Shows like *Empire*, *HTGAWM*, and *Scandal* lack these humorous overtones, but viewers still appear to uncritically accept the portrayal of the female leads as the Black Bitch. *Empire*'s Cookie, for instance, is presented as an aggressive and ambitious woman who will stop at nothing to get what she wants, a feat that Twitter fans picked up on seamlessly:

> Cookie's back and it ain't gonna be nothin sweet! #Empire #Empiresback #Cookiegonnatakeabite
>
> @kijkmultimedia

> Can we get an #Empire meets #Scandal? I just really want to see Cookie tear up the White House. #Eonlinechat
>
> @desiraevivian

Viewers appear to look forward to Cookie's antics (such as her fights with Anika in season one), revel in her unapologetic anger, and use tweets to relive their favorite moments or fantasize about what Cookie could do. Some tweets indicate an awareness that Cookie's behavior could be described as "thuggish," but in that same space indicate a desire to celebrate this characteristic which is argued to be inside everyone:

> WELCOME BACK #EMPIRE!! tonight, i'll b celebrating my "inner thug" w #cookie n 'em!!! (this tweet is accompanied by a bitmoji of an African American woman with short hair and glasses and the words "Thug Life" in gothic font)
>
> @myrrh423

Similar appreciation is shown for Annalise Keating:

> Wow. Annalise is a master manipulator, whether she knows it or not. #HTGAWM now and if she and #Empire's Cookie were to exchange notes . . .
>
> @LaurenHollyArmy

> You know Annelise is a badass because she can calmly discuss Rebecca's murder while eating a pint of ice cream. #HTGAWM
>
> @badnecklace

While Annalise's portrayal is not as violent as Cookie's, her drive and unwillingness to accept defeat is celebrated and viewed as on a par with Cookie's success.

One meme that was particularly popular during the season premiere of *Empire* was a picture of Cookie in a purple fur coat, with the words "ya'll ready or nah?" While Cookie is known for her outrageous wardrobe, it is interesting that numerous fans would use a picture of her in a fur coat to express their excitement for the show's premiere. As Hill Collins (2004) points out, African American women are often portrayed in animal prints or animal-like outfits to underline their animalistic sexuality, which in this case is reproduced by the audience. In this case, the meme reproduces dominantly held beliefs about African American women as uncontrollable and oversexualized.

Furthermore, Hill Collins points out that especially men contest the concept of the Black Bitch by reducing her to an angry, ugly, and loud woman, a notion reflected in several tweets, including the following where the users clearly express their dislike of Cookie's strident attitude:

> Can't wait to watching #Empire, just remember ladies you're not cookie . . .
>
> @Brucewayne_412

> DAMN ANOTHER SEASON OF #EMPIRE. GOOD LUCK RELATIONSHIPS, EVERY FEMALE TURNS INTO 'COOKIE' ALL OF A SUDDEN
>
> @etanylac

Retweeting the Tragic Mulatto

The tragic mulatto is one of the oldest stereotypes in existence, and yet it still used to make sense of some of the female characters in the shows under discussion. In *Empire,* Cookie is often juxtaposed against Anika, Cookie's ex-husband's new girlfriend, whose mixed heritage, ivy league education, and quiet, yet manipulative, demeanor has made her an easy target for Cookie's anger. While Anika has a college degree and years of experience running the business with Luscious, her presence is never discussed in in a celebratory manner. In fact, "#boobookitty" (the nickname Cookie bestowed on Anika in the first season) only appears on Twitter when users discuss her fight with Cookie in the first season, or in the second season when Anika falls from grace, and starts to act out of control:

> Goddaaammnn! #BooBoo kitty done push Ronda ass down the damn stairs ! She's done lost her damn mind ! #Empire
>
> @EriicaRochelle_

Interestingly, while Anika acts no different from Cookie in terms of hostility and aggression, Twitter users frame her behavior as "crazy" while Cookie's unwillingness to give in is admired. In this sense, fans frame Cookie as the Black Bitch (Hill Collins, 2004), i.e., a woman who is aggressive, hostile, and pushy, but successful. Anika, on the other hand, is framed as crazy because her endeavors tend to fai—an interpretation reminiscent of the tragic mulatto.

The same thing appears to happen when viewers try to understand *Scandal*'s Olivia Pope and her inability to have a fulfilling personal life. While professionally, Olivia Pope is very much the Black Lady, i.e., loyal, hardworking, ambitious, and aggressive (but only on behalf of others), and one who will always put work before her personal life (if she has any) (cf. Hill Collins, 2004; Springer, 2007), on a personal level, Olivia does not meet these qualifications. The cracks in her portrayal that Twitter users struggle with come from her secret relationship with the (previously married, now divorced) white president. Hill Collins argued that Black Ladies are allowed a sexual presence, providing this presence is restricted to a marital, heterosexual relationship, and this affair is clearly outside of those parameters. Olivia's role as the "other woman" coupled with the growing presence of the president's (ex-)wife in the show forces viewers to reconsider their interpretation of Olivia as a successful African American woman. A large number of tweets address Olivia's precarious psychological state, and debate how Olivia is her own worst enemy:

> Olivia won't let her self be happy, its the chase shes in the sun with jake, she runs away, white house with Fitz she runs away #Scandal
>
> @blackktarcloud

> #OliviaPope is a sociopathic (Lawyer) alcoholic w/ an eating disorder. An absent father who is used by married white men #Scandal
>
> @JannahLeeBird

Even though Olivia Pope is identified as having an African American mother and father, and viewers never question this, it is interesting that their tweets often focus on Olivia's problems with her father as well as her own personal demons. Viewers effectively reproduce the tragic mulatto who can never truly know happiness or success because of her troubled and distraught nature.

When a show does explicitly address mixed heritage, viewers appear to appreciate it. In one episode of *Black-ish,* Bow's heritage is addressed, and the respectful tone adopted by the show is reflected by its viewers:

> The honest and startlingly accurate depiction of race in America is exactly what everyone needs to be watching #Blackish #BowRacial
>
> @itsflawless19

The show thus created a discourse that countered the dominant beliefs about the tragic mulatto, and viewers appear to appreciate that as both a teaching moment and a form of empowerment.

Tweeting about Sexuality

African American female sexuality is often the topic for tweets, with Twitter users negotiating physical appearances and looks. Analysis shows that many users accept African American female sexuality as normal or something to be celebrated. This discourse, where African American women control their own sexuality, are aware of their good looks and use them to their advantage, is only a few decades old (Hill Collins, 2004). This becomes apparent, first of all, from the positive responses to Annalise Keating's newfound lesbian/bisexual identity. Many of the fans viewed these developments as an appropriate reaction to current social developments, viewing Annalise's behavior as a social commentary on the increasing acceptance of gay relationships in society.

This celebratory discourse was reproduced in tweets about women's own lives as well. Women discuss features that in the past have often been used to ridicule African American women and praise them as the features that make them beautiful and unique:

> YESSS they wanna joke our big lips and curly hair yet they spendin stacks to get just that #BeingABlackGirlIsLit
>
> @_AyyyeShawty_

> #BeingABlackGirlIsLit even though the DARK SKIN ones get shitted on daily, we still y'all faves
>
> @lydiaheaux

Tweets such as these indicate that the African American women in this sample, while under pressure to have a certain body shape or skin tone, do not experience the shame that others feel for not meeting these standards (e.g., Maragh, 2016; Poran, 2006; West, 1995). These tweets reflect an attempt to resist these pressures; even though @lydiaheaux acknowledges that having a darker skin is seen as less ideal by society, she rejects the claim immediately, stating that they are "y'all faves," i.e., implying that while people around her may say one thing, they really don't mean it. Twitter thus becomes a space for these women to build their self-confidence through connecting with women like them and reaffirming their beliefs.

At the same time, Twitter also creates a space for African American women to express frustration at social standards and how society makes it difficult for African American women to feel accepted or beautiful:

> struggling to find the correct shade of foundation and nice looking lipstick shades that fit my complexion #HowItFeelsToBeABlackGirl
>
> @xSilentScreams_

Tweets address examples such as white people wanting to touch women's hair, asking questions about their braids, and other instances that serve as proof that society views African American women as outsiders. The #AskRachel trend proved to be an excellent space for African American men and women to bond over experiences that are unique to African American culture, including ones related to looks, such as:

> How long do u take in the hair salon?
> A) 1 hour B) 2 hours C) 30 mins D) All fuckin day! I had other shit to do today! Damn! #AskRachel
>
> @tietie8705

Tweets such as this example indicate that while the media may have, somewhat, accepted African American women's sexuality, women themselves still need a space to commiserate over the beauty regimens they feel pressured to put themselves through.

The decades-old stereotype of the Jezebel has not completely disappeared from people's interpretations of African American women though. In discussing Olivia Pope, some tweets reflect interpretations that liken Olivia to a Jezebel or sexual siren; the seductive, hypersexualized African American woman (West, 1995), or as Hill Collins (2004) dubs her, "the sexualized Black bitch" (p. 128):

> HoeLivia is something else—no shame moving into Mellie's house—she didn't bring in her own plates or nothing #Scandal
>
> @malaikadiva

The discussion surrounding Olivia's status as a Jezebel intensified during the midseason finale, when Olivia chooses to have an abortion. Interestingly, it appears that fans either condemn Olivia as a "Bad Black Mother" (Hill Collins, 2004, p. 131) who would hurt her baby for her own selfish reasons (e.g., "That was his baby too. He deserves to know he is going to be a daddy. Olivia and her feminist ideas shouldn't take that away from him"—@celesteg75), or they applaud the show for discussing abortion in such an open way (e.g., "Conservatives shut it—@Scandal @Shondarhimes, @kerrywashington are brilliant! Imagine that, women have brains!"—@KreeBau). It appears that while Olivia, as the BBM is to blame for the abortion, the show's creator is to be praised for the courage to discuss a topic, as is perfectly captured by this tweet:

> I'm sad Olivia had an abortion on #Scandal but glad they showed the types of decisions women have to make!
>
> @DJSammieLee

The Educated Black Woman

The portrayal of African American women has traditionally focused on either her respectability or her lack thereof. When an African American woman is presented as successful, little attention is paid to how these women came to be successful; the intellect and studying it must have taken for them to get to where they are. This tends to be reflected in media portrayals of African American women. In *Black-ish*, for instance, Bow is a doctor, but, in line with the portrayal of the modern mammy, storylines never start at or center on her work, unlike her husband's work that often forms the backdrop for many of his storylines. Interestingly, viewers pick up on this, and outright reject it:

> Everyone does forget Rainbow is a doctor. #blackish
>
> @FilmsofColor

Similarly, viewers also reject storylines in *Scandal* where Olivia Pope's skills and talent are underestimated by other characters and overwhelmed by her personal drama (e.g., "Olivia isn't dumb Fitz, She's a powerhouse"—@ItsDrewOfficial).

The idea that African American women are often perceived as undereducated is reflected in other tweets as well, with women expressing their frustration at being treated as though they don't know what they're doing because they are African American:

> You asking to verify something with the person I supervise because I can't possibly know what I'm talking about. #HowItFeelsToBeABlackGirl
>
> @Engalicia

> People being surprised by the fact that you're smart #howitfeelstobeablackgirl
>
> @mehitofnuba

Due to the limitations of tropes such as the Black Bitch, African American women's success thus does not appear linked to their education or even hard work, but merely their attitude or quick-wittedness. African American women appear to take to Twitter to voice their discontent with these interpretations, opposing the dominant narrative that even an uplifting show such as *Black-ish* carries.

DEFINING THE AFRICAN AMERICAN MAN

While *Empire, HTGAWM,* and *Scandal* center on African American women, African American men also play central roles in the three other shows, and *Black-ish* features an African American couple. Subsequently, the roles played by African American men are part of the ongoing discussion on Twitter. Several themes were drawn from the tweets posted during the two episodes of the three shows.

The Female Gaze

While this study does not focus on the Twitter users' identity, and thus no statements can be made about the gender or ethnicity of the people posting the tweets, it is interesting that many tweets appear to subject the male characters to a female gaze. With the majority of the audience for the shows made up of women (e.g., Kissell, 2015; Prince 2014), it does not come as a surprise that a large number of tweets reflect the objectification usually reserved for women:

> Wes is so fine, he is perfection #HTGAWM
>
> @HiDeexDee

> I'm watching #Empire and Andre is hella fine ! He always used to be hot but he is hotter
>
> @Lovebreezayn

These tweets reduce Wes and Andre to their physical appearance. While there are numerous tweets about the appearance of the female characters too (especially the leading ladies' wardrobe, and the appearance of the younger female characters on *HTGAWM*), tweets where the men are reduced to objects are just as frequent.

Real Men are Tough

African American males are often presented as tough, unemotional, and aggressive. The main character on *Empire* especially embodies this stereotype, a feat accepted and celebrated by many Twitter users:

> Luscious is the original Don Gorgon #Empire
>
> @El_swaGz

> "Make it loud and make it long" Lucious Lyon #Empire
>
> @BaddieNay

In the second tweet, a fan reflects on Luscious's behavior while he is incarcerated on suspicion of murder. Luscious orders one of his lackeys to murder another prisoner using the words quoted above, which are the opposite of the command "make it fast and quiet" used by a rival inmate when he coordinated a murder. By quoting Luscious's command to do the opposite, fans underline not only his power (he is unafraid of any fallout from the murder) but also his desire for violence and revenge. This perspective on Luscious is reminiscent of the Black brute stereotype where African American men are viewed as violent, criminal, and hypersexual (Hill Collins, 2004). The Black brute trope includes a lack of respect for women, a behavior Luscious often displays, and one that fans appear to have no problems with either:

> "You ain't nothing but a black bitch in cheap shoes." #EmpireFOX
>
> @leshaJenee

This quote was directed at the prosecutor who put Luscious in prison, showing how Luscious reduces her to her race and sexuality. This quote and others like it were incredibly popular among the tweets analyzed, showing that viewers have no qualms accepting Luscious as the Black brute.

Interestingly, when characters act outside of this frame, Twitter users pick up on this behavior and reject it. When Dre starts binge eating after realizing his oldest daughter is about to leave for college, viewers mock his emotional response, making it clear this is unacceptable behavior:

> Hahahah the kit kats. . . . Oh no. Just no. #Blackish
>
> @MissMahlia

The expectation that African American males should be tough is also apparent through the fans' discussion of younger African American male characters. Several of the shows discussed in this chapter feature young African American men, many of whom often display behavior that could be described as immature. This behavior is often a point of discussion on Twitter, with users mocking their juvenile behavior:

> Hakeem hit him with the "I'm telling mom" #Empire
>
> @CupidKiller_

> Wes is really quite the douche. #HTGAWM
>
> @accio_ashley

This tweet discusses Hakeem, the Lyons's family youngest son who is still very dependent on his mother, and Wes, one of Annalise Keating's students. Hakeen exhibits behaviors such as pouting that might be viewed as childish. Wes, on the other hand, is very sensitive and a little naïve. Twitter users encourage them to grow up, and act more "like a man." The same thing happens with other immature male characters, like Junior from *Black-ish*. When a character, such as Junior, finally stands up for himself, viewers take to Twitter to rejoice, reflecting the stereotypical belief that African American heterosexual men should not adopt any kind of deferential attitude toward other African American men (cf. Hill Collins, 2004).

This notion is further reinforced by the use of memes. One popular meme on Twitter during the season premier was tied to *HTGAWM*'s Wes's ongoing pouting about certain narrative developments, which featured a gif of *Real Housewife* Nene Leakes, an African American woman, saying "trust that." Viewers were comparing Wes's behavior to Nene's, underlining the idea propagated by some that when African Americans males do not act tough and resilient, they act outside of cultural standards and are not seen as "real men."

Limitations to the Black Brute

However, there are limits to the acceptance of the Black brute as a designation for the African American males among Twitter users. Sometimes, this is due to the intertextual meanings attached to certain actors. This became especially apparent from Twitter's response to Chris Rock's guest appearance in *Empire*'s season premiere as a hardened gangster. Twitter users viewed Chris Rock's portrayal of Frank Gathers through the frame of his comedic work, and found him falling short of the Black brute qualifications:

> Chris Rock as a hardcore gangster? Everytime he spoke I thought of the Zebra from the movie Madagascar #Empire
>
> @ErkandJrk

This tweet and the many others like it reveals that viewers' understanding of a character is as much based on his previous work, as it is on his acting abilities. In the case of Chris Rock, his work as a comedian in shows and movies that could be described as "neominstrelsy" (Hoon Park, et al., 2006, p. 159) is seen as defining to his persona, placing the Black brute character far out of his reach.

Twitter users further explore the limits of the African American male as tough when considering characters like Dre, the dad from *Black-ish*, who addresses race-related issues in a comedic, palatable manner. In the season analyzed in this chapter, he treats one of his sons, Junior, with even less respect than he usually does. While his less-than-ideal treatment of his son is a running gag in the show, it appears that his behavior in this season has crossed a line with viewers:

> Disappointed in Dre's treatment of Jr. #blackish
>
> @SallyBalsamo

> #blackish @anthonyanderson as Dre acts like an even bigger DICK than Judge Kevin Ross on America's Court. He hates Junior.
>
> @ChaseTriton

It appears that people have a hard time accepting characters who are portrayed as funny and easy-going as embodying aspects of the Black brute stereotype. Viewers seem to expect Dre to act more like the Black buddy, the friendly and approachable African American man who accepts American values (Hill Collins, 2004).

Similarly, viewers' responses to the portrayal of Jamal on *Empire* show a clear line in what kinds of African American men can fit in the Black brute trope. In the first season Jamal came out as gay, a feat which has generally been embraced on Twitter (see below for a more detailed discussion). In the second season, however, Jamal sides with his father in the battle over the family business, and takes a very tough stance toward his mother and brothers, going as far as to kick them out of the house. This behavior received negative feedback from Twitter users, who were not comfortable with the soft-spoken, R & B producing gay man from the first season taking on a more brute-ish persona:

> Who the hell does Jamal think he is #Empire
>
> @_lovekee

> Jamal is so not credible as the bad guy. #Empire
>
> @ralf_0629

Hill Collins (2004) argues that because of the heterosexism that dominates Black gender ideology, the only way gay African American men are allowed to be present in the media is as "non-threatening lovable sissies"

(p. 173), i.e., the buddy or comic relief for the straight, mainly female, characters. Jamal's newly found assertiveness violates this trope, and Twitter users are not comfortable with how his portrayal challenges the heteronormativity that controls the cultural space in which shows such as *Empire* exist.

This is further underlined by a popular meme used in combination with tweets like the one above, which features a screenshot of Tyra Banks as the host of *America's Next Top Model*, with the words "We were rooting for you, we were all rooting for you!" across the bottom of the picture. This meme was taken from an episode where Tyra yells at a girl for not taking a chance when she was giving one. Using this meme to express displeasure at Jamal's behavior equates his feelings about how the family business should be run to that of a pouting teenage girl. Jamal's decision to act more aggressively is thus rejected by the viewers who see it as no more than a teenage girl having a lapse in judgment. So instead of this meme being a condemnation of Jamal's manliness, it's an expression of the role within which he is allowed to exist.

NEGOTIATING AFRICAN AMERICAN IDENTITY

Twitter also appears to be a space for users to celebrate their African American identity. Hashtags such as #AskRachel, #GrowingUpBlack, and #BeingABlackGirlIsLit appeared to especially function as a site for users to tease out their racial identity.

As discussed earlier, the Rachel Dolezal controversy created a huge backlash on Twitter, which in turn allowed African Americans to explore their racial identity. People used Twitter to mock Dolezal's attempt to take on the African American identity by creating "quizzes," where users posted questions about topics familiar to African Americans, such as the style of "Black" church services, getting one's hair done, or trivia about shows and movies featuring African Americans:

> What does Ciara bet?
> A. You want the goodies
> B. You talk about them
> C. Got you all hot and bothered
> D. All of the above
> #AskRachel
>
> @KimberlyKemjika

Tweets such as this one ran in the thousands, with Twitter users expressing enjoyment at sharing the quizzes and answering the questions. While some of the questions could be qualified as specific to being African Americans (e.g., @TheToast2015 posted a picture of a kitchen and the back of an African American woman's head with the question, "Which one of these is the kitchen"), many of the questions were about popular cultural expressions featuring African Americans that anyone with a passing knowledge of current movies, TV shows, and popular music could answer (e.g., @therealayedubya asked which "Gheri" was popular in the movie *Coming to America*, Tom and Jerry, Jerry Seinfield, or the curl). However, by linking these forms of popular culture to the #AskRachel hashtag, Twitter users took ownership of them as part of African American culture. Hence, while this hashtag provided users with a lot of entertainment and allowed African Americans to connect over shared experiences and knowledge, it also served as a space for African Americans to reinforce the different dimensions of their racial identity. Rachel Dolezal's claims to African Americanness were based solely on her looks, and Twitter users used this hashtag to make it very clear that being African American encompasses not just looks, but culture, religion, as well as shared expressions and experiences that are all the result of a shared heritage.

Besides using the #AskRachel hashtag to express one's identity, the topic was also utilized to express pride in one's ethnic origins:

> If you ever say "I'm ashamed to be black sometimes" you might as well go ahead and #AskRachel
>
> @zephaniiiah

> Black folks throwing away our blackness in the same aisle #AskRachel picked it up in. Don't run from your blackness. #JusticeOrElse
>
> @angelopinto720

Tweets such as these reflect the importance of recognizing oneself as a member of the larger African American community. Experiencing a connection to the larger community is generally seen as an important element of the African American identity (Oysterman, Gant, & Ager, 1995). Sentiments such as these were also reflected in hashtags such as #BeingABlackGirlIsLit, where African American women used Twitter to share their sense of pride of their African American womanhood:

> #BeingABlackGirlIsLit extremely proud too be black girl!
>
> @xnarryscakex

Hashtags such as these are also used to underscore the importance of African American women feeling proud of their identity:

> #BeingABlackGirlIsLit bc where else would y'all get "your" hair styles, slang, fashion, shit basically your whole life from?
>
> @Honeychalana

> We've always been lit we just have to recognize it for ourselves #BeingABlackGirlIsLit
>
> @_XoVeronica_

The majority of the tweets using the #BeingABlackGirlsIsLit hashtag reflect sentiments similar to these two tweets. While these two users express pride in their racial identity, their tweets also recognize the complexity associated with this pride. @Honeychalana recognizes that many of the beauty ideals and language use embraced by white people was culturally appropriated from African American women without any form of recognition. The tweet indicates that African American women should be proud of those things, even though receiving recognition for them is not a given. The second tweet acknowledges that even though African American are "lit," they often fail to have the self-confidence and pride implied in the hashtag.

Interestingly, there was also evidence of Twitter users "hijacking" or taking over hashtags such as this one to discount the importance of race. These Twitter users utilized the #BeingABlackGirlIsLit hashtag to share the neoliberal belief that skin color, or race, is irrelevant (this will be discussed in more detail in chapter 5):

> #BeingABlackGirlIsLit those who make everything about the color of their skin their very shallow lives
>
> @highin_love316

> @this hashtag #beingablackgirlislit, all girls are lit. there's no separation between blacks&whites, we're all people. #allgirlsarelit
>
> @fruityfranco

While tweets such as these could be said to undermine the celebratory character of this hashtag, it appears that users active in this hashtag expected this response, as evidence by the number of tweets addressing the "salty white people" (@elegantmani) who use the hashtag to "talk about racism" (@tRa_CiE_). Many users tweeted they anticipated the start of a #BeingAWhiteGirlIsLit hashtag because "they can't stand to not be the center of attention" (@longlivenova). It thus appears that Twitter users not only embraced the space provided by the hashtag to celebrate their Black womanhood, they were also expecting and willing to defend it against detractors.

Besides serving as a space to reaffirm and celebrate one's African American identity, African Americans also used Twitter to share their experiences with racism:

> #GrowingUpBlack when u are the only black kid in the class and the teacher starts talkin about slavery and all the white kids look at u. . . .
>
> @sellers__nathan

> #HowItFeelsToBeABlackGirl having everything you do wrong be pinned to the color of your skin
>
> @vvliencvit

> #GrowingUpBlack my parents talked to me about being black, what I could, & couldn't do but my friends parents didn't about being white
>
> @marq_corey

Learning how to cope with racism, discrimination, and prejudice is an unavoidable element of identity formation in African American young adults (e.g., Brittain, 2012), and tweets such as the one by @marq_corey reveal that African American parents commonly talk to their children about racism (Richardson, et al., 2015). This tweet, and the others like it, used Twitter as a space to share and seek recognition for very private experiences. This critique of current racial situations continued into other hashtags as well, as exemplified by this tweet:

> When you don't know if the cops are really here to protect & serve! #GrowingUpBlack
>
> @MekaPye100

Tweets like this one show that discrimination, prejudice, and fear of being targeted is an unavoidable part of being African American. Even when talking about how white women ""hijack our style" (@_superherospir), some tweets in the #BeingABlackGirlIsLit hashtag acknowledge the duality that comes with being African American:

> #beingablackgirlislit bc everybody wants to be us, but nobody wants to be us.
>
> @sh3darkskin

Moreover, Twitter was also used as a space to affirm one's racial identity, especially for African American women:

> #HowItFeelsToBeABlackGirl when every time you speak proper English you constantly get told you sound like a "white" girl.
>
> @xoMichellleeSxo

> Having "good hair" & being labeled as "mixed" or "biracial" because you're light skin. #HowItFeelsToBeABlackGirl
>
> @_Nise

Many tweets, like the two above, focus on how physical markers, such as skin color or accent, are used to assess someone's ethnic heritage. Twitter is then used as a space to express frustration with these assumptions and, through the use of the hashtag, connect with others with the same experience.

However, the vast majority of the tweets associated with this hashtag were positive, turning what could be perceived as a barrier to success as a source of pride:

> My Dad said I was born into this world w/ 2 strikes against me: Being black & a woman. Wouldn't have it any other way. #BeingABlackGirlIsLit
>
> @TheDCTurner

> We're out here breaking barriers regardless of obstacles the world throws at us #BeingABlackGirlIsLit
>
> @Cali_Lawrence10

RELATIONSHIPS

One dimension that many tweets touched on was the interpretation of relationships. Twitter users reflect on various aspects of these relationships, including family, loyalty, and sexuality.

Family

The African American family has been at the center of much academic debate. Scholars have pointed at the centrality of the family to the African American identity, with mothers at the center of the nuclear family as well as the extended familial network (Oysterman, et al., 1995). Research into the media portrayal of African American families has lamented the pervasiveness of single mothers (Hill Collins 2004), and has questioned and praised the portrayal of African American families in the situation comedies that have graced the screen in the past few decades (e.g., Sanneh, 2001).

When looking at the portrayal of African American families, research shows that they are often portrayed as conflictual and displaying little affection for the children of the family. While some have argued that this portrayal has improved, starting with *The Cosby Show* in the 1980s, others dispute this claim and posit that little has changed (e.g., Gray, 1989; Ward, 2004). Shows such as *Black-ish* and *Empire* feature, as discussed above, a family that is characterized by differing degrees of conflict and strife. While this could be seen as a way to reinforce the stereotypes about African Americans, viewers appear to revel in the conflict between the various family members, indicating approval for the strife:

> "Your father is a tampon" god I've missed #Empire—such great insults
>
> @K3SHV1

Viewers often quote what they think are the funniest insults used by the different characters, indicating an approval of the behavior. In the 2016 season premiere of *Black-ish,* Dre takes his family to Disney World and at one point loses his cool with his children, much to the amusement of people live-tweeting the episode, who especially indicate to enjoy the sense of familiarity this particular scene brought to them:

> A Black Daddy getting loud in the line at Disney World is toooo real #LetMeTellYouAboutWhenSecurityCame
>
> @WheresDaSpoon

> #blackish I'm fuckin dead! Dre just told his kids he hates them in front of a bunch of white folks at Disney World!
>
> @Nk3play2

Whether or not this portrayal is stereotypical appears irrelevant to the viewers, who reproduce similar conflictual situations for the hashtag #ThanksgivingWithBlackFamilies:

> when shit hit the fan at the kitchen table , & yo family start arguing #ThanksgivingWithBlackFamilies
>
> @CellyHOE

Again, Twitter appears to serve as a platform where users share experiences and seek confirmation of how they perceive the world rather than a site where people actively resist narratives.

Tied to the notion of the conflict-ridden family is the belief that African American parents are strict and demand respect for themselves and other elders. This trope returned time and time again in the hashtags considered for this chapter:

> When your mom and grandma give you permission to clap back at nosey relatives #ThanksgivingWithBlackFamilies
>
> @kenzie_yates

The above tweet was accompanied with a gif from *Fresh Prince of Bel Air* that showed Carlton and Will doing Carlton's dance. A large number of tweets from the #ThanksgivingWithBlackFamilies hashtag share similar stories, with users sharing "battle tales" of their strict parents and upbringing. In other words, it appears that people use Twitter to share childhood experiences common to many African Americans.

Similar patterns can be observed when it comes to religion, with many Twitter users commenting on the lengthy prayers they had to sit through before Thanksgiving dinner, or revel in *Black-ish*'s portrayal of Ruby as the religious, overbearing mammy:

> Tell me why my uncle took 10 minutes to bless the food #ThanksgivingWithBlackFamilies
>
> @tiarala162

> Ruby always trying to curse somebody out or beat them down in the name of Jesus
>
> @JamiesonDiaries

The purpose of these tweets is not to question the stereotypes that underpin these tropes, but to seek affirmation and have fun sharing experiences with other African American Twitter users. The collaborative construction of these particular aspects of African American culture thus links people who use these hashtags into networked (counter) publics, safe, exclusive spaces where counterhegemonic discourses can be created without interference (Boyd, 2011; Jaggar, 1999; F. Shaw, 2012), allowing for the creation of a discursive racial identity (Brock, 2012).

Loyalty

Families sticking together was a theme that recurred through many of the fans' discussions about *Empire*, and that reflects the familism, or the centrality of the family, common to the African American culture (Oysterman, et al., 1995). Tweets about *Scandal* and *HTGAWM* also frequently addressed the need to have someone who "had your back." In other words, loyalty is seen as an essential element of any relationship:

> #Empire "but I love cookie, if you got war with her, you got war with me" damn! Lucius hear me roar! @EmpireFOX
>
> @MsSimone1978

This tweet is particularly interesting as it is about Cookie and Luscious who have been divorced for years, and whose relationship is tumultuous at best. Viewers, however, look for proof that the two are still loyal to one another. In essence, they accept the trope of the African American woman as nurturing, strong, and caring, and the African American male as aggressive and possessive of his significant other (Hill Collins, 2004).

At the same time, viewers refuse to address the verbal (and sometimes physical) abuse that characterizes the relationship between the two, instead celebrating the fact that neither Cookie nor Luscious were willing to give up on each other. Luscious's poor treatment of Cookie during and after her time in prison could be seen as a "marker of Black masculinity" (Hill Collins, 2004, p. 189), where an African American male has to dominate a tough African American woman to prove his worth. This trend, though unnoticed in tweets about the show, is part of the discourse in hashtags about being an African American woman:

> I grew up learning to love men that hate me. #HowItFeelsToBeABlackGirl
>
> @Alicia_B_3

The importance of trust and loyalty among African American family members is expanded to include the extended family as well, and is an important element of African American identity (Oysterman et al., 1995). Twitter users are aware of this extended form of familism, as exemplified by the following tweet about Hakeem from *Empire:*

> HAKEEM LYON !!!! OVER SOME VAG REALLY YOU CHOOSE VAG OVER YOUR FAMILY cookie shud beat your ass with a broom again
>
> @SaluteMeImGabbi

Besides pointing to the belief that family ties trump everything, tweets such as this one also hint at the notion that perhaps the world outside the family cannot be trusted. But there is a limit to how far family loyalty goes:

> How quickly Jamal forgot that his father treated him like actual trash . . . nah, son.
>
> @shereegolightly

This viewer's tweet, echoed by many others, actually argues that putting family loyalty above acceptance (of Jamal's sexuality in this case) is unacceptable. Contrary to Hill Collins (2004), who argues that homosexuality is still a controversial issue in the African American community, these viewers appear to argue that acceptance of one's sexual identity trumps remaining loyal to one's family.

The need for loyal friends is also touched on in *Scandal*, where viewers lament Olivia's lack of true friends:

> Oh my word have mercy on my ancestors spirit! Olivia Pope needs a sista friend like yesterday! No . . . like season 1! #Scandal
>
> @CaLlyons

The need for a "sista friend" is especially intriguing, as Olivia Pope is the only African American female on *Scandal* in the season under analysis, and this viewer appears to see that as one of the reasons for Olivia's troubles. An African American woman needs another African American woman to have her back. Tweets such as these reflect the sense of connectedness that is seen as central to the African American identity, i.e., African Americans generally feel strongly connected to not only their family but the African American community as a whole (Oysterman et al., 1995). This notion is echoed by Tweets about *Black-ish*:

> Mommas supporting mommas Go for it Gigi and Rainbow! #Blackish
>
> @VonnieLowery

> Moms supporting moms- love it and love the convo between Bow and GiGi #blackish
>
> @Kiesh_box

The need for African American women to be loyal to one another and stick together in the face of oppression and racism was also embodied by the #BeingABlackGirlIsLit hashtag. Tweets bearing this hashtag listed reasons why African American women were great, including their looks and their attitudes, calling each other queens, and recognizing that "if we don't celebrate ourselves, who is going to?" (@_ItssMishon). The oppression faced by African American women was listed as a reason for this unwavering loyalty and support:

> I love ALL my sistas! Flaws and all, because only you all know the struggle@ of being a #BlackWomanInAmerica . . . #BeingABlackGirlIsLit
>
> @eyecmoneymusic

Sexuality

As discussed above, it appears the viewers of the three shows generally accept the LBGTQ characters in the shows, regardless of their race. This is contrary to Hill Collins's (2004) observations about the difficulties people have in making sense of gay representations of African American men and women in the media. Twitter users are not only accepting of the sexual identity of the characters, their tweets show a certain protectiveness of these characters, expressing disgust at people who attack Jamal's sexuality:

> Listening to 102.3 in LA. Disgusted by the guy's comment. "Gayness being shoved down my throat" Gross & Ignorant #Empire
>
> @voicesincolor

In fact, Jamal's homosexuality is so generally accepted, that when he expresses interest in another female in the last few episodes before the midseason finale, fans are confused:

> #Empire last week: Anika is cra—and over Jamal—like why? Carol. Cookie. & Candace need a web series. And I mean I thought Jamal was gay?
>
> @jessicaclayton

> Camilla married to a white woman, cookie done got skinny af, Jamal like pussy again #empire Mmkay
>
> @quomina

This confusion could be the result of audience's desire for consistency in their characters (when Cookie cut her bangs, this received almost as much backlash), or it could be attributed to the fact that audiences are truly comfortable with Jamal as a gay man. Increasing acceptance of LBGTQ relationships in society at large (as evidenced by the recent SCOTUS decision on gay marriage) could be at the source of this unhappiness—people are becoming more familiar and comfortable with LBGTQ relationships and are thus more aware that adult gay men do not usually experiment with women, subsequently viewing this plot development as unrealistic and unnecessary.

This same level of acceptance is seen in the two other shows, where Annalise's lesbian affair is applauded (e.g., "Viola Davis just made out with Jean Grey!!!!!!!"—@Danez_Smif), and the other gay relationships are uncontested (though these are between two white men). Hill Collins (2004) notes that while LBGTQ characters are more likely to appear on screen, they are never seen in romantic and/or sexual relationships. This does not appear to apply to any of these shows, and none of the tweets address the visible homosexual romantic relationships as problematic. Viewers instead applaud any romantic developments in these relationships.

However, tweets about *Empire*'s season premiere reveal that acceptance of homosexuality has its limits. Miss Lawrence, a well-known gay man from *The Real Housewives of Atlanta*, had a cameo on the premiere, flirting with Jamal, and viewers expressed dismay at his presence. They called his performance the "scariest most unsettling moment from #Empire last night" (@LucianSavant) and questioned the necessity of his role:

> :: Too much going on in one episode, should've been 2hrs & I despised Lawrence's part . . . unwanted & unnecessary!! #Empire #empirefox #sorry
>
> @Peach_29

It appears that homosexuality is acceptable as long as the characters' behavior falls inside predetermined social roles. Miss Lawrence, with his feminine name, dress, and demeanor, is outside the realm of prescribed gender behaviors and is thus not accepted by the Twitter users.

Besides homosexuality, fans also work on defining what kinds of sexual behaviors are acceptable for what kinds of characters. One scene from *Empire*'s season premiere received an inordinate amount of attention on Twitter. In this scene, Anika is seen twerking with a white female character who is lesbian, while wearing a modest white dress and pearls:

> The way Anika was twerking on #Empire last night reminds me of the niece trying to twerk! lmao geez that was too funny!
>
> @_cnj89

> Still not over Boo Boo Kitty wearing that sweater set in the club and dancing like Tina Belcher. #Empire
>
> @AngieWorldOrder

One of the most popular memes of *Empire*'s season premier was created as a result of this scene, too. The meme consisted of a gif of a twerking Tina Blecher, a white, bespectacled and overall nerdy character from the animated show *Bob's Burgers* with the words "Anita [sic] arched that back like that." As mentioned previously, Anika's behavior in that particular scene was viewed as so out of character, and so unacceptable for a woman like her, that it is not surprising that this particular meme went viral (Hamedy, 2015).

Expressions of female sexuality are, in the eyes of the viewers, not available to women who embody the Black Lady trope (Springer, 2007). Anika, with her mixed background, ivy league education, and high-class background, is the embodiment of the Black Lady, a woman who (at least up until the second season) is in a committed heterosexual relationship, in power (at Luscious's company), and whose sexuality is restricted to the home (cf. Hill Collins, 2004). Viewers' rejection of Anika's attempt to utilize her sexuality to get something done shows that they are unwilling to accept her as anything other than the Black Lady.

SUCCESS

The final theme that was distilled from the tweets was success. Interestingly, how success is discussed in hashtags such as #HowItFeelsToBeABlackGirl diverges completely from how the success of the main characters in the television shows under investigation here is considered.

The Twitter users who participated in hashtags like #HowItFeelsToBeABlackGirl discussed success as something that, while attainable, was often questioned by non-African Americans:

> When people assume that you won't make it and you'll be a single mother on welfare #HowItFeelsToBeABlackGirl
>
> @eby_xo

The tweets analyzed for this chapter showed a desire for success, but this desire was expressed in tandem with a wish to prove people wrong:

> Tbh I just want to be really successful when I grow up so people will now I'm not another stereotype #HowItFeelsToBeABlackGirl
>
> @motherabi

Even though research has consistently shown that African Americans, and especially males, face significantly more obstacles than their white counterparts when it comes to attaining success (Anderson, 2012), Twitter users ignore any barriers that might impede their success, and instead focus on not becoming a stereotype.

While all four shows feature highly successful African American females, allowing viewers to construct an understanding of what it takes for a woman to become and stay successful, none of the tweets about the women's success question how this success is presented (e.g., no one wonders about the struggles faced by Olivia Pope in achieving her success). What these interpretations do engage in, however, is the tendency to focus on the women's humble beginnings, as is the case with viewers of *Empire:*

> Cookie never forgets where she came from, I love that about her #Empire
>
> @_MissLovelyJas

Wilson and Gutierrez (1995) have argued that most media portrayals make a conscious effort to ensure that minorities are still associated with "where they came from." Flashbacks to the Lyons's time in the projects and Cookie's time in prison, coupled with Cookie claiming her poor background as a source of pride, ensures that viewers do not forget that the Lyons were once poor and powerless, and that most of their friends and family still find themselves in that situation. Twitter users appear to pick up on these cues, as they quote Cookie's statement about her ability to survive in "the streets" and praise her for not forgetting her roots. The juxtaposition between Anika and Cookie comes in part from their different backgrounds; where Anika is generally seen as spoiled and out of touch, while Cookie is "the real deal." So, for the Lyons, viewers associate their success directly with their ability to rise above a poor background, affirming the commonly held belief that that is the space most commonly occupied by African Americans.

Another trope addressed by the viewers is that women cannot depend on a man for their success and should instead be willing to do what it takes to be successful. When Anika fails to secure an investment from Mimi, the lesbian music mogul, she is blasted by Cookie, an exchange that made it into multiple tweets:

> "You can't even dyke right" -cookie that's gon be forever funny #Empire
>
> @SmileyTriece89

Viewers' enjoyment of Cookie's one-liner reflects a shared belief that a woman should be able and willing to do what it takes, in line with the Black superwoman trope discussed above. Anika's inability to deliver makes her a target of mockery for Cookie and the viewers, who have come to realize that while Anika may look like a Black Lady (as discussed above), the fact that she cannot succeed without her man means that trope is out of her reach, as both the Black Lady and the modern mammy can succeed on their own. This view is echoed by viewers of *Scandal*:

> Zamn . . . Your biggest accomplishment to date is waving & smiling See ladies. That's why you should always have your own
>
> @thereal_honeyB

This quote reflects, again, viewers' acceptance of the Black superwoman trope, which labels African American women as able to do it all, on their own. Women who are unable to meet these standards are somehow perceived as inferior, showing how far audiences have gone in accepting these stereotypes. At the same time, however, Twitter users acknowledge the dilemma this presents to African American women's relationships with African American men:

> "Men like to be in control, they don't like when women have a choice" #HowItFeelsToBeABlackGirl
>
> @MoseTheArtist

While African American women are thus expected to be independent and hold their own, this puts them at odds with the African American male who is also looking to take charge of his family (Hill Collins, 2004).

CONCLUSION

The findings indicate that Twitter serves an important role for users to make sense of mainstream representations of African Americans, and (re)construct understandings of African American culture, masculinity, and femininity. In addition, Twitter is used as a space to negotiate what it means to be African American and to celebrate one's racial identity.

The analysis indicates that whle Twitter users reproduce some of the hegemonic ideologies presented in the shows analyzed this chapter, they also use Twitter to create oppositional interpretations of the commonly accepted stereotypes and cultural understandings. The stereotype of the tough, maternal African American woman/mother is an interesting example of this negotiation: While Twitter users appear to reproduce this stereotype without questions, they take being seen as a strong, tough woman as a source of pride. In line with this, Twitter users reject the trope of the uneducated Black woman, and African American women are also seen to embrace their looks and sexuality. There are limits to this sexuality, though, with it seen as inaccessible to the proper, respectful Black Lady. These interpretations all align with the notion of the strong, independent African American woman who handles life on her own, an idea reflected in how Twitter users define success, namely as a woman who can achieve her goals without the help of a man. Twitter users also eagerly embraced the notion that all African American men are tough, but with limitations. Intertextual references as well as characters' sexuality played a role in how far viewers were willing to go in reproducing this stereotype. The analysis revealed that Twitter users constructed the African American family as conflictual, in line with dominant stereotypes, while discussions about success were limited to wanting to defy the stereotype of the unsuccessful African American, and recognizing one's humble beginnings. It thus appears that to some extent, Twitter users do create understandings in line with the dominant narratives presented through the media. More importantly, however, Twitter affords its users the space to deconstruct mediated meanings and then reassemble these in such a way that the newly created meanings are neither fully oppositional nor entirely accepting, but do fit with the Twitter user's views of reality. In other words, Twitter allows for the remediation and bricolage that is central to the creation of digital culture (Deuze, 2006).

This chapter revealed, in line with previous research, that Twitter allows African Americans to connect and form a networked public. The various hashtags under investigation showed that African Americans, women in particular, took to Twitter to celebrate their racial identity and build up others. More than anything, Twitter affords African Americans a space to create a networked public which affords them the ability to tease out their own racial identity in ways that match their lives but that both reproduce and renegotiate dominant myths and stereotypes.

In the case of African American cultural understandings, Twitter does not produce the countercultural narratives that some of the techno-optimists predicted. But because Twitter collapses interpersonal with mass communication, it does publicize many of the in-group renegotiations (such as the ones that took place within #BeingABlackGirlIsLit) to a larger audience. One the one hand, this means that such conversations are open to disagreements and "attacks" from outsiders, taking away the safe space that many Twitter users involved in this hashtag seemed to appreciate. On the other hand, this also means that the meaning making that would have otherwise been reserved for the African American community is now part of the public discourse and potentially capable of influencing those in other communities as well.

3

#NotMiAbuela and Tuco Salamanca

Exploring Latinx Masculinity and Femininity

I wonder what it would be like to exist on the mental plateau of Tuco Salamanca for a day Wooooh #BreakingBad #BetterCallSaul

@SouksSk

While the days of the mustachioed, unkempt bandido marauding the wide screen are far behind us, the portrayal of Latinx characters in the media still leaves a lot to be desired. Not only are Latinx characters often stereotyped, the Latinx community is traditionally underrepresented in English-language media content (Mastro & Behm-Morawitz, 2005; Ramirez Berg, 1990). In recent years, however, television has seen a slow rise in Latinx characters thanks to shows like *Breaking Bad*, *Narcos*, *Modern Family*, *Jane the Virgin*, and *Devious Maids*. In addition, because of social media such as Twitter, Latinx culture has gained visibility through trending tropics such as #NotMiAbuela, which allow individual Latinx to share their own understanding of cultural norms and values. Twitter thus provides the Latinx community more opportunities to play an active role in the construction of shared cultural understandings, and affords all viewers the ability to (re)negotiate their understanding of Latinx culture.

This chapter investigates how audiences use Twitter to create shared understandings of the Latinx community and culture. It examines tweets related to television shows that feature Latinx characters, as well as trending topics that centered on the Latinx community.

LATINX CULTURE IN THE PUBLIC EYE

Latinx have been stereotyped in media content as early as the first silent movies, where men were presented as the evil villain, the "bandido," or the male clown, and women were portrayed as sultry seductresses whose sole purpose was to provide entertainment for the male heroes. By the time sound was introduced, Latinx representations had been "broadened" with two additional stereotypes: the gangster and the caballero or Latin lover (e.g., Johnson, 1999).

In recent decades, Latinx characters in the media are often either portrayed as a criminal, as working in law enforcement, or as comic relief. They are frequently presented as lazy, angry, violent, sex-driven, and simple-minded (e.g., Dixon & Rosenbaum, 2004; Dong & Murrillo, 2007; Mastro, Behm-Morawitz, & Ortiz, 2007; Mastro & Tukachinsky, 2011; Merskin, 2007). Ramirez Berg (1990) identified six Latinx stereotypes that have dominated media representations: the uncivilized bandit; the sexy, passionate "harlot" (p. 294); the clown (female and male); the Latin lover; and the aloof yet sensual "dark lady" (p. 296). Latinx are also often portrayed with a heavy accent, as inappropriately dressed but attractive, and are likely to be ridiculed (Mastro & Behm-Morawitz, 2005; Monk-Turner, Heiserman, Johnson, Cotton, & Jackson, 2010). Media portrayals also tend to present the Latinx community as a unified culture with a shared language, values, and goals, while in reality, the Latinx community refers to people from multiple countries each with their own traditions, values, and agendas (Avil-Saavreda, 2010).

However, as the media industry becomes more aware of the sheer size and buying power of the Latinx audiences, and as more Latinx producers and directors make it in Hollywood, some of the portrayals of Latin Americans have become more complex and less stereotypical. Shows such as *Ugly Betty* have been hailed as examples of media content that is written so that Latinx audiences can construct their own interpretations, independent of dominant understandings of Latinx identity (Avila-Saavreda, 2010). Ramirez Berg (1990) points to movies such as *Stand and Deliver* to have broken the mold of traditional Latinx stereotypes, while Beltran (2004) argues that recent action movies have rendered the fiery, assertive Latina with the urban background more empowered by putting her in control of her sexuality and her surroundings. These changes in representation have been accompanied by an ongoing discussion about the label used to describe the Latinx community. From the language-based "Hispanic" to the region-based "Latino/a," to the gender-neutral, "Latinx"; efforts have been made to adopt a phrase that is inclusive of all the groups that identify as belonging to this community. In this book, the term "Latinx" is used as it is deemed a gender-neutral, inclusive term that can be used to describe men and women of Latin American descent (cf. deOnís, 2017)

In spite of these recent trends, research has found that traditional media content often remains stereotypical and does not offer viewers the space to contest these representations. While actors can subvert stereotypical portrayals by using their performance to create "performative excess" (Ramirez Berg, 2002; p. 90) such as humor or costume choices, many opt not to do so, thus offering viewers little space to create oppositional meanings. Subsequently, traditional media tend to "reinforce dominant ideology about race" (Mastro & Behm-Morawitz, 2005, p. 124).

As discussed in chapter 1, however, new media, and especially social media, provide viewers with the ability to construct their own cultural interpretations of race and ethnicity and circulate these ideas beyond their own social circle. When given the freedom to create their own understandings, do people rely on the stereotypes they have been exposed to for so long, or do they try to counter those hegemonic beliefs? Guo and Harlow (2014) investigated this in their study into popular YouTube videos and found that, similar to research that looked into the YouTube portrayals of African Americans, the majority of videos featuring Latinx confirmed existing racial stereotypes rather than counter them, and the number of comments or dislikes for videos that featured Latinx characters was not impacted by whether or not these videos reinforced negative stereotypes. In other words, even when ordinary media users are given the opportunity to produce their own media content, they will still adhere to the Latinx stereotypes that dominate mainstream media. Guo and Harlow's work examined the number of comments received by each video and speculated that the high number of comments could mean that people use that space to resist the dominant narratives reproduced in the videos.

Twitter is a platform where users generally do not "perform" in the hopes of getting signed by a production company, and where users tend to create communities of like-minded people with whom they can create countercultural narratives (Jackson & Foucault Welles, 2015). This then raises the question whether discussions on Twitter construct a less stereotypical view of Latinx culture than YouTube videos. In order to examine this in more detail, this chapter explores how Twitter is used to construct shared understandings of Latinx culture, femininity, and masculinity as presented in popular culture. I investigate how Twitter users comment on the mediated portrayals of Latin Americans and look into the conversations that arose from hashtags focused on issues related to Latinx culture.

Data for the analysis presented in this chapter came from two sources. One the one hand, I searched for tweets that focused on shows featuring Latinx characters: *Jane the Virgin, Devious Maids, Breaking Bad, Narcos,*

Better Call Saul, Weeds, Ugly Betty, and *Modern Family*. I collected tweets from the 24-hour period after each show's season premiere and finale from the 2016 season, or whenever the show's last season was in case the show was no longer on the air in 2016 (as was the case with *Devious Maids* and *Ugly Betty*). In the case of shows where the Latinx character was one of an entire cast (*Modern Family, Breaking Bad,* and *Better Call Saul*), I searched for the name of the show as well as the name of the character and/or actor/actress. Additionally, I analyzed trending hashtags that were featured in the 2015 and 2016 top trending lists and that focused on particular aspects of Latinx culture. These trends included #NotMiAbuela and #NotMyAbuela, two hashtags created in response to an ad created in December 2015 by the Hillary Clinton campaign stating she is "just like your abuela"; #HispanicGirlsUnited, a hashtag started in 2015 by a Twitter user that quickly gained a following (Pittman, 2015); #GrowingUpHispanic, a hashtag started in the summer of 2016 that produced millions of tweets (Briceño, 2016), and its accompanying hashtag #BeingLatino, and #TacoGate, a hashtag created in response to a 2016 cinqo de mayo tweet by then presidential candidate Donald Trump (Linthicum, 2016). A total of 11,234 tweets were included the final analysis.

The findings have been broken down into four major sections: What it means to be a Latina, Latinx masculinity, Latinx and immigration and citizenship issues, and Twitter users' understanding of the Latinx family.

VIRGINS, MAIDS, AND ABUELITAS: TWEETING THE LATINA

The construction of Latin-American femininity on Twitter appears to, in a lot of the cases, accept and reflect the stereotypes that have so often been attributed to Latina characters. This seems to especially be the case when people discuss the representation of Latinas on television shows.

One common Latina stereotype is that of the verbally aggressive, funny, and sexy woman who has also been described as a spitfire with street smarts (e.g., Beltran, 2004; Ramirez Berg, 1990; Valdivia, 1998). This stereotype appears to be at the foundation of many of the discussions on Twitter, with users reflecting on different aspects of this trope.

The Spitfire

The Latina as the spitfire, or the smart and sassy clown, is a stereotype that has been around as long as moving images. Ramirez Berg (2002) describes Lupe Velez, an actress from the 1930s and 1940s who perfected the Mexican spitfire, as a comedic and sassy caricature while simultaneously creating a performance that subtly resists this stereotype.

A character that comes close to Lupe Velez's spitfire characters is Gloria from the comedy *Modern Family*. Gloria, played by Colombian-born actress Sofia Vergara, is the second wife to Jay, the family's pater familias. She is beautiful, dresses provocatively, and her struggle with the English language and tendency to reference Colombian norms and traditions are the crux of many of the show's jokes. Tweets about the show and Gloria often reflect the clown stereotype. Viewers often quote some of Gloria's funniest lines or indicate an acceptance of this still stereotypical portrayal by showing appreciation for Jay's deadpan responses to his wife's antics:

> "You put egg on my house, I kill what you love!"—Gloria
>
> "psycho"—Jay (modern family)
>
> @JMondulick

> "I am going to call for a Russian masseuse, their hands are very strong from wringing laundry"—Gloria is crazy (modern family)
>
> @kumero

However, the clown stereotype is not limited to *Modern Family*. Many tweets about *Devious Maids* and *Ugly Betty* demonstrate how people pick up on the comedic aspects of this stereotype. They are comfortable viewing characters through this humorous lens, embracing the dominant interpretation of these personae. This is evidenced by the large number of tweets that summarize the characters' antics, such as these:

> "you are an attractive, intelligent, confident business woman . . ."—then Betty walks into a glass door #UglyBetty #storyofmylife
>
> @liliesblossom

> Zoila you have some esplaining to do. #deviousmaids @DavahAvena
>
> @cinnimin

This last tweet is particularly interesting, as the user references the 1950s comedy *I Love Lucy*, and a comment ("Lucy, you have some 'splainin' to do") that many viewers have attributed to Lucy's long-suffering Cuban-American husband Ricky (although he never said it). In this case, the user takes on the role of the frustrated Latinx husband to correct a Latina, rendering the racially inappropriate statement even more charged, and underlining the perception of the Latina as a bumbling, silly woman who is unable to execute anything properly.

A woman's voice is an essential part of her clown status, an idea discussed in numerous works (e.g., Ramirez Berg, 2002; Valdivia, 1998).

Latina characters are often portrayed with "thick, unshakable, often humorous, and self-deprecating accents" (Valdivia, 1998, p. 395). Their timbre and especially their accents are a continual source of entertainment:

> She's my best! Her expressions are SO silly! And says d dumbest tins! RT @ MsEmi88: I hate ds rosie, her voice is annoying . . . devious maids
>
> @FeyiFab

This particular tweet is about Rosie from *Devious Maids*, but Gloria from *Modern Family* is also known for her heavy accent. Her accent is an integral part of her character and a main factor in the comedy of the show, with family members often struggling to understand what Gloria is saying. Numerous tweets indicate an overall acceptance of this portrayal; people find her accent amusing and entertaining (e.g., "Jajajaj Watching TV "Modern Family" #SofiaVergara is so funny, with her accent :) Arriba Colombia!"—@luzes09).

At the same time, Gloria's accent also provides space for viewers to construct a less stereotypical interpretation of her character. Her accent is so thick that it could be said to be over the top, creating what Fiske (1987) calls semiotic excess, i.e., a space for subversive meaning making. This space allows audiences to create meanings that oppose the dominant interpretations of the text. This kind of meaning making becomes clear through numerous tweets that literally quote Gloria's lines, capturing her accent phonetically:

> Gloria pronouncing 'vegimite' in a Colombia accent is everything. Veh-heh-mee-tee #ModernFamily
>
> @me4scotus

> "Oh bicos in colombia wi trip over gouts and kil pipol in da strit?! Laik we ar peruvians!" #gloriaprichet #modernfamily
>
> @majoseo23

These two Twitter users seem aware that this is Sofia Vergara ridiculing commonly held ideas about Latinx' poor command of the English language. This interpretation was facilitated in the eighth season, when Gloria takes her son to a speech therapist who, upon hearing Gloria's heavy accent, offers speech lessons to Gloria. While attempting the exercises the therapists gives her, Gloria's English becomes almost incomprehensible, giving Twitter users the ability to formulate a non-stereotypical interpretation. Some use it to reflect on her acting ability and appreciate Sofia as a good actress rather than a vehicle for stereotyping:

> Gloria from Modern Family is so under-rated as a character, was trying so hard not to laugh on the train at her speech therapy scenes
>
> @PaulGold92

Not everyone shares this appreciation. Some view this particular scene as stereotypical, arguing that making her fail miserably at learning to speak without an accent is insulting and plays into the clown stereotype:

> we're on season 8 and dedicating half the episode to Gloria's accent? really?! #SMDH #DejaVu #ModernFamily
>
> @ThedMS90

> Eight years later, #ModernFamily still thinks that storylines about Gloria's accent are funny. I give up.
>
> @Jom_s

The stereotypical belief that Latinas lack the education or intelligence to turn their comedic or aggressive antics into productive action (e.g., Mastro, et al., 2007; Ramirez Berg, 1990) are visible in all the shows under discussion in this chapter. While the shows themselves offer little space for oppositional readings, Twitter users do find a way to challenge this stereotype. In many cases, this involves stepping outside of the show's narrative, and adopting an extratextual approach, addressing the show's writers or questioning a characterization:

> Dear Modern Family writers, we get it, Gloria is from Colombia. Colombia is backwards, hilarious.
> Write a new joke.
>
> @RossFrenett

> I'm so over Gloria on modern family. Having her place dumb for 8 years is overkill
>
> @SimplyLindZ

Individuals also use Twitter to directly challenge this stereotype by presenting facts that prove Latinas' intelligence, such as the Latinx heritage of one of the Supreme Court Justices, or citing the degrees they or their mothers earned. The frustration many Latin American women feel at this stereotype becomes apparent through the numerous conversations where Twitter users reach out to others to discuss the negative impact of this stereotype, as exemplified through the following tweets:

> #hispanicgirlsunited because we are not all HS dropouts, "cholas," or teenage moms. #mastersdegree #hardwork #overcomingstereotypes #latinas
>
> @Curiosa88

> "@GloStick: #HispanicGirlsUnited because my family has more degrees than some Americans yet were yelled at to "stop taking our jobs" SO TRUE
>
> @evillaugh

> #HispanicGirlsUnited because this "dirty Mexican" whose family picked your fruit has a masters in science
>
> @EducatedXicana

All three tweets capture the frustration expressed by many Twitter users about the negative impact of stereotypes on Latinas' lived experiences. In addition, the last two are especially interesting as they are retweets (@evillaugh) or were retweeted dozens of times (as was the case with @EducatedXicana's tweet). This exemplifies how Twitter in general, and the retweet function in particular, allows people to share, thus expressing approval of counterhegemonic ideas. In other words, Twitter provides the space for like-minded people to connect and construct counterhegemonic discourses, i.e., the construction of networked counterpublics (Jagger, 1999; F. Shaw, 2012).

Sometimes the actresses themselves help viewers create counterhegemonic interpretations. Ramirez Berg (2002) explained that many Latinx actresses add depth to their stereotypical role as a spitfire by how they perform their roles. In many situations, they actually get the better of their white counterparts, whether through the narrative, the way these women place themselves in the shot, or their costume choices. Báez (2015) agreed with this in her analysis of the Latina maids on *Devious Maids*, where the maids take the spitfire stereotype their characters embody and add to it to render their characters more complex. Twitter users appear to pick up on this in several of the shows that feature Latinas. Various tweets reflect on Pablo Escobar's wife (from the show *Narcos*) being "bad as hell" (@KingCvtty), and numerous Twitter users revel in several instances where Gloria outsmarts or critiques Jay:

> This was so funny! RT @Fiskey: @jordanMIA How about Gloria having Jay beat the devil out of the chicken "like in Colombia"? #modernfamily
>
> @kathybarbour

This last tweet references a scene in which Gloria has just fooled her husband after having Jay believe he had managed to trick her. This particular scene could be described as what Ramirez Berg calls "stereotype reversal"

(2002, p. 81), whereby viewers' stereotypical expectations (in this case: Gloria, the silly Latinx clown will fall for Jay's tricks) are proven wrong, thus negating the stereotype that guided their expectations in the first place. The fact that this stereotype reversal is noticed on Twitter shows that this is more than just a theoretical construct. Instead, it actually plays a pivotal role in viewers' interpretation of these shows, who take it to turn Gloria into something more than a one-dimensional stereotypical clown.

The Latina Temper

The harlot or "cantina girl" is another stereotype commonly used for Latina characters. It entails the portrayal of Latinas as hot-tempered, smart-mouthed, and sexualized (e.g., Merskin, 2007, p. 134; Ramirez Berg, 1990). Like Báez's study, which found that numerous Facebook posts about *Devious Maids* praised the sassy comebacks the maids had for their employers, many Twitter users appear to enjoy this particular aspect of the harlot trope:

> So Devious Maids low-key makes me want to be a sassy hispanic maid with a cute clique of eccentric maid-friends.
>
> @CourtRevolution

> #halloween episode of #ModernFamily volatile, temperamental, hot-headed Colombian woman! Gloria. (tweet accompanied by a gif of Sofia Vergara saying "You put egg on my house, I kill what you love!")
>
> @ImmieBroods

Twitter users praise characters for making good, show-stopping points, or for "throwing shade," i.e., giving other characters a hard time:

> Evelyn is the queen of shade! I swear! I think she could out shade wendy williams #DeviousMaids
>
> @ComputrBlue

> I am living for this shade fest! #DeviousMaids
>
> @jessixadelrey

> Someone give Marisol a mic, so she can DROP IT! #DeviousMaids
>
> @ClydeEDawkins

There appears to be some overlap in people's views of the Latina hot-tempered harlot and the Black Bitch from the previous chapter, with people comparing a Latina character's tendency to harshly critique others to an

African American talk show host who is known for her sharp comebacks. Báez (2015) observed the same pattern in her study of *Devious Maids* and argues that this is one of the few instances where the maids are able to take on, if only symbolically, the racism that dominates the show.

Very few Twitter users appear to contest this trope. In fact, a very popular vine that was retweeted numerous times with the hashtag #BeingLatino features a squirrel that attacks the person holding the camera and the words "This squirrel must be a Latino lol." Considering that #BeingLatino was mainly used by Latinx Twitter users, one can only assume that even the Latinx community embraces the idea of the hot-tempered Latina. Latinas' tendency to lose their temper is viewed as an innate characteristic, one that no one, not even the women themselves, can control. This is a belief underscored by several quotes from *Modern Family* that was retweeted a lot:

> "Yes . . . I shouldn't be so angry. But I am Latin. So I get to feel whatever I want."—Gloria, Modern Family #amensista
>
> @lexililysmith

> "I am not a hot head! I'm just Colombian! We get excited, my country is covered in coffee!" (this tweet is accompanied by a crying with laughter emoji)
>
> @OhhyonameTati

Accepting the stereotype was, at times, accompanied by a sense of empowerment, with users relying on the #HispanicGirlsUnited hashtag to express pride in their ability to get angry or emotional in two languages. Interestingly, some tweets openly rejected the notion of being hot-tempered as accepting a stereotype, arguing that doing so is to simplify human emotions:

> #HispanicGirlsUnited Because my emotions are a symptom of being HUMAN not from "spicy" latin woman stereotypes
>
> @HFTRR

The "Hot" Latina

The other dimension of the harlot stereotype; the sexualized woman who can, in spite of her overt sexuality, not seem to be successful in long-term relationships (Valdivia, 1998) is still highly visible in television series. *Modern Family, Weeds, Devious Maids* all feature very sexualized women who, in the case of *Maids,* are not capable of holding on to their significant others for very long. Many tweets reflect this understanding of Latinx women by showing appreciation for these women's looks and/or sexuality. Tweets in this category reflect the *tropicalism* trope, where Latinas are seen as seductive and physically attractive (e.g., Molina Guzmán & Valdivia, 2004):

> Binging on 'Modern Family.' They are all awesome particularly hot Colombia mom.
>
> @sandersonjones

> Carmen's daughter is the hottest Latina in devious maids right now.
>
> @fvckberry

In spite of the large number of Tweets commenting on the desirability of these women, Twitter users, mostly Latinas, did find the space to contest the notion of the Latina as a harlot, as well as the notion of tropicalism. They achieved this by discussing and rejecting attempts by others to turn them into sex objects:

> #HispanicGirlsUnited Bc im not considered mexican for my skin but i am when you want me to call you 'Papí'
>
> @unexpectancy

> Yes I speak Spanish. No I will not call you "papi" #HispanicGirlsUnited
>
> @lucyphurr

Both tweets reveal the hypocrisy of mainstream culture which associates the harlot stereotype with Latinx women but renders that the only valuable part of these women's ethnic heritage. The tweets reject both the harlot narrative as well as mainstream culture's tendency to judge people's heritage based on their looks or language skills.

Fregoso (1995) identified the "Pachuca-chola-homegirl" (p. 320) character as an extension of the harlot. This character, while still hypersexual, aggressive, and loud, shows solidarity to other women and takes charge of her life in a way that takes her outside the home, the space commonly reserved for Latinas. Fregoso makes the point that by helping each other out, these women are able to rise above the stereotypical constraints commonly placed on Latinx women. Many of the shows that feature Latinas provide space for the viewers to see these women through the lens of the Pachuca-chola-homegirl by creating a storyline that has females making the decisions that drive the plot. Twitter users appear to celebrate the Pachuca-chola homegirl trope. Several tweets, for instance, indicate a desire to see a "mash up" between *Queen of the South* and *Narcos,* in the hopes of seeing Teresa from *Queen* interact with Pablo from *Narcos*, indicating that people view Teresa at the same level of agency as Pablo.

Solidarity is an essential element of the Pachuca-chola-homegirl character. Viewers of *Devious Maids* picked up on this, especially in the show's finale, when the maids bond together to stand up to a common nemesis:

> "We're maids and we're not messing around."
> This is seriously the best line this season of #DeviousMaids. DONT FUCK WITH THE MAIDS.
>
> @CatrelCathey

> That's right Marisol (@TheRealAnaOrtiz) gals over pals! Sorry Mr. Powell. #DeviousMaids
>
> @Latina

Gloria from *Modern Family* does not have any female friends with whom she can bond and express female strength and solidarity, a feat that is lamented by some viewers. Whenever Claire (Gloria's white stepdaughter) and Gloria do have one-on-one time, Twitter users revel in the bonding, expressing a desire to see more of these kinds of scenes, possibly reflecting a desire to view Gloria as a more empowered Puchaca-chola-homegirl.

Of course, the #HispanicGirlsUnited trend capitalizes on the Puchaca chola-homegirl trope; its name alone references the notion that women need to be strong and stick together if they are to rise above the stereotypes commonly placed upon them. Tweets reflect a rejection of dominant stereotypes, share their success, and view Latinas as one collective made up of strong, resourceful women:

> #hispanicgirlsunited because we are (as my mom always said) mujeres de recursos. Resourceful women. There's nothing we can't make happen.
>
> @NataliaSylv

> #HispanicGirlsUnited because we are not a mustache and sombrero. We are not a costume. We are not a joke. We are mujeres fuertes.
>
> @ambernunyo

FROM THE LATIN LOVER TO PABLO ESCOBAR: INTERPRETING THE LATINO

Many of the stereotypes that restrict the portrayal of Latinos in the media can be traced back to the "grand narrative" of machismo that surrounds the Latinx male experience (Falicov, 2010, p. 310). According to this narrative, the Latino is a violent and overly sexual man who domineers the women in his life and demands respect from those around him. The machismo narrative also includes bravery, respect and altruism, and the need to defend one's family at all costs (Falicov, 2010; Warren & Rios, 2013). Mediated stereotypes include caricatures such as the bandido, the buffoon or clown, and the Latin lover, but also include portrayals of Hispanic males as socially disadvantaged, inarticulate, criminal, immoral, and angry (Dong & Murrillo, 2007; Monk-Turner, et al., 2010; Ramirez Berg, 1990).

Current television shows featuring Latinos tend to portray them as one of two stereotypes: the drug-dealing gangster (e.g., Pablo Escobar in *Narcos,* Tuco in *Breaking Bad* and *Better Call Saul*) or the Latin lover (as portrayed by Miguel in *Jane the Virgin*). However, the characters in these shows and others do allow for additional interpretations, as becomes clear from the discussions between viewers on Twitter.

The Gangster

Tweets about the criminal and violent side of many of the Latino characters in the media reveal that viewers have no qualms embracing these characters as the bad guy. Viewers appear to focus on the "machista" image (Falicov, 2010, p. 313), i.e., the Latino as violent, selfish, and lacking respect. Tweets call Pablo Escabor a "fucking savage" (@queeen_emilyy), rejoice in *Devious Maids'* Miguel's disrespect for his teacher ("Miguel is a little thug lol #DeviousMaids"—@YeahImFamous), and admit that the violence and crime are the main reasons for tuning into shows like *Narcos* and *Weeds:*

> I marathoned through Better Call Saul and its great but the lawyering is a bit much. Can we get to more gangster shit now? Mike and Tuco >>
>
> @CrownRoyal22

> Woohoo. Don't disappoint me weeds. Bring the drugs, sex, crAziness and of course Andy and a handful of Hispanic thugs.
>
> @pounds77

The importance of intertextuality again becomes apparent through the numerous tweets that describe other roles played by Giancarlo Esposito (the actor who plays Gus Fring) and Raymon Cruz (the actor who plays Tuco) and explain how these roles underscore their image as aggressive criminals (e.g., "Totally forgot Tuco from Breaking Bad/Better Call Saul is in Training Day."—@neontulips).

The analysis shows that one of the reasons people embrace the gangster trope is related to the success of these characters. The standard bandido caricature, i.e., the sloppy villain whose intellectual abilities are so limited that his plans inevitably fail (Ramirez Berg, 1990) appears to have been altered in these latest shows featuring Latino criminals. Many of these characters show a fair amount of ingenuity and success in their criminal dealings. And even though Tuco, Gustavo Fring, and Pablo Escobar end up being killed, their ingenuity is not lost on the viewers who celebrate their success through their tweets:

> Dey'll never suspected da 7th richest person in the world to be riding ah trunk of ah taxi #Narcos
>
> @_fat2kold_

> Gustavo in breaking bad is a genius
>
> @brayden_laidlaw

Gustavo Fring's character from *Breaking Bad* has actually been hailed as breaking the mold of the drug-addicted, impulse-driven, overly violent Latino gangster. He is instead presented as a well-organized, calculated criminal with sound business strategies, who is far removed from the original bandido (Howe, 2014). Viewers active on Twitter seem to appreciate this new, counter-stereotypical representation of the Latino criminal as evidenced by the tweets that celebrate Fring's criminal masterminding:

> I honestly love Gus Fring on Breaking bad. He was a smooth character, and ten steps ahead of everyone
>
> @soluminated

> Gus Fring is friggin' awesome tho. That deadly calm! Half his face blown off n he still adjusted his tie before dropping dead! #BreakingBad
>
> @bk_browne

However, an exchange that was frequently tweeted shows how viewers are also ready to view Fring from within a stereotypical frame:

> "What advice to you have for me?"—Walter White
>
> "Never make the same mistake twice."—Gus Fring #BreakingBad
>
> @JonathanWood

This particular quote is intriguing as it features a white criminal, Walter White, asking advice from a Latino gangster. In this particular scene, then, the Latino criminal is portrayed as the wiser one, touching on the "wise old man" stereotype identified by Ramirez Berg (1990, p. 296).

Interestingly, while shows like *Narcos* and *Breaking Bad* reflect the idea that the only way for an ethnic minority to be successful is by operating outside of the law (Ramirez Berg, 2002), viewers appear to not see their illegal behaviors as so problematic that they cannot admire these men. Twitter users appear to revel in the control these men exert over their world:

> Yesssss "Sometimes I feel like God . . . when I order someone killed; they die the same day. Pablo Escobar #narcos . . .
>
> @evrenmanchester

> Pablo Escobar was insanely powerful. Unbelievable. #Narcos
>
> @JayRGhost

And in some cases, people use these lines to express their own opinions, weaving the ideas propagated by these characters into their own lives:

> Hey, @SenTedCruz, did you ever see the Breaking Bad episode where Tuco says, "you're done"?
>
> @hg9703

> Random biblical thought: I don't know if there is anyone in the Bible more ruthless than Joab. He's like Gus Fring from Breaking Bad.
>
> @MikeAllenShow

While Twitter users may have created a negotiated understanding of the criminal stereotype so often foisted on Latino characters, one that negates their ultimate powerlessness to some extent, the fear that the bandido character inspires has not completely disappeared. This becomes clear from the numerous tweets that mention how people in the users' lives remind them of some of these characters:

> There's a guy who looks like Tuco from Breaking Bad / Better Call Saul on the Metro. I'm irrationally intimidated.
>
> @RainbowDee_

> Our Uber driver is literally Gus Fring from Breaking Bad, and I am equally terrified and amazed and SO FULL OF QUESTIONS.
>
> @fenwayjournal

All three criminals end up being killed by white men, embracing the "succeed and die" trope proposed by Ramirez Berg (2002, p. 124), where

Latinos' only chance at success is by abandoning all cultural and moral values, ultimately creating their own demise. As Warshow (1962) states, this is part of the satisfaction viewers gain from watching gangster films: enjoying the criminals' brutal crimes and then getting the satisfaction of seeing that brutality turned against them. This is evidenced by tweets such as this one:

> Gus Fring is such a badass in breaking bad . . . at least until Walter one ups him by blowing him up
>
> @rross421

However, not all viewers accept this "assimilationist narrative" (Ramirez Berg, 2002, p. 114) that easily. Especially in the case of *Narcos*, many Twitter users openly identify with Pablo Escobar, and, in spite of knowing the outcome of his story, root against the DEA agents that end up killing him.

> The problems with Narcos the show was I didn't want the DEA or the Colombian police to win, I wanted Escobar to succeed.
>
> @YoungMru

> If you root for the DEA in Narcos then I'm sorry, but we can't be friends anymore
>
> @olivia_amislay

This second example collapses a critical view of the show with a comment directed at the user's social network, which, whether it's serious or tongue in cheek, indicates an awareness of the community that is always monitoring one's expressions on Twitter. This following tweet takes this idea even further, when it prescribes other users what to think about the show:

> Only person you want to win is Don Pablo. Not the DEA. Not Cali. Not the President. Just Escobar. #Narcos
>
> @AllegedlyQ

This tweet, which includes a gif of Pablo Escobar saying "my eyes are everywhere," does not question whether people agree; it states that people should, indicating a belief that most everyone in this Twitter user's community agrees with their identification with Escobar and their rejection of the assimilationist narrative.

Other users take to Twitter to protest the "white gaze" that *Narcos* employs (@helloalegria) and critique the DEA agents featured on the show:

> Best thing about America: we made the show Narcos.
> Worst thing: our gringo DEA agents spend 18 episodes in Colombia NEVER LEARNING SPANISH
>
> @CharlieKasov

> Never thought I'd feel sad for Pablo. Also, it's messed up how the DEA are posing + smiling next to a dead body . . . literally. #Narcos E10 S2
>
> @StarLightsAbi

> Just finished Narcos it was class, but that pic of aw the DEA agents posing wae his dead body was well fucked man
>
> @WULLiiELoPEZ

The first example tweet uses the word "gringo": the Spanish word used for anyone who is not Latinx but in particular for, non-Spanish speaking Americans. While the ethnic background of this Twitter user, and the others who use this term is unknown, the fact that a large number of them resort to using this phrase again indicates that they identify with the Latinx characters on the show, rejecting the dominant ideology embodied by the white, American DEA agent who does not think that learning Spanish is a necessity for his job.

The Female Gaze

Tweets reveal that many of the male characters in these shows are subjected to the gaze that is usually reserved for women, with tweets expressing their admiration for the men's physique, indicating a desire for more shirtless scenes, and even a love for Pabo Escobar and his strange clothing choices:

> Can we please have more shirtless scenes for Jesse? #DeviousMaids
>
> @LatinaMami898

> I wanna do dirty dirty nasty things with the guy who plays Pablo Escobar on "narcos" My dad-bod thirst is real (this tweet includes several pictures of Pablo Escobar)
>
> @TheRealLizRose

What is especially interesting here is that while the male characters in *Devious Maids* and *Jane the Virgin* were clearly created to serve as "eye candy" for female viewers, Pablo Escabor is not. In spite of that, many tweets construct a sexualized interpretation of Pablo, citing his "dad bod" (@HotelFoxtrot) as an attractive physical quality. In *Narcos*, he is most commonly portrayed in the round-necked shapeless sweaters and loud Hawaiian shirts that the real Pablo Escobar used to wear, and which, according to modern standards, are far from sexy. It appears, however, that many viewers see these sweaters as an opening to challenge Pablo's otherwise commanding and aggressive presence:

> #PabloEscobar and his mom jeans #Narcos
>
> @miamiback2back

> Pablo Escobar is just out there murdering people, wearing the cutest nautical jumper I've ever seen. What a savage. #Narcos
>
> @Flynndra

So, while the narrative sets Pablo up as a threatening and violent individual, his outfits provide viewers with an unintentionally polysemic layer, allowing them to negate aggression that dominates his characterization.

In the case of Gustavo Fring, however, viewers interpret his costume choices in line with his anti-stereotypical portrayal of the calm, clever, and business-like gangster:

> Gus Fring is friggin' awesome tho. That deadly calm! Half his face blown off n he still adjusted his tie before dropping dead! #BreakingBad
>
> @bk_browne

> Gus Fring = ultimate frat bro. Fixes tie as last thing he does before he died. #TFM #BreakingBad
>
> @Shane_KCCO

When viewers discover that his ever-present tie is in fact, a clip-on, the show is lambasted for not aligning Fring's outfit with his otherwise calculated and professional demeanor:

> The only thing I don't buy in all of Breaking Bad is that Gus Fring wears a clip on tie.
>
> @bnacker

> It seems weird, but I just lost a lot of fear and respect for Gustavo Fring because he wears a clip-on tie . . . #BreakingBad #S4E13
>
> @DennisBlkAndAsn

While Pablo Escobar's sweaters are seen as a way to undermine his violent characterization, Fring's clip-on tie, which could be explained away by his personal background as a restaurant manager, is seen as a violation of his portrayal as the cool criminal. Twitter users, in line with the two examples shown above, view it as an interruption of the realism of his character. One possible explanation could be that Pablo Escobar, who was a real person, is expected to possess more contradictory features. Viewers accept his sweaters, seeing them not as a violation of realism but as part of his real-life persona, and work to incorporate that apparent contradiction into their understanding of his character. Fring, on the other hand, is fictional, and as such, all of his attributes are expected to fit his characterization. In this case, the clip-on tie violates the anti-stereotypical gangster trope that viewers so readily embraced, and it thus becomes a site of disappointment and even resistance.

Commenting on characters' looks, however, is most commonly used to affirm the trope of the Latin lover, i.e., the sensual, seductive, and attractive Latino. Tweets address *Jane the Virgin*'s Rafael's looks as well as the physical attractiveness of the Hispanic drug dealers on *Weeds*. Both characters were created to resemble this particular stereotype, and the viewers appear to accept this without much consideration.

The Hombre

According to Falicov (2010), another dimension of Latinx masculinity is the "hombre" (p. 313). This trope incorporates positive characteristics such as respect, loyalty, and the desire to take care of one's family and members of one's community (cf. Stein, Gonzalez, Cupito, Kiang, & Supple, 2006). Both Pablo Escobar and Tuco, in spite of their criminal activities, embody these characteristics, and viewers revel in the ability of such cold-hearted criminals to still express love for their family:

> tuco may be crazy af but every time he's introduced (breaking bad and better call saul) he's taking care of an elder. What a sweet maniac
>
> @NerdWithTheHair

> Pablo Escobar was a terrible man, the greatest/smartest drug lord of all time yet I'm like he's such a family man albeit THE WORST #Narcos
>
> @kevotano

> One scene got me like, "Pablo Escobar is a real scumbag" & another scene got me like, "aww Pablo Escobar family man" #Narcos #narcosseason2
>
> @miamiback2back

Viewers thus pick up on the contradiction inherent in Latinx masculinity and its media portrayal: the hombre and the machista, the caring, family-oriented provider versus the violent, unpredictable, and irrational criminal.

TWEETING THE LATINX IDENTITY

Even though the Latinx population is made up of a wide variety of cultural groups, each with their own struggles and background, the mainstream media and most non-Latinx view the Latinx community as a united group of people. The tendency to view Latinx as having one syncretic identity (cf. Guzman, 2006), where differences between groups are minimalized and similarities are celebrated, has led to the creation of what scholars have dubbed *Latinidad*, the belief that Latinx share common characteristics (e.g., Dávila, 2000). This trope is not without a struggle, as is reflected in many of the tweets analyzed for this chapter.

Latinidad

One of the top trending topics analyzed for this chapter, #Growing UpHispanic, captures both the desire to conceive of the Latinx culture as entailing a high number of shared experiences, as well as the conflicts that arise when one tries to bring the different identities under one denominator. On the one hand, Twitter users share hundreds of stories about having to use Vicks Vaporub for all medical ailments, having to deal with singing Happy Birthday in multiple languages, and having strict mothers and grandmothers. They rejoice in sharing these similarities:

> #GrowingUpHispanic relating to every single growing up Hispanic tweet because all Hispanic families do the same shit
>
> @Sophiasopapilla

> @Ughitsbrenda all these growing up Hispanic tweets are so true omfg
>
> @stephanieisok

On the other hand, however, Twitter also reveals the struggle that surrounds the phrase that makes up this hashtag and the hesitant embrace of Latinidad that it implies:

> #GrowingUpHispanic caused much of my conflict and doubt because hispanic is a label I cannot identify with #latina #chicana #mexicanamerican
>
> @YoursTruly_Liz

> #GrowingUpHispanic means growing up as a Spanish person (from Spain). Learn the difference!
> Hispanic and Latin are wrong labels.
>
> @miguel0mana

This tweet, and the many like it, reveals the issues that Latinx have with the term "Hispanic." While the term Hispanic can be used to refer to anyone who speaks Spanish, and the vast majority of Latinx in the U.S. are Spanish-speakers, this is not how many Latinx view it. The implied suggestion of a shared identity and history creates a great deal of resistance, as evidenced by @YoursTruly_Liz tweet, because Latinx identify themselves by their national roots (i.e., Mexican), instead of an overarching category.

This negotiation of one's identity also becomes apparent through a second popular hashtag #HispanicGirlsUnited. Numerous tweets indicate that Latinas have no qualms identifying as Hispanic, using the hashtag to discuss achievements and barriers common to Latinas, while others use the hashtag to contest the implied unified identity:

> #HispanicGirlsUnited just bc I speak Spanish doesn't mean I'm Mexican, and just cuz I look white doesn't mean I am . . . I'm Venezuelan.
>
> @Sylvana_baby

> #hispanicgirlsunited bc if you speak spanish or look Hispanic your automatically Mexican
> #soyguatemalteca
>
> @Carveddaisies

These tweets are two examples of many used to express frustration with people's tendency to lump all Spanish speakers together, using a hashtag that does exactly that. Ironically, this is the only way for Latinas to call for a change; to first acknowledge the generic label that is used to define them before they can call on others under that same label to make a change (cf. Dávila, 2000). Twitter is the ideal space for these calls for change, as it allows its users to acknowledge the usefulness of Latinidad in the construction of their identity while providing them with the space to challenge those constructs that do not work for them. In a way then, Twitter provides Latinx with the ability to create an identity that is the result of a negotiated understanding of Latinidad (Aparicio, 2003).

Language

As Zentella (2007) points out, language is an important factor in defining the Latinx identity. The understanding of the Latinx culture as one unified whole is in part based on the fact that the vast majority of Latinx speak Spanish (cf. Davila, 2000). Zentella ties language to belonging, arguing that the language one speaks as well as one's accent is an important marker in defining who does and does not belong. The ability to speak

English without an accent is seen as a sign of one's willingness to integrate into American society. Within the Latinx culture, though, the ability to speak flawless English is often seen as a loss of national identity. The importance of and struggles surrounding language are reflected in numerous tweets. Many tweets discuss the idea that one's ability to speak Spanish as an essential part of one's Latinx identity:

> When you see the #beinglatino IG page, and realize. How you're hella not that Latin. And you can't understand any of the posts in Spanish
>
> @TheeMcSkeez

> #HispanicGirlsUnited because not speaking Spanish doesn't make me any less of a Chicana
>
> @mujerista

Some users commiserate with those who identify as Hispanics but who cannot speak Spanish as though this is a sign of an incomplete identity (e.g., "to all my Hispanic girls that grew up only speaking English, I feel you and I love you #HispanicGirlsUnited"—@lindabreeezy). These tweets reveal an acceptance of the traditional notion that one's language skills is tied to one's cultural identity, a notion that is challenged by others, as exemplified by @savjeafi's tweet:

> #HispanicGirlsUnited because even if i don't speak spanish & am constantly being told I don't "look Hispanic," I am a proud puertorican

> #hispanicGirlsUnited just because I don't have an accent and can't speak Spanish very well that doesn't mean I'm any less of a Latina
>
> @FearlessMode661

Tweets like these center on pride and being equal to other Latinas, indicating that their "Latina-ness" is a central part of who they are; and although they recognize the importance of language in one's identity, they reject it as a defining feature.

Numerous users also address the link between language and race. Among other things, Latinx appear to use Twitter to express their frustration with non-Latinx tying their accent (or lack thereof) to their ethnic heritage:

> #HispanicGirlsUnited because assuming my mom doesn't speak English because she's darker-skinned than me is some white standard bullshit.
>
> @feministafataIe

Users like this one unapologetically point at the racist assumptions that underpin a lot of the attitudes toward Spanish speakers in the U.S.: If you are going to claim a Latinx identity by speaking Spanish, then you need the embody tropicalism, i.e., the stereotypical physical features assigned to Latinas by the mainstream media such as darker skin and long dark hair (e.g., Martynuska, 2016; Merskin, 2007; Molina Guzmán & Valdivia, 2004). Within tropicalism, there is no room for a mixed ethnic identity, a belief that these Twitter users recognize and reject:

> #HispanicGirlsUnited bc they want us to sound american but to look hispanic. #Confusing #LOL
>
> @karlasolarte

> Debunk #HispanicGirlsUnited b/c folks hear me speak spanish n say "I thought you were black tho. How'd u learn the language?." #Afrolatina
>
> @nkento

In this case, Twitter provides Latinas with the space to dissect and confront this perennial stereotypical view of Latinx identity.

The #HispanicGirlsUnited hashtag also captures the duality that many Spanish speakers face: they are expected to speak Spanish to claim the Latinx identity, but when they do, they are confronted with the belief that their desire to speak Spanish indicates a lack of interest in assimilating into U.S. culture:

> #HispanicGirlsUnited When I speak Spanish to my family at the grocery store, I get ugly looks & am told that I need to go back to Mexico
>
> @_klaramarieg

Again, though, Twitter offers users with the space to resist this interpretation:

> #HispanicGirlsUnited bc when i speak spanish i get told "this is america speak english" but they are pressuring me to teach them Spanish
>
> @realgot7s

> #HispanicGirlsUnited Because I grew up speaking Spanish at home, & I still have better English language grammar skills than most Americans.
>
> @BlueEASM

Many Latinas propagate the advantages of being bilingual to debunk the stereotype that Spanish speakers are less educated or integrated. By doing so, they propagate the traditionally held belief by the Latinx community that raising children to be bilingual is the best way to preserve their Latinx identity and help them succeed in the U.S. (Zentella, 2007).

The discussion about language is not limited to Twitter users' personal experience, but extends to how Twitter users view shows featuring Latinx:

> That show narcos pisses me off because all the accents are so bad
>
> @_Stephanie_19

> Whyd you guys put a guy who doesnt even looklike Pablo OR have that colombian accent to play Pablo @NarcosNetflix so wack
>
> @Manuu_V

As mentioned above, the mainstream media has created a unified perspective of Latinx identity without any regard for the differences between the various national groups and/or accents. While to a non-Spanish speaker, Pablo Escobar's Spanish sounds just fine, to a Latinx, the use of a Brazillian actor to portray a Colombian is yet another reminder of the mainstream media's refusal to acknowledge the diversity inherent to the Latinx culture.

Physical Features

Even though Zentella (2007) noted that physical features are no longer seen as markers for race or ethnic identity, Guzman (2006) and numerous others (e.g., Merskin, 2007) contested this. It appears that the tendency to group people based on their looks is still very much alive, and something frequently disputed in social spaces such as Twitter.

> When your not considered "dark enough" to Latina.
> #HispanicGirlsUnited
>
> @SonniaisFearles

> #ThingsIGetAlot "You're Mexican???? What??? You don't look like it!!!!"
> #HispanicGirlsUnited
>
> @emmaseguraa

Again, Twitter allows Latinas to share their daily experiences with an audience beyond their peers, revealing the stereotyping still prevalent in today's society and allowing them to connect to users with similar experiences. Many use Twitter to rebel against these norms, mainly through the use of jokes or sarcasm:

> #HispanicGirlsUnited because apparently I'm not curvy enough, or tan enough or ethnic looking enough to fit your stereotype.
>
> @HeavyMetalLovr_

> Feel free 2 use this: "You don't look Hispanic." "I killed a white bitch & I am wearing her skin like an Aztec priest," #hispanicgirlsunited
>
> @lauramariaflora

Twitter then provides Latinx users with a space to form a networked counterpublic and create counterhegemonic narratives away from the mainstream media.

Citizenship and Immigration

In recent years, the topic of immigration and citizenship has been inexorably linked with the Latinx community. Subsequently, many television shows featuring Latinx characters reference immigration. In *Ugly Betty*, Betty's father Ignacio is an undocumented immigrant whose immigration woes drive a large part of the plot in season 1. In *Devious Maids*, one of the maids, Rosie does not possess the appropriate immigration paperwork either. Her employer, Peri turns her in to the authorities after finding out that her husband has been having an affair with Rosie.

Numerous tweets address these two plot lines, with some lamenting that America Ferrera (the actress who plays Betty in *Ugly Betty*) always appears to struggle with immigration issues, implying that the "undocumented parent—documented child" trope is perhaps becoming too much of a staple in popular culture:

> RT @stayingin: Daddy immigration issues just follow America Ferrara around, don't they? #TheGoodWife #UglyBetty
>
> @amandapham

Viewers discussing Peri's betrayal and Rosie's subsequent arrest are a great deal more vocal of their disapproval of this course of events:

> Oh Naw If That Heifa Called Immigration On One Of My Friends, We'd Have To Square Up #DeviousMaids
>
> @OhGirl_SoFancy

> "@jesssicacastroo: That white bitch called immigration on Rosie!! #DeviousMaids"
>
> @jennxneg

These tweets, which reflect the tone of the majority of tweets on this topic, focus more on the act of betraying someone to the authorities than Rosie's immigration status. Twitter users condemn Peri and her desire for revenge, accepting the system that allows for such situations to occur without question.

Real critique of attitudes toward immigrants in the United States can be found in the hashtags created by Latinx themselves, such as #HispanicGirlsUnited. Here Twitter users express their frustration with the assumptions about legality held by many white Americans:

> #HispanicGirlsUnited because every Hispanic is assumed to be Mexican & people still think Puerto Ricans are "undocumented" in the US
>
> @_harlemworld

> This is a real issue that is not being addressed "#HispanicGirlsUnited because no I am not mexican and yes I am here legally"
>
> @vanessasx29

@vanessasx29's tweet used a quote from someone else's tweet, showing how individuals can use Twitter to engage in conversation, amplify others' ideas, and come to a consensus with like-minded people about social issues. What renders these tweets, and the ones in this category, even more interesting is that they point to the invisibility of Puerto Ricans in both Latinx and mainstream American culture. As U.S. citizens, Puerto Ricans are not subject to the any immigration rules, yet they are part of the Latinx community, as pointed out by @_harlemworld.

Some tweets use the hashtag to express anger at the double standard that white Americans frequently employ when it comes to the Latinx community:

> #HispanicGirlsUnited bc we constantly get called dirty "illegal" immigrants when white people fail to see they are too.
>
> @Anna_Murillox3

> #HispanicGirlsUnited because people like to celebrate our holidays but still tell us to go back to our country.—Kathy @2chainzamore
>
> @projectenye

Tweets such as these reveal how people use Twitter to be heard on issues relevant to their community, and in ways that are generally not shown in the mainstream media.

RECONSTRUCTING THE FAMILY

Latinx understandings of the family have been described by the term *familismo* or familism, which captures the cohesion and interdependence that characterizes many Latinx families (e.g., Guilamo-Ramos, et al., 2007; Stein, et al., 2013). Collectivism, the understanding that one can turn to one's family for anything but that the family takes precedence over the self, is a driving force in the Latinx family (Miranda, Bilot, Peluso, Berman, & Van Meek, 2006). Latinx families generally value harmony over conflict, believe in respecting authority, and view loyalty and attachment as important family values. In addition, Latinx family structure is characterized by specific gender roles, with the males in charge of important family decisions (*machismo*), and the women's role centered on being a mother (*marianismo*) (Guilamo-Ramos, et al., 2007), who sacrifices everything for her family (*la madre abnegada*,, Fregoso, 1995).

Familismo

One theme that recurs in a wide variety of tweets is interdependence, or the idea that family members should and will depend on one another for a host of issues. This ability to count on one's family is generally seen in a positive light:

> mi abuela raised 12 kids & others that weren't hers bc family & her barrio were more important than her politics. Clinton is #notmiabuela
>
> @hypeisnow_

> #HispanicGirlsUnited because my parents work hard every day to make my dreams come true and happen easier.
>
> @xlurenxp

In many cases, this tendency to sacrifice everything for one's family is seen as something to be grateful for:

> #HispanicGirlsUnited I try my hardest in school and in life because my parents didn't struggle for nothing. I'm forever grateful.
>
> @itsgenebaby

> Growing up disadvantaged . . . With hardworking Hispanic parents who came from nothing . . . I will never not appreciate them.
>
> @imnotorionxx

This idea is reflected in shows such as *Ugly Betty*, where the Suarez family is not only portrayed as a close-knit family, but as extending this closeness to characters who exhibit behaviors that are usually reserved for family members; i.e., helping each other out, standing up for one another.

This idealization of the interdependence that characterizes Latinx families is met with nothing but approval:

> And then Justin gave Daniel his own stocking for the tree & Betty's dad thanked him for standing up for his grandson. I'm crying. #uglybetty
>
> @LilyMiranda07

In some cases, however, users appear to rely on Twitter to express their frustration with this tendency toward interdependency. Tweets reflect frustration or embarrassment at the "family before everything" notion, labeling it as a burden to someone who is trying to acculturate to a society where familism is not a pivotal part of the family structure:

> MY ABUELA WANTS TO BRING MARACAS TO THE GRADUATION FOR WHEN THEY CALL MY NAME BYEEE
>
> @gracemoreoreless

> Mom: "hey Mia your grandma made chicken you can eat that right?" Problems of being Hispanic and vegan
>
> @mianorton28

In Tweets like these, one never mentions resolving the conflict; they simply appear to use the platform to express dissatisfaction, but simultaneously, an understanding that this is how things are done in Latinx families.

The acceptance of familism is such that even when a comedy such as *Modern Family* does not make any concerted effort to address it, viewers still see Gloria as a carrier of traditional Latinx values, such as familism:

> "But you mess with us, we mess with you. Thats the custom" Gloria #modernfamily *Lmao. I love #Colombia*
>
> @Rimzzzeee

This particular quote is from a scene where Gloria has just fooled her husband into slapping a chicken arguing that these are Colombian customs. While the full quote reads, "I made it up. It's not a real custom in Colombia. We're not lunatics. But you mess with us, we mess with you. That's the custom," many tweets only focused on the last part, implying they are mainly focused on the idea that in Colombia, people stick together, embracing the principles of loyalty and cohesion that lie at the foundation of familism.

At the same time, Twiter users readily accept *Modern Family*'s humorous, but critical, take on familialism as is evident from the following tweet:

> Gloria <3 RT @edmundanchi—Where I come from, brothers respect each other.—That's why Colombia is such a peaceful utopia. #ModernFamily
>
> @Gerson_S

This particular quote captures an exchange between Gloria and Jay, her American husband, and numerous Twitter users tweeted this exact quote. In doing so they show appreciation for Jay's critical analysis of the reality of familism; it may apply to one's family but no further, thus explaining the crime rates that people commonly associate with Colombia. The humor in *Modern Family* thus allows viewers to see the apparent contradictions inherent to the practice of familism, a contradiction that viewers readily embrace

At times, the idea of a family that looks out for one another, with parents sacrificing themselves for their children has become a weapon in political battles. This became particularly apparent when, in December 2015, the Hillary Clinton campaign created an advertisement aimed at Latinx voters that claimed that Clinton was "just like their abuela." The pushback was swift and relentless, with #NotMiAbuela and #NotMyAbuela dominating Twitter for days after the ad was released. The majority of tweets responded by reiterating the sacrifice that was implied in the familism trope, reflecting the belief that in Latinx families, mothers sacrificing for family members is the norm:

> Hillary is #NotMiAbuela because she didn't have to cross any border to give her kids a better life.
>
> @puzzleshifter

> Both of my abuelas immigrated to this country. Neither were allowed to pursue a career because family came first. #NotMiAbuela, Clinton.
>
> @mcastimovies

The tone of these tweets and others like it appear to associate "abuela" with the familism typical to Latinx families; the grandmother becomes synonymous with the loyalty and sacrifice that characterizes Latinx families. The sacrifice becomes both an identifying characteristic as well as a badge of honor.

Other tweets directly address the presidential candidate, and appear to create a dichotomy, with the "us" representing the Latinx community, and Hillary Clinton (and the whiteness she represents in this discussion) making up the "other:"

> #NotMiAbuela @HillaryClinton u will nevr know BEAUTY of HOW we embrace r familias thru it all. With story,music,food,prayer,laughter,tears
>
> @TonantzinKansas

Whereas this tweet uses the hashtag to demarcate a boundary between Latinx and all others, emphasizing familism as a unifying factor, many other users instead utilize the hashtag to describe how Latinx are actively excluded from American society:

> And raised 10 grandchildren in a place that never accepted her, they grew to know perfect English & Spanish. You could never. #NotMiAbuela
>
> @LiztheGodfather

> @HillaryClinton my abuelita took care of me after my mom was deported due to your husband immigration policies that u supported #NotMiAbuela
>
> @alexistnava

These two tweets extend the "us versus them" dichotomy to touch on the theme of belonging (or lack thereof). Instead of focusing on aspects of Latinx culture that set it apart from other ethnic groups, these users define who they are by looking at ways in which society did not accept them.

Respeto

Respect for one's elders is another characteristic typically linked to Latinx families, and one that returns in many tweets about Latinx families. Twitter users discuss fearing their mothers after acting out in public, being told to eat whatever someone's mother or grandmother cooks for them regardless of whether they like it or not, and criticize scenes from shows featuring families that do not feature the level of respect standard to a Latinx family. One example is this tweet about the show *Weeds:*

> Wait . . . Silas punches Shane, and Nancy just lets him run out the house? That would not happen in a Hispanic household. #Weeds #SeasonOne
>
> @BrianRentas

The concept of *respeto* is clearly a central part of Latinx culture that is faithfully reproduced in these tweets (Guilamo-Ramos, et al., 2007). Another tweet that got a lot of attention featured a picture of Kermit the Frog giving his nephew Robin the Frog a disapproving stare and pinching his shoulder tightly and the words, "Si no te paso esto no tuviste infancia (if this didn't happen to you, you did not have a childhood). We all know that grip! #Beinglatino." The tweet received dozens of responses and likes, making clear that there is an expectation of respect for one's elders in the Latinx culture that these social media users embrace and reflect. In addition, this meme also shows how easily mainstream cultural icons can be used to convey a message outside that same mainstream.

The centrality of respect is also reflected in the tweets surrounding Tuco's kindness toward his grandmother, where viewers juxtapose Tuco's consideration with his violent and unpredictable behavior to everyone else, expressing appreciation for this gentler side. Not one tweet questioned this sudden change in character, accepting the dominant discourse that as a Latinx male, Tuco knows that his family comes first, and respect for his elders is everything.

Interestingly, the discussion about respect is the second time when Twitter users reference other ethnic groups:

> Growing up everyone was allowed to whoop you if you were being bad and your parents weren't around #BeingLatino #BeingBlack
>
> @GIJO_siah

Twitter users thus appear to recognize similarities between African American and Latinx child-rearing practices, using Twitter to highlight the connections between distinct networked counterpublics.

Marianismo

The tweets that reflected on the woman's place in the family reveal that most Twitter users are comfortable viewing Latinx mothers as the sacrificing, child-rearing, strong housewives captured by the marianismo trope. While this role encompasses various characteristics, the one that most Twitter users mention is women's tendency to work hard for others, sacrificing their own goals and dreams in the process:

> my guela raised tons of ppls kids, including me, made us mangu daily & let ppl take what lil she had, turning the other cheek. #NotMiAbuela
>
> @bad_dominicana

> My abuelas didn't see the inside of a college classroom because they were too busy taking care of their families. Hillary is #NotMyAbuela
>
> @high_femme

Mothers are also seen as responsible for the running of the household, and thus are often portrayed as a strict matriarch. Twitter users discuss being forced to learn how to make tamales by their mother, called up to come home and do the dishes, or their mothers not allowing them to stay home from school when they are sick.

The ease with which users reproduce the marianismo role became especially apparent when analyzing tweets about one particular storyline on *Devious Maids*. This narrative arc follows Carmen who gave up her daughter Danni for adoption when Danni was a baby. The two are reunited when Danni is grown up, and Danni is seeking revenge on her mother for giving her up as a baby. Some viewers clearly side with Danni:

> Hey Carmen, pay back is a bitch #DeviousMaids
>
> @malice316

Carmen, by giving up her child, did not adhere to the marianismo-based notion that mothers need to be there for their children regardless of the circumstances. Had Carmen stayed true to her Latinx heritage, she would have embraced the role of *la madre abnegada* (the selfless mother), instead of putting herself first. Therefore, these tweets reveal, Carmen deserves whatever Danni does to her. When Carmen finds out her daughter secured an acting role she really wanted, she, in true marianismo spirit, forgives, an act that many tweets applauded, thus further underlining their reproduction of the marianismo role:

> I like that Carmen was still happy for Dani, even though she was jealous too. #DeviousMaids
>
> @leahsingworld

Interestingly, once Danni starts carrying out her plans for revenge, many Twitter users express disapproval of her behavior, indicating a desire for Carmen to stand up to her own daughter. Many of these sentiments appear to be based on an adherence to the role generally assigned to daughters in Latinx culture: they should be obedient, well-behaved, sacrificial, and pure (e.g., Fregoso, 1995; Guilamo-Ramos, et al., 2007). When daughters act out, the mother should step in:

> "She was mean to me 1st"? When? When she gave your ungrateful, stuck-up ass to loving parents? #DeviousMaids
>
> @RealMissJuicee

> Danny is about to get served! I don't feel sorry for her for doing Carmen dirty like that. #DeviousMaids
>
> @Rx_Fay

This disapproval ties into another stereotype commonly associate with Latinx families: the roles assigned to daughters. Latinx daughters are expected to respect their elders just like their brothers per the cultural construct respeto, but they are generally held to higher standards and stricter rules (e.g., Guilamo-Ramos, et al., 2007). In addition, they are expected to ready themselves to be mothers and wives, and not chase a career that will take them away from the home (Fregoso, 1995). Danni's behavior violates not only the expectation of respeto, it also goes against the behavior expected of daughters. Interestingly, while viewers of *Devious Maids* appear to embrace the idea of the ideal daughter, other Twitter users take to the platform to actively argue against this stereotype:

> #HispanicGirlsUnited because we were taught to clean up after men and make their food
>
> @jenniferr_perez

> "@SOMEXICAN: #HispanicGirlsUnited because my brother was allowed to go out & stay out but since Im a girl I have to stay home & do chores"
>
> @_dxniellla

In the case of these tweets, the hashtag #HispanicGirlsUnited has become a battle cry, a call to resist dominant ideals about Latinx men and women's behaviors. These tweets and others reflect an acute awareness of the differential treatment parents give to sons and daughters often discussed in literature (e.g., Guilamo-Ramos, et al., 2007), and the hashtag is used as a way to express dissatisfaction with this inequality, as well as a desire to change this. Change is seen as coming from individual empowerment, i.e., Latinas standing up for what they want to do, and using the hashtag as a call to action (e.g., "I will not be the stereotypical 'mexican' housewife, I will succeed in life and make my parents proud.#hispanicgirlsunited"—@Jazmin1271).

At the same time, the hashtag is also used to revere the sacrifice that women make for their families. Many tweets that discuss mothers' and daughters' success again circle back to the marianismo role so often bestowed on women, where women's success is tied to their desire to sacrifice for their family:

> #HispanicGirlsUnited because my mother's "American Dream" wasn't 2 buy a house. It was the chance 2 give our family a decent life
>
> @JohanaAmaya00

> Unlike HRC, mi abuelita has lived in poverty all of her life and worked to give her children and me everything that we needed #NotMiAbuela
>
> @possiblykarla

Reconstructing the Father Role

Conversely, the roles allotted to the men in the house, sons and fathers, is questioned more critically:

> Hispanic men have deep emotional problems stemming from the relationship they have w they mother
>
> @Adgile_Dol

> Having dinner ready and waiting unable to make a plate till your dad sits down to eat—#hispanicproblems
>
> @steffy_time_tho

These tweets do more than just summarize a problem and make the victims of the problem responsible for alleviating the issue—they actually include a clear condemnation of the behavior under discussion. Boys, who are coddled by their overprotective, overbearing mothers more than girls (cf. Ramirez Berg, 2002), are seen to have emotional problems, while being made to wait on a father who is late is seen as simply not done.

CONCLUSION

Twitter affords its users with the ability to take popular cultural understandings of Latinx culture and to reproduce these or alternatively create their own interpretations. The platform also affords the Latinx community with the ability to share their experiences, seek affirmation, and call on like-minded individuals to start changing certain aspects of the Latinx identity. As evidenced by the high number of replies, retweets, and quotes, Twitter's technological affordances for conversation and collaboration are used extensively, with users mainly expressing agreement with ideas expressed by others, thus using the platform to magnify the original expression.

The analysis presented in this chapter showed that, like in chapter 2, the discourses used on Twitter reflect, negotiate, and contest some of the dominant stereotypes prevalent in mainstream culture. Users appeared to draw clear lines about how far they would go in accepting certain stereotypes, but don't outright reject all stereotypical portrayals either. So, while most Twitter users seemed to accept the notion of the comedic Latina, analysis revealed they did not necessarily appreciate how writers used women's accents to mock them, and they also rejected the idea of the Latina as uneducated. Similar to the findings from chapter 2, most of the Twitter users embraced the notion of the smart-mouthed Latina, and appeared to be proud of their temper. In line with this, the Pachuca-chola-homegirl trope was readily embraced and projected on many of the Latina characters currently on television. At the same time, while many people on Twitter showed appreciation for the looks of the Latinx actresses, many Latinas themselves used Twitter to contest tropicalism. Twitter users also readily reproduced the stereotype of the Latinx male as the aggressive, selfish gangster, but instead of rooting for their downfall, viewers of the various shows rooted for their success. At the same time, viewers viewed these gangsters as sex symbols, tweeting about their looks and outfits. Many viewers took to Twitter to express their appreciation of the hombre stereotype, i.e., the Latino as respectful for his elders and his family, and an understanding of the contradiction Latinos faced in balancing all these different stereotypical expectations. Twitter users appear to wholeheartedly embrace the stereotypes associated with familismo, praising Latinx mothers who sacrificed everything for them. Conversely, Twitter users who saw themselves in the role of the daughter fought the place that they were expected to take in the family, and critiqued the passive role taken on by the men in the family. Again, it appears that Twitter users rely on the practice of bricolage to create an understanding of the world that encompasses both hegemonic and countercultural interpretations.

The social media platform appeared to especially serve as a space to connect with like-minded people and create networked (counter)publics, where Latinx constructed a discourse of shared experiences. Latinx took to Twitter to share stories about growing up Latinx, but also to contest the notion of Latinidad, and how non-Latinx culture has constructed Latinx identity. Twitter is used to express and share frustration at how the dominant culture has framed topics related to immigration, and at the same time serves as a platform where Latinx affirm their belonging in the U.S. as rightful citizens. More so than in the previous chapter, tweets analyzed for this chapter show that Twitter affords Latinx a space to express their frustration at social inequalities and injustices. Twitter then renders discussions that used to take place in (semi-)private conversations to become public and gain visibility across communities.

4

#AsianProblems

Constructing Cultural Understandings of Asian Americans

"What kind of Asian are you, Chinese or Japanese?"
"Neither."
"Then what are you? Asian-ese?"
#BeingAsian

@chubkyun

The stereotyping of Asian Americans made major headlines a few years ago with the infamous "Asians in the library" YouTube video, in which a white college student complained about the Asian American students on her campus in racially charged terms. Up until that point, the representation of Asian Americans in the media, while far from unproblematic, had remained mainly invisible to the majority of media users.

Like other ethnic minorities, Asian Americans have always been, and still are, underrepresented in the media (e.g., Ono & Pham, 2009). The past years, however, have seen some positive changes when it comes to the presence and portrayal of Asian Americans. First, there was the increase in television shows centered on Asian Americans—*Dr. Ken*, *Quantico*, and *Fresh Off the Boat*, to name the major ones. Second there was increased attention for the lack of representation in mainstream media on Twitter, through hashtags such as #StarringJohnCho and #White WashedOut. In spite of all these positive changes, though, there is still much to be done about the portrayal of Asian Americans (Hess, 2016). Considering the popularity of social media among Asian Americans (Facebook IQ, 2015; Nielsen, 2015b) and the young adults who view the shows featuring Asian Americans, this chapter investigates how Twitter is used to construct shared interpretations of Asian American culture, and if these interpretations challenge or accept dominant understandings of Asian Americans.

ASIAN AMERICANS IN THE MEDIA

In the 1990s, the show *All-American Girl* was hailed as the beginning of the end for Asian American invisibility and stereotyping in mainstream media. When the show, which was based on Korean-American Margaret Cho's life, was canceled after only one season, it was clear that this was not to be. While some viewed the show as providing a positive counterpoint to existing negative stereotypes, the overall consensus was that the show did little more than re-create a white view of the Asian American experience. This was especially apparent through the fact that while the entire cast was Asian American, only two were actual Korean-Americans. This casting choice is indicative of the mainstream narrative that erases differences between the various ethnic groups and that assumes all Asian Americans, regardless of their national origin, share the same cultural background, perspectives, and experiences (Ono & Pham, 2009; Hong, 2006).

Asian American identity is often rendered invisible in mainstream culture. This is reflected in the failure to recognize Asian Americans as a separate ethnic group, as well as the use of white actors to play Asian American characters ("yellow face"). Moreover, the invisibility is apparent through the media's tendency to ignore the Asian American roots of multiracial actors such as Keanu Reeves and Dean Caine (Hess, 2016; Kawai, 2005; Nishime, 2014; Ono & Pham, 2009; Sue, Bucceri, Lin, Nadal, & Torino, 2007).

In the late 19th- and early 20th-century American fears of increasing numbers of Asian immigrants led to the birth of the "Yellow Peril" trope, where Asian Americans were viewed as a direct threat to the country (Kawai, 2005; Kim, 1999; Sun & Starosta, 2006). This stereotype was reflected in many of the first movies turned out by Hollywood: Asian American men were often portrayed as the villain, a threat to America and Western society in general, and white women in particular (Ono & Pham, 2009).

By the 1960s, mainstream American perceptions of Asian Americans switched from that of the Yellow Peril to that of a model minority. According to this trope, Asian Americans are the most successful minority group, characterized by close-knit families, low crime rates, and a lack of mental or social problems, as well as a good work ethic. Subsequently, Asian Americans are generally perceived as having achieved high levels of education and financial success (e.g., Chu & Kwan, 2007; Kawai, 2005; Ono & Pham, 2009; Sun & Starosta, 2006; Wang, 2010). While this sounds like an overall positive portrayal, the success of this model minority is often perceived as a threat by the mainstream culture which is then neutralized by invoking a modified version of the Yellow Peril trope. This modification entails attributing Asian Americans' success to characteristics that are labeled as distinctly Asian, including a lack of creativity, a tendency to avoid social interactions, and insistence on putting one's career before one's personal life. By ascribing Asian Americans' success to features that are characterized as un-American, Asian Americans are essentially painted as not truly American and thus not equal to white Americans, even if they are equally or more successful (e.g., Chu & Kwan, 2007; Kawai, 2005; Ono & Pham, 2009; Wang, 2010; Shen, Wang, & Swanson, 2011).

As a result of the model minority–Yellow Peril trope, Asian Americans are generally portrayed as good at math and sciences, smart, hardworking, driven, loyal to their families, and respectful of authority (Shen, et al., 2011). Their perceived desire for good careers and financial stability is portrayed as leading to a frugal, self-disciplined, and self-sufficient lifestyle. Asian Americans are portrayed as apolitical and, unlike other ethnic minorities, very much able to pull themselves up by their bootstraps. In other words, Asian American are seen as the ideal but perpetual immigrant (Huang, 2012; Kim, 1999).

The representation of Asian American men has been characterized by the dialectic of the threatening gangster trained in martial arts and the physically unattractive "nerd." Asian American men often provide comic relief, and as such are clearly positioned as inferior to white characters. Asian American men are also portrayed as asexual, effeminate, emasculated, and are portrayed as possessing a more feminine physique than their white or African American counterparts (Keum, Wong, & DeBlaere, 2014; Ono & Pham, 2009; Wong, Owen, Tran, Collins, & Higgins, 2012).

The portrayal of Asian women has been strongly influenced by the manner in which the first Asian women migrated to America: as sex workers or "picture brides" in the late 19th century. Subsequently, Asian American women have never been able to shake the image of the overtly sexualized seductress (Perez, 2013). In the past, this image was expressed as either the innocent, naïve Lotus Blossom, the self-sacrificial Madam Butterfly, or the manipulative, sex-driven Dragon Lady. As Ono and Pham (2009) point out, while these blatant stereotypes have long disappeared, they still persist in today's mediated presentations, albeit in a subtler way, with actresses like Lucy Liu portrayed as smart, almost aggressive, and willing to use her sexuality as a weapon. As a result of the model minority trope, Asian American women are also portrayed as driven, hardworking, but lacking empathy (Ono & Pham, 2009), which aligns with the Western view of Asian American mothers as the "tiger mom," i.e., the authoritarian mom whose tough love and focus on education creates successful children (Nishime, 2014; Shin & Wong, 2013).

Like Latinx families, Asian American families emphasize the importance of maintaining positive relationships: a focus on collectivism ensures that a family member's sense of self is closely tied to one's familial relationships, resulting in behavior aimed at bringing honor to the family and preserving face. Sacrificing oneself for the good of the family is a common value in Asian American families (Shin & Wong, 2013), as is holding on to traditions (Facebook IQ, 2015). This collectivism extends outside the family too, with Asian American culture focused on promoting social harmony and giving up one's own desires to conform to the group's norms and expectations (Chu & Kwan, 2007).

RECONSTRUCTING ASIAN AMERICAN IDENTITY

Even though the days of Fu Manchu and Madam Butterfly are far behind us, the representation of Asian Americans in mainstream media has a long way to go before it can be considered diverse, realistic, and fair. With the rising popularity of social media, Asian Americans, like other ethnic groups, have started to use these platforms to reflect on existing media content and create their own, expressing themselves in ways that they do not see in mainstream media (Balance, 2012; Guo & Lee, 2013; Nakamura, 2008). The question this raises is how Asian Americans use these platforms to (re)create their own understandings of age-old stereotypes presented throughout popular culture. Research has looked into how Asian Americans use YouTube to construct a cultural identity, arguing that YouTube offers Asian American producers the possibility to resist hegemonic discourses (Balance, 2012). In spite of this optimism, research has consistently shown that YouTube videos created by Asian American YouTube celebrities recreated dominant understandings of race and masculinity, a finding attributed to the producers' desire to get as many views as possible (Chun, 2013; Guo & Lee, 2013). The main space of resistance, according to Chun (2013), who analyzed YouTube celebrity Kevin Wu, lies in the comments on this particular video: this is where viewers can and do in fact create alternative interpretations.

This chapter starts where these studies left off and focuses on the one space specifically designed for people to comment on popular culture, namely Twitter. Unlike YouTube, Twitter is not often used as a place to build a reputation or get the attention of major record labels or production companies, so if viewers desire to express counterhegemonic views, this would be the space to do so. In this chapter, I examine how people commenting on Asian Americanness in popular culture through Twitter reflect, re-create, and negotiate dominant understandings of Asian American culture. Asian American in this chapter has been defined as broadly as possible, and encompasses anyone that claims an Asian background, including but not limited to people from countries such as Japan, China, Korea, the Philippines, Taiwan, India, and Vietnam (cf. Humes, Jones, & Ramirez, 2011).

The analysis presented in this chapter is based on data taken from publicly available tweets. Like the previous chapters, the data came from two sources. First, I looked for tweets that were about shows that featured Asian American characters: *Fresh Off the Boat (FOTB), Quantico, Dr. Ken, Hawaii Five-O,* and *The Unbreakable Kimmy Schmidt*. I collected tweets from the 24-hour period immediately following the show's 2016 season premiere and midseason finale. In the case of shows where the Asian American character was one in a cast made up of a variety of ethnic groups, I also searched for tweets with just that character's name. This chapter also examined top trending topics that addressed specific Asian American issues over the past few years. I included tweets that used the hashtags #NotYourAsianTigerMom (and its much less popular counterpart, #NotYourAsianTigerDad), and #HowIMetYourRacism. The former two hashtags were a response to Amy Chua's latest book early in 2014, while the latter was a response to a 2014 episode from *How I Met Your Mother* where the show was accused of relying on Asian American stereotypes and using yellow face (Broder Van Dyke, 2014; Wu, 2014). Other trending topics this chapter analyzes include #BeingAsian, #AsianProblems, #WhiteWashedOut, #OscarsSoWhite, and #MyYellowFaceStory. #MyYellowFaceStory trended in the spring of 2016 and addressed people's concerns with the lack of Asian American representation on stage, while #WhiteWashedOut was a top trending hashtag around the same time and was started to put a halt to the use of yellow face (Cheng, 2016; Viagas, 2016). #OscarsSoWhite trended in February 2016 and focused on the lack of diversity at the Oscars (Ryan, 2016). #BeingAsian and #AsianProblems trended a few months earlier, while #StarringJohnCho, a trend whereby people put the face of actor John Cho on to movie posters featuring white actors, was started around the same time (Lee, 2016; Rogers, 2016). Finally, the analysis also included #NotYourAsianSidekick (a hashtag started in 2013 that focused on Asian American actresses; Capachi, 2013). A total of 12,477 tweets were included in the analysis.

LOTUS BLOSSOMS AND DRAGON LADIES: RECONSTRUCTING THE ASIAN AMERICAN FEMALE

In this section, I address how people on Twitter look at current representations of Asian American women and negotiate the tropes commonly associated with Asian American femininity.

The Struggle over the Mail-Order Bride

The mail-order bride industry, which started in the 1970s and persists today as an online venture, plays into white hegemonic views of Asian women as Lotus Blossoms. It commodifies Asian women's bodies, allowing white men to re-create themselves as the knight in shining armor, ready to save Asian women from their plight (Perez, 2013). The question raised by the increased use of digital technologies is whether these can provide Asian American women with the agency needed to create an oppositional understanding (Sciachitano, 2000) The analysis carried out for this chapter showed that a large number of tweets that used hashtags centered on Asian American culture and identity such as #BeingAsian, addressed the dominant narrative surrounding Asian American women. In fact, #NotYourAsianFetish was actually a "spin-off" from #NotYourAsianSidekick, indicating that Twitter has provided Asian American women with the space to take back the conversation about their bodies.

The first finding to come out of the analysis was that a large number of Asian American women took to Twitter to describe the experiences they had with the trope of the sexualized, commodified Asian body:

> #beingAsian means "exotic, permissive, submissive, petite," and other hypersexualized words are used to describe my whole race and gender
>
> @VananhPHNerd

> #BeingAsian means being told you're attractive bc said guy has a "[insert ethnicity] fetish" for you
>
> @megsnewcar

While these tweets involve mere observations, without any critical assessment or pushback, they are posted in a public forum. Just the act of recording one's experiences can be seen as creating visibility for Asian women, as a form of pushback against dominant narratives, and thus as an act of empowerment.

Others use Twitter to express their disapproval of the objectification of Asian women, utilizing it to broadcast feelings and opinions that, without

Twitter, might have gone unheard or remained restricted to the user's circle of friends:

> Type in "Filipina" on Google and see what you find. Tired of these dating sites fetishizing Filipino women. #notyourasiansidekick
>
> @kalihischolar

> #BeingAsian doesn't mean that im merely a sex object for white consumption as an AsAm woman. I will always be a multifaceted
>
> @CuteAngryAsian

@kalihischolar's tweet shows how the use of a hashtag that provides a critical frame for current discourse about Asian Americans can change the tone of a tweet from a personal expression of frustration to a call for empowerment. Many women echo this sentiment, using Twitter as a place to safely express their feelings. For some, Twitter becomes a platform they can use to mock these white, postcolonial views of them, and regain some of the power that this hegemonic discourse took away:

> It's safe to say I won't be accepting your FB friend request when your friends list is composed of ONLY Asian women. #notyourasianfetish
>
> @jen_wbdalliance

> No, I will not "ruv you rong time." #NotYourAsianFetish #MyAsianAmericanStory
>
> @keikoinboston

Some use Twitter to express their disapproval of what happens to them in real life, which can, as seen by the tweet below, lead to support from others:

> a guy just called me his "spicy little spring roll" uhmm nah #NotYourAsianSidekick #NotYourAsianFetish
>
> @lucandyy

> RT #zeynep: Nothing prepared me his spicy little spring roll uhmm nah #NotYourAsianSidekick #NotYourAsianFetish
>
> @puppet_ebooks

While these hashtags provide Asian American women with the space to contest dominant stereotypes, Twitter is also used to perpetuate the trope of the sexualized Asian women through the discussion of the Asian women on television. Large numbers of tweets comment on how viewers think Jessica Huang from *FOTB* is hot, how Grace Park from *Hawaii Five-O* is sexy, and how Priyanka Chopra, who plays Alex Parrish on *Quantico,* is beautiful. Some viewers take this objectification a step further, expressing their personal fantasies about the characters (e.g., "Can someone please write an episode of *Hawaii Five-O* that gets Grace Park and Katee Sackhoff on a beach!"—@dementedtwist). Although Twitter provides some women with a space to resist dominant narratives, it equally allows others to perpetuate those same narratives.

The Strong Woman

Even though some tweets objectify Asian American females in the media, there are also many tweets like this:

> #AlexParrish #Queenofquantico Strong as hell Smart as hell Hot and Sexy as hell #PriyankaChopra @SweetZzoya
>
> @AakashGanguly

This tweet reflects how Alex Parrish is not only hot, but also tough, smart, and strong. Similar tweets were found about Grace Park and Alex Parrish's characters "kicking butt," being "badasses," and not needing a man to rescue them. Jessica Huang is also described as the epitome of the Tiger mom, as well as Twitter users' personal hero, and someone they aspire to be. These interpretations appear to bypass any of the Asian American stereotypes; the women are perceived as strong, but for others' good, thus steering clear of the Dragon Lady trope. Twitter users admire these three women for doing the right thing, even when situations are tough, as such creating an entirely new interpretation of Asian American women.

Closely related to the idea of women as tough and resilient is the perception that Asian American women are efficient, hardworking, and dedicated. This is mirrored in the portrayal of female Asian characters in the media, whose behavior fits the model minority archetype. Twitter users do notice this, but appear to celebrate it rather than critique it:

> Yeah Molly is handling business! You go girl hahaha yet another reason to love this lady!! #DrKen @kristamarieyu #HandleIt
>
> @ColeJones83

> "You white people love throwing around that word. Impossible. 'Oh Jennifer, my bangs are IMPOSSIBLE.'" @ConstanceWu I love you @FreshOffABC
>
> @symbolicth0t

The first tweet praises Molly, the oldest daughter on *Dr. Ken* for taking charge during a party where the Dean of Admissions for Stanford, her school of choice, was in attendance. The second tweet reflects on a scene where Jessica from *FOTB* refuses to give up on a problem that seems to be unsurmountable. Viewers revel in the women's dedication, and in Jessica's case, the blunt racially charged statement that white people will give up on things a lot more quickly than Asians. While this is as a celebration of Asians' perseverance and their subsequent success and a jab at white Americans' lack of tenacity (and thus, it is implied, achievement), it also feeds directly into the model minority stereotype.

Renegotiating the Lotus Blossom

Finally, Asian Americans appear to use Twitter to negotiate the stereotype of the Lotus Blossom, i.e., the idea that all Asian women are demure, obedient, and sacrificial (Ono & Pham, 2009). The tweets above reveal that Twitter users applaud strong, outspoken Asian American women on television. On the one hand, these beliefs are mirrored in tweets which indicate a clear disagreement with the belief that Asian women should be quiet and reserved. The platform provided by Twitter becomes a tool to broadcast one's rejection of the Lotus Blossom:

> This tag #NotYourAsianSideKick is so important for Asian female! We are not submissive or sex symbol! Say it LOUD!
>
> @Hanapleek

> we're not here to be the butt of your jokes, the helpers of your homework, the weaker ones, we're #notyourasiansidekick
>
> @dontkatsu

Some Asian American women use Twitter as an outlet for their frustration with the responses they receive when their behavior is not in line with people's expectations:

> BeingAsian means hearing 'you're quite outspoken for an Asian woman' @naisA_Global #BeingAsianWomen
>
> @JamieYSheen

> #BeingAsian means being told multiple times that my anger is cute
>
> @octavia_sun

> being an opinionated Asian American is really hard bc ppl expect you to shut up & become a doctor & I'm sick of that #NOTYOURASIANSIDEKICK
>
> @Liaa_Fernandez

Others use Twitter to express frustration at the limited sexuality that the Lotus Blossom offers Asian American women:

> i'm not allowed to be demure or submissive without it being fetishized/ stereotyped #beingasian
>
> @kimmaayy

But, on the other hand, Twitter is also used to applaud one specific aspect of the Lotus Blossom: the woman as self-sacrificial:

> #NotYourAsianTigerMom I wldn't b the actor,writer that I am if my Mum hadnt made the ulitmate sacrife 4 me so that I cld live & hve a life
>
> @LucySheen

> For sacrificing everything to make sure that your daughters could only strive to be half of what you ever were. #NotYourAsianTigerMom
>
> @sadiasmusings

In short, while these Asian American women appear to reject the stereotypical view of them as quiet, shy, and reserved, the self-sacrificing associated with maternal behavior a la Madame Butterfly is still accepted and applauded.

THE KOREAN CHANNING TATUM: INTERPRETING THE ASIAN AMERICAN MAN

For the first few decades of film, Asian American men were relegated to the role of the villain. They embodied the concept of Yellow Peril through their hostility, cunning, and unstoppable desire to challenge the Western world. Since these early portrayals, Asian men have been presented in a wider variety of ways, although they are still limited in their characterization (e.g., Ono & Pham, 2009). In this section, I examine how Twitter users negotiate their interpretation of Asian American males.

The Effeminate Male

A returning theme in the representation of Asian American males is their emasculation. One way that the media have rendered Asian men less threatening is by portraying them as effeminate and asexual (Ono & Pham, 2009; Keum, et al., 2014). Portrayals of characters like Ken on *Dr.*

Ken, Louis Huang on *FOTB*, and Dong on *The Unbreakable Kimmy Schmidt* are examples of the stereotypical, geeky, and emasculated males. The argument could be made, though, that their comedic antics create space for oppositional interpretations through the semiotic excess produced through their performance (cf. King, 2002; Seethaler, 2013).

When analyzing how Twitter users discuss these men's portrayals, however, it does not immediately become clear if viewers actively challenge the stereotype of the effeminate male, or whether their appreciation of the humor merely validates the trope:

> "Because I'm petty and dramatic." #DrKen
>
> @givemesometruth

> Perfectly summarizes my life, @kenjeong "This is not the time to mock my slight frame and delicate features." @DrKenABC #DrKen
>
> @DrArtemusPrime

These particular tweets quote Ken, in two scenes where he appears to poke fun at the stereotypical emasculated Asian male he portrays. However, tweets like these provide no clue as to how viewers interpret these lines. People who tweet quotes generally do so while live tweeting, as a way to emphasize information or ideas that they thought was important (Bruns & Burgess, 2012; Jungherr, 2014). The fact that these Twitter users quoted these lines indicates these lines somehow touched a nerve with them. But without any clear indication of what they meant for them, other than that they were funny or reminded them of the rough time they are going through right now, their quoting could mean an endorsement of the stereotype as it is.

Dong, Kimmy Schmidt's Vietnamese love interest on the show *The Unbreakable Kimmy Schmidt,* is a highly contested character. Numerous reviews touch on the fact that while his portrayal appears to underscore every male Asian stereotype in the books, he does eventually become Kimmy's love interest, taking him out of the standard "Asian sidekick" role (e.g., Chow, 2015). Viewers grapple with their understanding of Dong as well, with some indicating appreciation for the relationship between him and Kimmy and expressing anger when Dong marries someone else to secure a green card:

> Damn it Dong. I WAS ROOTING FOR YOU WE WERE ALL ROOTING FOR YOU #UnbreakableKimmySchmidt #titusandromedon #KimmySchmidt
>
> @kerrilynpaloma

The tweet is particularly interesting, as it references the famous scene from *America's Next Top Model,* in whichTyra Banks loses her temper at one of the contestants and tells her "we were all rooting for you" discussed in chapter 2. This particular viewer thus equates Dong's behavior to that of a spoiled teenage girl, indicating that Dong's association with Kimmy is what elevated him above the stereotypical, geeky and effeminate Asian immigrant, and that once he divests himself from that, he is no more than your average emasculated Asian male.

Other viewers outright reject Dong's portrayal, calling his performance "old school racism" (@janhopis), critiquing the producers of the show, and showing frustration at how audiences seem OK with his portrayal:

> I can just imagine Tina Fey thinking of Dong's character in Kimmy Schmidt "Ok so we need an Asian . . . immigrant.
>
> @kayyweeezy_

> Because y'all white people ignore the treatment of Dong's character when you are talking about Kimmy Schmidt #whitewashedOUT
>
> @deidrene

@deidrene takes to Twitter to render visible the different interpretations that white and non-white viewers will have of Dong's story arc, showing not only a refusal to accept his portrayal but a critical awareness of the influence of ethnicity on the acceptance of stereotypes.

Interestingly, in spite of viewers' tendency to accept the portrayal of Asian American men as effeminate, the tweets analyzed also showed that Dong is viewed as attractive:

> Dong from kimmy Schmidt is such a hottieeeeee
>
> @BrookeCompton_

> I started watching the unbreakable kimmy Schmidt today and WHO plays Dong I need to marry him
>
> @fleurdelis

This interpretation runs counter to the view of Dong as the emasculated male, positing him instead as a sex symbol. Dong is not the only Asian male seen as "hot"; in one *Dr. Ken* episode, Dr. Ken feels threatened by a rival Korean doctor who is very attractive. Ken calls him "The Korean Channing Tatum," a statement that is retweeted numerous times, with people indicating their agreement that this particular man is very handsome. In addition, during the #StarringJohnCho campaign, Twitter users took great pleasure in retweeting posters of John Cho in a variety of action and romantic roles played by white actors, demonstrating a willingness to see Asian American men in action-heavy, masculine roles. Similarly, when discussing Daniel Dae Kim's character on *Hawaii Five-O* Twitter users mainly focus on his good looks, using Twitter to objectify him. This in itself is a countercultural interpretation. Asian American men are generally not viewed as sexy or attractive: In order to erase their earlier image as virile but aggressive and threatening, the media have taken extra care to portray Asian men as nonthreatening and thus asexual. The fact that women view Kim as attractive is thus a step forward in people's interpretation of Asian American men.

However, tweets also show a reliance on a gaze usually reserved for females, where the object of the attraction is rendered passive ("eye candy") and reduced to their bodies:

> Daniel Dae Kim is wandering around in a v. v. tiny towel and I forgot half my complaints about the show
>
> @MarySueSays

> Daniel Dae Kim from Hawaii Five-O had the strongest cheekbone game that I have ever witnessed with my own two eyes
>
> @ayyyimani

This last example, with its focus on Kim's facial structures, reflects Nishime's (2014) analysis of Keanu Reeves, where she notes how the fans' focus on his eyes and cheekbones reflects "stereotyped exaggerated femininity" (p. 29). While viewers do sexualize Daniel Dae Kim, counter to the dominant narrative, they appear to view Kim through a feminine lens. This feminine view of Daniel Dae Kim is exacerbated by his endorsement of Clinique skin care products for men. As part of Clinique's #BehindTheFace campaign, Kim talks about his experiences as the child of Korean immigrants, and how his wife inspired him to take better care of his skin, accepting not only his status as a perpetual foreigner, but also firmly placing himself in the feminine discourse often applied to Asian American males. When Daniel Dae Kim shared this campaign through a tweet, one Twitter user responded with:

> @danieldaekim @Clinique @VanityFair How do I convince Daniel Dae Kim to go on a date with me lol he is so beautiful!
>
> @ParisLibby

Kim is described as "beautiful." Not the more masculine "handsome" or sexualized "hot," but "beautiful," a very feminine term, effectively undermining the countercultural movement of recognizing Asian American men as attractive.

Tweeting about the Robot Asian

Asian American males have also been rendered unthreatening through their portrayal as the "Robot Asian"; i.e., a work-focused, nerdy professional without any social life (Guo & Lee, 2013, p. 398). As @Taedaelay notes:

> #BeingAsian not seeing any asians on tv shows unless they're playing nerds or ninjas

The Robot Asian is a trope common to mediated representations and reappears in both *Dr. Ken* and *FOTB*. These shows touch on these stereotypes through two of the children in the shows, who love school, work hard, and are a little naïve and geeky (Dave in *Dr. Ken* and Evan in *FOTB*). The shows, through the excess in their portrayal of both boys, provide viewers with the space to contest these stereotypes, and on Twitter, users pick up on several specific scenes:

> MY NORMAL AESTHETIC. I LOVE EVAN. #freshofftheboat
>
> @containthechloe

In this scene, Evan compliments his Taiwanese cousin on his school uniform by calling it "close to his normal aesthetic." Evan is far too young to comfortably use a phrase like that, and viewers find humor in his precociousness, recognizing the Robot Asian stereotype, but not necessarily challenging it. On *Dr. Ken*, the trope of the Robot Asian returns in several episodes too. While the show obviously mocks this stereotype (at one point, Dr. Ken tells his nerdy son who is about to join the robotics club that the best way to make friends is to build them), viewers do not pick up on this challenge at all. Viewers merely retweet a tweet from the Twitter account associated with the show that includes an excerpt from this scene. Some include the words "seems like solid advice" (@aliciamaryweath), which appears to join the show in mocking the stereotype, but there is never any clear recognition of the implied subversion. In the 2016 midseason finale, Dave is approached by his sister Molly who needs help understanding her cute but nerdy lab partner. When Dave admits to knowing all about anime, Molly tells him, "See, you speak dork," to which Dave responds, "Fluently." This particular exchange is retweeted numerous times, with most viewers adding an "lol" or a laughing emoji, but not indicating any critique of this exchange or the stereotype it implies and appears to subvert. The same happens when Allison, Dr. Ken's wife tries to convince Dr. Ken that he really needs a hobby, and he replies that he doesn't because he has his job, "his sweet khakis," and his wife, in that order. This exchange gets retweeted several times, and the only user that adds any meaning on to this, does it as follows:

> "I've got my job . . . my sweet khakis." J. #Midlifethuglife #DrKen
>
> @rofodaruler

In this tweet, the user calls Dr. Ken out for being middle aged and boring by using the hashtag "midlifethuglife," a hashtag people use when they describe mundane dull activities that they undertake that are responsible and mature but anything but "thug." The hashtag is thus a tongue-in-cheek acceptance of how life changes when one gets older. This tweet could be seen as a recognition of the subversion of the Robot stereotype. At the same time, the tweet is sufficiently vague that the author could have also intended an acceptance of the Robot stereotype by calling Ken out for being as far removed from cool and interesting as possible.

WHAT I AM IS WHAT I AM: NEGOTIATING IDENTITY AND BELONGING

Asian Americans' presence in the US is characterized by a dialectical opposition between perpetual foreignness on the one hand, and racial invisibility on the other. Asian Americans are, above everything else, always seen as the outsiders, a group that is "immutably foreign and unassimilable" (Kim, 1999, p.107), a perception in part the result of their success. As discussed earlier in this chapter, Asian Americans are permanently invisible due to limited media representations, and faced with the fact that non-Asian Americans fail to distinguish between the different ethnic groups in the Asian community. In the next section, I discuss how Asian Americans negotiate this invisibility and foreignness on Twitter.

Ethnic Identity

In 2016, the #BeingAsian and #AsianProblems hashtags produced thousands of tweets about the quirks of being an Asian American. Asian Americans took to Twitter to write about experiences they thought were common to the Asian American culture, such as eating rice with every meal, the embarrassment at admitting they did not know how to eat with chopsticks, and having friends' parents serve them pork because "that's what all Asian people like" (@olygeeks). Besides allowing Twitter users to share common experiences, numerous tweets also reflected the struggles Asian Americans experienced in constructing their identity.

One of the issues that comes up on Twitter time after time is the conflation of different Asian nationalities by non-Asian Americans:

> #BeingAsian
> Having to explain to people that not all Asians look alike, that the term Asian is not a look or style. (this tweet is accompanied by a picture of four different Asian women)
>
> @brendarambitan

> #beingasian means people get confused when you tell em you're Korean and then they're like ? I thought you're Asian?
>
> @Yuudi_yuudi7

> When asked by a coworker if I want to be called by my Thai name in a meeting. We've worked together for a while & I'm not Thai. #BeingAsian
>
> @tannienguyen

More than anything else, these tweets reveal non-Asian Americans' tendency toward *orientalism*, the notion that the Western world is superior to the east and that therefore it is not relevant for Westerners to know and remember all the different ethnic groups in Asia (e.g., Kim & Chung, 2005; Said, 1978).

Like the Latinx Twitter users in the previous chapter, some Asian American Twitter users express frustration at the ongoing questioning of their background:

> #BeingAsian as a South Asian & mixed race person means that 1) no one thinks you're Asian 2) everyone invalidates your identity constantly
>
> @mayag_j

> #BeingAsian but also having a lot of people tell you, directly or indirectly, that you are too dark-skinned to be "truly Asian"
>
> @sunshowerwitch

When *Dr. Ken* plays on this by having one of the characters mistakenly assume Ken is Chinese, several tweets quote the line, as an indication of enjoying the comedy, but there are no signs of recognition or frustration at something that apparently happens quite often. The same happens when Dr. Ken admits to not being a member of the local Korean club and calling himself a "bandwagon Korean." People took to Twitter to indicate their agreement and their enjoyment at this particular statement. There appeared no desire to challenge this description of himself as not really invested in his ethnic identity. This could be because the people tweeting about this particular episode were not Asian American and thus did not recognize this issue as salient. However, it could also be the result of the fact that many Asian Americans identify as American (Cheryan & Monin, 2005). It is possible that jokes like the ones on *Dr. Ken* merely reinforce what Asian Americans experience on a daily basis and don't touch on their core identity, which is American, and not Korean or Chinese.

However, Asian Americans are often faced with "identity denial" (Cheryan & Monin, 2005, p. 717), i.e., white Americans refusing to acknowledge them as full-fledged Americans and instead emphasizing their Asian identity through questions like "Where are you from?" This kind of experience that was reflected on a great deal throughout both #AsianProblems and #BeingAsian:

> I'm a proud American citizen. Stop with the "No really where R U from?" when I say that. At least phrase it better! #NotYourAsianSidekick
>
> @arielwang13

> "Where are you from?"
> "Oh, I was bored here"
> "No, I meant, where are you REALLY from?"
> #AsianProblems
>
> @UpTownAsians

> #BeingAsian, living in North America means automatic assumptions that you're not a citizen, even though you've lived here your whole life.
>
> @cathusiast

Tweets such as these demonstrate that the belief that the American–white trope, proposed by Devos and Banaji (2005) is very much alive, but that Twitter provides Asian Americans with the space to challenge it.

In a discussion about the invisibility of Asian Americans in Hollywood, @Wong00T shared a post about this topic, upon which another user told him to "go back." @Wong00T then responded with:

> @kartikeysehgal @mikesteinberg13 @DragonNanoha @NerdyAsians "Go back" where? How long your family been in US? #whitewashedOUT
>
> @Wong00T

In this tweet, @Wong00T touches on the crux of identity denial, the refusal to acknowledge someone's core perception of themselves. In response, @Wong00T engaged in what Cheryan and Monin (2005) dubbed "identity assertion" (p. 718); i.e., reaffirming his/her American roots and identity.

Another way in which white Americans define Asian Americans as the "perpetual foreigner" is by focusing on their "Asian name." It is common for Asians who spend a lot of time interacting with foreigners to take on English first names, and Asian Americans who have non-American first names tend to do the same (Hsu, 2009; Kwon, 2016). While this is a common practice, many Asian Americans have taken to Twitter to express their displeasure at it:

> #BeingAsian is being reminded of ur perpetual foreignness b/c you don't have an easier aka "American" name.
>
> @sayutaka524

> "So, what's your real name? Like the Asian one." #BeingAsian
>
> @PKrompicha

The idea that one's "real" name is the Asian name, and that every Asian American must have one is an obvious reminder that as Asian Americans, these Twitter users do not truly belong, and Twitter is the space where they reject these interpretations. Asian Americans also take to Twitter to mock non-Asian Americans' lack of cultural awareness through tweets such as these:

> your name is weh #beingasian ¿
>
> @sherenbadlishah

This particular tweet is interesting, as it is very much an insider joke; "wei" is how Chinese-speaking people answer the phone. It's the equivalent of "hello," and obviously not someone's name. By only repeating the question @sherenbadlishah has received, s/he is making it impossible for anyone who does not speak Chinese or is familiar with Chinese culture (i.e., anyone who could ask that question) to get it: the ultimate resistance.

Both *Dr. Ken* and *FOTB* play with this convention. In the *FOTB* episode where the family travels to Taiwan, Eddie finds out that one of his Taiwanese cousins has "Hennesey" for his English name (because he's "smooth and always in the club"), while on *Dr. Ken*, Ken gets worked up about one of his wife's ex-boyfriends whom he assumes, based on his last name (O'Connell), is white, only to find out the man is actually Korean. Both of these scenes lead to much appreciation on Twitter:

> No that child didn't pick Hennessey for his name, lol #FreshOffTheBoat
>
> @ReadInColour

> @DrKenABC #DrKen hilarious-cubicle monkeysKorean Channing Tatum-lesson-never assume who someone is by their name.Dr O'Connell was adopted
>
> @peacewyns93

Viewers appear to appreciate these jokes as they subvert commonly held assumptions about Asians having either Asian names or conventional English names.

Besides struggling with recognition from non-Asian Americans, Asian Americans also use Twitter to point at the struggle they face in gaining acceptance from their own culture:

> #BeingAsian people say I'm not Asian bc I act white
>
> @highlightkth

> #BeingAsian is an odd experience—only recent brush w/racism was from other Asians for not being "Asian enough" in their eyes.
>
> @nakamachirabu

Tweets such as these one reflect the problem surrounding "acculturation" and "assimilation," i.e., the line between joining a new culture and changing your own cultural patterns to match those of the host culture, and completely integrating into the new culture without recognizing one's old traditions (Berry, 1997, p. 7). This feeling of being "stuck" between two cultures was captured by the opening episode of the 2016 *FOTB* season which focused on Jessica's struggle to feel at home during a visit to Taiwan, and viewers took to Twitter to express their pleasure at this storyline. They retweeted her lines, recognizing that in spite of what the dominant white culture may think of them, America is their home. As @kawaiiinnyc summarized:

> Stuck between 2 worlds, belonging to both, belonging in neither—the Asian American story #FreshOffTheBoat

Invisibility

One of the tropes of Asian representation that many tweets touch on is the lack of it. Asian Americans have been underrepresented in mainstream media for decades, and so when Asian Americans do make it on television, people take to Twitter in overwhelming numbers to express their delight at seeing Asian Americans in the mainstream media. At the same time, the nature of the representation is not without its problems, and Asian Americans on Twitter are more than aware of that:

> excited for Fresh Off the Boat, pissed that having a show w/ POC means sanitizing it to make it fun for white people
>
> @jazzedloon

In fact, Twitter often becomes a space where people discuss the white privilege that enables producers to create shows that stereotype Asian Americans. This became especially evident from the discussion surrounding the use of yellow face in *How I Met Your Mother*

> The yellowface is unreal. But White privilege allows whites to act out minority culture, & not suffer the consequences. #HowIMetYourRacism
>
> @S_Hill23

Twitter became a site of organized resistance when Margaret Cho and several other Asian American writers started the #WhiteWashedOut hashtag to protest the lack of Asian Americans in Hollywood movies. Tens of thousands of tweets picked up the banner, calling on producers to cast Asians in roles that were meant for Asians. Some tweets used sarcasm, other displayed anger, and others wondered why stories that were obviously Asian in nature could not feature Asian actors:

> Oh phew, 'Lone Wolf & Cub' will have an "essentially Japanese" cast . . . ESSENTIALLY! What a relief! #whitewashedOUT
>
> @mynette

> I find it REALLY insulting that 'Hawaii Five-O' is trying to play Daniel Dae Kim (A KOREAN) off as a Hawaiian. #really?
>
> @dylan1doyle

> um, the new #sailormoon takes place in japan there is #literallynoexcuse for making the characters white #whitewashing #notyourasiansidekick
>
> @jpmeyer

These Twitter users aggressively point out the prejudices that underpin the studios' casting decisions, using the social media platform as a site to unite individual voices in a protest against the mainstream media's tendency to render Asian Americans invisible.

Physical Features

Asian Americans also took to Twitter to discuss their physical characteristics. Many of them, mostly women, use Twitter to express frustration with their looks, which are deemed to be "too Asian" and reflecting on the desire to adhere to European beauty standards (Lau, Lum, Chronister, & Forrest, 2006):

> -Flat Face
> -No boobs
> -No ass
> #AsianProblems
>
> @AsiansForTheWin

> #beingasian means having some days where you feel the weight of your nose, wishing it was smaller, pointier, and didn't flare
>
> @nikathefreaka

What is interesting about these tweets is that they remain focused on the self and do not incorporate a critique of the social standards that create these feelings in the first place. Some Twitter users are unhappy with how they look, and by using #BeingAsian and #AsianProblems, they attribute it to their ethnic background. It appears that users have internalized Western expectations for their bodies, and then take to Twitter to express their unhappiness at the inability to meet these expectations. Tweeting about these issues and receiving likes and positive replies in return makes Twitter very much like a support group, where Asian Americans can connect in a networked counterpublic to share experiences and feelings, and receive support in return, as evidenced by @kterakita's use of "guys" in his or her tweet:

> Guys . . . I think I'm getting an ass J #squats #asianproblems

Asian Americans also use Twitter to vent about experiences where others rendered them aware of their physical inequities:

> I'm going to see Ghostbusters for the 2nd time at a VIP 19+ theatre & was asked if I was actually 19. I'm WAY older than 19 #asianProblems
>
> @pipey21

> #BeingAsian your weight constantly criticized by everyone you know or meet. Hearing thought Asians where skinny.
>
> @ChaoticAngel7

These users rely on Twitter as a safe space to express their unhappiness with how they look, rendering visible the intersection between racism faced by many Asian Americans.

The tendency of non-Asian Americans to use a racist yardstick to assess Asian Americans' looks returns in other hashtags as well, in particular in the #MyYellowFaceStory. This hashtag was used by Asian American actors and writers to share their experiences with racism. A returning theme in discussions using this hashtag was white Americans' ideas about Asian eyes. Eyes are an important element of the stereotypical portrayal of Asian characters in Western media (e.g, Nishime, 2014) and many Asian American actors used the hashtag to express dismay at non Asian-American people attempting to re-create these eyes:

> Non-Asian moms teaching other non-Asian moms how to make their kids' eyes "look right" when I was in 'The King & I.' #MyYellowFaceStory
>
> @justinwyu

> That time a castmate asked if he should tape his eyes to look more "oriental" instead of just using makeup. #MyYellowFaceStory
>
> @AndiM_AndiM_

The hashtag also appeared as a safe space for Asian American actors to connect and share stories about rejections because their appearance did not meet the stereotypical Asian physical features:

> I auditioned for a commercial & they loved that I was tall for an asian but hated that I was too dark for being one. SMDH #myyellowfacestory
>
> @BionicGoneFunk

> That time when my Agent called for feedback and they said 'She is a GREAT singer, but she is too fat for an Asian' #MyYellowFaceStory
>
> @Equill

This is another expression of orientalism, where Westerners not only believe they are superior to Asians to such effect that they know what Asian are supposed to look like more than Asians themselves, but also where Asians are exoticized to further separate them from white Americans (Leong, 2005).

All of these tweets relay stories that are disturbing and discriminatory, yet the people who shared them did nothing more than that: sharing. There was no call to action, no anger, no aggression. Again, the decades-long invisibility of the Asian population and the problems they face meant that this hashtag was probably one of the first times that actors could publicly discuss what goes on behind closed doors. As a result, the hashtag remained the mere sharing of stories it set out to be.

Language

The stereotype of the Asian American as the perpetual foreigner includes the portrayal of Asian Americans as having poor English skills (Shen, et al., 2011). Both *FOTB* and *The Unbreakable Kimmy Schmidt* play with this stereotype by including two characters whose English is not perfect. Jessica Huang has a tendency to use the incorrect words, while Dong, from *Kimmy* starts off with a thick Vietnamese accent and then, after listening to the Kardashians, speaks like a "valley girl." Dong's accent is described as racist and offensive while viewers find Jessica's mangled use of the English funny:

> Her "karate tortoise" line was the best part! @FreshOffABC #Ninjaturtles
>
> @sugarbriches82

What is interesting here is that both characters express themselves in unrealistic ways. The chances of anyone, especially a non-native speaker, confusing "'Teenage Mutant Ninja Turtles" for "Karate Tortoises" are as slim as someone having as exaggerated of a foreign accent as Dong. Yet viewers on Twitter express deep offense at Dong's character, while they find Jessica's mistake hilarious. One possible explanation is that Dong's portrayal makes him sound uneducated, while Jessica's mistake involves a relatively big word ("tortoise") that just makes her seem out of touch. It could be that viewers, in line with the model minority, cannot accept a representation that makes an Asian American seem uneducated.

The perception of Asian Americans as the perpetual foreigner and the subsequent expectation that they have an accent is reflected on Twitter as well, where viewers of shows that feature Asian Americans talk about their accents (or lack thereof). Twitter users comment extensively on how they expected Daniel Dae Kim's character on *Hawaii Five-O* to have the same Korean accent his character on *Lost* had, while also referencing Alex Parrish's accent on *Quantico* as something to love. This suggests viewers of these shows seem to take the idea that Asian Americans should have accents for granted, and that it's part of their exotic appeal. To take that away removes their identity, which is, in the eyes of these viewers, above all that of an Asian American.

The orientalism that informed non-Asian Americans' attitudes about what Asians should look like also translated to Asian Accents. #MyYellowFaceStory often shared anecdotes that revealed this kind of orientalism, where Asian Americans were told by white Americans what an Asian accent sounds like:

> The lady told me my accent was so good. She lived in Chinatown for a while. So she knew "mine" was good #MyYellowFaceStory
>
> @stephanelycuong

> "Your Chinese accent doesn't sound authentic." #MyYellowFaceStory
>
> @IsaacHoWriter

While all these stories show a lack of respect and understanding of Asian Americans, the Twitter users merely record the event, without any judgement. Again, #MyYellowFaceStory provided actors and writers with a space to share and educate, no more and no less.

DEFINING SUCCESS AND THE MODEL MINORITY

A large portion of the portrayal of Asian Americans in the media and in mainstream society centers on the successes achieved by members of this minority group. Subsequently, this theme is often the focus of discussions on Twitter, with users addressing several aspects of the model minority trope.

One facet that is addressed on numerous occasions is the belief that all Asians are smart and are expected to do well in school. Twitter users reflect on this without any sign of critique or resistance, but instead appear to be resigned to this definition:

> #BeingAsian "Of course you'd get an A, you're Asian!!!"
>
> @steff_choe

> #beingasian having college admissions hold you at a higher standard
>
> @guojilu

The only time Twitter becomes a site where people contest and negotiate what it means to be a smart Asian American is when they discuss television shows that address this trope. On the 2016 season premiere of *FOTB*, Evan, the family's most school-oriented son, has the opportunity to go to school in Taiwan with his cousin. After expressing joy at finding out that Taiwanese students have year-round school, Evan demands to be taken to the American Embassy when he sees a teacher slap his cousin. This scene, which is clearly meant to poke fun at the model minority concept, is well-received on Twitter with viewers quoting Evan's lines from this scene (e.g., "please take me to my embassy," and "It's like they read my wish journal") to indicate their appreciation of this perspective.

Some viewers, however, opt for an oppositional interpretation, and tie the notion of year-round school to the success that Asians have:

> #FreshOffTheBoat we don't have summer break. Year round school. #asian success
>
> @PeterRchai

These viewers thus propagate the model minority myth and the belief that Asian success hinges on their dedication to education. Others lambast Evan for not knowing that Taiwan doesn't actually have an embassy, indicating they believe that a child as smart as Evan should know better:

> The AIT "isn't" an embassy. #FreshOffTheBoat
>
> @givemesometruth

Others use this scene to point to the privilege that Evan as an Asian American has:

> "I am an American citizen. Take me to my embassy" #privilege #FreshOffTheBoat
>
> @BJGEsq

Unlike the other Taiwanese children in the classroom. Evan has a way out. In the eyes of this particular viewer, this reeks of entitlement.

> Evan pulled a white man's "HELP, I'm a American!" #FreshOffTheBoat (this tweet includes a gif of a group of Asian people laughing)
>
> @shortiduwop410

In this tweet, the user actually compares Evan to a white man, indicating that only white Americans would use their nationality as a way to get out of anything, and that this should really be beneath any Asian. The rejection of the show's narrative and focus on privilege and Evan's "whiteness" appears to reproduce the view of Asians as smarter and harder working than "the white man."

In the 2016 midseason finale for *Dr. Ken,* one particular storyline focuses on the family's daughter Molly's application to Stanford. When the Christmas party where the Dean of Admissions for Stanford is also in attendance threatens to flop, Molly steps in and saves the whole affair through some quick thinking. Her portrayal of the quick-witted, dedicated Asian American is accepted and appreciated by many Twitter users:

> How about Molly saving this party? She did one heck of a job. She is Stanford material no doubt. #DrKen
>
> @Magic20099

> @kristamarieyu You kept it together and got in to Stanford during a blackout. Nicely done. #DrKen
>
> @LAlupusLady

These tweets, and the many others like them, firmly place Molly in the camp of the smart Asian daughter, reproducing the model minority myth. Very few tweets strayed away from this interpretation. Even the actress who plays Molly reflected the idea that getting into Stanford should be Molly's main goal, by tying the show's storyline to her real-life brother's achievements, adding a level of realism to the storyline and implied model minority myth:

> My real bro got into Stanford . . . this is why Molly MUST get in #DrKen @RobsterYu #proudofyou
>
> @kristamarieyu

The only alternative interpretation of Molly's behavior was offered by a viewer who likened her actions to what they did to get into college:

> Molly being a kiss up to college admissions . . . it was like watching my past self #DrKen #Cringe
>
> @flyingchong

In this case, Molly isn't seen as smart or hardworking, but as sweet-talking to get what she wants. This takes the model minority myth and adds in touches of the Dragon Lady, i.e., the Asian woman who is manipulative and cunning, and will do what it takes to attain success (e.g., Ono & Pham, 2009).

Another dimension of the model minority myth is the notion that Asian Americans are dedicated and hardworking, which is the key to their success (as opposed to creativity or ingenuity). This too is often discussed on Twitter, although tweets render the hardworking trope more multidimensional, claiming that Asian Americans work hard to survive, not to win. Tweets move beyond the "Asians work hard" trope, revealing some of the contradictions that underpin this theme:

> Cuz we hustle financially to survive not beat others, and hustle in preserving our non-western cultures. #NotYourAsianTigerMom
>
> @bidrohicreed

> I love #BeingAsian—obstacles and all. We are a resilient and hardworking lot with perseverance like no other
>
> @AlexMallariJr

These tweets accept the model minority myth, but focus on the obstacles faced by Asian Americans. The desire to survive, to preserve one's culture, is what drives the resilience and dedication that is seen to characterize Asian Americans, which renders the myth much more sympathetic.

Asian Americans also took to Twitter to fight the common conception that the success associated with the model minority myth comes natural to them:

> people say, "of course you got an A." as if it didn't take hard work for me #beingasian
>
> @kimmaayy

> #BeingAsian means being told I did well in school because I am Asian, not because I worked hard.
>
> @charltonys

Others remarked on the same preconceived notion, but from a social perspective:

> #BeingAsian means having been told—"but its easier for you and less discriminating compared to other POC groups" bc of #modelminoritymyth
>
> @leanghuphea

@leanghuphea uses the hashtag #BeingAsian to remark on the unfair comparisons made between Asian Americans and other groups as a result of the model minority myth. This tweet thus points to the invisibility of the struggles faced by Asian Americans. However, even this tweet, like the other examples shown above, does not show any critique of the myth. It remains an observation, not a challenge. It is possible that the model minority myth is not seen as highly problematic since the myth acknowledges the hard work that goes into the success.

Asian American success is often tied to their ability to be careful with money (e.g., Oysterman & Sakamoto, 1997). The stereotype of Asians as frugal is one of the drivers behind the plot of the 2016 season opener for

FOTB, and viewers mention key scenes as a way to reflect on their own experiences with frugal Asian parents:

> I've missed you Fresh off the Boat. Nothing is more Asian than not going on vacations and sleeping on the floor.
>
> @lebronaldjames

Again, even though the portrayal of Asian American frugality on *FOTB* is excessive and most likely not meant to be taken seriously, most tweets merely express recognition. This finding is reflected in other hashtags as well, where large numbers of Twitter users share stories of parents jumping through hoops to save money. As @Thesueshi points out after a long discussion where several Twitter users shared tales of frugal parents:

> @fiveshinki we're such a frugal group; I'm proud of our skills, but as a kid I was a little embarrassed;)

In line with Oysterman and Sakamoto's (1997) findings, Asian Americans embrace the model minority stereotype and everything that comes with it because it means they can take pride in all the things their ethnic group can accomplish.

When it comes to Asian American success, this is often perceived as taking place in the STEM (Science, Technology, Engineering, and Math) fields (e.g., Shen, et al., 2011; Leong & Hayes, 1990). A large number of tweets focus on stereotype, with numerous expressing the limitations and expectations that it brings with it:

> #BeingAsian in America means growing up with only a few "respectable" career paths that you are encouraged to follow.
>
> @KalaMendoza

> #beingasian getting asked for ur papers in math class bc "you're asian you're supposed to be smart"
>
> @asamiiisato

Many Asian Americans used Twitter to discuss how their parents responded when they did not get a degree in a STEM-related field. While some indicated that parents had to learn to adjust (e.g., "In the end, she was proud of me and my English degree. #NotYourAsianTigerMom"—@shelzhang), others described how their parents never had these stereotypical expectations in the first place:

> #NotYourAsianTigerMom my mom always, always supported my art and was proud of me despite her hopes that I would go to law school
>
> @AngrygirLcomics

> #NotYourAsianTigerDad When I lost sight of my dreams after dropping computer science, my dad encouraged me to apply for art school.
>
> @Kaxbeokay

Even though these tweets question the STEM-oriented Asian American student trope, they still embody the stereotype of the Asian American as smart, college-educated, and desiring their parents' approval.

Due to their perceived success in school and focus on science and math, Asian Americans are often stereotyped as geeky (e.g., Oysterman & Sakamoto, 1997). This particular dimension of the hardworking immigrant trope is generally rejected across the Twittersphere.

> That time my PE teacher told me it was ok if I didn't do well in gym since "my people weren't athletic." Um . . . thanks? #MyYellowFaceStory
>
> @sarayublue

TIGER PARENTS: CONSTRUCTING THE ASIAN AMERICAN FAMILY

Asian American parenting styles came to the forefront a few years ago with Amy Chua's book on tiger moms. Tiger parenting can best be described as "competent yet unsociable" (Huang, 2012, p. 41), whereby the parents exert large amounts of control over their children's lives in order to ensure their academic success (e.g., Juang, Qin, & Park, 2013). Moreover, Asian American families are portrayed as collectivistic, i.e., they focus on social harmony and the importance of maintaining good relationships with family members. Familism, the belief that the importance of the family unit supersedes the needs of any one individual member, also plays a role in Asian American family life, and Asian Americans are generally seen as respectful of authority figures, obedient, and loyal (Oysterman & Sakamoto, 1997; Yeh, Inman, Kim, & Okubo, 2006).

Twitter users spend a lot of time discussing their understanding of Asian American families. This is no surprise considering that the two most popular shows that feature Asian Americans as the main characters, center on a nuclear family (*FOTB* and *Dr. Ken*), and the hashtag #NotYourAsianTigerMom gained a widespread following.

While the parents on *FOTB* and *Dr. Ken* are supportive of their children, the children appear completely self-motivated when it comes to their academic performance. In fact, in the 2016 midseason finale, when Molly, the oldest daughter on *Dr. Ken,* is stressing out about her application to Stanford, her parents appear completely unconcerned about their daughter's worries, assuring her that serving meatballs to the Stanford Dean of Admissions is fine. Molly's repartee, "Well, there's always community college" led to numerous mentions and conversations on Twitter which appeared to support the parents' laid back approach. Because the actors live-tweeted during this episode of Dr. Ken, there were also numerous interactions between viewers and the actors themselves about the "meatball" incident, such as this one, which involved a viewer (@ColeJones83) and the actress who plays Molly (@Kristamarieyu):

> Stanford standards. #anxiety #DrKen
>
> @kristamarieyu

> @kristamarieyu don't worry there's always community college
>
> @ColeJones83

> @BoyColeJones83 lesigh #drken #actuallyithinkmeatballsarethebest
>
> @kristamarieyu

This interaction is particularly interesting as it starts off with @kristamarieyu staying in character, reflecting Molly's anxiety about the party. One of the show's viewers plays along by quoting one of her lines from the show, at which point @kristamarieyu uses a hashtag to step out of character and indicate her agreement with the show's ridiculing of demanding, high-performing Asian American parents.

When examining *FOTB,* it becomes apparent that especially the mother, Jessica, embodies the tiger mother stereotype. She appears to aspire to the perfectionism and high demands of the tiger mother, and viewers pick up on this:

> I like Fresh Off the Boat but I always feel really bad for the kids
>
> @elizaeffect

> am i the only one who's been reading tiger mother in the voice of the mother from fresh off the boat
>
> @RyceDoria

But what the writers of *FOTB* have done is made Jessica fallible, and thus opened her character up for oppositional decoding. She often falls short or makes mistakes, like in the 2016 midseason finale, which spoofs, among other things, *Home Alone*. Jessica and her family go to the movies, accidentally leaving one of their children behind who then booby-traps the house to protect himself from intruders. Jessica's unapologetic response to leaving Evan at home is the exact opposite of *Home Alone*, where the mother is extremely contrite. The writers of *FOTB* juxtaposed the caring white mom who moved heaven and earth to get home to the cool, calculating Asian American mom who sat through the entire movie before going home and then refused to show any remorse. Interestingly, some viewers critique her for that:

> @FreshOffABC Darn marbles! And you tell Mommy, Evan . . . how could she forget her baby at home then sit thru a 90 min movie? #FreshOfftheBoat
>
> @Fab4tune

> @TheIanChen @FreshOffABC @therealraywise Loved the Home Alone allusion so much! Can't believe Jessica left you home!
>
> @_KennyUong_

Tweets such as these indicate that these viewers do not use the space the show offers them to create alternative interpretations of Jessica's character, and instead apply the tiger mom trope to her character without questioning.

The tiger parent trope is further discussed in hashtags such as #BeingAsian, #AsianProblems, and of course #NotYourAsianTigerMom and #NotYourAsianTigerDad. There does not appear to be any consensus about whether Asian American parents are tiger parents. Some users revel in sharing stories of strict parents with high demands, while others explained how their parents really weren't that protective or demanding. In addition, many Twitter users showed gratitude for their strict parents to getting them where they are now, as well as a desire to defend their strict upbringing:

> Whether our parents were strict or not has nothing to do with race. There are demanding parents everywhere. #NotYourAsianTigerMom
>
> @arissoh

> #BeingAsian means your parents want you to be a doctor or lawyer because they risked everything to come here so you can have what they didn't
>
> @shxhzil

These particular tweets (and others like it) acknowledge yet another aspect of the tiger mother trope: Parental willingness to sacrifice everything for their children's success (Huang, 2012). This tweet also reflects the hard-working immigrant trope, by referencing "the risk" a parent took "to come here," as well as the familism trope: One's parents risked everything for you, so you owe them. It seems that these particular tropes are commonly accepted among Asian Americans.

What is especially interesting here, however, is how Twitter users attempt to prove that their parents did not adhere to the tiger parenting model:

> My mom actually bragged to her friends that I interviewed indie bands (after I got a business degree & a day job . . .) #NotYourAsianTigerMom
>
> @txc84

> After getting degree in biochem from Yale, told mom I'd rather plan weddings. Her reply:"Proud of you no matter what." #notyourasiantigermom
>
> @ejpevents

While tweets like these attempt to debunk the tiger mother myth, they seem to do the exact opposite by indicating parental approval after the children had received the desired degrees. In their efforts to counter the stereotype, these users in fact further perpetuate it. Other Twitter users rely on the same strategy, they indicate parental approval of choices that were outside the norm (e.g., "taking art lessons instead of piano"—@ssoyunum) subsequently affirming that these normative expectations are still very much alive in the Asian American community. The same happens when Asian American mothers use the #NotYourAsianTigherMom topic to discuss how they refuse to have their children use an after-school math program, and explain this choice by stating they want to create "life-long learners" (@JulieJungKim). This reasoning reflects the tiger mom's desire to raise children to always want to learn and better themselves more than she realizes. Only a few Twitter users picked up on this, for example:

> "My mom cried when I wanted to be a writer not a doctor. But she was #NotYourAsianTigerMom!" Give me a break.
>
> @AskAKorean

In this case, the user does not directly engage with the unnamed user they quoted, but uses Twitter to critique people's eagerness to disavow the Asian tiger mother trope.

Several users critique Chua, the author of the book on the tiger mom. Some criticize how she uses a white narrative in her description of her parenting style, making it sound abusive while it is no more than a push for success ("Pushing me to succeed to make sure I'd survive and thrive. It wasn't abuse. White lens of Chua as damaging as her #NotYourAsian TigerMom"—@Hermit_Hwarang). @seanmiura echoes this perspective:

> Honestly, I think my mom is a #TigerMom. Not cause she ate her young like Chua, but cause she taught me how to roar. #NotYourAsianTigerMom

This user reframes what the tiger mother trope means, arguing that Chua's definition is detrimental to children, but that their mother's version was one that made them strong and powerful. In effect these users claim that while the tiger mom narrative as presented by Chua is both racist and ineffective, the way it is practiced by Asian Americans has great success.

An additional facet of the stereotypes surrounding Asian American parenting is the lack of emotional involvement. While this stereotype is applied to Asian Americans as a whole, it is especially poignant when discussing familiar relations. The combination of parents focused on education achievement and their inability to express love or warmth elicits the "fear and envy" (Huang, 2012, p. 42) that leads to the perpetuation of the Yellow Peril trope. Twitter provides Asian Americans with a space to hash out this stereotype, and they do so in a variety of ways. Some tweets reflect on how this stereotype was a reality in their lives:

> #BeingAsian Strict Up-bringing. Bad childhood. Prideful Parents don't express Love very well. Unfulfilled High Expectations.
>
> @T_Qiang_C

> #BeingAsian is when your mom asks "have you eaten yet?" because saying "I love you" is a little less awkward.
>
> @aileenymariposa

While others list examples of the different ways in which their parents were emotionally involved in their lives:

> #NotYourAsianTigerMom Mom (and dad!) saw that I was pushing myself too hard and taught me the value of self-care.
>
> @calvinhyj

> Mama wanted to spend more time w/her kids, left the corporate world, and started her own business from home. #NotYourAsianTigerMom
>
> @sadiasmusings

What is interesting about these tweets is that the ones that question the stereotype fall under the hashtag created to negate the tiger mother trope, while the ones that indicate the stereotype is still very much true use the #BeingAsian hashtag. The hashtags frame the discussion, bringing out different opinions on the same topic.

A final element that is seen as a part of Asian American familial traditions is the adherence to traditions and respect for authority. Twitter allows users to show how this stereotype does not reflect their lived experiences:

> #NotYourAsianTigerMom because my mother lets me voice my opinions and is willing to let me exercise my views instead of shooting me down.
>
> @tofugrandma

> My Korean-American mother gave me the freedom to express myself. If I had an opinion, she listened & we talked. #NotYourAsianTigerMom #Mom
>
> @aechjay

Only a handful of Tweets, again, using the #BeingAsian hashtag, disagree and argue the stereotype is still very much alive.

At the same time, whenever television shows display children behaving in ways that do not reflect this stereotype, users will take to Twitter to express their displeasure, as is evidenced by this tweet:

> @TheIanChen @FreshOffABC How can Evan dare treat his mom or parents like that?!! That's disrespectful!! #FreshOffTheBoat
>
> @tammyyim1

Twitter thus serves as a space for users to discuss the anti-stereotypical reality of their own lives while also providing a platform for people to critique that same reality if it is shown in the media.

CONCLUSION

Asian Americans have taken to Twitter to let their thoughts about race be known in overwhelming numbers. Hashtags such as #NotYour-AsianSidekick and #BeingAsian raise a host of issues that would have remained out of the public eye if it had not been for Twitter. The analysis shows that Twitter is seen as a safe space for Asian Americans to share negative experiences and express their insecurities. In addition, the platform serves as a space for people to renegotiate their understandings of Asian American culture.

One the one hand, the digital culture that arises out of the interactions on Twitter appears to embody some of the hegemonic views of Asian Americans. The idea of the model minority and Asian Americans as a hardworking community is generally embraced. The notion of parents in general and women in particular sacrificing themselves for others (either as immigrants or as the sacrificial Madam Butterfly) is seen as an essential element of Asian American culture, as is the perspective of the attractive Asian American woman and the effeminate male. On the other hand, tweets clearly reject mainstream society's tendency to view Asian American as the perpetual foreigners, and people take to Twitter to seek acceptance from the dominant culture as well as their own. The construction of the Asian American family is clearly a site of struggle. Users reject the white lens inherent in the tiger mom trope; they applaud the parenting style's success, but also reject it as unrealistic. However, these rejections often are undermined by the users' explanations which still include an embrace of the ideology of the hardworking success-driven Asian American. Findings show that like in chapters 2 and 3, people's understanding of Asian American culture and identity is a bricolage made up of oppositional and dominant understandings. However, it appears that these constructions are more likely to accept hegemonic beliefs about Asian American culture than the constructions examined in the previous two chapters.

This chapter's analysis also revealed the power of hashtags to frame the constructions about Asian American culture. Depending on the hashtag, people either accept or reject stereotypes. While users, when framing their tweets with #BeingAsian for example, accepted the tiger parenting trope, when they would discuss the same topic using #NotYourAsianTigerMom, this idea was far more contested. The diversity in people's understandings of Asian American culture is thus rendered more visible by the different hashtags.

In general, when compared to the previous chapters, the tweets in this section appear less countercultural. Many of tweets merely presented an observation, eschewing the critique, empowerment, or calls to action that were witnessed in previous chapters. It thus appears that Asian Americans use Twitter to reflect on the concerns they have, to write about what they observe around them, and to seek support for issues they face.

In this first section, I have examined how Twitter users construct African American, Latinx, and Asian American culture and identity. I have specifically looked at how this construction takes place in response to popular cultural portrayals of these ethnic groups. With an increase in the number of shows that feature African American, Latinx, and Asian American actors, the popularity of Twitter as a second screen, and the use of Twitter as a space for different ethnic groups to rally around specific hashtags, this analysis provided insight into how Twitter is used as a platform to negotiate dominant understandings of these three ethnic groups. Overall, findings show that Twitter users create an understanding that is a mixture of countercultural and hegemonic understandings, and use Twitter to connect with like-minded individuals in networked counterpublics. Twitter provides these users with a space to celebrate their racial identity and call attention to issues that, in their opinion, have gone unnoticed in the mainstream media.

TWEETING WITH A PASSION

Twitter, Politics, and Social Justice

5

From #PantSuitNation to #AllLivesMatter

Understanding User-Driven Social Media Movements

> #BlueLivesMatter or do #AllLivesMatter makeup your mind please. If both are ok to you then why not #BlackLivesMatter
>
> @KingKuma93

Twitter is seen as one of the moving forces behind many of the social movements that have shaped public discourse, altered political agendas, and, in some cases, overthrown governments. The Arab Spring, the Occupy movement, #BlackLivesMatter, these are some of the most famous movements that have been associated with social media. Attributing all of their success to the affordances offered by social media platforms such as Twitter would be overstating the power of these sites and ignoring the other sociopolitical forces at play, but movements such as #BlackLivesMatter and #Occupy did grow their roots in these spaces, while the social movements associated with the Arab Spring owe at least part of their success to the connectivity available through social media (e.g., Castells, 2015; Cottle, 2011; Freelon, et al., 2016; Gerbaudo, 2012). In addition to these well-known movements, Twitter has also been host to a variety of user-driven social justice campaigns that intended to change something about the world as well, but that never quite attained the same real-world momentum these larger movements did, such as #YesAllWomen and #BlackPowerIsForBlackMen. While some scholars dismiss these online campaigns as "clicktivism" or "slacktivism," I argue that these "virtual" campaigns are an essential part of today's public sphere. They help shape public discourse, contribute to digital culture, and as such are worthy of study. In fact, the argument could be made that without feeling pressured to act on their ideas, people are more likely to construct meanings that better reflect their opinions, which means that these campaigns possibly capture a fairly accurate snapshot of public consciousness. Subsequently, in this chapter I analyze the discourse that makes up virtual movements focused on race and gender. I investigate a select number of these virtual movements, explore how tweets negotiate the meaning of each movement, how these expressions counter or support dominant cultural narratives about race and gender, and take a closer look at the dialogue that shapes each movement.

ONLINE ACTIVISM: A NEW KIND OF SOCIAL MOVEMENT

In the past, taking on social injustice and being a part of a social movement meant joining sit-ins, walking in marches, or starting a "conscious-raising" group. Today, all it seems to take is a 140-character tweet with a predesignated hashtag. The raises the question whether joining a protest in, for instance, Ferguson, or sending a tweet labeled #BlackLivesMatter are both forms of activism, demarcating the individuals behind the actions as members of the same social movement. Have internet-based technologies in general and social media platforms in particular, enabled more people to more easily join a social movement, broadening the scope of these movements? Or are these technologies no more than extra-fancy trappings that, while receiving a lot of credit and attention, either falsely placate people into believing they can make a difference with the click of a button, or merely act as tools for movements that are already in motion?

In contemporary society, we are quick to label something as a form of activism or a "social movement." #BlackLivesMatter is seen as a social movement, but so is #PantSuitNation, #SayHerName, #AllLivesMatter, and #BackTheBlue—not to forget hashtags such as #WhiteWashedOut and #NotYourAsiansSidekick, which not only dominated Twitter for some time, but created a wave of mainstream media attention as well. Do these hashtags deserve that label though? All these movements support social justice causes and have a strong online presence. Some have an offline presence too, although the forms this presence takes are different; some involve a counterpresence at demonstrations, others involve T-shirts, buttons, and posters. Whatever their physical presence looks like, these hashtags represent public sentiments, or movements toward or away from a certain way of thinking. But does this qualify these hashtags as a form of activism?

Traditional scholars have argued that any social movement must include physical action. If not action, then at least the (re)appropriation of a physical site, a stage to showcase the group's resistance to the world.

The taking back of urban public space is seen by as crucial to any social movement's existence and, more importantly, their ability to engender change (Gerbaudo, 2012; Castells, 2015). This would seem to suggest that a single tweet, or even an avalanche of single tweets, does very little in terms of social change and cannot be considered a form of activism, unless accompanied by collective, public, physical action.

Debates about the value of a single tweet aside, researchers do agree that social media can play a role in building momentum for social movements. A movement like Black Lives Matter, with its protests and local chapters, is an example of modern-day social movement that started in a virtual space (i.e., Twitter), but quickly created its own physical space as well. Others have pointed to the role played by social media in the #Occupy movement as well as the political upheavals in Tunisia and Egypt as an indication that social media have forever altered how social movements are formed and sustained (Cottle, 2011; Freelon, et al., 2016; Gerbaudo, 2012; Howard & Hussain, 2011).

In spite of success stories like Black Lives Matter, skeptics have cautioned against awarding too much power to social media in the shaping of social movements. Obviously, when discussing the role that social media play in forming social movements, it is important to acknowledge that these social movements were the result of sociopolitical factors, not the availability of a new medium (e.g., Cottle, 2011). In addition, questions have been raised about the long-term impact sustained by social movements that were created online. Morozov (2013) points at the leaderless and horizontal structure of these movements as a risk to their potential success. Moreover, and most important for the discussion in this chapter, skeptics have argued that the popularity of online social movements can be misleading, as most participants do little more than tweet, like, or share and are unlikely to participate in a physical sense. Participating in a social justice movement solely through social media has also been called a form of "slacktivism" (Morozov, 2009) or "clicktivism" (White, 2010). Not only has slacktivism been argued to have little to no impact on real social issues, according to these critics it can render people less compelled to engage in "real" action because they think their online actions have already made a difference. These techno-skeptics warn for technological determinism, i.e., endowing a technology, in this case social media, with powers and abilities beyond those of the individuals using it. A medium's technological affordances hinge on the individual using the technology more than the technology itself, and so the power of a social movement to engender change lies not in the medium but in the people and social issues driving it (Fuchs, 2012; Gaver, 1991; Gerbaudo, 2012; Tudoroiu, 2014).

Dismissing online activism as a form of slacktivism, however, has been challenged by scholars who question the traditional understanding of "engagement" and "activism" in lieu of the new kinds of behavior afforded by social media (e.g., Edelman, 2001). They argue that to define these terms to only include action taking place in physical public spaces ignores and negates the actions undertaken in online spaces by younger people, women, and other marginalized groups and the meaning these actions hold for them. Linking activism to "real" action no longer matches the reality of many, and what they view as engaged activism. To many, especially younger people, online activity is as "real" as physical, outdoor activity (Harris, 2008; Keller, 2012), The focus on the reappropriation of physical public spaces also restricts "activism" or "participation" to those who can access such traditionally exclusive spaces, many of which are not necessarily open to alternative voices (Keller, 2012; Harris, 2008; F. Shaw, 2012). The traditional conceptualization of social movements then in effect propagates the same white, patriarchal ideology many movements are trying to combat.

Moreover, limiting social movements to physical actions negates the effectiveness of discursive activism, or the challenging of dominant norms and values, in engendering change. The ability to be heard is the essence of political change, and as such discursive activism should not be discounted. The feminist movement has long recognized the importance of this kind of activism. Their 1960s "consciousness" groups, used to share experiences and create a community (Kennedy, 2007) have moved online, creating what Clark (2014) dubbed "hashtag feminism." Hashtag feminism, the use of hashtags to redefine dominant narratives, is an excellent example of discursive activism as well as "subpolitics": small, online acts that show political engagement and can have a cumulative real-life impact but are not always recognized as such (Barker-Plummer & Barker-Plummer, 2017; Clark, 2014; Lindgren & Lundström, 2011, p. 1015). The virtual public space created by Web 2.0 is the ideal space for this new kind of social and political engagement (F. Shaw, 2012; Papacharissi, 2002). Discursive activism and subpolitics have been facilitated by the networked publics afforded by social media, i.e., the ability for people to collaborate to reappropriate dominant narratives (Boyd, 2011; Lindgren & Lundström, 2011). Contrary to face-to-face discussions, social media allow for the inclusion of previously unheard voices such as minorities, as well as the creation of safe, exclusive counterpublics (Jaggar, 1999; F. Shaw, 2012).

In short, to dismiss online movements that have no real-life counterpart as a form of "clicktivism" does not do justice to the current shifts taking place in activism and social movements. In fact, scholars have called on the critics to reconsider what participation and social change looks like (Conley, 2014; Carroll & Hackett, 2006). Movements that are solely online reflect the current trend toward a more discursively driven, collaborative, subpolitical activism. These virtual movements are capable of countering dominant narratives, offering up alternative ideas about politics for people to consider, and shaping public discourses. By relying on an online platform already popular among marginalized groups, these online movements have the potential to include a wide variety of voices and ideas that might go unheard in traditional social movements. Subsequently, in this chapter I examine those movements that were characterized by a mainly virtual presence to shed light on the narratives that dominated them, analyze how the values in these narratives reflected or opposed hegemonic understandings of gender and race, and gain insight into the dialogue that shaped the movements.

PANTSUITS AND PRIVILEGE: VIRTUAL MOVEMENTS

The social media landscape has been the site of many movements aimed at creating social and political change. #Occupy, #BlackLivesMatter, and the Arab Spring are probably the most famous of these contemporary social movements. These are also social movements in the true, traditional sense of the word: Their online presence was accompanied by a real-life physical movement in the form of protests and occupations (e.g., Freelon, et al., 2016; Hardt & Negri, 2011; Howard & Hussain, 2011; Juris, 2012; Tudoroiu, 2014). In the past few years, Twitter has also seen a number of social justice-oriented hashtags dominate the top trending list that never materialized into a "traditional" social movement with a consistent physical presence. These are examples of discursive activism or "virtual movements," and examples include #PantSuitNation, #SayHerName, #AllLivesMatter, and #WhiteWashedOut. These hashtags touched on social and political issues such as racism, discrimination, and feminism. Their high rates of participation indicate that these hashtags obviously carried meaning to some segment of the larger population, and allowed for the creation of networked (counter)publics where people connect, debate, and create the contemporary social movements that Lindgren and Lundström (2011) envisioned. While some of them were accompanied by small forms of physical activities (e.g., yard signs, buttons, T-shirt, a flash mob, an occasional counterprotest in the case of #AllLivesMatter), their main activities remained online. According to the traditional definition then, they cannot be not qualified as a "real" social movement, and with the exception of #AllLivesMatter (Carney, 2016) have not been subjected to the intense academic scrutiny that their "real" counterparts have.

In this chapter, I focus on these virtual movements as case studies of discursive activism. Because they lack an organized physical presence, all the dialogue and action taken to define the movement and engender change takes place online, providing excellent insight into the networked publics that are the result of these hashtags. Examining these virtual movements will thus provide insight into the dialogue that is seen as essential to any social movement, traditional or not (Bennett, 2005; Ganesh & Zoller, 2012). This will shed light on the narratives that underpin each of these movements and to what extent these reflect or counterdominant cultural understandings. Examining the dialogue that underpins these movements will also provide insight into whether the interactions that take place on Twitter qualify the platform as a public sphere.

Subsequently, I have selected some of the most popular social justice hashtags from the past few years to serve as case studies. As described in chapter 1, theoretical sampling was used to select these hashtags. Relevant hashtags were identified by a survey of top-trending topics as well as hashtags mentioned in the news in the past few years. Hashtags were selected if they represented social justice issues related to race and/or gender and had garnered sufficient of a following to make it into Twitter's top trending list. The hashtags focused on gender issues included in the data collection for this chapter were #SolidarityIsForWhiteWomen, #SayHerName, #BlackPowerIsForBlackMen, #YesAllWomen, #PantSuitNation, #NotYourAsianSidekick, #MasculinitySoFragile, #FeminitySoFragile, and #NotAllMen. Hashtags that focused on race-related issues that were analyzed for this chapter included #AllLivesMatter, #BackTheBlue, #AsianPrivilege, and #WhiteWashedOut. #BlackLivesMatter was included to serve as a counterpoint in the analysis of #AllLivesMatter, Tweets were taken from the periods when the hashtag trended on Twitter. Black Lives Matter (BLM) tweets were taken from the second half of 2016, while #AllLivesMatter and #BackTheBlue tweets were drawn from the summer of 2016. A total of 6,300 tweets were analyzed for this chapter.

REWRITING THE NARRATIVE: THE CREATION OF VIRTUAL MOVEMENTS

How virtual movements came to be provides useful clues about what they aim to achieve and the narratives they construct to do so. In this section, I discuss the goals of the virtual movements considered in this chapter in order to construct an idea of their different narratives.

The most famous and successful social movement to come out of Twitter in the past few years is probably #BlackLivesMatter. In-depth analyses of development of the movement, the tweets about #BlackLivesMatter, and the people behind them revealed that African Americans used Twitter as a networked subaltern counterpublic to create a narrative about police brutality that countered the dominant color-blind ideology and accompanying narrative propagated in the mainstream media. The narrative created by #BlackLivesMatter resonated across society (Carney, 2016; Freelon, et al., 2016). The movement received national media coverage, and was the target of "a sustained high-profile oppositional narrative" created by conservative pundits (Freelon, et al., 2016, p.25) that quickly translated into the #AllLivesMatter hashtag. This virtual movement used the post-racial color-blind ideology that dominates American discourse to counter BLM's resistance (Carney, 2016; Garza, 2014). As the public dialogue about police brutality against African Americans intensified, topics showing support for police officers also appeared on Twitter, using hashtags such as #BackTheBlue and #BlueLivesMatter. The appearance of these hashtags can be seen as a form of co-optive dialogue (Ganesh & Zoller, 2012), where an attempt is made to erase oppositional narratives by co-opting them into the dominant discourse. In the case of these counterhashtags, they generally explained police brutality by blaming the African America victims as responsible for their own demise:

> If you resist arrest you deserve to have excessive force used on you! #Back TheBlue #ThinBlueLine
>
> @Andrew_F1997

Tweets like this invoke the trope of enlightened racism, an element of color-blind ideology. This ideology has informed the majority of discussion surrounding race in the U.S. since the 1960s. Color-blind ideology argues that racism is over and that personal behavior and not institutionalized racism is the driving force behind both success, failure, and any inequalities (e.g., Bonilla-Silva, 2013; Doane, 2007; Jhally & Lewis, 1992). These hashtags re-establish the dominant color-blind, neoliberal narrative that racism is a thing of the past in the U.S. (cf. Carney, 2016). As the remainder of this chapter will show, countermovements such as these are very common responses to discursive activism, reflecting the power that dominant groups attribute to Twitter in giving voice to the marginalized.

One of the most recent virtual movements discussed in this chapter is Pantsuit Nation, which started as a Facebook page in October of 2016 as a way for Clinton supporters to rally behind their candidate. The movement quickly made its way to Twitter, where #PantSuitNation was used to call people to vote, wear a pantsuit on Election Day, share encouraging stories, and support Clinton (Ohlheiser, 2016). The name of the movement was drawn from the outfit favored by Hillary Clinton, in itself an act of resistance to social expectations for female politicians. Pantsuit Nation, while formed to support Clinton, became a feminist counterpublic after the election, its purpose to provide a space for women to share their stories and resist patriarchal understandings of femininity (Pansuit Nation, n.d.).

#SayHerName, #BlackPowerIsForBlackMen, and #SolidarityIsForWhiteWomen were created to bring attention to the issues faced specifically by ethnic minority women. In 2015, the African American Policy Forum launched #SayHerName to bring attention to the many African American women killed at the hands of police and the systemic problems faced by "marginalized Black women" (African American Policy Forum, 2015, p. 32). In a similar vein, #SolidarityIsForWhiteWomen trended in 2013. It was launched in response to the feminist discourse that has dominated the discussion surrounding women's rights for decades and which has been accused of ignoring the intersectionality of race and gender that comprises much of the struggles faced by women of color (Little, 2013; Ortega, 2006). The hashtag quickly caught on, with women from minority backgrounds and their supporters using it to express their frustration at feeling ignored by mainstream feminism and to renegotiate what feminism meant to them. The equality and inclusion that characterizes Twitter means that women could do this without risking exclusion from the movement, as had often happened in the past (Kendall, 2013; Loza, 2013). In response to this hashtag, #BlackPowerIsForBlackMen was created in the same week, to address the sexism faced by African American women. This hashtag spawned a host of responses, both on Twitter and in the mainstream media, including outrage at the issues African American women have been facing and apologies from African American men (Blades, 2013; BrothersWriting to Live, 2013).

The name of the hashtag plays an important role in defining the movement, in part because of the attention and subsequent pushback it engenders from opponents. #MasculinitySoFragile is an excellent example of how a movement's name can attract negative attention and force proponents into a dialogue about the meaning of that movement. This particular hashtag trended in the fall of 2015, and mainly consisted of people tweeting examples of "toxic masculinity" in order to criticize how society has created a restrictive view of what "real men" can and cannot do. Examples included the claim that men needed to add "man" to anything that could be conceived as feminine in order to preserve their manhood (e.g., purse = manbag). Other examples were more serious, with tweets referencing how men need to demean women to feel empowered, or how transgender women are murdered by men who feel their heterosexuality is under attack. While the purpose of the hashtag was to call out male stereotyping, it led to a large amount of backlash from men who used the hashtag to indicate their disagreement. Opponents used the original hashtag to counter the ideas it propagated and created a countermovement by the name of #FemininitySoFragile. Here, detractors of the #MasculinitySoFragile hashtag attacked women for being the "weak" ones by needing special considerations:

#masculinitysofragile, targeting people based on gender is #cyberviolence. But it's men so who cares.

@AlexSmith1964

@johannamayblack #FemininitySoFragile that you need Pantenne and Tresemme
because you can't use X-treme mountain surf scented bath products

@94Smith1

Ironically, the original countermovement defined masculinity as fragile because its construct requires so many "linguistic gymnastics" (Wynn, 2016) to be maintained, e.g., men cannot just like each other, they have a "bromance," and then used the hashtag to question these gymnastics. The men who felt attacked by this movement did so exactly because the tweets touched on that fragility, i.e., it laid bare the constructs that underpin their male identities, and they thus felt threatened in their masculinity (Lachenal, 2015; Romano, 2015). The debate between the original countermovement and its detractors demonstrates how Twitter enables the dialogue that forces supporters of a movement to better define their movement. At the same time, it also shows how quickly the safety of networked counterpublics can be negated by the openness of the platform.

Using Twitter to rewrite dominant narratives has been used by other oppressed groups as well. As mentioned in chapter 4, #WhiteWashedOut was created in May 2016 to critique the representation (or lack thereof) of Asian Americans in major movies. In December 2013, Asian American women jumped on the #NotYourAsianSidekick hashtag created by Suey Park to identify and critique stereotypes about Asian American women and renegotiate a space for Asian American women in the dominant feminist discourse (Capachi, 2013). However, this hashtag almost immediately led to a countermovement: #AsianPrivilege. This hashtag argued that Asian Americans, because of their success, could not be the victims of racism or sexism. The tweets in this hashtag went beyond the trolling common to Internet-based discussions, where a few users will purposefully try to derail a conversation (Hardaker, 2010). Instead, #AsianPrivilege represented the stereotype-filled hegemonic narrative about Asian Americans that has dominated public discourse about Asian Americans for decades.

Similarly, #YesAllWomen and #NotAllMen were created in part in response to each other. Both gained traction in the spring of 2014 as a reaction to the killing spree that took place near the campus of University of California, Santa Barbara, where the killer explained his actions in written and recorded testimonials that reflected both racist and misogynist ideas. The hashtag #NotAllMen was created by men to explain that not all men were like Elliott, the killer, while the #YesAllWomen hashtag gained worldwide popularity in its attempt to clarify that while not all men were misogynist or sexist, all women were victims of such behaviors. #YesAllWomen succeeded in gaining national attention and creating a counternarrative that was picked up by many mainstream media outlets (Barker-Plummer & Barker-Plumer, 2017; Bridges, 2014; Pachal, 2014; Thrift, 2014; Weiss, 2014). The purpose of #NotAllMen was to undermine the feminist discourse that informed #YesAllWomen by arguing that acts of sexism or misogyny are the exception to the rule and that therefore, women cannot claim systemic oppression or exclusion (Zimmerman, 2014). However, #YesAllWomen tweets took on the challenge to their narrative, countering a large number of attempts by the #NotAllMen tweets with oppositional responses.

The vast majority of the movements discussed in this chapter were faced with counterhashtags. This finding undermines the idea that online platforms create a safe, exclusive space for marginalized voices to create counter hegemonic discourses (e.g., F. Shaw, 2012) and instead points to the role played by dialogue in defining an online social justice movement. The next section addresses the importance of dialogue in online activism and virtual movements.

COLLABORATIVE RESISTANCE: CREATING VIRTUAL MOVEMENTS THROUGH DIALOGUE

Social movements require a collective identity and a strong sense of solidarity to come into existence and, more importantly, to persist. Social media have facilitated the first steps in the formation of social movements, as they have made it much easier to connect with like-minded people and create a shared set of ideological beliefs (Gerbaudo, 2012; Howard, 2000). The creation of this collective identity, and thus the core values that underpin a social or virtual movement, occurs through what Ganesh and Zeller (2012) dubbed collaborative dialogue. This kind of dialogue occurs when all parties are equal and open to new ideas. Subsequently, it can be used to cement the internal workings of a social movements.

Unlike "old-school" social movements, where the debate over what the movement would entail took place away from public scrutiny and among the leaders of the movement, the direction and meaning of virtual movements is created through the public discussions that take place around the hashtag. The fact that this discussion takes place on a public platform means that it in itself is a form of resistance to dominant narratives and qualifies as discursive activism. Analysis of the collaborative dialogue within the virtual movements described above reveals two key themes that drive the movements: the need for recognition and the desire to reframe social problems.

Can You Hear Me? Twitter as a Soapbox

One of the major themes to come out of the analysis was the need for recognition. The virtual movements become communities where people share experiences in an effort to gain support and understanding from people inside the movement (whom they target with the use of the hashtag) and people on the outside (such as their own followers) (cf. Barker-Plummer & Barker-Plummer, 2017; Thrift, 2014). Searching for recognition took on two different forms: Sharing personal experiences and highlighting the social problems that underpinned inequality are two of the ways that online movements define themselves. In addition, #BlackLivesMatter and #PantsuitNation will be discussed separately, as they sought recognition for the issues these movements addressed in specific ways.

Hear Me Roar: Sharing Stories of Inequality

The analysis showed that many of the tweets from the movements focused on women's issues shared experiences reflecting the inequality the participants experience on a daily basis. The sheer volume of these tweets implies that the issues addressed by these hashtags are often denied, and participants view these hashtags as a way to bring their issues to the attention of the general public (for an in-depth discussion of #Yes AllWomen, see Barker-Plummer & Barker-Plummer, 2017; Thrift, 2014). Some of the tweets take a very personal approach, bridging the divide between the private and the public to bring attention to a political issue:

> So my girlfriend got catcalled last night and she laughed at him. He then wanted to fight me. #MasculinitySoFragile
>
> @Joey_St0cks

> #YesAllWomen bc every time I report gender bias-every single fucking time-a man tells me not to jump to conclusions. Wake up and support us.
>
> @annerloo

Movements like #NotYourAsianSidekick and #SayHerName center on sharing similar personal stories of inequality, only these specifically address the complexity created by the intersectionality of gender and race:

> When as the sole employee at a Pasadena restaurant I was the target of all the old White Asian Fetish men #NotYourAsianSidekick
>
> @shortnmorose

> My friends and fam see it enough. I don't want to retweet or post anything. #sayhername
>
> @The_Laxboy

These tweets show how people use social media to create a "carefully orchestrated performance with the other in mind" (Papacharissi, 2009, p. 238), i.e., how, while this tweet and others like it are very personal, they are written with the aim of garnering support by providing information, and subsequently shaping public consciousness. They reflect the intertwining of personal identity with the political that has become so commonplace with the rise of Web 2.0.

Addressing the Big Picture

Many of the tweets associated with hashtags aimed at addressing gender inequality and the intersectionality of gender and race went beyond sharing personal experiences that capture the inequality issues. Instead, these tweets addressed the "big picture" of inequality, i.e., they asked for recognition by framing current events (such as the release of convicted rapist and athlete Brock Turner) as examples of inequality, or pointing at examples of systemic oppression instead of focusing on the lived experiences that are the result of the problem:

> #SolidarityIsForWhiteWomen when you're #1 on every privilege yet claim to be victim & hold 100% of feminism power; nothing for WoC.
>
> @WoCSilencedbyWW

> Gender is socially constructed, WE put up the walls, not some biological instinct encoded by mysterious ghost operons #MasculinitySoFragile
>
> @N_Ver_Sean

> Black women are outnumbered by White women 5:1 in the United States, yet are killed by police in nearly the same numbers. #SayHerName
>
> @thephw

Hashtags like these as well as #NotYourAsianSidekick and #BlackPowerIsForBlackMen argue that women of color in general and African American and Asian American women in particular suffer from more inequalities than Black men and white women because of the intersectionality of race and gender.

Virtual activists also use Twitter to frame current events from the perspective of gender/racial inequality, drawing attention to specific dimensions that they believe are ignored in the media:

> Dear media, #Renisha matters too. #solidarityisforwhitewomen #blackpowerisforblackmen
>
> @TheFireNexTime

> #SolidarityIsForWhiteWomen Sandra Fluke attacked by Limbaugh results in protests, Michelle Obama insulted by Limbaugh results in ecrickets
>
> @drupkins

> #solidarityisforwhitewomen When they care more about the rights of a white man in a dress than the rights of oppressed Latina/Black women
>
> @VanHernandezz

Interestingly, while the previous category included tweets that kept the call for recognition almost personal, the tweets that eschewed the personal approach adopt an "us versus them" tone. The use of "you" in the tweet by @WoCSilencedbyWW, "they" by @VanHernandezz, and "we" used by @N_Ver_Sean, and in the tweet below, create a separation between victims of the discrimination and those who perpetuate the inequality:

> Truth. #wearenotsilent RT @bdeguzman94: We are the people of color that don't get to be people of color. #NotYourAsianSidekick
>
> @jessikachi

The "us versus them" experience was enhanced by the controversy surrounding the "Harriet Tubman sex tape." This online skit, created by Russell Simmons, featured Harriet Tubman recruiting another slave to secretly film her having sex with her master so she can blackmail him into releasing her. While this video led to a huge cry of outrage among the Black community (see e.g., Robinson, 2013), other social justice movements remained silent on the matter, as noticed by many participants in the #SolidarityIsForWhiteWomen hashtag:

> so where is the outrage white feminist? A Harriet Tubman sex tape has been made. crickets aint she a woman? #SolidarityIsForWhiteWomen
>
> @RstewartJewelry

> #SolidarityisForWhiteWomen when nothing is being said about the degrading of an original feminist #HarrietTubmansextape
>
> @NisiNirvana

Both #Solidiaryisforwhitewomen and #NotYourAsianSidekick identify the "other" as the white woman, who is seen as much of a roadblock to equality for women of color as men:

> White feminists, 1st step in ending racism is SHUT UP 2nd LISTEN 3rd UNDERSTAND yr experience is not universal #SolidarityIsForWhiteWomen
>
> @thejenn

> #NotYourAsianSidekick: a movement for #Asian American women against oppression, racism, patriarchy, white feminism
>
> @chui108

> The white feminist reaction to #NotYourAsianSidekick is EXACTLY the reason feminism isn't for women of color.
>
> @YaaAsantewaaBa

The idea that white feminists need to take on different perspectives is reflected in a large number of tweets, although many users doubt whether this will matter:

> Yes. RT @king_alexsarah: when every discussion of privilege means a meltdown #solidarityisforwhitewomen
>
> @adelinekoh

> The last time a group of white women "sat down and listened," George Zimmer(Hitler)man was acquitted. #SolidarityIsForWhiteWomen
>
> @Trans_Tammy

The last tweets reflect the belief prevalent throughout this hashtag, namely that even if white women were to try to understand or listen, it would not make a difference to the issues faced by women of color, because of their inability to take on other women's perspectives, as evidenced by the outcome of George Zimmerman's trial.

The "other" isn't always white, though. #BlackPowerIsForBlackMen, instead, targets African American males as part of the discrimination faced by African American women.

> #BlackPowerIsForBlackMen who preach about breaking away from European beauty standards but hold onto Eurocentric superiority over women.
>
> @complexitiiiiii

> #blackpowerisforblackmen when underneath the "conscious" talk, black men imply that a "queens" place is behind her "king."
>
> @Minniemette

These tweets express a desire for recognition by sharing tweets about larger social issues, instead of personal experiences. By doing so, these participants make their movement less about individual members' lives, and more about the social injustices wrought upon the entire community. This strategy makes it more difficult for opponents to detract from or erase their message, i.e., it's easier to explain one women's experience with a sexist customer away as "that was just one man" than it is to deny the presence of Eurocentric beauty standards.

At the same time, the use of "us versus them" discourse is sufficiently provocative to invoke the creation of countermovements, as evidenced by a movement like #AsianPrivilege. This hashtag undermines #NotYourAsianSidekick by claiming the success of the Asian American community as evidence that there is no discrimination against this particular ethnic group. However, this countermovement did not go unnoticed either, and the analysis showed that #AsianPrivilege tweets actually helped the #NotYourAsianSidekick fine tune the problems faced by Asian Americans in general:

> #AsianPrivilege is when an incredibly diverse & large group of people gets lumped as 1 entity with 1 experience. #NotYourAsianSidekick
>
> @AleksieAleksie

Still Tweeting to Be Heard: Black Lives Matter

Even though #BlackLivesMatter is one of the older examples of hashtag activism in existence, the tweets analyzed for this chapter came from 2016 and still expressed a desire for people to recognize the issues facing te African American community. As opposed to the other hashtags discussed in this section, however, #BlackLivesMatter tweets show more frustration at not having been heard yet. Tweets using this hashtag did not focus on people's personal experiences, but instead sought recognition by referencing past and present instances of racially motivated police brutality. Tweets reflect the belief that mainstream discourse does not value African American lives the same way it values white lives. The only way to change is to seek recognition for the victims:

> It happen again, damn #America. #BlackLivesMatter #SayHerName #Black Twitter
>
> @LeBaronLordKing

> Terrence Crutcher. Terrence Crutcher. Terrence Crutcher. Terrence Crutcher. Say his name. Terrence Crutcher. #BlackLivesMatter #SayHisName
>
> @ItssLuisa

In addition, many tweets show frustration with the lack of change after years of online and physical activism:

> I'm tired of seeing another name as a simple hashtag #BlackLivesMatter
>
> @Faith_Sugar143

> How much hurt can my spirit take? . . .
> I am tired.
> We are tired.
> #BlackLivesMatter
>
> @princesss_iza

These tweets, and others like them, reflect frustration and anger but also highlight a clear sense of community, indicating that #BlackLivesMatter has created a truly shared identity and purpose.

By the summer of 2016, with the shooting of five Dallas police officers during a Black Lives Matter protest, the countermovements that had been created gained traction on Twitter once again (e.g., #AllLivesMatter and #BackTheBlue). Many of the tweets posted during and after the birth of these movements reflect frustration with outsiders' inability to see the problems, and an ongoing desire for the same outsiders to understand the issue:

> if you still don't understand the point of this movement, you're apart of the issue. #BlackLivesMatter
>
> @bdfriederichs

> How do people not understand #blacklivesmatter ?? it's that simple. Black. Lives. Matter.
>
> @cicily_riggs

Some tweets, especially those from the second half of 2016, express outrage at opponents' attempts to discredit the movement:

Wtf. Black lives matter = cop killer. Anti-racist = anti-white. Not just lies. Perversions of truth. #trumpisdeplorable #basketofdeplorables

@deemallon89

Fact for the #foxnewsnazi 's who say #blacklivesmatter makes the job of police harder, 71percent of cops killed are by white men #crutcher

@freedomatters2

These tweets show that Carney's (2016) findings about tweets posted in 2014 still apply two years later. Proponents of the #BlackLivesMatter movement still struggle to gain recognition for the racism that underpins a lot of the problems facing African Americans, while, as discussed in more detail below, #AllLivesMatter tweets still propagate a color-blind ideology. Combating the color-blind ideology that underpins movements like #AllLivesMatter has become part of the #BlackLivesMatter movement's purpose. Part of that includes active engagement of opponents, which will be further explored in the next section of this chapter.

From Hope to Highlighting Inequality: #PantSuitNation

When it comes to women's movements, #PantSuitNation is an interesting case study. Unlike the other virtual movements discussed in this chapter, it started off as a movement that was firmly rooted in the belief that sexism and misogyny were in the distant past. Tweets that used the #PantSuitNation hashtag can be divided up into two periods: pre- and post-election. Prior to the election, the tweets associated with this movement did not address personal experiences of racism or sexism but instead expressed optimism and encouraged others to believe that change was about to come:

@thehill Trump might be a monster but average American voters are not monsters. Trump is going to be beaten BIGLY! #pantsuitnation

@NurseShield

We're entering the last week in America that we'll say we've never elected a female president. #frommylipstovotersears #pantsuitnation

@MargoLezowitz

Just heard a UPS guy say to two other men "you're voting for Hillary tomorrow, right?"
"Me too!" I shouted.
#pantsuitnation #ImWitHer

@1chicklette

Tweets praised other members of the movement, lifted up other members, and generally worked hard to create a positive, uplifting atmosphere:

> Wow, if you want to see the resilience, courage, creativity, kindness and support HRC's leadership inspires, get into #PantSuitNation.
>
> @cbn2

> You guys, the #pantsuitnation hashtag is pretty nice. It's refreshing to read optimism.
>
> @MungoMonster

Tweets also expressed a desire to make a change, using additional hashtags such as #ReadyToRoar, and discussing plans for Election Day and the Clinton victory that they were expecting. These tweets were in line with Pantsuit Nation's goals ("Posting guidelines = no memes, no articles, no attacks. Yes personal stories and pictures! We <3 #PantSuitNation" @pantsuitnation), and very much reflect the exclusive space marginalized groups needed to reflect on their beliefs that F. Shaw (2012) talked about.

After the election, the Pantsuit Nation did not disappear but instead grew in membership. Its aims changed from electing Hillary Clinton to creating a safe space for Hillary supporters to share their stories and plan for action. This action took place both on an individual level (which organizations to donate to, for instance), and a social level (the movement played a role in the Women's Marches that took place on January 21, 2017). Twitter thus became the platform for a subaltern counterpublic (Fraser, 1992; Jaggar, 1999) where women could regroup, and prepare for actions against the dominant culture. With the realization that their earlier belief that "sexism is a thing of the past" had been proven wrong, the tweets that reference #PantSuitNation become a lot more like tweets from other women's movements, and focused on sharing experiences of inequality:

> On the train listening to some guy mansplain the election to his girlfriend. Looked over at her—we both rolled our eyes. #PantSuitNation
>
> @brielledb

> Had a discussion with a man who finally said, "calm those emotions, sweetheart." We have so much work to do #ImWithHer2020 #pantsuitnation
>
> @kalliem

Tweets also shared stories of encountering people with similar beliefs, expressing joy at finding like-minded people in a world that post-election seemed a lot less equal:

> Ladies in Starbucks talking about #PantSuitNation and their #nastywomen shirts and going to DC and I just wanna yell HELLO SISTAS
>
> @mhd7593

Like with the other women's movements I have discussed so far, the post-election tweets center on sharing thoughts and experiences that underline this inequality in a search for support.

At the same time, a large number of tweets focused on the action that people were now going to take:

> Joining the protest! We will NOT go quietly and let our country let hate take over! Marching in DC on 1/21! #PantSuitNation #notmypresident
>
> @KimSchwan

> #pantsuitnation: Set up monthly donations for @PPFA & donating blood tmrw. How else can I #dothemostgood in @HillaryClinton's honor?
>
> @bethaleh

Contrary to virtual women's movements such as #YesAllWomen and even #SayHerName and #NotYourAsianSidekick, the outcome of the election made #PantSuitNation evolve from an almost entirely online movement, to a "real" social movement in the traditional sense of the word, with performative action in public, urban spaces generally reserved to support dominant cultural discourses.

Using Twitter to (Re)Frame Social Problems

The "original" virtual movements discussed above focus on inequality and discrimination as the driving issue behind the problems they identify. These movements view the lack of equality for marginalized groups as the root cause of the problems faced by these groups and use Twitter to construct a counternarrative and magnify their voices. The countermovements described earlier in this chapter, however, exist only to dispute the claims made by these original virtual movements. They do so by reframing the social problems addressed by the original movements so the inequality that these movements fight appears to be a nonissue. When looking at these countermovements in more detail, it becomes apparent that they and the original virtual movements have very distinct ideas about the problems that plague American society, and subsequently, proponents of the original and the countermovements could be said to live in different realities.

All of the countermovements (#NotAllMen, #AllLivesMatter, #BackTheBlue, #FemininitySoFragile, and #AsianPrivilege) propose a discourse that preaches unity, equality, and color-blindness. The argument made by tweets associated with these hashtags is that the original movements perpetuate the racism and discrimination they're claiming to fight by generalizing about white people, police officers, or men. According to these countermovements, the solution is to respect everyone:

> Generality is an open door to the path of discrimination. Just as culture is scapegoat for villainy. #YesAllWomen #NotAllMen #equality
>
> @JamesCaud

> How about this: #LetsALLBeBetter As much as I support #YesAllWomen, I also support #notallmen Why can't we all protect & respect each other?
>
> @reinventingerin

In addition, many tweets from these countermovements argue that the virtual movements they agitate against fail to acknowledge that all races and genders face inequality. The countermovements posit that by ignoring the universality of these inequalities, the original movements only contribute to the divides that characterize society:

> #AllLivesMatter is a cry against #racism— against singling out any #race for unfair*or* special treatment "@SpryGuy: @ MkSpeaksHisMind Wow, you still don't get it, do you? No, you don't. Saying "Black Lives Matter" isn't racist, it's a cry AGAINST racism."
>
> @MkSpeaksHisMind

> #YesAllWomen needs to be turned into #YesAllPeople . . . because it seems like most are forgetting both genders go through these issues.
>
> @Honey_sickle

These tweets indicate a belief that discrimination is not something that only affects ethnic minorities or women, but that white men can equally be the victim of unfair treatment. In a way, these tweets are reminiscent of the battle against affirmative action of the mid-1990s, when, using color-blind ideology, white men argued against affirmative action programs, claiming they were instances of reverse racism (e.g., Bonilla-Silva, 2013; Chang, 1996; Doane, 2007). According to the color-blind ideology, racism is no longer an issue, and so programs to promote ethnic minorities are not only irrelevant but they could also be seen as an attack on the U.S. as a whole and white males in particular. These tweets represent a similar line of thinking, where, like in the narratives surrounding affirmative action, the white male is framed as a "victim" of attacks from the enemy, which both the affirmative action narrative and the countermovements on Twitter identify as racial minorities and feminists (Chang, 1996).

Analysis revealed that countermovements focused on race took a different approach to reframing social issues from gender-oriented countermovements. Below, I elaborate on the nature of this reframing for the two types of countermovements, starting with those addressing race and followed by a discussion of the ones that center on gender.

Challenging Racism

When digging deeper, it appears that proponents of the countermovements focused on race have indeed embraced the color-blind ideology, echoing Carney's (2016) findings. Starting with #AllLivesMatter and #BackTheBlue, findings show that these countermovements do not see racism as the root cause of the problems plaguing African Americans, but instead point to individual behavior and a lack of respect for basic American values as the real problem:

> @Cassosphere The Unheard should comply when a Police Officer tells you to drop your Gun. #CharlotteProtest
>
> @airwolf1967

> As long as you idolize gangsters, call women "bitches," insult cops, use drugs, refuse an education & only complain. #AllLivesMatter
>
> @DeepDarkFear

> This this and more of THIS. #BLACKLIVESMATTER
> #AllLivesMatter #BlueLivesmatter #PJNET #Trump #TrumpTrain #MAGA
>
> @k3at

@k3at's tweet was accompanied by a picture of an African American police officer named Sheriff David Clark and a quote, "Stop trying to fix the police. Fix the ghetto." These tweets all center on the idea that any police violence or other forms of perceived racism are the result of individual behaviors. By quoting an African American police officer who appears to acknowledge that the problem lies with the African American community, not the police, an attempt is made to validate this argument. However, the use of name-calling ("the unheard") and generalization ("as long as you") captures the "veiled racism" (Carney, 2016, p. 192) that characterizes the color-blind, post-racist discourse used by these countermovements.

While Carney's work focused on tweets from 2014, it appears that by 2016 the adherence to a post-racial discourse had become a marker for one's respect for American values. Challenging the police tears at the foundation of what the United States stands for, as captured by this tweet:

> America this has got to stop . . . #BlueLivesMatter #AllLivesMatter The senseless killing of individuals who protect us
>
> @ScottSaxman1

This tweet was accompanied by a picture of a police badge and the words "killing some for wearing one of these should be considered a hate crime! Like, comment, and share if you agree." While murdering someone for their occupation does not fall under the official definition of a hate crime, this picture and ones like it were very common on Twitter, showing that many people adhered to this belief. This underlines the notion that police officers and people in uniform in general are seen as members of a special class of people, believed to protect American values, and thus worthy of respect.

This trope resurfaced and was magnified during the summer of 2016 when the Black Lives Matter movement crossed paths with the NFL. Colin Kaepernick, an NFL quarterback, kneeled during the national anthem as protest to the police shootings of African Americans, and the NFL refused to let the Dallas Cowboy players put decals on their helmets to show support for the Dallas police officers killed during a #BlackLives Matter protest. These two events led to an outcry on Twitter, one that further cemented the belief that supporting the police is a basic American value, and critiquing them is the equivalent of criticizing the country:

> Nobody should boycott the one team that stands for American values @dallascowboys who #BackTheBlue #boycottNFL
>
> @KeilaTownson

> I know these hero's fought and died for you to protest Black Lives Matter__SF QB Kaepernick
>
> @wdcgator

@wdcgator's tweet is accompanied by the famous picture taken inside a military cargo plane that features three rows of coffins draped with the American flag. Two uniformed military members are straightening the flags. The words "would the suppressed millionaire, NFL quarterback, who would not stand for the National anthem please point out which of these guys are black so we can remove the offensive flag" have been added beneath the picture.

These two tweets as well as the majority of the tweets discussing these two events using #AllLivesMatter or #BackTheBlue do so from an "American values" frame, i.e., the belief that failure to acknowledge the anthem, the flag, or support the police shows a lack of respect for basic American values that the military and the police fight to protect. @ wdcgator's tweet is an especially poignant example, where Kaepernick's action is juxtaposed with the deaths of military members overseas, somehow implying that he is not worthy of the sacrifice of these "real" American heroes. This shows how police and people in uniform are seen to embody what America stands for: freedom, democracy, and justice. Subsequently, any attack on these people is seen as an attack on these values. Supporting Kaepernick and Black Lives Matter is the equivalent of betraying the U.S. and all the values it stands for, as captured by @ Mysammysam95 below:

> Makes me sick to watch Obama stand there on ground 0 after supporting black lives matter, supporting Kaepernick and giving billions to Iran

Ground zero (the site of the 9/11 attacks in New York) has come to represent America as a whole, and in particular, its sense of justice, its pledge to freedom, and the bravery of its men in uniform. Obama, because of his support for the Black Lives Matter movement, is seen as un-American and thus not allowed to visit "hallowed ground," i.e., ground zero. Moreover, Obama's support of the Black Lives Matter movement and Kaepernick is equated to his alleged donations to Iran, a longtime enemy of the U.S., and a country that does not support freedom, equality, or democracy. Supporting Black Lives Matter is thus seen as anti-American as donating to Iran.

Some Twitter users take this frame and make it very personal, claiming that they, unlike Kaepernick and the NFL, are "true" Americans:

> I proudly #BackTheBlue. I offer no apology. I stand for the Flag of the only FREE nation on Earth. #spine #liberty @Kaepernick7 @NFL
>
> @btwoodward

> @bMarshh54 @Kaepernick7 @NFL At my house we stand #BackTheBlue #supportthetroops #standupfortheAnthem
>
> @jchrisking

@jchrisking's tweet is accompanied by a picture of a white family standing while the national anthem plays on television before a football game. These tweets, and others like them, juxtapose the user's support for "God and country" (as embodied in the flag, the anthem, and the men and women in uniform) with Kaepernick's and the NFL's refusal to respect that same country. Many of these tweets also call out

Kaepernick for disrespecting the same country that gave him the freedom and the opportunities to become who he is today. This again embodied post-racial thinking, where African Americans are seen to have the same opportunities as anyone else, and a demand for more is unfair and unacceptable. What's interesting is that the majority of tweets use the "@" function to directly address Colin Kaepernick, indicating a desire for him to hear their protests, and a belief that the conversation option offered by the platform works.

From these tweets, it is obvious that these countermovements were based on the color-blind ideology. Supporters appear to adhere to the idea of enlightened racism (Jhally & Lewis, 1992), believing that institutionalized racism no longer exists and people's ethnic background is no longer of any importance in daily interactions (cf. Gotanda, 1996). Challenging this belief, as Kaepernick did (the first of many athletes to do so), is seen not only as challenging the premise that the U.S. is the land of freedom, equality, and opportunity, but as a threat to the future of the nation:

> @ashleyc479 @PierreBalian EVERY Race and nation is on fire not just blacks and not just the USA. It is PREVENTION. Yes #AllLivesMatter
>
> @cmconcepts

> #AllLivesMatter @BarackObama this one way show of support MUST END for America to survive @CNN @WhiteHouse @StateDept @USATODAY @CBSNews
>
> @demsnomore

These tweets, and their extensive use of the @ symbol, indicate the genuine fear that these users experience and the desire to counter what they see as a wrong direction for the nation by directly addressing those involved. Just like in the 1990s, when some people felt that affirmative action was threatening to undermine the country (Chang, 1996), today, many feel that movements like #BlackLivesMatter threaten to undermine the country again, failing to acknowledge the opportunities given to them, and attacking basic American values.

Challenging Justice and Equality

Countermovements focused on women and Asian Americans (#NotAllMen, #FemininitySoFragile, and #AsianPrivilege) argue that the calls from the original movements deserve to be ignored because they come from groups who already have achieved more than equality:

> super privileged asian american woman going to an expensive as hell grad school whining publicly about white privilege
>
> @Senpai_Kun_Sama

> #socialjustice warriors— toddlers throwing tantrums because the're not allowed to have every toy in the store #YesAllWomen #SJW
>
> @TheOtherAtheist

The idea that white men can never do or give enough ties in to the trope of the white male as a victim discussed in the previous paragraph. In the current cultural climate, white men are seen as under attack, specifically from women and ethnic minorities (Chang, 1996). These countermovements reframe issues of inequality and white privilege to reflect their post-racial and neoliberal beliefs.

> Screw #NotAllMen and #YesAllWomen . . . You both are promoting supremacy. What about #equality?
>
> @Nick_Beitz

This example captures the idea that arguments from women demanding equality is really a call for female supremacy, as well as a failure to recognize that equality should mean equality for all, a notion embodied by all of these countermovements.

In his discussion of reverse racism, Chang (1996) describes how ethnic groups and feminists are seen as the "enemy within" (p. 1123), a belief that these particular countermovements adhere to as well:

> Modern feminism is built on hatred and dehumanization of men #YesAllWomen #Notallwomen #NotAllMen #yesallmen
>
> @randomfox

> #YesAllWomen Because apparently feminism isn't about empowering women but belittling men. Fear leads to Hate, Hate leads to Anger. #yoda
>
> @mcargul

Reframing feminism's call for equality as a hate-fueled push toward female superiority was a common thread among these countermovements. Many members of these countermovements identified feminism as a direct threat to men. A common defense was to call feminists sexist, or to accuse them of "weird, vicarious fear shaming" (@gabrielapetrie). This argument stems from the belief that men and women are equal, and that there is no need to change anything in the relationship between men and women anymore. Any additional call for action is thus a form of reverse sexism, aimed to give women power over men, which would defy the equality that defines the nation.

THE LOOKING GLASS SELF: WHEN VIRTUAL MOVEMENTS COLLIDE

As discussed earlier in the book, Twitter is the ideal space for interactions to occur between people from vastly different backgrounds. Hashtags create temporary communities that unite people who share common interests or dislikes (e.g., Acosta, 2014; Brown, et al., 2014; Lim, 2012). The virtual movements outlined above center on controversial topics, and use names that easily draw the attention of both supporters and opponents when they appear in the top trending list on Twitter. Subsequently, a large number of the tweets analyzed for this chapter were focused on engaging with a real or imagined outsider about the meaning and value of the social movement, instead of working with supporters of the movement to share knowledge and create a shared identity inside an exclusive "deliberative enclave" (Dahlberg, 2007, p. 828).

These interactions are a central aspect of the movement's identity. An individual's identity is the direct result of one's interactions with others. How someone sees themselves is tied to how they think others see them, i.e., the "looking glass self" (Howard, 2000; Shrauger & Schoeneman, 1979, p. 549). What matters in this interaction is not so much what others think, but one's interpretations of others. According to symbolic interactionism, interaction is based on people's understanding of the things and people around them. How people perceive the other will inform their interaction with them, and thus their understanding of themselves. Subsequently, identities are constructed and negotiated through social interactions (Howard, 2000). Dahlgren (2013) referred to this as "intervisibility" (p. 55), and argued that the ability to perform for and interact with others to shape one's identity is an essential prerequisite for participation in the public sphere. How members of different movements interact to define their group is thus not only essential to understanding what that group stands for. It is also a fundamental part of participation in the public sphere.

This constructivist view of identity is reflected in many of the tweets that mentioned the various virtual movements, with individuals negotiating what a movement stands for by engaging with others:

> If your argument to #MasculinitySoFragile is #FemininitySoFragile, you don't understand that's already the societies understood position
>
> @LiToast

> When the police brutalizes & kill innocent white people then that's when I'll rep #AllLivesMatter until then bitches #BlackLivesMatter
>
> @QueenAmazi

Simply providing one's own interpretation was not sufficient for supporting the collective identity hinging on the virtual movement; supporters had to further specify the movement's meaning by interacting with opponents. This is no surprise when one considers that collective identity is essential for the formation of social movements (Gerbaudo, 2012). This shared identity hinges on a sense of belonging, the feeling that the group has shared ideological beliefs, and more importantly, a common enemy (Howard, 2000). While most "old-school" social movements relied on face-to-face meetings to cement this shared identity, the virtual movements of the past five years instead rely on the collision with other virtual movements to create that sense of belonging and solidarity. Defending the virtual movement's collective identity is essential to its survival, and the negotiations that take place in these online discussions are paramount to understanding how its members view the movement's meaning.

Responding to the Imagined Other

As mentioned above, the formation of one's identity depends on real and imagined interactions (Howard, 2000; Shrauger & Schoeneman, 1979). A person does not have to interact with someone else to imagine their thoughts or ideas and work those into their self-concept. The same applies to the virtual movements discussed in this chapter: A lot of tweets are directed against a movement's opponents without any real interaction preceding or following those tweets:

> Hey, #NotAllMen, if you think that #YesAllWomen is an attack on you, you are part of the problem. Not starting a war, just a conversation
>
> @Mimo_Movie

In this case, @Mimo_Movie uses two hashtags in his or her tweet to address the followers of #NotAllMen and explains to them what #YesAllWomen is really about. While this tweet is not the result of a tweet directly aimed at @Mimo_Movie, this user has apparently kept up with both hashtags and felt the need to clarify what one movement stood for to its countermovement.

Many of the tweets that come from the Black Lives Matter or All Lives Matter movement reflect the frustration and fear inherent to their movements:

> Y'all Killing Me With This #AllLivesMatter Shit. . . .
> You Know ALL OF THEM Don't Give A Fuck About Us???!!
> #BlackLivesMatter Over Here. . . .
>
> @CauzNEffect

> #AllLivesMatter
> The hypocrisy of BLM supporters. Gang up on a white guy, then wonder why you get labeled a thug
>
> @D_Moore2006

Tweets like these clearly embody an idea of the "other" and what the "other" thinks or does. @CauzNeffect argues that people who support All Lives Matter definitely do not care about African Americans, a reason to continue his or her support for Black Lives Matter. On the other hand, @D_Moore2006 equates the people who ganged up on a white man (this tweet is from July 2016, it is unclear what event he or she is talking about) with all Black Lives Matter supporters, labeling them as thugs and unaware of how their behavior causes the actions they protest against. Both of these tweets and others like them define the opponent of the movement, and in doing so provide a reason for their movement to persist.

Some of the opponents of virtual movements only use the hashtag of the movement they are critiquing in their tweets. This is called "content injection" and is generally used to expose opponents to one's ideas (Conover, Ratkiewicz, Gonçalves, Flamini, & Menczer, 2011, p. 94). As is shown from these tweets, this type of content injection is commonly used to address the other to better define the self, or in this case, the social movements:

> If you say #AllLivesMatter, you do know you're saying you value the lives of Adolf Hitler, Ted Bundy, Dylann Roof & Anders Breivik, right?
>
> @FrankCastr0

> Yal racists corny w| that #AllLivesMatter mess
>
> @_dxtn

> Ppl whining about #whitewashedOUT #appropriation #culturevultures #whiteprivilege #racismthisracismthat r #SJWdumbassplayedOUT tired of it.
>
> @H2drOh

In addition to defining the self, the purpose of tweets like these is also to undermine the power and purpose of these movements. They are, in effect, an example of individuals trying to co-opt dialogue in an attempt to regain power (cf. Ganesh & Zoller, 2012).

Some, including Twitter users themselves, will argue that these attacks as well as the countermovements themselves are little more than trolling:

> #AllLivesMatter is basically a negative response group to #BlackLivesMatter they have no mission or goal except to troll
>
> @BookofFrank

To argue that these attacks are no more than an attempt to disrupt conversations or create arguments (Hardaker, 2010), however, ignores the meaning inherent in these tweets. The sole purpose of trolling is to create amusement for the "troll," and while one cannot surmise intentions from tweets alone, the repetition of similar themes (All Lives Matter supporters are racists; Black Lives Matter supporters are criminals, etc.), indicates that these Twitter users are articulating a clear political concern using tools and methods common to Web 2.0 users (cf. Burroughs, 2013).

Engaging with the Other

In some cases, critiquing a movement leads to a dialogue between opponents and supporters of a movement. The analysis showed that this kind of dialogue does not aim to create common ground but instead can be described as a form of agonistic dialogue (cf. Mouffe, 1999, 2000), where interactions are conflictual, passionate, and not geared toward building consensus, but still essential to democracy. More specifically, the dialogue with "the other" can be labeled as diachronic, i.e., as a one-way form of communication that is open to contestations by outsiders (Ganesh & Zoller, 2012). While not the collaborative, respectful dialogue envisioned by Habermas, this kind of dialogue can still be viewed as constructive, as shown below (Mouffe, 1999, 2000, see also chapter 6).

This kind of dialogue usually starts with someone using a hashtag for content injection. While many of these injections or "hashtag hijacking" go unanswered, sometimes they lead to dialogue with other opponents as well as proponents of the movement. One example of such dialogue starts with this tweet:

> #BlackPowerIsForBlackMen really???? Yall reaching for real. Black women voices aren't being heard by black men??? Really?? When? Where? Lol
>
> @BOB_Boblaw

This tweet questions how African American women can feel unheard by African American men, denying the notion that African American women are victims of both gender and racial discrimination. With African American females often constructed as the Sapphire or the Black Bitch (see chapter 2), this interpretation is a natural defense to the calls for recognition. What makes this particular tweet interesting, however, is that proponents of the movements engaged in interaction with @BOB_Boblaw to further tease out the meaning of #BlackPowerIsForBlackMen:

> @BOB_Boblaw when black men date white to find submissive girls who ARENT heard.Not against IR dating but Im against that reason for doing it
>
> @Minniemette

> @Minniemette why is dating white women even part of the discussion?
>
> @BOB_Boblaw

> @BOB_Boblaw You wanted an example of how black women voices aren't being heard. Interracial dating is often used as a tool to do that.
>
> @Minniemette

> @BOB_Boblaw @Minniemette It doesn't sound like you're trying to understand this discussion let alone dismissing it before you even listen
> @BOB_Boblaw @Minniemette to the issues that black women face so therefore you proved a point, were not being heard by many black men
>
> @LiberalArtsDiva

Both @LiberalArtsDiva and @Minniemette engage with @Bob_Boblaw as the "other" to explain the relevance and meaning of the movement. There does not seem to be any attempt to ensure @Bob_Boblaw understands their message. In fact, these tweets are the extent of the conversation. But the dialogue allowed @LiberalArtsDiva and @Minniemette to connect and feel strengthened in their shared purpose. This interaction is also an excellent example of agonistic dialogue, with the participants passionately defending their positions. This type of interaction will be further teased out in the remainder of this chapter and the next one.

Not everyone agrees that these kinds of interactions help a movement that is attempting to counter hegemonic narratives (e.g., F. Shaw, 2012). Constructing a nonhegemonic identity in an open, public space means that one is vulnerable to oppositional viewpoints. This means that the focus on constructing a meaningful counterhegemonic message is diluted with the need to address potential attacks from outsiders. However, I posit that the ability to defend oneself in public and find others defending the same idea helps to create a stronger snse of self and augments the solidarity essential to any social movement. Gerbaudo

(2012), in his analysis of social movements, points to the creation of the "cultural narrative and . . . common collective identifications among participants" (p. 41) as an essential first step of a social movement, and these kinds of debate, where individuals supporting a movement band together to defend that movement against outsiders is imperative for the shaping of their cultural narrative.

This desire to create a collective identity and shape the narrative that informs the movement through interaction with opponents becomes especially apparent when proponents and opponents of a movement jump on tweets that are not associated with a movement in the hopes of tying that tweet to their cause. On September 11, 2016, @benhiggi tweeted:

> I understand @Kaepernick7 has a message to share, but please today everyone STAND in unity for our National Anthem. #NeverForget

While @Benhiggi didn't situate himself as a proponent or detractor of either the All Lives Matter or Black Lives Matter movement, supporters of both movements immediately weighed in, situating the discussion about Kaepernick's behavior and the meaning of 9/11 in either a discourse that underlined the importance of equality, or a discourse driven by colorblind ideology. Proponents of the racial equality promoted by Black Lives Matter responded to @benhiggi's tweet by underlining the importance and continuing lack of racial equality:

> @benhiggi @Kaepernick7 disagree. His cause doesn't change just because of a date on the calendar.
>
> @megstoll

> @megstoll @benhiggi @Kaepernick7 imagine 9/11 outrage being felt on a smaller scale in minority communities everyday.
>
> @dexbot

> @benhiggi would be nice if Tamir rice could stand.
>
> @maximillionb23

> @benhiggi @Kaepernick7 #NeverForget is funny thing to say when we ask everyone else to get over it. Natives, slavery, racism
>
> @Rachelle_jdh

These tweets reiterate the main themes of the Black Lives Matter movement described above: a need for equality. Demanding respect for a commemoration does not appear fair when other traumatizing events, such as the death of Tamir Rice or the injustices felt in ethnic communities, go unnoticed. Users respond to one another with approval and additional comments, using @benhiggi's tweet to strengthen their social ties as well cementing the movement's original position.

Others reiterated the importance of respecting the country and the values it embodies:

> keep the camera on the flag and not on him, or any of those who refuse to stand. It's not about them today
>
> @lizzybean3712

Tweets shared pictures of the twin towers and football teams decked out in gear featuring the American flag, underlining the belief that respect for one's country trumps a call for justice.

These tweets are a good example of agonistic dialogue, where the various discussants share ideas without seeking agreement or consensus. Both sides reiterate their stances, cementing the values the movements were built on. At the same time, however, they used interactions with like-minded individuals to collaboratively reaffirm their movement's goal.

Interestingly, in this discussion several tweets took a softer stance, arguing that 9/11 is a special day, where unity should trump all differences. These tweets appear to seek common ground between the two movements, attempting to create a more collaborative dialogue by insisting that in spite of the disagreement and injustices, unity is the key American value that trumps everything else. Two tweets in particular appear to try to build a bridge between the two narratives by calling on unity as a defining American characteristic and one that could resolve both movements' issues:

> @benhiggi @Kaepernick7 I agree. But will you STAND in unity tomorrow against inequality?
>
> @lawrence_author

> Thx @benhiggi ! UNITY for today is the key word here. No injustice was ever solved without the coming together of our great nation.
>
> @mindlyne

However, these tweets never got any response from people supporting either Black Lives Matter or All Lives Matter, indicating that the discourses that create these movements are situated in opposing ideologies without room for compromise.

Sometimes, however, the dialogue between opponents can change from highly antagonistic to the deliberative, reflexive dialogue Habermas envisioned when he introduced his ideas about the public sphere. One such discussion came out of a tweet by Jamilah Lemieux (@JamilahLemieux), who started the #MasculinitySoFragile movement. Her tweet read:

> #MasculinitySoFragile that it's more important to teach women to reject men politely than it is to teach men to accept rejection peacefully

This tweet received 790 retweets and 139 responses. When looking at the responses in depth, some interaction between supporters and detractors is visible, but a lot of it is antagonistic, i.e., the conversation partners view each other as enemies, not as adversaries, and appear to be set out to annihilate the other (Mouffe, 1999, 2000):

> @OaklandElle @JamilahLemieux You don't get that men are attacked too, by women & men alike. Assuming our ignorance is condescending
>
> @RemyNorth

> @RemyNorth @OaklandElle @JamilahLemieux men are attacked by women over rejection as a norm? Please stop your lying.
>
> @cashless

This conversation carries on in this vein for a few more tweets, with @RemyNorth arguing that men need advocacy too, while @cashless points out that men's issues do not need to be on any agenda. The conversation clearly shows how both sides, @cashless and @RemyNorth, dig their heels in and reiterate their points without giving the other person credit for their beliefs, an excellent example of the kind of antagonistic conversation that does little to strengthen democracy.

But then a second conversation starts, in response to @RemyNorth's comment about men as the majority of suicides, homeless, murder victims, and workplace fatalities:

> @RemyNorth @JamilahLemieux these all stem back to hyper masculinity though, an issue that feminists are trying to address. Just saying . . .
>
> @reezybreezyy

> @reezybreezyy @JamilahLemieux Men will determine how to express OURSELVES & if we want your help, we'll ask. Please and thank you.
>
> @RemyNorth

> @RemyNorth this was a convo about women & the fear we face in social situations, not about men expressing anything. You made it about you
>
> @reezybreezyy

The conversation then turns to a discussion about what #MasculinitySoFragile means, with @RemyNorth making statements like:

> @reezybreezyy No, no, no. #MasculinitySoFragile is about how much certain women <3 cattily bashing men all the live long day.

And @reezybreezyy responding with tweets such as:

> @RemyNorth the tag was about the ways that archaic notions of masculinity affect people. Some were small observations e.g brogurt

While tweets are still very passionate, the name-calling has disappeared, and the two users appear to be genuinely engaging with the other, in a highly agonistic manner. This conversation thus demonstrates how antagonistic conversations can become agonistic, which, according to Mouffe (2000, p. 16), is "the aim of democratic politics." As the conversation continues, both @RemyNorth and @reezeybreezyy's tones soften. Even though both continue to uphold their own positions, they seem to be enjoying the conversation. This becomes apparent when others jump in on the conversation with provocative statements, and @reezybreezyy asks them to step out, as "I'm having a convo with the other guy and there's actual interaction so please don't fill my mentions."

While they never reach a complete agreement, the conversation between @reezybreezyy and @RemyNorth becomes less hostile, and they appear to find common ground in the issues they have with feminism. Toward the end of the conversation, @RemyNorth drops his hostility completely, and @RemyNorth responds in kind:

> @reezybreezyy Men are not how you present us anymore. As a gay man, feminist women have made fun of me more than straight men.
>
> @RemyNorth I'm sorry to hear that is your experience, especially as feminists are overwhelming pro LGBTQ+ but your experience isn't the norm

@RemyNorth ends the conversation as follows:

> @reezybreezyy Thanks for at least not calling me a woman hater for giving a shit about men like most feminists do. I appreciate that.

While this dialogue is not the collaborative dialogue that helps build a movement or understanding between movements, it is also not the co-optive or antagonistic dialogue that characterized the beginning of the conversation. While there is no way to know how or if this conversation changed @RemyNorth or @reezybreezyy's minds about the hashtag or feminism, it did allow two people from opposite ends of views on feminism gain insight into each other's perspective. They are, in effect, engaging in the "diverse discussion" that Conroy, Feezell and Guerrero (2012, p. 1536) argued is necessary for political participants to gain a deeper understanding of political issues.

CONCLUSION

This chapter examined how social media in general and Twitter in particular have changed our understanding of social movements. This chapter discussed the traditional understanding of social movements as reappropriating urban space, and discussed how this conceptualization needs to change with the arrival of new media and the changing ways in which people interact and engage. While some techno-skeptics warn of the dangers of "clicktivism," denying the importance of online activism is equivalent to refusing to recognize the alternative means used by marginalized groups to create change.

This chapter examined various "virtual movements," i.e., movements that started, and in most cases remained, in the online environment of Twitter. An in-depth analysis of virtual movements that fought against racism and discrimination revealed that supporters of these movements used Twitter to gain recognition for their issues, to bring social issues to life, and to express frustration at the lack of progress. These social justice movements used Twitter to express a firm belief that inequality between gender or race was the root cause of the problems facing society. Countermovements created in response to these social justice movements instead focused on the lack of respect for American values as the cause of the issues facing the country. Many supporters of these movements also saw the nation under threat.

Dialogue is essential to the collective identity of each social movement. The dialogue between supporters and opponents of the various movements reveals that much of it is agonistic, i.e., it is not aimed at finding common ground or reaching a consensus and instead consists of little more than people restating their views and discrediting the other side. However, the lack of collaborative dialogue between the different movements should not be viewed as a detractor of Twitter's democratizing potential. As Ganesh and Zoller (2012) point out, the refusal to search for common ground that characterizes agonistic dialogue actually helps social movements resist hegemonic interpretations of their cause and facilitates genuine intragroup dialogue that questions commonly accepted understandings. As such, this kind of dialogue is imperative to the pluralism that underpins democracy (see Mouffe, 1999, 2000; discussion in chapter 6). But this lack of collaborative intergroup interaction does mean that, although people on Twitter occupy the same online platform, they seem to live in different worlds.

In short, Twitter allows for the creation of countercultural movements, but it also allows for dominant narratives to be re-created in movements that oppose these social justice activists. The use of hashtags does allow supporters of different movements to seek each other out, and when they do, the dialogue that ensues is not the rational deliberation that Habermas envisioned. Instead it more closely resembles the agonistic struggle that Mouffe (2000) saw as characteristic of the modern-day public sphere. This idea will be further elaborated on in the next chapter.

6

#MAGA, #ImWithHer, and #Snowflake

Politics and Twitter

> I'm a Latino with a college degree who likes pumpkin spice lattes, wine, and Taylor Swift but NOOO, #BernieMadeMeWhite!
>
> @ahhhhhlecks

In the past few years, Twitter has become an integral part of almost every political campaign, serving to inform, mobilize, persuade, and entertain constituents and potential voters (Kreiss, 2016). The 2016 election especially showed how influential Twitter has become in the decade since its inception. With a presidential candidate as active on Twitter as some of the platform's most engaged users and voters taking to Twitter in record numbers to share information and opinions, Twitter's relevance to politics is unparalleled (Isaac & Ember, 2016). This has raised questions about the dialogue that takes place on Twitter and the extent to which it contributes to the possibility of Twitter to serve as a virtual public sphere (e.g., Colleoni, et al., 2014).

Extant research has examined the role played by Twitter in shaping political opinions, as well as its potential to create dialogue between opposite sides of the aisle, checking the sometimes unbridled enthusiasm about Twitter's potential against the reality of Twitter usage (e.g., Bruns & Highfield, 2013; Kalsnes, Krumsvik, & Storsul, 2014; Merry, 2016; Parmalee & Bichard, 2011). This chapter contributes to this growing body of knowledge by exploring how supporters and opponents of a candidate utilize Twitter to negotiate the meanings attached to the various political campaigns. It examines if and how these negotiations reflect the deliberative dialogue that is deemed one of the foundations for a public sphere.

The tweets that came out of the 2016 U.S. presidential campaign serves as a case study, and I will examine tweets related to campaigns initiated by politicians as well as those that were created by Twitter users. This campaign, with a female presidential candidate and both parties' platforms focused on issues related to race, such as immigration (Andrews & Kaplan, 2015) and criminal justice, as well as issues related to gender, such as abortion (Kukreja & Green, 2016), provides an opportunity to examine how the political dialogue on Twitter reflects on and construct cultural tropes about race and gender. In this chapter, I first provide a brief overview of what is already known about Twitter, political communication, and the potential for dialogue. Next, I examine how the two hashtags that promoted the Clinton and Trump campaign, #MAGA and #ImWithHer, and hashtags that came out of events surrounding the 2016 campaign (e.g., #NastyWoman and #BernieMadeMeWhite), were used to construct shared understandings of gender and race.

WEB 2.0: A NEW AGE OF POLITICAL DELIBERATION

Ever since the rise of the Internet in the mid-1990s, scholars and political commentators alike have debated the usefulness of Web 1.0 and later 2.0 in providing access to political information and affording possibilities for political engagement (e.g., Papacharissi, 2009). Recent numbers show that the majority of American adults obtain their news from social media (Gottfried & Shearer, 2016), and that the bulk of social media users are politically engaged through these platforms (Rainie, Smith, Schlozman, Brady, & Verba, 2012). Opinions about the role played by social media in political discussion and engagement diverge. Some see social media platforms as an excellent space for expanding political knowledge and participation (e.g., Obar, Zube, & Lampe, 2012; Vitak, et al., 2011). Others disparage the optimists. A few scholars, like Morozov (2013) question techno-optimists' focus on the importance of sharing opinions and online discussions. Morozov argues that to reduce politics to the online sharing of ideas does not do justice to the complexity of political deliberation and democracy. Other techno-skeptics question whether social media really are that important for political decision-making. They argue that social media platforms do not increase political engagement (e.g., Kushin & Yamamoto, 2010) but only have a small effect (Valenzuela, Park, & Kee, 2009), or only ad to the knowledge and participation of those already engaged with politics (e.g., Carlisle & Patton, 2013; Dimitrova, Shehata, Strömbäck, & Nord, 2014).

The key factor in the debate between the techno-optimists and the techno-pessimists is the potential of social media to afford users with a space for meaningful deliberation. The presence of meaningful dialogue between political actors with different political and ideological backgrounds is seen as essential to the public sphere and key to maintaining a democracy. Proper deliberation encourages consensus-building, eschews polarization, and involves people from different backgrounds and communities (Dahlgren, 2005; Habermas, 1989, 2006; Jaggar, 1999; Wells, et al., 2017). Optimists have argued that the Internet in general and social media in particular provide a space for political dialogue (e.g., Mihailidis, Fincham, & Cohen, 2014), alleviating the polarization that has marked contemporary society (e.g., Farrell, 2012), and creating a platform for inclusive participation and discussion as well as the relationship-building required for political participation (Carlisle & Patton, 2013; De Zúñiga, Puig-i-Abril, & Rojas, 2009; Levenshus, 2010). Critics, however, have questioned whether social media provide such a space, arguing that the dialogue is limited to like-minded users, reproduces existing disparities, and lacks the depth and quality to qualify as deliberation (e.g., Halpern & Gibbs, 2013; Huckfeldt & Mendez, 2008; Papacharissi, 2009; cf. Conroy, et al., 2012). In the remainder of this section, I unpack some of these claims, and explore the dialogue that characterizes social media platforms.

One issue addressed by numerous scholars is whether or not social media platforms encourage cross-political discussion, i.e., dialogue between people from different ideological backgrounds. The diffusion of information afforded by social media on the one hand encourages the diverse discussion that demarcates political deliberation, while on the other hand social media's "tendency to reinforce group cohesion" (Colleoni, i.e., a space where people are solely exposed to those sharing their opinions. This is a concern, as conversation between diverse points of view is what is needed to build political understanding (Conroy, et al., 2012). Research has found that online conversations are often ideolo,gically homogeneous, i.e., they take place between people who share political viewpoints. This is known as homophily and is understood to be facilitated by social media (e.g., Farrell, 2012). In other words, social media encourage multiple parallel conversations as opposed to across-the-aisle interaction (e.g., Conway, et al., 2013; Merry, 2016; Poell, 2009). Conversely, Parmalee, and Bichard (2011) discovered that cross-political conversations do take place on social media. Only people with ideologically extreme views appear to practice selective exposure and avoidance, while others have no qualms following people with whom they usually disagree. People who are politically active and those who use Twitter for news will expose themselves to opposite ideas, whereas young users, as well as those who rely on Twitter for social interaction, are more likely to practice selective exposure. (cf. Colleoni, et al., 2014).

Examining the use of technological affordances specific to Twitter (hashtags, retweets, and mentions) nuances the findings regarding Twitter's potential to become an echo chamber. Hashtags play an important role in facilitating cross-ideological conversations. In line with the findings from the previous chapter, research has demonstrated that people often tweet using the hashtags used by both sides of an argument to rally for or against an opinion, exposing both ends of the political spectrum to their ideas (Boulianne, 2016; Yardi & Boyd, 2010). In contrast, retweets are generally used only when the argument in the original tweet reflect the user's opinion, increasing homophily and polarization. This polarization is further augmented by people's tendency to follow like-minded others. At the same time, research has shown that tweets that make use of mentions (@) tend to reflect the entire spectrum of political opinions, and that people will use their tweets to address those on the opposite end of the political spectrum, indicating that people want those on the other side of the aisle to at least hear their ideas (Bruns & Highfield, 2013; Conover, et al., 2011; Lorentzen, 2014).

A related question here is how much people actually interact on social media. Reciprocity is paramount if online communication is to contribute to democracy (Papacharissi, 2009). However, Twitter's defining characteristic is that it affords its users with the ability to broadcast their thoughts and ideas, and interaction is a secondary trait (Boynton, et al., 2014). Some research has found that people tend to use the platform as such, and merely tweet to share information, foregoing engagement with others (e.g., Jungherr, 2016; Larsson & Moe, 2011; Small, 2014). Conversely, others have found that Twitter is used as a town square, and political communication on Twitter tends to be far more interactional than other forms of communication (e.g., Boynton, et al., 2014; Grant, Moon, & Grant, 2010). Further research pointed to the importance of the mention and the hashtag in creating meaningful interaction and political deliberation, debunking any belief that Twitter is merely a broadcasting medium (e.g., Bruns & Highfield, 2013; Kalsnes, et al., 2014; Tumasjan, Sprenger, Sandner, & Welpe, 2010). However, a great deal of this interaction takes place between a small group of highly engaged users, who dominate most conversations. As a result, the interaction on social media platforms may not reflect the broad-base deliberation that scholars such as Habermas had in mind (e.g., Dean, 2010; Jungherr, 2016; Bastos, Raimundo, & Travitzki, 2013; Poell, 2009).

Besides the extent of reciprocity on social media sites, the nature of the dialogue is also important to consider. Social interaction between different groups is only valuable if this conversation occurs in a respectful manner, where people listen to the other side and are willing to compromise (Vargo & Hopp, 2017). Again, research has produced contradictory findings. Some investigations showed that discussions between social media users with diverging political opinions tend to be polarizing rather than consensus-building. If conversations between people with diverging opinions do take place, they are often heated and inflammatory and can in fact lead to the creation of more extremist views on both sides. Cross-political dialogue has also been found to do little for the creation of a deeper understanding of the issues at hand, and it often derails into personal attacks (e.g., Al-Tahmazi, 2015; Conover, et al., 2011; Dean, 2010; Duggan & Smith, 2016; Woolley, Limperos, & Oliver, 2010; Way, 2015; Van Zoonen, Vis, & Mihelj, 2011). This has been attributed to the level of anonymity afforded by social media, which leads to more inflammatory and antagonistic interactions (Halpern & Gibbs, 2013). Conversely, research has also shown that balanced, respectful cross-political interactions can be a reality. Groshek and Al-Rawi (2013) found that conversations on Twitter and Facebook during the 2012 presidential election reflected a very balanced and nonconfrontational view of both candidates. This finding is echoed by Merry (2016) whose analysis of conversations on Twitter did not find any indication of antagonism or polarization.

Research to date thus shows that while Twitter has the potential to create the political deliberation that lies at the foundation of a public sphere, the question remains if this potential is realized.

TWITTER AND POLITICS: CHANGING THE RULES?

Twitter has inexorably changed how political communication takes place, and is, as Loader and Mercea (2011) point out, capable of disrupting existing dominant discourses (cf. Dimitrova & Bystrom, 2013). The question is just how far this disruption can go. Ideally positioned, with the affordances needed to create the diverse and open dialogue required to form a public sphere (Colleoni, et al., 2014), Twitter was at the forefront of social media interactions during the 2016 presidential election.

In the remainder of this chapter, I examine how Twitter served as a platform for dialogue about the 2016 presidential election. I focus specifically on topics related to gender and race, exploring how people construct understandings of related themes, while also considering people's interactions and how these reflect the deliberative dialogue associated with the idealized public sphere.

In order to gain a better understanding of the discourses that surrounded the 2016 presidential election, I analyzed several sets of tweets. First, I looked at the hashtags that came out of both campaigns: #MAGA and #ImWithHer. I collected data for the four weeks prior to the election as well as the four weeks after Election Day. Next, I examined tweets bearing hashtags created by Twitter users in response to candidates' actions that dominated the top trending lists during the 2016 primary season and general election. Considering the focus of the book, namely the collaborative constructions of race and gender, I focus on those hashtags that touch on issues related to either. The hashtags that were used to collect data were #BernieMadeMewhite, #NastyWoman, #IAmANasty WomenBecause, #BasementDwellers, #Deplorables, #WomenWhoVote Trump, #BadHombres, and #TacoGate. I also discuss some of the top trending political hashtags that occurred in the two months after the election, including #NoBanNoWall, #TheResistance, #Resist, #Snowflake, #ShePersisted, and #LetLizSpeak. These hashtags were the direct result of the election outcome, and provide a good insight into the discourses that were created in response to the framing of ongoing events in the mainstream media. A total of 2,491 tweets were analyzed for this chapter.

#IMWITHHER AND #MAGA: INFLUENCING THE TWITTERSPHERE

This section takes a brief look at how the tweets associated with two main hashtags created by the 2016 political contenders, Hillary Clinton and Donald Trump, evolved during and after the election. The main hashtag employed by the Clinton campaign, #ImWithHer, grew out of a tweet sent out by Hillary Clinton's husband, Bill Clinton. While the Clinton campaign had tried to launch several other hashtags prior to this particular tweet, none of them caught on the way #ImWithHer did, and it quickly became the campaign's main slogan (McGrown-Levy, 2016). The slogan "Make American Great Again" was first employed by Ronald Reagan in his run for presidency in 1980, and Donald Trump used it in his successful bid for the White House in 2016 (Taibbi, 2016). On Twitter, the slogan became #MakeAmericaGreatAgain or #MAGA for short.

Campaign slogans are created to direct voters' thoughts and drive the narrative about a particular candidate. In a world where people got their information from mainstream media, and the media turned to politicians, press releases, and other major organizations for their news, controlling the narrative surrounding slogans and politically relevant events was not as difficult as it can be today. Gerodimos and Ward (2007) argue that the Internet has led to a "decline of a dominant narrative" (p. 125), as well as a loss of control over the narrative by political organizations, which raises the question if tweets that use either #ImWithHer and #MAGA follow the dominant narratives created by either candidate. In this section, I explore this question by examining tweets bearing either hashtag from the month before and after the 2016 election.

Preelection: Hope, Frustration, and Fear

Analysis of the tweets prior to the election revealed several themes. These include a desire to explain one's vote, expressing the belief that the opponent was completely unfit for office, and a call for people to vote for a particular candidate. The difference between the two hashtags lies in the sentiments expressed by both sets of voters. It appears that #ImWithHer tweets are more focused on a hopeful future, while #MAGA tweets show a fear that this is America's last chance to get things right.

Explaining the Vote: A Future at Stake

The largest category of tweets was focused on explaining why people needed to vote for a particular candidate. While the purpose of the tweets was the same, the two hashtags showed different ideas and feelings, providing interesting insight into the psychological underpinnings of both campaigns. Supporters of both sides felt their country was in danger, expressing this mainly through concerns for their children's futures:

> for the love of your brothers and sisters, your future children, please please please vote tomorrow #imwithher
>
> @katiefayeoliver

> #ImVotingBecause I love my children and their future is important to me. #maga #TrumpPence16 #specialneedsmom @realDonaldTrump
>
> @EVStoneRo

But #MAGA supporters tie the fear for their children to a larger concern about the direction of the country as a whole. Tweets reflect the belief that America's safety, its economic prosperity are lost or at risk, and that the country has lost its connection with its "Christian roots" (@aWeibs25). Many of the tweets bearing the #MAGA hashtag take this belief a step further, expressing a conviction that without Trump, the country that they know will be lost ("this is our last chance America"—@Pete_Bald). These tweets voice the conviction that Trump is the only person who can restore the power and respect that the U.S. used to have:

> #draintheswamp #LockThemUp @realDonaldTrump will restore the Greatness of America! and our respect by the world N fear from tyrannts! #MAGA
>
> @TommyGOP

> True PATRIOTS know @realdonaldtrump is our last chance to save America! #ImVotingBecause #MAGA #DrainTheSwamp "@VoteTrumpPics: Bill Belichick and Tom Brady Voted Trump! They really are PATRIOTS!"
>
> @Suzost

There is a clearly expressed fear that if anyone but Trump is elected, the America as these people know it will cease to exist. People tie this fear to a hatred of the establishment by reiterating hashtags like #DrainTheSwamp, as well as a belief that America needs to come first, and a belief that Trump stands for "we the people," an implication that he represents the common man as well as the values encapsulated in the U.S. constitution:

> WE THE PEOPLE: DOESN'T MATTER RACE, COLOR OR ETHNICITY . . . WE GO DOWN TOGETHER! #UNITY #MAGA #FIGHT #BlackVotesMatter #LatinosWithTrump #NOW "@StopQatarNow: THIS IS YOUR FIGHT AMERICA! YOU HAVE AN OPPORTUNITY TO WIN!!!! LETS OVERWHELM THE POLLS AND FINISH THE #TrumpRevolution #Retweet #MAGA #TCOT"
>
> @StopQatarNow

This tweet uses a post-racial discourse to convince ethnic minorities to vote for Trump. With a campaign that embraced color-blind ideology and embodied "Americanism," i.e., the belief that American values are superior, tweets like these show how this user perfectly reproduced the intended narrative. References to this Americanist ideology abounded through Tweets that used #MAGA, with references to the constitution, American independence, the "American patriot" and users likening this election to America's fight for independence from Britain:

> @NBCNightlyNews @PeteWilliamsNBC I smell a 2016 #AmericanRevolution brewing if #hitlery gains office! #maga #HillaryForPrison #ComeyMustGo
>
> @bobjohnson1180

This tweet and the many others like them reflect the values captured by the #AllLivesMatter and #BackTheBlue movement discussed in chapter 5: The belief that America is different from other nations in its freedom, its opportunities, and its power, and that Clinton poses a unique threat to these qualities. These findings also reflect Sylwester and Purver's (2015) work, who showed that Republicans on Twitter were more likely to invoke themes of national identity and religion.

Conversely, #ImWithHer tweets reflect similar fears for the future of their children but frame these fears at a more personal level:

> Honestly worried for this election, america please make the right decision !! #imwithher
>
> @kurtsrachels

> #ImVotingBecause I love the children in my family. I want them to live without fear. Just love & freedom to pursuit their dreams #ImWithHer
>
> @puppymnkey

Tweets like these capture similar fears to the ones expressed by the #MAGA tweets above: a fear that a core American value, namely freedom, is at stake. However, the choice to present this fear at a personal level and appeal to other Twitter users as family members softens the fear, hiding the condemnation of society as a whole behind maternal concerns. Only a few tweets use a bolder approach, similar to the ones used by the #MAGA tweets:

> #ImVotingBecause I care about the future of my country & cannot let @real DonaldTrump destroy our country. #ImWithHer #HillaryClinton #Trump
>
> @the_other_kimk

Again, though, the use of the words "I care" personalizes the fear, rendering the tweet less of a condemnation of the country as a whole. The Twitter users thus, in line with Sylwester and Purver's (2015) findings regarding the tweets of Democratic voters, frame their issues more as a personal concern, based on their feelings, and not on a perceived threat to their national identity.

Mudslinging: Condemning the Opponent

The second largest category of tweets from both hashtags were those that bashed the opponent and praised one's preferred candidate. Both Trump supporters as well as Clinton voters took vociferous swipes at the other side. Trump supporters accused Hillary of being untrustworthy and crooked, while those in the Clinton camp called Trump a sexist, a racist, and a demagogue. These tweets reflect the political polarization that characterizes American society as a whole, and that has seeped over into social media conversations (Duggan & Smith, 2016).

What is interesting to note, however, is that #ImWithHer tweets did, when attacking Trump, frequently include a comparison to Hillary Clinton:

> #ImWithHer because I don't believe that being kinda careless with emails is actually even comparable to sexual assault.
>
> @kokonutmeg

> #ImVotingBecause it's time for strong experienced woman to take office not for an man who uses racial slurs and thinks it's okay #imwithher
>
> @capt_ameriKARA

#MAGA tweets that attack Clinton merely focus on her as the object of their frustration, without any reference to their candidate's weaknesses or strengths.

> Going to be the second Clinton impeached once her skeletons are out. #MAGA
>
> @LeslieLynnLamb1

> The Clintons are rotten to the core.
> They have betrayed us all.
> #MAGA #SpiritCooking #Benghazi #PayForPlay #PodestasPizza
>
> @RaptorRAF

This theme returns when considering tweets that only sung praises of their candidate. When categorizing the tweets, it quickly became apparent that maybe a handful of tweets from the #MAGA hashtag did nothing but show unequivocal support for Donald Trump.

Only a few tweets talk about Trump as a "great" man, without any specifics (e.g., "I have no doubt in my mind that if @realDonaldTrump could campaign on Tuesday, he would have. What a great man who genuinely wants to #MAGA!"—@satya_matters), but the majority of the tweets that show support for Trump do so by critiquing Clinton or by expressing fear about the country's future:

> This scumhag deserves to occupy a prison cell . . . NOT THE WH!! #Hillary-Indictment #TrumpPence16 #MAGA #draintheswamp
>
> @dc10466

The particular tweet included a retweet by @TaraHollyGoFigure that said "This arrived at bookstores today. The arrogance is truly unbelievable. Newsweek claiming she won already #draintheswamp" with a picture of that week's *Newsweek* cover, which featured a picture of Hillary Clinton and the words "Madam President." The vast majority of tweets that use the #MAGA hashtag are of this tenor, critiquing Clinton and expressing anger and disgust at her candidacy.

Conversely, tweets that use the #ImWithHer hashtag are much more likely to unequivocally share their support for Hillary Clinton, without any reference to Donald Trump. Interestingly, when users shared reasons why they like Clinton, they became very reflective, sharing stories about who they are, as well as their feelings, and why they support Clinton:

> I am a 1st gen MBA in finance, business owner and #iAmWithHer #Bad-Hombres
>
> @Oscarca0731

> Gonna miss you, @POTUS. The work continues. #LetsGoChangeTheWorld #FiredUp #ReadyToGo #ImWithHer
>
> @Benny_Bananas

> Sad that the end of Obama's term is coming up. Here's to hoping his legacy / work can develop with @HillaryClinton in @WhiteHouse. #ImWithHer
>
> @Nusrath_H

Twitter users talk about Clinton's election being a great birthday present, they mention the anger they have felt when thinking about the election, and they share stories about children supporting Clinton. In short, the support for Clinton is very much personalized, reflecting the campaign's message as indicated by the personal hashtag #ImWithHer.

These particular tweets show little to no interaction; users appear to utilize Twitter mainly to broadcast their beliefs. They could be said to engage in what Papacharissi called "civically motivated narcissism" (2009, p. 238), i.e., a form of self-expression not meant to contribute to the dialogue in the public sphere or necessarily increase political participation. While these tweets could be said to render the Twittersphere more diverse, they ultimately exist to share a person's feelings (cf. Boynton, et al., 2014).

At the same time, content injection, or hijacking the other side's hashtag to attack their candidate was a common occurrence:

> #imwithher Hillary, Bill, &Chelsea scam and steal from charity and the poor to pay for their lifestyle. Utter and totally evil people #MAGA
>
> @MegHedges

> #ImWithHer Hillary, can't we all just get along? Why are you so trigger happy with your Nuclear Codes talk? Things that make you go #MAGA
>
> @Verity2016

This trend toward using a hashtag from the opposing party to express disapproval for that party has been noticed in previous research as well (e.g., Conover, et al., 2011), and it could be said to be a way to "inject partisan content into information streams" (p. 89), encouraging responses from other Twitter users. In this body of tweets, however, the use of the opposing party's hashtag does not appear to lead to any more mentions or replies.

What is interesting is that Trump supporters overwhelmingly use the #ImWithHer hashtag to tweet their support for Trump and their disdain for Hillary, while only a few Clinton supporters appear to do the same with the #MAGA hashtag (e.g., "How about explaining to your #MAGA how you are moving all your factories back here @realDonaldTrump"—@anchorstine). This could be tied to the finding discussed above: Trump supporters were much more focused on critiquing Hillary Clinton and expounding on the danger she posed to the country than they were on celebrating Trump's values. This behavior is in line with Trump's campaign which focused on "draining the swamp" and returning America to greatness by rescuing it from the establishment as embodied by Hillary Clinton.

Getting out the Vote

People's tendency to use Twitter as a broadcasting platform becomes apparent in this category as well, with tweets calling on voters to support their candidate. Both sides call on ethnic minorities to support their candidate, with Trump supporters claiming Obama has done nothing for ethnic minorities and Clinton voters arguing that Donald Trump is a danger to all ethnic groups. The tone between the two hashtags is very different, however. When examining #MAGA tweets, the fear about losing the country for good described above is very much apparent, with Twitter users talking about taking America "back" (e.g., "Time to take our country back yet??? #MAGA"—@djslyd01) and using the election to get the country on the right track:

> America has suffered enough the last 8 years. God will help Trump #MAGA. Don't worry about exit polls or early election predictions. Vote.
>
> @bibifl59

Tweets like these capture the feeling that the country is in danger, which is also reflected in numerous other tweets. A few of the #ImWithHer tweets reflect the same urgency:

> Is the next 36 hours THE END of our dystopian, quasi-Fascist Trumped up Nightmare . . . or only the beginning? GO #VOTE! #StopTrump #ImWithHer
>
> @jinzilla20

But whenever calling on people to vote for Hillary Clinton, #ImWithHer tweets tended to be more inspirational and whimsical:

> Ok ladies now let's get in formation. #ImWithHer
>
> @waveravemaeve

Other tweets include quotes by Hilary Clinton ("When you divide us, you weaken us. We are stronger together!"), Edmund Burke ("All that is necessary for the triumph of evil is that good men do nothing"), and calling on followers to "do the right thing." The overall sentiment is less fearful, less frustrated, and shows more hope about the upcoming election and its outcome.

Postelection

After Trump won the election, both hashtags persisted on Twitter well into 2017. Besides using Twitter to express joy or despair at the outcome of the election, supporters of both candidates used the hashtags to interact with other Twitter users, express fears about the future of the nation, and discuss issues surrounding race and gender.

Talk to Me: Cross-Political Interaction

One of the main trends to come out of the analysis of these postelection tweets is the increased interaction between opponents and supprters. A large number of tweets were part of a larger discussion, sometimes between people who agreed with each other, but equally, between people who did not agree, or people who were addressing politicians they either did or did not agree with:

> @mike_pence @realDonaldTrump @TIME Hitler was Person of the Year in 1938-that about sums it right up-WE THE PEOPLE voted Hillary #imwithher
>
> @pmohs

In this tweet, @pmohs doesn't just express their discontent with the outcome of the election, but they explicitly address Donald Trump and Mike Pence. This qualifies what Conover, et al. (2011) found, namely that people will use mentions to connect to people with a diverse set of political beliefs. Although @pmohs did not receive a response from either leader, this tweet is one of many that use Twitter to personalize their discontent by addressing specific people, thus indicating a desire for interaction.

There are also a number of discussions between supporters and opponents of Trump, which can best be understood if framed within the debate surrounding different kinds of deliberative dialogue. Simply looking for collaborative dialogue (see chapter 5) does not do justice to the different kinds of dialogue that can enhance a democracy. In fact, Mouffe (1999) argued that the "dialogic pluralism" (p. 754) that underpins the Habermasian public sphere and which is rational, dispassionate, and aimed at creating consensus does not reflect the reality of discussions in today's democracies. She proposes "agonistic pluralism" (p. 754) as a more realistic alternative, i.e., discussions where people don't necessarily strive for consensus but do acknowledge their adversaries' right to speak up (Mouffe, 1999, p. 754). Agonistic pluralism is seen as more viable perspective on today's society than the deliberative democracy that informs Habermas's work, as it recognizes the passion and conflict that characterizes contemporary political dialogue. Agonistic pluralism is based on agonism, or agonistic dialogue, i.e., argumentative confrontations between opponents aimed at reinforcing one's point, rather than compromise or increasing mutual understanding (see also chapter 5). Mouffe (1999, 2000) also recognizes the existence of antagonistic dialogue, which views the other as an enemy that one needs to vanquish in order to move forward. This dialogue, while not necessarily helpful to democracy, can, as demonstrated in chapter 5, evolve into the agonistic dialogue that helps build constructive political relations.

When looking at the discussions between Clinton and Trump supporters, it is apparent that these conversations take on both an agonistic as well as an antagonistic form. In one example, opponents accused Trump voters of not supporting Obama, and supporters responded by denying that claim, presenting pictures of family members in uniform with Barack Obama, and then telling opponents:

> @michaelwild2198 @ProblemPanacea @CortneyWarwick Make no mistake @realDonaldTrump will #MAGA. Now go lick your wounds. I'm done with U
>
> @MikeHimsworth

These types of conversations appear highly antagonistic, with Twitter users unwilling to give the other side a space to voice their opinions or be taken seriously (Mouffe, 1999). They reflect the lack of civility that has been observed in the larger society, thus raising questions about these kinds of conversations' contributions to democracy (Vargo & Hopp, 2017).

Other interactions are less confrontational, with people from different sides arguing their case, and confronting the other side with reasons why their arguments are incorrect, as shown by the following exchange:

> Good luck with your union collapsing and your social security fund privatized to fund bad investment
>
> @CTSadler

> With Hilary I'd have more union working rights, but no work, so what good is that?
>
> @DwayneMcDevitt

> What jobs do you think Trump is going to bring back? Manufacturing and coal, those are gone 4ever
>
> @CTSadler

> gone 4ever, yes under @hilaryclinton which is why she's not my president #MAGA
>
> @CarlosV77424716

This exchange qualifies as agonistic (e.g., Van Zoonen, et al., 2011), i.e., both sides, while not aiming to build consensus, are acknowledging the other's right to be heard and engaging in an exchange of ideas, albeit a passionate one. The conversation also shows the civility that Vargo and Hopp talked about, implying that it could contribute to the kind of interaction that underpins democracy. This exchange, does not, however, mean that people are open to changing their ideas. These conversations could instead, as Yardi and Boyd (2010) posited, lead to a mere strengthening of one's opinion and an increased polarization. But, while this conversation and ones like it may not lead to the compromises and consensus that were on Habermas's mind, they do show the foundation of agonistic pluralism that Mouffe (1999) proposed. In other words, Twitter does help expose people to opposing views and ideologies, and is not, at least as far as this case study goes, the political echo chamber that some feared.

Another interesting observation was an increase in the number of retweets, especially of tweets and posts with which the retweeter disagreed. Several studies (e.g., Conover, et al., 2011; Lorentzen, 2014) found that retweet networks lacked diversity; people tended to retweet only those ideas with which they agreed. But the results were not unequivocal; Lorentzen found, for instance, that members of a Swedish minority party did retweet messages from other parties, although lack of qualitative analysis meant that the project could not make any statements about the nature of the retweet. The sample of tweets examined here contained examples of users retweeting news that reflected their beliefs (e.g., a story on the Daily Kos about how Trump voters were starting to feel remorse was retweeted several times by Clinton supporters using the #ImWith-

Her hashtag). At the same time, the analysis also revealed numerous instances of Clinton supporters retweeting news from outlets such as Fox news, and disagreeing with their content:

> Actually, her message was that I have stood up for women & children & freedom & equality for all Americans since I was a kid. #ImWithHer "@FoxNews: .@ericbolling: "[@HillaryClinton] never touched the hearts of voters. Her only message was, 'It's my turn' and 'He's terrible.'"
>
> @shelleychhabra

This tweet shows people do interact with oppositional beliefs, and while this may not lead to deliberative interaction, people's exposure to this kind of content could be helpful in fostering a more agonistic conversation which could enhance democracy. Again, while the results from this study are by no means representative, they do hint at possible patterns of behavior and provide the qualitative insight called for by Lorentzen.

Finally, I also noticed an uptake in the content injection, or the "hijacking" of each other's hashtags. In the preelection tweets, Trump supporters appeared far more likely to use #ImWithHer to make disparaging remarks about Clinton, but in the month after the election, both sides used each other's hashtags to critique the other. It appears that the anger that the Trump supporters experienced prior to the election transferred on to the Clinton supporters after the election:

> @BreitbartNews brilliant. Like putting Joker in charge of the justice league. #whatcouldpossiblygowrong? #MAGA
>
> @EatYourOwnHead

> Why do people vote for those who oppress them?
> #ImWithHer #MAGA #GreenParty #LibertarianParty #independants
> (this tweet included a survey with one vote and the following results posts: 0% They are wannabees; 0% Stockhom Syndrome; 0% Fear; 100% Misinformation)
>
> @KOMBUCHABABY

Without the campaign's narrative centered on unity and moving forward, the discourse utilized by Clinton supporters began to reflect the tone of the pro-Trump tweets.

A Country in Danger

The focus on a country that is at risk that was present in the preelection tweets also returned in the postelection discussions. This time, the #Im WithHer tweets expressed the fear about losing their country that was previously voiced by the #MAGA supporters:

> These people will endanger your country. #NeverTrump #ImWithHer #Im-StillWithHer @HillaryClinton (tweet included a link to a CNN story about Trump transition team requesting security clearance for Michael Flynn)
>
> @Herbiv4

> Please, Hillary Clinton, don't leave the country to Trump. Please fight for us, @HillaryClinton #ImWithHer (contains a link to a news article by The Independent about how Hilary could still win the presidency if she challenged the electoral college)
>
> @SheviStories

Conversely, #MAGA supporters rejoiced at Trump's desire to put America first and fix all the problems that had been threatening to bring the country down:

> America has a chance because we the people have spoken. We now have a leader who loves our country and will work to protect her and us. #MAGA
>
> @cindy_crawley

> We are on our way to better days & perhaps a little roughness but in end #MAGA @realDonaldTrump #MASA #TrumpTrain #HillaryIndictment "@EricSpracklen: This could be shared a million times and it wouldn't be enough (tweet includes a picture of several Times magazine covers featuring Donald Trump as losing the election, and then finally the cover that features him as the winner)"
>
> @jdavis3

In addition, #MAGA tweets appear to have identified a new threat to their current stability, activists, or social justice warriors:

> #Trump pick for #EPA has enraged "activists." Sounds like he's the right man for the job (this tweet includes a link to a news story about Trump's pick for head of the EPA) #MAGA
>
> @oldhickory49

Again, the finding that Republicans tend to focus on national identity as well as their opponents (Sylwester & Purver, 2015) is confirmed.

Discussing Gender and Race

Some of the tweets from both hashtags also touch on issues of gender, arguing that gender inequality is a thing of the past. One thread argued that the "I'm with her" slogan played the gender card; i.e., it was trying to convince people to vote for Hillary Clinton because she was a woman. The two Twitter users involved in this discussion agreed that:

> Also #Imwithher is weak. You shouldn't have to prop up your candidate, it doesn't create confidence. #sheswithme is stronger.
>
> @AlyssaSharpe

Another discussion posited that gender inequality is no longer an issue, as evidenced by Trump selecting women for his cabinet. When @Welly_World expresses her pleasure at Trump's picks, @AlwayanAmerican chimes in with the remark that race and gender should not matter, but results should, to which @Welly_World responds with:

> @AlwayanAmerican There is no inequality as long as "you are the best and brightest choice." The left has brainwashed the masses for votes.

This tweet reflects the neoliberalism that underpins the color-blind ideology discussed in chapter 5. These Twitter users feel confirmed in their belief that the U.S. is the country of opportunities and equalities by Trump's picks for cabinet.

#NASTYWOMAN AND #BADHOMBRES: USERS SPEAK UP

I now turn to the hashtags created by supporters of the respective campaigns. A host of hashtags were created in response to the various events surrounding the campaign.

A lot of these hashtags, such as #Deplorables, #BasementDwellers, and #NastyWoman to name a few, were a response to statements made by one of the candidates, one that was usually meant to insult or hurt the opponents' supporters. The groups affected by these phrases took to Twitter in response, using the insult as a hashtag to engender support for their candidate or to express their anger:

> #Obama is the #GreatDivider. #Trump is the #GreatUniter! #Deplorables #WeAreGonnaNeedaBiggerBasket! @waynedupreeshow @marcydw1
>
> @WalkingSeaWater

In this tweet, @WalkingSeaWater references Clinton's full statement, "You could put half of Trump's supporters into what I like to call the basket of deplorables" (Blow, 2016), and undermined its meaning by talking about needing a bigger basket for all the Trump supporters. Similar responses were uncovered in the #NastyWoman and #IAmANasty

WomanBecause hashtags where Clinton supporters shared personal stories of strength and resilience using the hashtag as a badge of honor.

In addition, many tweets referenced popular cultural expressions in their subversion of the phrase:

> Do You Hear the People Sing? Les #Deplorables. The #Trump #anthem. The new conservative revolution
>
> @JamesNavaCom

This particular example reflects the role played by Twitter's extratextual affordances in creating meaning. In this case, @JamesNavaCom used a picture of the Broadway show "Les Misérables," and replaced the title of the show with the words "Les Deplorables," and the red flags that are generally flown by the crowd in the show with Trump banners. This tweet captures a sentiment shared by many of the Trump supporters, namely that they are a small but justified minority fighting for the good of the country, just like the uprising presented in Les Misérables.

#BernieMadeMeWhite and #TacoGate both trended during the 2016 primary season. #BernieMadeMeWhite was started in March 2016 in response to the media's tendency to ignore Sanders' young ethnic minority supporters (Sanders, 2016). #TacoGate trended in response to a tweet sent out by Donald Trump on Cinco de Mayo, expressing his love for Hispanics (Kos, 2016). The #WomenWhoVoteTrump hashtag trended in October 2016 in response to a call from a Trump support group called "National Women for Trump," which asked that female Trump supporters use social media to express their support for the candidate using the hashtag (Rushton, 2016). #BadHombres and #NastyWoman as well as #IAmANastyWoman trended during and after the third and final presidential debate in October 2016, in response to statements made by Trump about illegal immigration and Hillary Clinton, respectively (Gray, 2016). Qualitative analysis of these hashtags revealed three major findings: the use of these hashtags to build communities, using the hashtags to give voice to a sense of marginalization and relying on the hashtag to provoke one's opponents and engage in antagonistic dialogue.

Building Networks and Creating Solidarity

First, these hashtags revealed that Twitter provides a space for like-minded people to connect and express their ideas. People used the hashtag to express emotions and beliefs, tweeted notes of encouragement, and addressed other users of the hashtag as members of a group.

While the tweets showed similarity to the tweets using hashtags created by the campaigns themselves by expressing support for one candidate and disdain for the other, the main difference was their tone. While the #ImWithHer and #MAGA tweets tended to be fairly serious, these tweets took a more tongue in cheek approach:

> Guys, really, no one has more respect for women than he does. He was only saying bad HOMBRES #DebateNight #badhombres
>
> @natsayth

> A good woman goes to heaven; a #nastywoman goes everywhere including the #WhiteHouse @HilaryClinton #leader #independent #strong
>
> @DebraLefebvre

> Can we call Clinton a #badmujer ? #badhombres
>
> @JulapiumEmentha

Considering the fact that #Nastywoman, #BadHombres, and #Bernie MadeMeWhite were created as ironic comebacks to undermine the remarks made by the candidates or the media, this is no surprise. In spite of their whimsical undertones, the use of hashtags such as these to create counternarratives leads to a clearer sense of a community among different users of the hashtag. In these examples, this is shown by the use of the words "guys" and "we." Even a hashtag such as #Women WhoVoteTrump, which was not meant as ironic, but which was created in response to the mainstream belief that women could not possibly like Donald Trump, led to a similar sense of community:

> us women and us MINORITIES are for trump!!! trump is on our side ladies and he looks out for minorities! #WomenWhoVoteTrump #Trump2016
>
> @hyunascult

> @TeamTrump #WomenWhoVoteTrump in Florida we are for you All the Way!! Trump for President
>
> @supkat12

When looking at the data, users frequently addressed other people using the same hashtags, and often relied on the word "we" or "us" to communicate a sense of belonging:

> Raise your hand if you identify as a #nastywoman @HillaryClinton (tweet is accompanied by a picture of two women on a staircase with their hand up)
>
> @karbuckle35

> SHOUT OUT TO ALL OF MY TWITTER PEEPS #BernieMadeMeWhite #TOTALLY MADE MY DAY #WeAreTheRevolution #BernieOrBust #Ber nieSanders #loveandpeace
>
> @smile33

Twitter users also often commented on the nature of the people who used a certain hashtag, pointing to the existence of an online community:

> Reading through the #BernieMadeMeWhite tweets, can't help but feel proud of all this intelligent people that really know who #Bernie is.
>
> @305Cristian

> You guys are really trending this one, excellent!
> #WomenWhoVoteTrump
> #ImWithYou
>
> @AlisonSpalding2

A last category of tweets referenced the actions taken by people to build the existing off-line support for their preferred candidates. People talked about phonebanking, knocking on doors, and wearing and buying merchandise:

> Has anyone created "Make America Nasty Again" hats? Because someone should. #nastywoman #nastywomenvote
>
> @ELWegener

Asking about products or sharing their latest purchase with just the hashtag again points to the sense that the hashtag doesn't just bring together people with similar beliefs; it has created a community. These tweets are particularly interesting, as they hint at the notion of the "prosumer," i.e., the media user who, through the consumption of products, is portrayed as a producer of meaning (e.g., Van Dijck, 2009). Tweets such as the one above indicate that Twitter users view the purchasing and owning of objects as another way to undermine dominant narratives. This will be further discussed in chapter 7.

On Your Side: Marginalized Voices

The tweets analyzed for this chapter also revealed that people view Twitter as a platform where they can safely express and discuss ideas not popular or commonly recognized in mainstream society. Many of the tweets centered on giving voice to feelings of discrimination and marginalization.

The #BernieMadeMewhite and #BadHombre hashtags were mostly used to share people's experience with racism and/or stereotyping. People used Twitter and these hashtags as a space to give voice to feelings of marginalization. Some were serious:

> The media needs to stop erasing & shaming young women of color, like me. We stand with Bernie & we will not be silenced. #BernieMadeMeWhite
>
> @RichaKamboj7

> We're not just the #MexicanThing but as immigrants we're the #BadHombres. @realDonaldTrump your hateful rhetoric continues. #HeretoStay
>
> @armancarr1990

While others captured feelings of discrimination in a more tongue-in-cheek fashion:

> I guess now #BernieMadeMeWhite i'm no longer a super-predator that needs to be brought to heel.
>
> @mydevastated

> Since #BernieMadeMeWhite I haven't been called *articulate* and not one person has asked to touch my hair! Thanks, #Bernie! #BernieSanders
>
> @smileydevil

> sooo #badhombres is the new Trump latinx outreach program? #debate
>
> @a_for2day

The majority of tweets using #BadHombres and #TacoGate address racial discrimination in a humorous way. For instance, #TacoGate was utilized by many to mock Trump's promise to build a wall on the Mexican border (e.g., "#TacoGate wait until you see the tortilla wall I'm going to build. Also will hire displaced workers to fire hot guac down on border crossers"—@ReelTronaldDump). Some took Trump's taco bowl tweet and applied it to other ethnic groups, jabbing at the racist undertones of this tweet:

> Trump's 1816 POTUS Campaign: The best African food is made at my plantation. I love blacks! #TacoGate #Racist
>
> @MatthewSwihart

> Donald Trump is one Miller Lite away from posting a picture of himself eating fried chicken, while claiming 'I love negroes!' #Tacogate
>
> @aristocritique

These tweets relied mainly on humor to subvert commonly held stereotypes, showing the importance of humor as a tool to counter the narratives created by the political candidates and the mainstream media. This especially came to the fore in the #BadHombre hashtag, where numerous Twitter users proposed ideas about who the "real" bad hombres were, including avid Trump supporters and the actors from the movie *The Three Amigos*. Others took on Trump's pronunciation of the term:

> what's worse is. dude mispronounced Hombres. If im Hispanic, Im double offended, because you didn't even offend me correctly.
>
> @Dj_TruBlu

Or indicated that they thought the phrase was so ludicrous by comparing it to a hair coloring technique called "ombre" (e.g., #badhombres—what happens when you dye the tip of your hair yellow #trump2016"—@stufunny). While a few tweets were more serious, with users mentioning the deportation of male family members if Trump got his way, the vast majority took a humoristic approach in countering Trump's insults.

The humor that was so apparent in tweets that addressed issues of race disappeared when looking at tweets that discussed gender discrimination. The #NastyWoman tweets show a frustration at the stereotyping and marginalization that women have faced:

> #IAmANastyWomanBecause I will not tolerate the good-old-boy mentality that says I'm a bitch when I stand up for what is right.
>
> @HotLav_a

> #IAmANastyWomanBecause I believe women's rights are human rights and human rights are women's rights
>
> @Donna_West

While both the phrases "nasty woman" and "bad hombre" were meant to insult specific groups, it is interesting to note that #BadHombre became a far more whimsical hashtag, and #NastyWoman and #IAmANastyWoman adopted a much more combative tone.

Women adopted the label "nasty woman" as a badge of honor, in essence reclaiming the phrase (e.g., "#IAmANastyWomanBecause #NastyWoman is the new badass"—@LastLatinHippie). Through their reclaiming, they redefined "nasty woman" to indicate that they were independent, smart, and not afraid to stand up for themselves (e.g., "#IAmANastyWomanBecause I don't apologize for my intellect, attitude or success"—@CrosetDesign). Tweets indicated that they clearly saw this as juxtaposed against Trump's view of women:

> #IAmANastyWoman Because I'm educated, beautiful & strong. Mr. Trump only likes mail order brides and/or pretty looking with no brains women
>
> @BonnerMegan

Women took to Twitter to describe how they fit the label of "nasty woman" by providing examples from their personal lives that showed their strength and a desire for change:

> #IAmANastyWomanBecause I divorced a malignant narcissist and I'm not about to vote for another to "rule" over me.
>
> @KimberyHough

> #IAmANastyWoman Because I'm working my ass off to become a lawyer so I can help others & aid in diversifying the legal community
>
> @jenniichristine

These tweets indicate, like the #ImWithHer tweets discussed above, that the election was highly personal for these Twitter users. In addition, this personalization again reflects Sylwester and Purver's (2015) findings that Twitter users who identify as Democrats are more likely to tweet about personal issues.

Interestingly, the tweets also revealed that Twitter is a space for anyone who feels marginalized to express themselves, even if they may not be viewed as marginalized by mainstream society. The #WomenWhoVoteTrump hashtag made it clear that Trump voters feel as symbolically annihilated by the mainstream media as women and ethnic minorities do; they often address the "lies" spread by the mainstream media and the media's tendency to demonize Trump supporters. Tweets are used to address others using the hashtag and encourage them to remain positive, in spite of all the pushback they are receiving:

> #WomenWhoVoteTrump care about our children and their future. We care about having a safe country.We care about our men and women in uniform. "@lingling23: #WomenWhoVoteTrump are strong & beautiful! Don't let the Liberal liars tell you any different!"
>
> @mrpac09

> #WomenWhoVoteTrump are smart women who aren't about to let the corporate media tell them who to vote for.
>
> @libertyin2016

There appears to be an overwhelming belief among Trump supporters that the mainstream media ("MSM") are not only liberal but that they support Clinton and will lie to get her elected:

> @seanhannity @JudgeJeanine @wikileaks WE MUST KEEP PUSHING THE TRUTH BC MSM LIES #WomenWhoVoteTrump #StealthTrumpVoters
>
> @MakeitRight16

> That's right Beverly!! Me too! #WomenWhoVoteTrump "@Bevansley1017: #WomenWhoVoteTrump are tired of corrupt politicians, Washington elite, Celebrities telling us who to vote for, MSM bias, the establishment"
>
> @flredheadmom

This is in turn tied to the belief that the nation is under the threat, i.e., not only are the mainstream media lying and supporting a partisan cause, in doing so they are attacking the U.S. and everything it stands for, including those who fight for its freedoms:

> #MSMbias is a threat to the democratic process & theft of our right to a fair election! Shame on you! #WomenWhoVoteTrump do our own research "@terrymendozer: @realDonaldTrump statement on Facebook. Democrats and the left are attacking WE THE PEOPLE. Not just Trump. Threat to our democracy."
>
> @smp0711

What is interesting about these tweets is that Clinton received more negative press attention than Trump during the general election (Patterson, 2016a, 2016b, 2016c). It appears that Trump voters do not view it that way. This could be the result of their tendency to rely on a few very conservative news sources (Mitchell, Gottfried, Kiley, & Matsa, 2014), which most likely created the image that Trump was being demonized by the media (e.g., Goodwin, 2016) or people's propensity to expose themselves to information that confirmed what they already believed (e.g., Knobloch-Westerwick & Meng, 2009). As a result, Trump supporters saw themselves as ignored and trivialized by the media and excluded from the mainstream public sphere and took to Twitter to create a networked counterpublic, i.e., to express their frustration and develop their own counternarrative together with other Trump supporters (cf. Papacharissi, 2009).

Twitter and Cyberbalkanization

The tweets discussed in the previous two sections underline the potential of Twitter to create bonding social capital, i.e., the strengthening of ties between like-minded people. Hashtags such as #Nastywomen or #WomenWhoVoteTrump expose people to others like them who have similar worldviews, and allows them to form connections with these people. These kinds of ties produce high levels of trust and connection and can have a host of positive consequences (e.g., Putnam, 2000). At the same time, it can also result in antagonistic relationships with people who are not members of their group. This bridging social capital, connections between people from different backgrounds, is seen as essential to democracy (Kavanaugh, Reese, Carroll, & Rosson, 2005; Putnam, 2000). Twitter has been shown to promote the creation of bonding social capital, but the creation of bridging social capital usually does not occur without the help of moderators (Sajuria, VanHeerde-Hudson, Hudson, Dasandi, & Theocharis, 2015).

The final theme uncovered in this analysis echoes these quantitative findings, as it revealed the division between Twitter users. Tweets revealed that the user-generated hashtags provided Twitter users with an opportunity to provoke their opponents and engage in antagonistic dialogue with outsiders. Instead of encouraging cross-political dialogue, these hashtags appear to inspire the feeling that the world is pushing people around, giving them all the more reason to not back down and stand their ground.

As mentioned in previous sections, the hijacking of hashtags, or content injection (Conover, et al., 2011) is a very popular way to express one's thoughts to the other side, but again, it seems to reflect no more than a desire to bash the opponents:

> #WomenWhoVoteTrump are ok with Trump's multiple divorces and cheating but say the sanctity of marriage is being ruined by LGTBQ folk
>
> @thewritelove2

> The HRC #CrookedHillary supporters are so weak they can't even get #NastyWoman to trend. LOL
>
> @bakerjmw2016

A great deal of content injection centers on challenging the hashtag's views on race and/or gender. Especially the #BernieMadeMeWhite hashtag received pushback from people who did not agree with the proposition that mainstream media had thus far ignored Sanders's non-white supporters and the larger underlying trope that ethnic minorities were under recognized in general:

> Bernie didn't make you white. Bernie spoke to your perpetual victim hood status given to you by the mainstream media #BernieMadeMeWhite
>
> @muayfarang555

> #BernieMadeMeWhite is ridiculous and endless whining from the people who make race their main thing will turn Bernie against you.
>
> @terriveganmom

> #BernieMadeMeWhite everything is about race, blacks seem to have some type of inferiority complex, jealousy? Get over it you simpleton losers
>
> @yongaryisback

Besides capturing the color-blind ideology common among opponents of the #BernieMadeMeWhite topic, these tweets also underscored the sense of marginalization experienced by white conservative voters who believe that race is a nonissue, blown out of proportion by the mainstream media. These people then turned to Twitter to express their disgust at the direction of the media's representation and/or Clinton's campaign and to "regain" their voice:

> Disgusted by #Hillbots implying being white is a bad thing. Hint: the majority of the US is white & most of its voters. #BernieMadeMeWhite
>
> @C_Truth_

While the tweets did lead to interactions, these were characterized by the polarization and lack of civility noted by other researchers (e.g., Halpern & Gibbs, 2013):

> #WomenWhoVoteTrump are teaching their daughters that it's okay to disrespect females; that it's okay to look at females as a piece of meat
>
> @drewryanscott

> @drewryanscott No they're voting for #Trump as a protest against @Hillary Clinton because #SexismTrumpsCorruption
>
> @crimsonboudoir

> @crimsonboudoir @drewryanscott @HillaryClinton you think trump isn't corrupt? What about the bankruptcies? The taxes? The women?
>
> @MollyJongFast

> @MollyJongFast @crimsonboudoir @drewryanscott @HillaryClinton He paid all the legal taxes. Hillary did THE SAME THING, look it up ignorance
>
> @NickCappuccino

This particular interaction is one of many; the tweet by @drewryanscott alone got 423 replies, many of which were like the example shared above.

While the interaction started off agonistic, with @crimsonboudoir explaining why @drewryanscott's conclusion is incorrect, it quickly became antagonistic. Twitter users dig in their heels and attack their opponents, calling them ignorant, and showing all the signs of uncivil, antagonistic noncollaborative dialogue that does not build mutual understanding (Ganesh & Zeller, 2012; Mouffe, 1999; Vargo & Hopp, 2017).

Whenever Twitter users do interact in a collaborative manner, this is only with people with whom they agree, and in a way that focuses on clearly defining the other as the enemy, the outsider who is uninformed, biased, or simply unable to see "the truth":

> @drewryanscott I guess the other side is teaching their daughters it's ok to stick up for a rapist and threaten his victims?
>
> @Peters1Aaron

> @Peters1Aaron @drewryanscott It's amazing how the left ignores the compounding crap on the left, but quick to overreport a Trump story.#Trump
>
> @Trump_Boss

The kind of dialogic pluralism that underpins Habermas's view of the public sphere thus appears limited to people who are already in agreement with each other. This will help augment bonding social capital, but does very little for the bridging capital that is seen as a necessity for the kind of dialogue that builds democracy.

In other words, Twitter does provide a space for groups, especially those that feel marginalized, to connect, grow, and create political momentum. However, even though Twitter creates the affordances needed to reach across divisions, people's online behavior reflects their offline tendency to only expose themselves to ideas and beliefs that matches their worldview. When they reach across divides, the dialogue is mainly antagonistic, seeing the opponent as a true enemy. These particular case studies thus show that Twitter has led to a cyberbalkanization, i.e., the creation of separate, but parallel online spaces where people only communicate with those like them (e.g., Suhay, Blackwell, Roche, & Bruggeman, 2015).

#NOBANNOWALL, #SNOWFLAKE: POSTELECTION POLITICAL COMMUNICATION

The political debate did not end with the 2016 election. In fact, with some of President Trump's decisions came a firestorm of controversy. Once again, Twitter became a primary tool for defending and opposing the new president's actions. In looking at the hashtags that were created after

President Trump's inauguration, it again becomes clear how Twitter is a space that is specifically attractive to marginalized voices and that encourages collaborative dialogue between like-minded people. Conversely, the conversations between opponents can be described as agonistic at best and antagonistic at their worst.

Within a few days of Trump's inauguration, Twitter became a focal point of Donald Trump's new presidency as the new administration placed numerous federal agencies under gag orders, banning them from using social media. Federal agencies such as the National Park Service were ordered to delete tweets about the size of the crowds at Trump's inauguration (Lartey, 2017), while the Badlands National Park Service deleted several tweets it had posted about climate change. While widely critiqued, the order probably would have disappeared from the media agenda had someone not created an alternative account for the National Park Service (@AltNatParkServ). The first tweet from this account read: "Can't wait for President Trump to call us FAKE NEWS! You can take our official Twitter but you'll never take our free time!" (Repanshek, 2017). This "rogue" account was quickly followed by other alternative accounts for federal agencies, such as @BadlandsNPSFans, @RogueNASA, and @RogueEPAstaff, which mainly focus on tweeting out facts about climate change that Trump supporters have denied (Davis, 2017). In some cases, though, the accounts also call out for followers to resist the current administration, using the #Resist hashtag commonly employed by anti-Trump movements.

This development points to the (real or perceived) power of Twitter in shaping public discourse and forming a space for resistance. The current administration clearly saw Twitter as a primary platform to inform people of new developments and findings, hence the ban. At the same time, the creation of these alternative accounts and their immense popularity (@RogueNASA alone has 990,000 followers) shows how eager Twitter users are to unite around a discourse that resists the perceived mainstream narrative.

Twitter stayed at the forefront of the public and media agenda with the creation of numerous hashtags in response to decisions made by the new administration. Hashtags such as #TheResistance, #Resist, and #NoBanNoWall were top trending topics in the days after Donald Trump's inauguration. They were part of the public's response to Trump's executive order that included the construction of a wall on the Mexican border, a reduction in the number of refugees allowed admittance to the U.S., and that blocked citizens from seven countries from entering the U.S. (David, Sanger, & Haberman, 2017). While only #NoBanNoWall was created in response to this particular executive order, and the others had been around since Trump was elected, #Resist and #TheResistance did not gain the widespread public traction until Trump's order was made public. These hashtags share a few characteristics. First, they are used to call to action and organize protests focused on the immigration ban. They were, among other things, linked to the Women's March on DC the day after Trump's inauguration. Subsequently, a number of tweets share information about protests, marches, and other steps people can take to oppose the current administration:

> Call your leaders every week to demand Trump's removal. #TheResistance #resist #trumpleaks #womensmarch #AlternativeFacts #RT #voterfraud.
>
> @DaShanneStokes

> I look forward to going to D.C. next weekend to protest Donald Trump & march for women's rights!
> #TheResistance #NotMyPresident
>
> @GilTPolitics

These kinds of tweets serve to engage people in action, and as such do not serve to create social capital, whether bridging or bonding, but are a form of "connective action," where social media "allows people to organize" (Sajuria, et al., 2015, p. 717).

Second, the hashtags produced tweets that were very much focused on strengthening the bonding social capital between people who agree. Some tweets, like the ones below, serve to encourage the people who follow #TheResistance, implying the experience of shared concerns and fears in an online community:

> All I'm saying is don't give up
> Don't you dare give up
> That's how freedom & liberty dies
> Our strength is in numbers
> #TheResistance
>
> @CaptainsLog2017

> Vive la #Bresistance! Long live #TheResistance! Let's get ready to get in #goodtrouble. We are the avalanche. "@repjohnlewis: Even though I was arrested, I smiled bc I was on the right side of history. Find a way to get in the way #goodtrouble"
>
> @clacksee

Again, many tweets invoke the trope reflected by both conservatives and liberals, that the nation is under threat, either as a result of Trump's immigration policy or Trump's election as shown below:

> Say goodbye to democracy, freedom of speech, peace, equality . . . Mourning in America #InaugurationDay #TheResistance #SocialRights
>
> @realbellasworld

> We are dissidents.
> We are legion.
> We are everywhere.
> We are powerful.
> We are motivated like never before.
> WE ARE AMERICA!
> #TheResistance
>
> @France4Hillary

As evidenced by @France4Hillary's tweet, the idea that Trump is a threat to the country was utilized to further cement the community implied by #TheResistance and #Resist.

Other tweets respond to specific events, such as the Women's March on DC or Tillerson's appointment as Secretary of State:

> Tillerson got in. We are screwed. The sanctions will be lifted next. This isn't good #TheResistance
>
> @PrincessBravato

> Today is the largest mass protest in American history, maybe in world history. Today I am proud of my country. #WomensMarch #TheResistance
>
> @ProgPoli

These tweets and the others like it rely on "we," again implying the existence of a group of like-minded people who share bonding social capital. A lot of tweets shared pictures about protests that the Twitter users had attended. The argument could be made that tweets that underline shared experiences and beliefs strengthen bonding capital. However, they are also highly self-serving ("look at me! I'm at the women's march"), and subsequently, could also be labeled as "civically motivated narcissism" (Papacharissi, 2009, p. 238).

Other political hashtags that trended in the first six weeks of 2017 reflected a liberal perspective on events and appeared to be aimed at creating bonding social capital. #LetLizSpeak and #ShePersisted, for instance, were created in response to the silencing of Senator Elizabeth Warren by Republican Senator Mitch McConnell. The tweets reflected outrage at McConnell's behavior, with Twitter users rallying behind Senator Warren, and people using the hashtag to share personal stories of females persisting in the face of adversity. Like the hashtags discussed above, these tweets show the creation of bonding social capital, but also, to some extent, the civic narcissism that Papacharissi (2009) talked about.

Furthermore, the findings also revealed an uptake in the number of tweets that hijacked left-leaning hashtags like #TheResistance. These attacks indicate a fear of the community that is being created through the hashtag and the threat it potentially poses to the new administration:

> The Bikers for Trump will have a soothing effect on the delicate snowflakes from #theresistance
>
> @Tomvegas1

> The #snowflake tantrum will not stop the will of the #SilentMajority who spoke when they elected TRUMP! #MAGA (this tweet includes a picture of 8 US Code § 1182 on Inadmissable Aliens)
>
> @HilaryForTrump

Tweets such as these attempt to interject opposing information into the discourse utilized by Democratic Twitter users, and relies on the conservative insult "snowflake" (see below for an elaboration of this term). It is clear that attacks such as these are not meant to encourage deliberative or even agonistic dialogue. The use of an insult implies that the speaker does not take the other side seriously and is unwilling to consider them as an equal discussion partner, hinting at antagonism.

The hashtag #snowflake is particularly interesting. The term "snowflake," meaning someone who is overly sensitive and convinced of their uniqueness, has been around for a few years. It has recently evolved to describe young liberals, especially those who oppose Trump and the Republican Party (Goldstein, 2017; Tait, 2017). When looking at tweets that use this hashtag, however, it quickly becomes apparent that after the election liberals embraced the term, as evidenced by these tweets:

> Funny how #Trump supporters call us snowflakes. Fine by me—the joining of snowflakes is how storms are created. #TheResistance
>
> @PalatePrincess

> #snowflake enough snowflakes cause an avalanche
>
> @diemcarey

@diemcary's tweet was accompanied by a picture that provided an alternative definition of the term snowflake. It included statements like: "I am not a liberal snowflake, my feelings aren't fragile, my heart isn't bleeding. I am a badass believer in human rights," "There is nothing more fierce than formidable, unconditional love" and "but if my belief in equity, empathy, goodness and love indeed makes me or people like me snowflakes, then you should know, winter is coming." This picture and the tweet captures how liberals have embraced the term snowflake as a badge of honor, subverting the meaning that the alt-right movement initially attached to it. Like #NastyWoman and #BadHombres, a phrase meant to insult a group became a weapon used against the people who initially coined the phrase. In spite of this subversion, many of the pro-Trump tweets still rely on the use of the hashtag to insult opponents, indicating that it is a factor in the high level of antagonism between both camps.

Finally, the data also revealed a pattern regarding the evolution of dialogue between people with opposing points of view. The tweet below is an interesting case study into the evolution of dialogue across the aisle:

> The most common liberal response to facts and logic is?? #TheResistance #MAGA #FlynnResignation #NoDAPL #NoBanNoWall #ToImmigrantsWithLove
>
> @MyInfidelAnna

The tweet includes a survey with the options: "1. Racist!!, 2. Worse than Hitler!!, 3. Sexist!!, 4. Putin Puppet!!." While the tweet is obviously meant to insult liberals, and could definitely be seen as a form of antagonistic interaction, where the speaker seeks to annihilate the opponent, it actually leads to interactions that could easily be qualified as agonistic, if not as a form of deliberative dialogue.

> @MyInfidelAnna Here's my liberal reaction to your tweet: How do you feel about the #FlynnResignation? Do you understand why it happened?
>
> @sineadrousse

> @sineadrousse yes. And I think he should've stayed. I love the double standard of you people. Ensures a GOP super majority next year.
>
> @MyInfidelAnna

Then the discussion becomes almost deliberative:

> @MyInfidelAnna Oh, & here's another: When you go out, do you eat at Denny's or Applebee's? Cuz me, I'm all #ToImmigrantsWithLove bcs yum!
>
> @sineadrousse

> @sineadrousse I love immigrants and I wish you wouldn't insult them by implying they're all illegals. Its offensive and vote losing
>
> @MyInfidelAnna

> @MyInfidelAnna ok, a fair point. But when your president has banned green card holders & legal refugees . . . he looks kinda xenophobic . . .
>
> @sineadrousse

The "fair point" here implies that the two are reaching some kind of consensus, at least about the labeling of immigrants, which hints at the openness and moral deference that Jaggar (1999) discussed as paramount for democratic discourse,

On the other hand, other responses copied the antagonistic tone of @MyInfidelAnna's original tweet:

> @MyInfidelAnna I'm thinking Anna's brain got grabbed, logic is hard for Trumptards.
>
> @jdgirl99

This pattern is reproduced in the vast majority of other conversations observed within these hashtags: They often start out as antagonistic jabs at the opponent, and any attempt at a movement toward agonistic dialogue is usually thwarted by an antagonistic remark by one or more Twitter users, who then band together to insult the original poster.

While this discussion is far from exhaustive, it does provide several interesting insights. As became evident from previous sections, Twitter functions as a platform where people can engage in agonistic interactions and deliberative dialogue, but conversations tend to veer toward antagonistic interaction. Although this could be interpreted to mean that Twitter does not support the kind of discussions essential to democracy, as Mouffe (1999) points out, "the aim of democratic politics is to transform an 'antagonism' into an 'agonism'" (p. 755), implying that the presence of antagonism, while not beneficial to democracy, does create the opening needed to shift the conversation to a more agonistic one. The prevalence of hashtags created by liberals in the postelection period also hints at the notion that Twitter is a platform particularly popular among marginalized groups who feel ignored by the establishment and want a space where they feel heard and create a networked counterpublic.

CONCLUSION

The themes that were observed in the virtual movements in chapter 5 resurface in the political discourse surrounding the presidential campaign on Twitter. There is a clear sense that the country is in danger, but the reasons behind the danger vary depending on one's political perspective.

Twitter serves as a space where people can collaboratively construct understandings of what is going on in the world, in the country, and with the election, affording users the platform to augment their bonding social capital. At the same time, results do reveal attempts at outreach to people outside these networks, although not to the level that would be necessary according to the ideals of a deliberative democracy. Interactions between groups are often fraught with accusations and insults, and only rarely lead to mutually increased understanding.

In conclusion, while Twitter provides the affordances for people to engage in the deliberative dialogue that is the foundation of the Habermasian public sphere, this dialogue is only observed between like-minded people, leading to the creation of bonding social capital, but foregoing the cross-political interaction and related bridging social capital that is seen as an essential element of the public sphere. However, the interactions between opponents that were discussed in this chapter do not necessarily detract from democratic ideals either. Instead, they point to a different kind of interaction, one that is more passionate and more focused on speaking one's mind than reaching a consensus. This kind of dialogue has been dubbed "agonistic," and unlike Habermasian deliberative dialogue, it centers on the struggles with an "adversary" and does not aim for consensus. These kinds of interactions may not fit in with the ideal of the public sphere, but they do help maintain and strengthen democracy (Mouffe, 1999; Papacharissi, 2009). In a society where both sides feel marginalized, having a platform like Twitter where they can engage with each other, no matter in what form, can thus be said to help democracy, even if it does not reflect the deliberative dialogue essential to the formation of a public sphere.

WHO TELLS THE STORY

Analyzing Twitter Users

7

Is It #WorthSaying?

Twitter, Marketing Campaigns, and Controlling the Narrative

Who cares about Makeup when people in #Flint don't have clean drinking water #WorthSaying #FlintWaterCrisis

@TheBookBabe84

Social media is not just a space for individuals to connect and share. Companies, large and small, profit and nonprofit, make up an indelible part of the social media landscape as well. In recent years, more and more companies have adopted an active social media marketing strategy. This strategy can include Facebook pages, YouTube channels, a Twitter presence, and advertising campaigns that integrate this social media presence with traditional media exposure. Most social media users will, in fact, at one point or another engage with a brand, whether it is to tweet their frustration with a company, link to an inspirational ad, or critique a company's stance on social issues. Sometimes, when companies fumble, like Cinnabon's poorly designed tribute to actress Carrie Fisher's death in December 2016, or when a particular campaign really takes off, as was the case with the ALS association's #IceBucketChallenge, the brand will hit the proverbial Twitter jackpot and make it into the top trending list.

With the majority of (potential) consumers active on social media, using social media to bring attention to a company's cause, sell their brand, and increase sales and/or engagement is a logical step for any corporation. Social networking sites like Twitter afford companies the opportunity to directly engage with their consumers, a desirable feature for any marketer, although this does come with the risk of relinquishing control over their intended message. In traditional media campaigns, major corporations have a firm grip on the narrative they construct for the promotion for their products. Their commercials and PR activities tell the consumer what to think and/or, hopefully, do. This was facilitated by the fact that before the advent of the internet, the dissemination of oppositional interpretations by consumers was usually limited to their own social circle. Not so with social media. As discussed in previous chapters, social media platforms such as Twitter provide users with the opportunity to share their interpretation of the corporate narrative with others, creating the possibility of a counternarrative that could usurp the intended campaign. While social media sites allow companies to attempt to control the narrative through interacting with their consumers directly, it is possible for platform users to distort the message and engage in a dialogue that does little for the company, as was the case with Starbucks' #RaceTogether campaign (e.g., Logan, 2016). This is a risk that corporations take when engaging in social media marketing and is one most of them are willing to take.

This raises the question of who tells the story on Twitter when it comes to marketing companies: Do the corporations that start the campaigns run the narrative, or do users find and exploit spaces in the offered narratives to tell their own story, appropriating the original message? Are there any patterns that can be observed regarding how users respond to social media marketing campaigns? This chapter explores these questions with a specific focus on race and gender through a few select case studies of marketing campaigns.

In this chapter, I first provide a brief overview of how companies use social media to advance their brand and/or cause. Next I present a brief exploration, using five case studies, of how consumers make sense of corporation-created campaigns. The specific case studies selected for this exploration center on campaigns related to race and/or gender, and provide preliminary insight into how consumers make sense of these campaigns and if their sense-making counters or supports the intended meaning.

SOCIAL MEDIA, PR, AND MARKETING

In recent years, social media have been heralded as the panacea of marketing and sales. The platforms' popularity among consumers of all ages and backgrounds, the wealth of information these media produce about their users, and the ability to quickly reach and interact with consumers have all been pointed to as excellent opportunities for companies to expand their brand, sales, and consumer engagement (e.g., Baird & Parasnis, 2011; Kietzman, Hermkens, McCarthy, & Silvestre, 2011; Lee, et al., 2015).

The days when consumers were seen as mere recipients of marketing campaigns are definitely over. Contemporary consumer experiences center on potential customers feeling like a participant rather than a bystander to a campaign. Customer engagement is seen as essential for a brand's success (Casaló, Flavían, & Giunalíu, 2008; DeVries & Carlson, 2014), and this engagement is best achieved through social interaction, both between consumers as well as between the company and its customers. Research has shown that interaction is most effective if it represents real-life conversations, complete with reciprocity (Kelleher, 2009; Schmitt, 2012). Social media are the ideal place to create this kind of interaction as communication is the foundation of these platforms. Not only do people use social media to engage with others and build social capital, they also rely on these platforms to feel like a part of major events, most notably through live-tweeting. Corporations have capitalized on this by designing multiplatform marketing campaigns that integrate advertising through traditional media with social media marketing (Davis, Piven, & Breazeale, 2014; Hanna, Rohm, & Crittenden, 2011). These campaigns aim to foster an emotional connection between a consumer and the brand by encouraging consumers to share personal experiences on social media. This emotional connection is essential to customer loyalty and positive word of mouth (Brown, Willis, Havard, & Irwin, 2015). In practice, this can mean designing a traditional television campaign that has been augmented by a hashtagged social media presence, or asking social media users to contribute personal stories which are then used to create a television commercial. Many companies have taken this to heart, as evidenced by the #WeAccept ad that AirBnb aired during the 2017 Super Bowl, or the #NotNuyingIt campaign launched by Project Representation, an organization aimed at ending gender stereotyping in the media during the 2014 Super Bowl (Clark, 2014). In either case, consumers are invited to participate in the campaign, to interact, and collaborate. These kinds of requests all serve to increase customer engagement and, hopefully, improve consumers' attitudes toward a brand (Ashley & Tuten, 2015).

However, just because social media provides users with the ability to interact about brands, it doesn't guarantee that all users do. In fact, many social media users prefer to keep a low profile and only post or engage ocassionally (Baird & Parasnis, 2011). The desire to interact with and/or about a brand or its company, or lack thereof, can in part be explained by the extent to which that brand is part of a social media user's identity performance (Ashley & Tuten, 2015; Schmitt, 2012). The self-expansion theory holds that whether or not a brand is seen as a positive contribution to this performance depends on the perceived correspondence between an individual's identity and that of the brand. If a consumer perceives (dimensions of) a brand's identity to be similar to theirs, they are more likely to have a positive view of this brand and communicate with and about it (Ashley & Tuten, 2015; Huang & Mitchell, 2014). In order for a brand to be considered a part of one's online identity, consumers need to be able to personify it, i.e., the brand needs to be perceived as having human characteristics (cf. Cohen, 2014). In addition, a consumer needs to believe that publicly identifying themselves with the brand on social media will have a positive effect on their self-image and not violate any social norms (Ashley & Tuten, 2015). In other words, not all brands are suitable to be a part of someone's online identity performance.

While social media platforms such as Twitter encourage the kind of interaction necessary for a marketing campaign to succeed, the nature of the interactivity on these platforms also pose a threat to brand managers. In the past, marketing campaigns could control the meanings associated with their brands fairly easily: They would put out an advertising campaign with the desired brand story, and that was the end of it. While research has shown that audiences could, and often would, misconstrue the ad's meaning by appropriating, parodying, critiquing, or modifying the content of the ad, these ideas and productions hardly, if ever, moved outside the audience member's own social circle. With the advent of social media, that all changed (Gensler, Völckner, Liu-Thompkins, & Wiertz, 2013). Social media have made these different interpretations visible for the world to see, enabling other users to modify the interpretation and share it with their network, turning consumers into co-creators of a brand (DeVries & Carlson, 2014). While this level of consumer engagement can be a great push for a product's popularity, it can also backfire as consumers can and will create narratives about the brand that may not align with the company's intended brand image (Ashley & Tuten, 2015; DeVries & Carlson, 2014; Gensler, et al., 2013). Research into brand selfies, for instance, has shown that these selfies can create a narrative that does not match the brand's envisioned narrative, instead constructing competing or conflicting meanings (Presi, Maehle, & Kleppe, 2016; Rokka & Canniford, 2016).

The connectivity afforded by social media platforms could also be described as both an opportunity and a threat for marketing campaigns. On the one hand, social media platforms have been hailed as the ideal platform for the creation of brand communities and the subsequent dissemination of electronic word of mouth (Brown, et al., 2015). Electronic word-of-mouth (or eWoM) functions in ways that are similar to offline word of mouth but with a much wider reach as well as the immediacy provided by online environments—a posted review can be read by thousands of people within minutes after having been posted. Electronic word-of-mouth or "influence impressions" (Ashley & Tuten, 2015, p. 17) spread among a user's network could impact the brand attitude among a vast network of connected users, and as such is deemed highly desirable by most campaigns. On the other hand, once a corporation starts an online word of mouth campaign, they have little control over what is said about them on which platform (Cabosky, 2016; Gensler, et al., 2013; Jansen, Zhang, Sobel, & Chowdury, 2009). While online engagement with consumers can help direct the narrative (Lee, et al., 2015), this level of company-user interaction is unlikely to be representative for a corporation's usual social media strategies. As a result, the meaning attributed to a brand is no longer just the result of an idea concocted in a marketing firm's boardroom but is instead the outcome of a negotiation between the company, its stakeholders, and social media users (Gensler, et al., 2013). This raises the question what Twitter users do when confronted with a narrative that is part of a marketing campaign. Do they embrace the story presented to them? Or do they find ways to tweak its meaning? In other words, who, in the end, gets to the tell story?

CONSUMPTION, PARTICIPATION, AND TWITTER USE

How people make sense of social media marketing campaigns is a central component to understanding collaborative meaning making. Rejecting consumerism as irrelevant to considerations of citizenship ignores the fact that consumption is as much a part of civic engagement as political dialogue (Burgess, Foth, & Klaebe, 2006; Dahlgren, 2013). Inherent in the view that consumerism is irrelevant to discussions about meaning making is the premise that consumers are passive and detached from social issues, a view that no longer matches reality. Consumption itself can be seen an act of active meaning making, and as such has become inexorably intertwined with civic expression. People often use their consumption behaviors to make political statements and challenge or support authorities, and political expressions and discussions are often characterized or even shaped by consumerist references. In that sense, consumptio is not only informed by political opinion, it becomes a form of civic action itself (Cabrera & Williams, 2014; Cherry, Ellis, & DeSoucey, 2011; Gil de Zúñiga, Copeland, & Bimber, 2013; McGuigan, 2005; Papacharissi, 2010).

At the same time, it is important to acknowledge that the online spaces that these consumers use for civic expression, e.g., Twitter, YouTube, Facebook, are controlled by for-profit corporations whose goal is to make money off their users. This money is made by exposing users to as many ads and/or sponsored links/promoted tweets as possible, and by selling user data (Gadkari, 2013; Hackman, 2015; Tsukayama, 2012). This means that these social media platforms benefit the more users are active, regardless of the nature of their interaction. But the extent to which social media users are exploited for profit goes further than that. As Maragh (2016) noted, social media platforms like Twitter thrive on their image as a grassroots, anti-establishment network. Subsequently, whenever members of marginalized groups join these platforms, or users protest current events or mainstream ideas, this benefits Twitter's image and only serves to increase its popularity. Using social media as a second screen or live-tweeting an event can be seen as equally exploitative, whereby users' interactions, even if negative or subversive, draw attention to the event, show, or advertisement under discussion, as well as providing the producers with valuable feedback about their work and their audience (Maragh, 2016; see also Jin & Feenberg, 2015).

This does not mean, however, that consumerism as expressed through these platforms is a passive, disempowering activity, one that should be disregarded as somehow irrelevant to civic and political considerations. The importance of considering consumerism as a part of active citizenship is further underlined by ongoing debate about people as "prosumers," i.e., people as producers and consumers (Ahluwalia & Miller, 2014). While in the past, the concept of the prosumer was framed in terms of exploitation and capitalist control, with the advent of Web 2.0, the prosumer has more options to resist this exploitation and turn the traditional notions of capitalism (scarcity of resources, paying for products, doing something for someone else's enjoyment) on their head. As a result, today's prosumers are less influenced by and more likely to resist the push from corporations trying to control them (Ritzer & Jurgenson, 2010). Even in spaces controlled by for-profit corporations such as Twitter and YouTube, people are still producing and consuming in ways that show an active, at times oppositional, engagement with content (Maragh, 2016; Papacharissi, 2009). This demonstrates how consumerism is an expression of the participatory culture that characterizes social media (van Dijck, 2009), where social media brand consumption should be seen as a "social co-production of shared meanings" (Davis, et al., 2014, p. 468). Claiming that this participatory culture is entirely commodified does not consider the fact that while people's expressions on these platforms are sold for profit, this particular process of commodification does not change the meaning of these expressions, or their potential democratic impact (Jin & Feenberg, 2015). But when considering this participatory culture, the various ways in which this participation, subversive or not, benefits the companies that own the platforms and even the brands against which users are agitating should be kept in mind. As such, examining marketing techniques and how Twitter users respond to these is relevant considering the overarching purpose of this book to examine the participatory culture that characterizes Twitter.

This chapter does not aim to provide a comprehensive overview of the large number of marketing campaigns on Twitter and how users interact with those. A single chapter is not sufficient to do justice to such a topic. Instead, it seeks to provide preliminary insight into how Twitter users negotiate narratives created by organizations by investigating Twitter trends associated with five of the most popular advertising campaigns related to race and gender between 2015 and 2017. The case studies examined in this chapter were selected for their popularity (each came from a list of most impactful branding campaigns published by *AdWeek, MediaKix,* and *Marketing Week*), as well as their relevance to this book. Two case studies focus on gender, or more specifically, the beauty ideology and associated beliefs about feminism, namely the #ChooseBeautiful campaign by Dove and L'Oréal's #WorthSaying campaign (MediaKix Team, 2016; Millington, 2015). Three campaigns centered on race and related issues: #RaceTogether; #WeAccept, the campaign launched by Airbnb; and the responses to the advertisement by 84 Lumber (hashtagged as both #Lum ber84 and #84Lumber). These campaigns were selected because of the high number of tweets as well as their relevance to the current social and political climate (Benner, 2017; Masunaga, 2015; O'Reilly, 2017). A total of 1,569 tweets were analyzed for this chapter.

#WORTHSAYING AND #CHOOSING: BEAUTY, ADVERTISING, AND TWITTER

Advertisement campaigns focused on beauty have been at the center of much debate for decades. Companies have been condemned for creating unattainable beauty ideals and numerous studies have examined the influence these campaigns may have on the women who purchase their products (e.g., Bissell & Rask, 2010). Corporations have responded by incorporating modified versions of these oppositional ideas into their campaigns to appease and draw in customers. These modifications placate the protestors without hurting the brand, in effect "commodifying dissent" (Taylor, Johnston, & Whitehead, 2016, p. 124; Johnston & Taylor, 2008).

Dove is probably the best-known beauty product company to attempt to incorporate resistance into their ads. Its "Real Beauty" campaign, launched in 2004, questioned traditional beauty standards and has since spun off a series of similar campaigns (Bahadur, 2014). Advocates of the campaign have argued that Dove challenges dominant norms about beauty and empowers its consumers by providing alternatives to the beauty ideal (Millard, 2009). Critics claim that the campaign perpetuates the hegemonic views of femininity it claims to undermine. Dove is said to propagate feminist consumerism, whereby feminist ideals are watered down just enough to pay lip service to the cause and not harm people's consumerist tendencies (Bolt, 2014; Johnston & Taylor, 2008). Even though Dove's unconventional campaign has been imitated by others in an attempt to meet consumers' supposed preferences, research has shown that consumers' responses to the Dove campaign are not unequivocally positive and involve a large amount of negotiation to connect the implied beauty ideals to the women's own body-image (e.g., Millard, 2009; Rayworth, 2014; Scott & Cloud, 2008)

While women have always challenged, negotiated, and accepted the meaning of advertisement campaigns, social media like Twitter render these discussions public, making a possible "takeover" of a company narrative a distinct possibility. In this section, I more closely examine this negotiation by looking at two beauty product campaigns: Dove's #ChooseBeautiful and L'Oréal's #WorthSaying's campaign. These two campaigns were selected because while they claim to fight hegemonic beauty ideals, they could also be said to embody feminist consumerism by using clichéd ideas about feminism to gain attention. In addition, each campaign created quite a following, producing a large volume of tweets, indicating popular involvement with the topic, and were seen as two of the most influential Twitter campaigns of 2015 and 2016 respectively (Millington, 2015; Pilon, 2016)

The #ChooseBeautiful campaign started in April 2015 with an advertisement that featured normal looking women, clearly not presented as models, faced with two doors, one labeled "average" and the other "beautiful." While women were shown making the choice, with most of the women choosing the door marked "average," the voices of the women themselves can be heard talking about the choice they made and what inspired that choice. The ad ends with the hashtag #ChooseBeautiful, encouraging viewers to continue the discussion online (Vaglanos, 2015). The campaign received some backlash, with critics wondering about the central focus on beauty and scholars labeling the ad as patronizing. In spite of this, or perhaps because of it, the hashtag did go viral relatively quickly (Chumsky, 2015). L'Oréal's #WorthSaying campaign was launched during the 2016 Golden Globes ceremony and expanded on its existing tagline "Because you're worth it" by proposing that all women have something worthwhile to say and therefore should be heard. The #WorthSaying campaign aimed to provide that space for women. The launch of the campaign coincided with the Golden Globes with the idea that if women on the red carpet would share something they thought was worth saying, the regular consumer would not hesitate to follow suit, capitalizing on people's tendency to live-tweet during major television events (Monilos, 2016). #ChooseBeautiful tweets were collected during the month after the campaign was initially launched, in April 2015. Tweets from the #WorthSaying campaign were collected during the ten-day period after the Golden Globes awards ceremony (January 10–20, 2016).

#ChooseBeautiful: Loving Yourself

When looking at the #ChooseBeautiful tweets, the one trend that immediately became visible is the large number of tweets that embrace the premise of the campaign, i.e., the idea that all women are beautiful; they just need to see that in themselves:

> I #choosebeautiful and you can too
>
> @ASMOKEE1

> The #ChooseBeautiful commercial of #Dove is just so wow! Yeah right—its indeed one's choice to be beautiful. Beauty comes within us. :)
>
> @iamjeanyrose

Tweets like these use Dove's message to construct a positive self-presentation, seeing the idea that beauty is a choice as a form of empowerment with which they can readily identify. Besides embracing the campaign, users also thank Dove for creating the campaign and talk about the impact the campaign had on them personally:

> So in love with @Dove #ChooseBeautiful campaign such a simple but powerful message it sends across
>
> @zoya_altaf

> This actually made me teary eyed. Always choose beautiful! #choosebeautiful
>
> @TheSteelDoll

> Well done @Dove #ChooseBeautiful
>
> @MegMurphyTX

In short, Twitter users rally around the #ChooseBeautiful hashtag, using it as a vehicle to express their own beliefs about self-worth and to support others in accepting themselves for who they are, reproducing Dove's message without question.

Some users tie the campaign's message to bigger ideas such as motherhood or equality:

> Moms, let's be the example of what beautiful is for the next generation. #ChooseBeautiful #postpartum #parenting
>
> @CandidMamaLife

> @DoveCanada I #ChooseBeautiful because we all are- no matter our size, skin colour, nationality, education, economic status, we R beautiful!
>
> @lilideluxe

Tweets like these expand Dove's message to a larger social platform, tying the concept of confidence through beauty to social justice issues. Twitter users appear to have embraced Dove's message that women themselves define what beauty is, and by not viewing themselves as beautiful, they are the ones holding themselves back, as captured by these two examples:

> Average or Beautiful? Which are you? Its your choice Ladies! #Choose Beautiful
>
> @TheAdamAntonio

> How are you feeling today? Average? Beautiful? Did you know the power is in your hands! #ChooseBeautiful
>
> @Becomingyoublog

A lot of Twitter users retweeted various versions of the original message from Dove, asking women what they will choose today, average or beautiful.

The hashtag and its underlying message that self-acceptance is both a choice and a necessity resonates with a large number of people on Twitter, which is evidenced by the large number of for-profit and nonprofit organizations that jumped in on the #ChooseBeautiful hashtag. Numerous companies retweeted the original message, adding in their company name or a hashtag specific to their brand, as shown by these examples from a magazine on women's fitness and a wellness center:

> Beautiful or average? Which door would YOU choose? #GORGOgirl #choose beautiful
>
> @GORGOmag

> I love #essentialoils. This is my new #NaturalBeauty secret. @42 you want to reduce #wrinkles and #choosebeautiful!
>
> @MilatesWBcenter

Companies recognized not only the fact that social media users were responding positively to the cause addressed by the Dove campaign but also the reach of the #ChooseBeautiful hashtag to potential consumers. The fact that consumers interpreted the message within a consumerist, neoliberal perspective that matched these companies' goals made the hashtag an attractive vehicle for marketing.

Implied in these tweets is the message that feeling beautiful is a choice. These tweets show a reproduction of the hegemonic belief that beauty and womanhood are inexorably intertwined and that "every woman should feel beautiful" (Johnston & Taylor, 2008, p. 954), i.e., beauty is something every woman should want to aspire to. At the same time, this ideology argues that feeling beautiful is a choice. It is not the result of outside pressures, of decades of exposure to ideals that are far out of reach; it is solely up to the women herself. Choosing to feel a certain way is seen as the ultimate form of empowerment. These tweets reproduce this ideology by ignoring the internal struggle that many women face when trying to accept themselves for who they are and failing to acknowledge the role played by society's beauty norms. Instead, they place the responsibility for how women feel about themselves on these women themselves, effectively reproducing "postfeminism," which argues that women are now equal and subsequently free to make their own choices (McRobbie, 2004, 2009). In a postfeminist discourse, making choices is seen as a highly individual process and a sign of empowerment, a trope reflected in the tweets discussed above (Taylor, et al., 2016).

Some users do more than just reproduce the message put out by Dove though. They use the hashtag to render visible the struggle between women's ideas about their looks and society's norms about beauty:

> How come according to society I can't be fat and pretty? I can only be fat or pretty. #ChooseBeautiful #ImThatWCW #beYOUtiful #lovelife
>
> @YoulikeLove

> I #ChooseBeautiful because I finally embrace who I am as a person. Society says one thing, but I say DIFFERENT! I accept ME and that matters.
>
> @Phyla3000

Both @YoulikeLove and @Phyla3000 uses Dove's message to reject society's views of them, making visible the process women who genuinely accept themselves for who they are have to go through, which includes a rejection of societal standards. This process is made invisible by the Dove ad, which presents it as a personal choice and one that has nothing to do with the beauty ideology propagated by society at large. Tweets like these thus renegotiate the #ChooseBeautiful message to include the struggle women face when attempting to achieve self-acceptance. These two users tweak the brand's message to strengthen their own identity performance. However, they do not critique Dove or the advertisement campaign for making this self-acceptance appear like nothing more than a choice to make.

Only a few tweets openly contest the ideas put forth by the Dove advertisement, and many of them retweet the same posts from two or three professional bloggers (Scary Mommy, Verily, and Color Lines). A select few discuss the profit-motive that lies at the root of this campaign:

> "All right team! Time for some good clean* corporate greed!" #Choose Beautiful
>
> *literally soapy
>
> @HowtobeaHippo

Others turn to the themes underlying the advertisement:

> @Dove #ChooseBeautiful What's sad is not that women don't choose the beautiful door, but that beauty discourse dominates & shapes our lives.
>
> @LauraHegge

In this tweet @LauraHegge makes visible the beauty discourse that Johnston and Taylor (2008) argued was present but ignored by Dove's Real Beauty campaign. Another user, @elsachaag, extends this idea:

> Beauty as choice=women convniently bcome responsible 4own self-denigration. Well said @Colorlines on #ChooseBeautiful

In this tweet, the user recognizes how Dove takes the collectivity out of feminism and turns what is supposed to be a societal conflict it into a personal choice. This development has been recognized across the board by feminist scholars (e.g., hooks, 2004; Jaffe, 2016; McRobbie, 2004, 2009; Taylor, et al. 2016) and is a vital component of postfeminism. Feminism has been reduced to issues centered on identity and consumption rather than a collective struggle, rendering it much more acceptable to a neoliberal society centered on individuality (Jaffe, 2016). This development, as evidenced by the tweets collected for this case, generally goes unnoticed. Most people who use the #ChooseBeautiful hashtag appear to embrace the narrative that empowerment lies in individual choices and the days of collective struggle for acceptance are over. They utilize #ChooseBeautiful to augment their identity performance with a sense of empowerment, effectively reproducing and broadcasting the company-created narrative that accepting yourself is a matter of walking through the correct door.

#WorthSaying: Empowering Yourself and Others

The #WorthSaying campaign had a slightly different tenor from #Choose Beautiful. Most importantly, the hashtag was not focused on physical attributes. Instead it aimed to empower women by giving them a platform to speak out about issues important to them. It was launched to coincide with a major television event, the Golden Globes, counting on people to live-tweet their thoughts using the hashtag.

One theme that jumps out from the tweets analyzed for this case study is how many people use the hashtag for empowerment, i.e., to send out a message intended to lift up others (or possibly themselves). Tweets touched on a wide array of topics, from overcoming challenges to self-acceptance:

> Never change yourself for another person. If they can't see how kick butt you a're then it's their loss #WorthSaying
>
> @AliceBadgero

> When we fall completely apart it's actually a good thing, from rock bottom we can build an even stronger version of ourself. #WorthSaying
>
> @lanaia22

Some tweets quoted famous women, such as Audrey Hepburn and Condaleeza Rice, while others retweeted messages from stars like Jennifer Lopez and Susan Sarandon. While the majority of the tweets that fit into this category addressed empowerment as an individual achievement, a group of users addressed women that deserved recognition as a collective:

> You educate a man; you educate a man. You educate a woman; you educate a generation.—Brigham Young #WorthSaying #GoldenGlobes
>
> @LauraNRuddy

Others talked about women serving as inspiration to others and applauded Matt Damon for thanking his mother during his award acceptance speech. A few even talked about the importance of female equality:

> "If you want to know how civilized a culture is, look at how they treat its women." #worthsaying (this tweet is accompanied by a picture with this quote and the source Bacha Klan underneath them)
>
> @svetlanainla

> Conclusion of the #GoldenGlobes: okay but we need more. #womeninfilm #strongfemalecharacters #bitchflicks #WorthSaying #AskHerMore
>
> @sgypsyfilmmaker

Tweets that focused on empowering women specifically, though, also included references to beauty, echoing the importance for women to feel beautiful as expressed through the #ChooseBeautiful campaign:

> @LOrealParisUSA every woman is beautiful, no mater size, hight or features. Being a woman is beautiful, we are all beautiful #WorthSaying
>
> @datondra

> Make-up is only truly powerful when you know you're beautiful without it @LOrealParisUSA #WorthSaying
>
> @rachaelrforster

While the last tweet would seem to undermine L'Oréal's business, it in fact reflects McRobbie's postfeminism discussed above, whereby women, not social norms, are responsible for their feelings of worth. Some women took this same theme and made it more personal by tweeting what they saw as physical shortcomings (e.g., stretch marks) and explaining why they were proud of them (in this case, the poster had several children), reiterating the belief that feeling beautiful is a choice.

However, because of the semiotic space offered by the hashtag, not everyone who talks about beauty does so in a physical sense or as a choice:

> Teach your kids that beauty is all about kindness, helpfullness, and generally being a good person #WorthSaying
>
> @itispattif

> @CrissyBeam True dat!! #WorthSaying "@CrissyBeam: Confidence is beautiful #Worthsaying"
>
> @Ryder_Knightley

Twitter users really enjoyed the campaign, which is not only reflected by the large number of tweets with the #WorthSaying hashtag, but also the amount of positive feedback directed at the company:

> Excited to help my friends @LOrealParisUSA celebrate the inspiring things women say on and off the red carpet. What's #WorthSaying to u
>
> @LupesujeyCuevas

> Who doesn't love @LOrealParisUSA #worthsaying
>
> @harleysoftail06

Users encouraged others to speak up, thanked L'Oréal for the campaign, and overall, seemed very happy to reproduce the intended narrative as a positive addition to their online identity performance.

This is also reflected by the high number of companies, both profit and nonprofit that jumped in on the hashtag. A large number of for-profit businesses, all related to the makeup industry in some way (e.g., beauty magazines and advertising agencies), used the hashtag to tweet about the Golden Globes, share ideas in line with the "empowerment through speech" narrative, or they used the hashtag to advertise their own upcoming projects:

> Congrats @thekatewinslet for all the #GirlPower you have given us! #GoldenGlobes #WorthSaying
>
> @VeedaUsa

> #WorthSaying #mondaymotivation @dustinpari It's okay to have differences. Kindness and love win. #PariPrint (this tweet includes a picture of a man with the words "it's okay to have differences, our commonalities greatly outweigh them. Kindness and love win. Dustin Pari. Official site: www.dustinpari.com"
>
> @PariPrints

Nonprofit organizations showed similar interest in the hashtag, although they tended to adhere more to the original intention of the hashtag, i.e., sharing thoughts worth talking about. In their case, these thoughts often reflected the aim of their organization. Examples of this are these tweets from two nonprofit organizations, the first one aimed at creating playgrounds that include children with disabilities, the second one from a senior citizen advocacy group:

> "I can do the same things as my friends. I just do them a little differently." —Lourdes #WorthSaying @catcurrywill
>
> @ShanesPlay

> @LOrealParisUSA Seniors are valuable people #WorthSaying touch them with #kindwords#kind acts@beautybecomesyou
>
> @AlisonONeil

Nonprofit jumped in on the opportunity to gain attention outside their usual circle of influence by using the highly popular hashtag to tweet out beliefs that reflected their causes.

Some Twitter users used the invitation to speak out on worthwhile topics to call people to action. Some posted tweets calling on people to volunteer, while others took the opportunity to ask for specific donations. Like the nonprofit organizations, these people expanded L'Oreal's narrative to include social justice causes, a possibility afforded by the openness of the hashtag. Some took the invitation to speak out to link the hashtag to specific political opinions. This campaign took place at the beginning of a very heated primary season, and tweets reflect this:

> Has anyone even seen a @HillaryClinton bumper sticker in the wild? I swear it's like an urban legend. #FeelTheBern #WorthSaying
>
> @freckledninja

Tweets such as these took L'Oréal's intended narrative and altered it to meet their own needs.

A few tweets directly undermined the campaign's intentions, using the hashtag to create a narrative that ran counter to L'Oréal's intended story. Some did so in a whimsical way, making random statements followed by the hashtag:

> Turtles are rad. #WorthSaying
>
> @annamichhh

Other Twitter users took a more serious approach and took on L'Oréal itself. Some questioned the company's intentions, with some pointing to the fact that at the end of the day, L'Oréal is about selling beauty products using beautiful women:

> Share you you think is #WorthSaying . . . as long as you look pretty.
>
> @heyprofbow

And others question the company's ethics in promoting this campaign, as well as their business practices in general, raising questions about the chemicals in the company's products for instance.

Similar to the #ChooseBeautiful campaign, only a small minority of Tweets question the fact that a company whose goal is to sell beauty products seemingly propagates women empowerment:

> It is #worthsaying that makeup companies that want $$ should not be the driver of feminism and women's empowerment.
>
> @SarahBtotheS

The question how a company whose goal is to sell products that perpetuate hegemonic beauty ideals can truly help women achieve equality is only picked up by a few of the thousands of people who joined the hashtag conversation. This underscores the belief that postfeminism and the accompanying neoliberalist capitalist view of society is so firmly embedded in today's dominant discourse that campaigns that claim that women can talk about things other than beauty are no longer perceived as patronizing, perpetuating gender inequality, or taking away the space needed for political deliberation and resistance. Instead, narratives such as #WorthSaying are seen as affording the already equal and empowered woman with additional spaces to express herself as a consumer of the company's products (cf. Taylor, et al., 2016).

In summary, #WorthSaying, with its more generic phrasing, offers consumers more semiotic space to create additional interpretations than #ChooseBeautiful, where interpretations generally adhere to the script set out in advance. However, while both campaigns have resulted in some diversion from the company's intended narrative, tweets in general follow the story set out by the corporations, using the campaign as a building block in users' online identity performance.

RACE, ADVERTISING, AND TWITTER

In spite of the controversy surrounding race and diversity, several corporations have created campaigns that address these issues. While such campaigns can backfire, hurting the company's image as well as their bottom line, companies are finding more and more that corporate activism isn't much of a choice anymore. Today's consumers expect businesses to take a stand on important social issues and a failure to do so can hurt the company's profits in the long run (Corcoran, Newman, & Devasagayam, 2016; J. Davis, 2016; Davis & White, 2015). The question that leaves is how consumers respond to a campaign centered on contentious social issues: Will they accept the narrative the company presents, or will they reject it and construct an alternative story?

In order to explore the answers to these question, I examine three campaigns where race and diversity were the central topics of the company's message: Starbucks' #RaceTogether campaign, 84 Lumber's "The Journey" ad, and the #WeAccept campaign launched by Airbnb. These three campaigns were selected because they each utilized the highly contested issues of race and/or diversity to advance their brand, creating a narrative focused on acceptance, inclusion, and conversation between groups. Each campaign took a clear stand on issues that consumers are still very much divided on, thus taking a risk in how consumers would interpret their proposed narrative. In addition, each campaign went viral on Twitter, producing thousands of tweets, demonstrating popular investment in the topics at hand, and a shared desire to share one's opinion about the proposed narrative.

Of the three campaigns, Starbucks' #RaceTogether is the oldest. It was launched in March 2015 in response to rising racial tensions across the

U.S. and aimed to increase conversations about race between its customers. Baristas were asked to write #RaceTogether on consumers' cups, be open to discuss issues related to race, and the company launched several forums about race and diversity (Company, 2015). The initiative immediately drew enormous response, especially on social media, where the majority of the responses were critical of both the campaign and the company (Feng, 2016; Logan, 2016; Masunaga, 2015; Sanders, 2015).

The 84 Lumber advertisement called "The Journey" aired during the 2017 Super Bowl. While this ad did not include a specific hashtag to channel online conversations, it sparked such intense responses on Twitter that it is worthy of inclusion here as an example of people using Twitter as a second screen. The commercial follows a mother and daughter leaving an unnamed country assumed to be somewhere in Central America and traveling by car, train, and on foot to the U.S. border. This sequence is interspersed with shots of men working on a construction site. When the woman and her daughter reach the border, they come upon a large wall. The mother notices a light shining from what turn out to be two large doors in the wall. She and her daughter open the doors and use them to cross the border, walking into the bright sunlight. The ad ends with a shot of one of the construction workers from earlier driving in a truck filled with construction materials and the words, "The will to succeed is always welcome here." The ad led to a huge response on social media, especially Twitter, where #84lumber and #lumber84 trended while people debated the meaning of the ad and their opinions on immigration in general (Heath, 2017; Payne, 2017).

Finally, #WeAccept was created by Airbnb. The commercial aired during the 2017 Super Bowl, immediately going viral on social media. The ad featured a montage of faces of people from different ethnic backgrounds, where one face would slowly morph into the next, accompanied by the words, "We believe no matter who you are, where you're from, who you love, or who you worship we all belong. The world is more beautiful the more you accept. #WeAccept." According to the company's CEO, this campaign is part of a larger effort by Airbnb to provide housing for those in need, including refugees and people not allowed into the U.S. due to the (temporary) travel ban imposed in January 2017 (Graham, 2017; Palazzo, 2017).

The tweets for #RaceTogether were collected the week after the launch of the campaign, in March 2015, the tweets for the #WeAccept campaign as well as tweets about the 84 Lumber ad (both #84lumber and #lumber84) were collected in the 24-hour period after the ad was aired during the 2017 Super Bowl.

#RaceTogether: The Complexities of Talking about Race

This campaign has been examined from various angles, both by scholars and journalists alike (e.g., Corcoran, et al., 2016; Feng, 2016; Morrison, 2015). Logan (2016) compared the coverage of the campaign in the news to how people discussed the campaign on Twitter and found that both reporters and Twitter users questioned the legitimacy of the campaign, brought up Starbucks' own record on race, and questioned Starbucks' motives, wondering if the whole campaign was just a ploy to sell more coffee. Another theme that came out of Logan's analysis was the logistical challenges of the campaign (how can you sell coffee to people in a rush and talk about race?). On Twitter, detractors of the campaign used the hashtag to argue that #RaceTogether was an attack on white people, while the few supporting tweets acknowledged the problems that the U.S. continues to have with race and applauded Starbucks for taking a stand.

Logan's thematic analysis hints at how consumers took Starbucks' intended narrative and interpreted it to better match their understanding of race relations in this country. The analysis conducted for this chapter found similar themes: People questioned whether baristas were qualified to discuss race, they wondered about the logistics of buying coffee and having a serious conversation, they challenged the company's record on race, they questioned the company's motives, while others used the hashtag to promote racist ideologies, and only a few actually applauded the initiative. But the analysis carried out in this chapter moved beyond Logan's critical race analysis. By using interpretive content analysis, it was possible to reconstruct the narrative that detractors constructed in response to the Starbucks campaign, as well as the discourses and ideologies that informed this narrative. The analysis helps to explain why both liberals and conservatives, African Americans and white people, opposed the idea. The overarching narrative that all detractors of the campaign appear to agree on is that a discussion about race is not the answer. But when this opposition is teased apart, it reveals two very separate sets of beliefs about why such a conversation does not make sense.

True Colors: #RaceTogether and Color-Blindness

On the one hand, there is the conviction that talking to someone about race is unnecessary and thus an infringement of someone's freedom. The idea that a conversation about race can be forced on someone who is trying to do business with a company is unacceptable to many Twitter users. They repeatedly state that all they want from Starbucks is a cup of coffee and anything beyond that is too much:

> No #Starbucks I don't want a Social Lecture when I order coffee. I am done with you forever!
>
> @CureOurCountry

> It's 6 a.m., I have a long commute, I need coffee. What I don't need is a sanctimonious white kid babbling to me about race.
>
> @fuzislippers

Many Twitter users use examples to prove why their view of the campaign as ridiculous is correct. The examples involve what they see as similar situations with other companies:

> YEAH, RIGHT! LOL MT @KurtSchlichter: "Welcome to Chick Fil-A. Before you order, lets discuss my personal savior, Jesus." #RaceTogether
>
> @GadsdenBabs

> Hobby Lobby now forces employees to discuss w/customers the Pro-life by sayin how many children they have bc no birth control #RaceTogether
>
> @averykayla

What is interesting about tweets like these is that they all feature corporations that have raised liberal ire with their decisions. Twitter users thus frame their dislike of #RaceTogether through the lens of the struggle for cultural domination between liberals and conservatives. Conservatives reason that if there is no space in mainstream culture for Chick-Fil-A or Hobby Lobby's views because they're potentially exclusive, they should not have to tolerate narratives they view as exclusive either.

This particular discourse flows from the color-blind ideology introduced in chapter 5, which argues that all races are equal in today's America (e.g., Bonilla-Silva, 2013; Doane, 2007). Therefore, these Twitter users reason, making consumers talk about problems related to race is equivalent to making customers talk about their religious beliefs. Both are the outcome of personal choices, not systemic social inequalities, and therefore, the reasoning goes, they have no place in a business environment. According to this ideology, making race visible through dialogue is a form of racism in itself; equality between races means there is no need to discuss race at all (e.g., Carney, 2016). This becomes apparent through a large number of tweets, many of which turn the tables on Starbucks:

> @Starbucks wants people to talk about race. If you believe race exists, you are a racist. Enjoy getting your morning coffee. #RaceTogether
>
> @vilagereactonry

> So if I want nothing in it, do I have to ask for "coffee of color" now? #Race Together Seriously get my coffee & stop keeping race pertinent.
>
> @SFoulard

Some users went as far as to claim that African American civil rights leaders supported color-blindness, and would have thus opposed this campaign as well ("MLK wanted us to be BLIND to race."—@TallulahStarr; "#RaceTogether I'll remind the color conscious barista of MLKs "judge not by the color of one's skin, but by the content of one's character""—@RosabelRose). People who adhere to this ideology believe that if there are inequalities, these cannot be blamed on race, but on a host of other issues:

> Hey In glad to talk about race, but let's talk what really holds people back, culture. #RaceTogether
>
> @GOPtalk

> #RaceTogether? How about stop bringing it up, and judge people on the content of their character?
>
> @SamValley

Both @GOPtalk and @SamValley make it clear that talking about race is not an issue; people whose discourse is shaped by a color-blind ideology generally do not eschew discussing race, but race is not seen as the cause of any social problems. Instead, they point to character and culture as defining factors in inequality.

It is interesting how many times the word "guilt" or "white guilt" are used in tweets, with users expressing no need or desire to experience any guilt while ordering their coffee:

> I just want coffee. Hold the racist guilt. #RaceTogether
>
> @maryfernandez31

> Is the whole purpose of @Starbucks #RaceTogether to have honest discourse on race or just to implement white guilt?
>
> @TheStowBilly

The second tweet is accompanied by a picture titled "The color of murder 2005–2013," which lists the following statistics: "Whites killed by Blacks: 4,348. Blacks murdered by Blacks: 23,812. Blacks killed by whites: 1,915." This tweet captures how post-racial discourse operates to maintain the color-blind ideology: It offers an alternative explanation for racial inequality and racism that absolves white people of any responsibility (Bonilla-Silva, 2013). In this case, this is accomplished by presenting statistics that show that African Americans are responsible for their own demise, not white people. The implication is that any dialogue about race should not point fingers at white people, but at the "real" cause. When dialogue does point to race, it is clearly aiming to make white people feel guilty and victimize them.

This idea of white victimhood is reflected in other tweets as well, where Twitter users equate the #RaceTogether slogan on their cups as a form of judgment, one that they did not ask for, and is thus reason to stop going to Starbucks altogether:

> All I want is coffee from my Barista. Not something equivalent to the scarlet letter on my cup. #RaceTogether to @DunkinDonuts I say.
>
> @Nasedo

The idea of white victimhood is thus an important part of this narrative, with users inserting the bane of color-blind ideology into their tweets: Affirmative action.

> #Starbucks Barista, I know u gotta make coffee but I need to tell u about being the victim of affirmative action #tcot #gop #RaceTogether
>
> @DebbieSchlussel

The belief that racial inequality is a thing of the past is so firmly embedded in this ideology that users like @DebbieSchlussel view affirmative action as equally discriminatory toward white people as any kind of racist action is toward members of other ethnic minority groups (cf. Bonilla-Silva, 2013). As opposed to non-white people though, white people's problems are not recognized, not made the center of a Starbucks' campaign, again reaffirming the victimhood trope discussed above. The sarcasm reflected in the "I know you gotta . . . but I need to tell you" makes it very clear that the user does not see a need to share her racial struggles with the barista, implying she doesn't understand why the barista would do the same to her. Just like in the tweets about Hobby Lobby and Chick-fil-A, there is a sense that since there is no space in mainstream society to talk about being a victim of affirmative action, there shouldn't be room to talk about racism either.

#RaceTogether and the Need to Listen

On the other hand, there are those people who opposed the #RaceTogether campaign because while they see racism as a problem, they do not see (white) people talking about race as the solution. For one thing, there is the belief that ethnic minority voices have gone unheard for too long, and that instead of discussing race, white people need to listen to and acknowledge the minority perspective on racial issues:

> We don't need *to talk* about #racetogether—white folks need *to listen* about race. Hey white ppl let's #ShutUpAndListenTogether instead.
>
> @YaYaAshley

> But now is an excellent opportunity for Corporate White America to listen to people of color. #RaceTogether
>
> @capetownbrown

This sentiment was further reinforced when Starbucks' VP for Global Communications shut down his Twitter account after feeling "personally attacked in a cascade of negativity" (duBrowa, 2015). The tweets that made up the cascade questioned him about Starbucks' race record in terms of employment, education, and store location (Geier, 2015). Twitter users expressed their disbelief and disapproval of duBrowa's refusal to engage with them:

> But out of the gate, @coreydu, VP of @Starbucks Global Communications, is playing the victim instead of listening. It's wild. #RaceTogether
>
> @local_maxima

This user's description of @coreydu (duBrowa's Twitter handle) as a victim links the Starbucks' campaign to the color-blind ideology discussed above, reducing the campaign to nothing more than an attempt to assuage white guilt. This sentiment was echoed by other users, who mocked the VP for claiming he was attacked by people of color, and expressing the belief that a conversation implied the need to listen to all parties:

> @coreydu Agreed. People of color are speaking out about real issues and we as white people should really listen (1/3) #RaceTogether
> .@coreydu It may feel like attacks, but when PoC speak about trauma and injustice, they're giving an opportunity to hear (2/3) #RaceTogether
> .@coreydu If we can listen first, that's when real dialog can start. Please listen to those voices (3/3) #RaceTogether
>
> @HeyChrisEdwards

Furthermore, there is a clear understanding that talking alone isn't sufficient. Not just because white people need to listen instead of speak but because race as a topic of conversation has been exhausted:

#RaceTogether: Starbucks wants to start a cnversation about race. We've been doing this for yrs. It's an exhausted topic. #thefive

@JoeDavi1

Twitter users are also very clear about what they do think will solve the country's institutionalized racism: action.

AAs have been talking to ourselves for 400 yrs. I want action. @starbucks how many of your board mbrs & employees are Black? #raceTogether

@BougieBlackGurl

@Starbucks want to #RaceTogether ? Fund efforts to end racial residential segregation. Talking about race wont change ppl's opportunities

@Steph_Llanes

Twitter users give Starbucks all sorts of alternatives that would help resolve the racial issues they wish to address such as funding efforts to end residential segregation, hiring more ethnic minorities, and educating people on Black history. There was a clear understanding that "Talking about race won't change ppl's opportunities" (@Steph_Llanes). Beneath the frustration with the campaign and the lack of people listening and taking action was a recognition of the color-blind discourse that these Twitter users saw as informing the campaign:

Between Common's #HandInLove, Starbuck's #RaceTogether and St. Pattys Day, today has been jam-packed with White Privilege and condescension

@BreeToniRose

@Starbucks It's well intended, but the CEO lost me at the "we are all human" piece b/c that reinforces colorblindness #RaceTogether

@MsAriV

Both of these tweets view the refusal to recognize different racial categories, and the belief that simply extending a hand and talking is sufficient to end racism, as symptomatic of white privilege and the post-racial color-blind ideology this informs. Reducing the solution to centuries of oppression to a simple, "we're all human" fails to acknowledge inequality and struggle, a narrative familiar to most ethnic minorities, and one that is firmly embedded in the color-blind, post-racial, neoliberal ideology. Twitter users also reflected on the appropriation of civil rights symbols by the campaign as a sign of the color-blind ideology that they felt informed the campaign. One example that was addressed in the Tweets was the use of "We Shall Overcome" in the #RaceTogether ad:

> How disrespectful is #RaceTogether ad using "Shall We Overcome?" We shall overcome refers to Black liberation, not bs corporate PR moves.
>
> @lolitasaywhat

Tweets identified this as the ultimate sign of symbolic annihilation and appropriation of Black cultural symbols for hegemonic (i.e., color-blind) purposes. While the campaign meant to make members of nonminority groups aware of the issues surrounding racism (Logan, 2016), and the use of these symbols was probably meant as educational, the tweets analyzed here show how these symbols were seen as a sign of the failure to understand issues facing ethnic minorities.

Ultimately, Twitter users interpreted the #RaceTogether campaign as another post-racial color-blind attempt to assuage the majority's feelings about race:

> Black slavery, plunder, redlining, imprisonment, and correctional control are somehow symptoms rather than causes. Convenient. #RaceTogether
>
> @z0x1c

The use of the word "convenient" indicates a resignation to the fact that this ideology assigns the blame to the people it subordinates, instead of recognizing the systemic racism that is perpetuated by society. This same resignation is reflected in @ThunkinOutloud's tweet about the campaign:

> Watch: this stupid #racetogether thing will be an excuse to do nothing . . . "But, we TRIED and you blacks didn't like it so . . . GTFOH!"

The campaign will fail, this tweet reasons, and African Americans will be blamed because they didn't accept the construction of the problem and subsequent solution.

The Narrative of #RaceTogether

In short, #RaceTogether was rejected by people from a variety of ethnic backgrounds and from across the political spectrum. On the one hand, people rejected #RaceTogether because their acceptance of the color-blind ideology that led them to see a desire to discuss race as an attack on them. On the other hand, #RaceTogether was seen as the perfect embodiment of the color-blind ideology it was trying to fight.

The Journey: Analyzing Responses to 84 Lumber's Super Bowl Ad

The next campaign this section addresses is the single 84 Lumber commercial that aired during the 2017 Super Bowl. This ad left many viewers confused about its meaning—the presence of a door in a border wall that allowed people to cross without presenting any papers seemed to support illegal immigration. When news got out that the owner of 84 Lumber was a supporter of Donald Trump, this seemed to turn this interpretation on its head. The CEO herself claimed the ad wanted to show the company as one that celebrated opportunity and hard work, and was not meant to be political (Payne, 2017). Many viewers, however, disagreed and took to Twitter to debate the meaning of the commercial. Analysis of the tweets revealed three frames that underpinned people's interpretation of the 84 Lumber ad.

Keeping the Dream Alive: E Pluribus Unum

Viewers who saw the commercial in a positive light relied on a frame that centers on the American dream, i.e., the belief that the U.S. is strong and successful because it gave a chance to all who came, becoming one out of many. The commercial's narrative is interpreted as opposing the current anti-immigration discourse, and instead promoting the "true" American values that make the U.S. successful, which include opportunity, unity, and compassion.

People who use this frame see mother and daughter overcoming hardships in search of a better life, and applaud this as one of the pillars of the nation:

> We ARE and always will be a nation of immigrants and the land of opportunity for ALL people wishing to dream #84lumber
>
> @jayoung1892

> This is what makes America great: decency, opportunity, fairness & the dream of a better life #84Lumber #SB51
>
> @Centurion480

> Brave and Bold—so VERY American. Loved the ad #84lumber. Thank you!
>
> @michelleleff

Many Tweets rely on an Americanist ideology (Hall, 2013), where they appropriate the U.S. constitution and other symbols and phrases that reference the founding of the country, to applaud the commercial's positive stance toward immigration:

> Some still believe in the #Americandream: #ImmigrantsMakeAmericaGreat. #lumber84
>
> @AmAnDayinCA

> #WeThePeople all came here for a better life to live the land of the free. Thx #84Lumber #WeAreAllImmigrants
>
> @ezziesmommy

Tweets such as these, especially the second one, makes the woman's actions part of the fabric of the country's history, connecting her border crossing to the success of the country.

In the interpretations that came out of this frame, the use of the door was seen to signify the need to keep America open to all who wish to enter it; as one Twitter user said, "Build ALL the doors & bridges" (@col leenhoover). This need to keep the U.S. open was directly tied to a liberal discourse and a subsequent rejection of the short-lived travel ban Trump imposed in January 2017, with many tweets using the #NoBanNoWall hashtag or even #NotMyPresident.

The presence of the door was also used to argue for unity and inclusion as central American values, with Twitter users making statement such as "If you knock over a wall, does it not then become a bridge?" (@JasonJ Thomas), and tying the need for inclusion directly to the opportunities that make the U.S. succesful:

> Let's build bigger opportunities that open up doors, not walls that separate us! #84lumber #TheJourney
>
> @v_fatti

The only way, these Tweets argue, to make America great is to keep it the open and welcoming country it was in the past. In other words, Trump's plans to build a wall are not just wrong, they are in fact anti-Americanist. This argument shows how this particular frame is very much informed by liberal discourses, as evidenced by the many tweets that call out President Trump and his opposition to immigration as anti-American and unproductive:

> Hope @realDonaldTrump you are enjoying the #superbowl ads. #Lumber84 #Coke #Airbnb. All show #truth and #love for #America. #notmypresident
>
> @dgatterdam

> #Libertarians for #Immigration. Can't create #jobs without immigration. #lumber84 #AintNoTimeToHate
>
> @OldFatBaldDude

Compassion was also seen as a central value to come out of this commercial, with Twitter users thanking 84 Lumber for showing the human side of immigration, and warning them for the wrath they were about to experience for showing compassion. There is a clear sense that current political discourse has reduced immigrants to either faceless criminals or a number, and people who adhered to this frame saw this commercial as challenging that discourse:

> Please watch the end of the #Lumber84 ad. We MUST stop dehumanizing people with real suffering, they are HUMAN. EMPATHY IS PARAMOUNT #SB51
>
> @TheRealHcount

> Thank you for sharing some humanity when so many were watching. #lumber84 #SuperBowlCommercials #superbowl
>
> @seanbruna

In short, when viewing the 84 Lumber commercial through the frame of the American dream, the commercial is a celebration of the diversity that characterizes the country, one that recognizes the "true" nature of the nation:

> Thank you #lumber84 for standing up for our country, celebrating our diversity & the beauty of our human spirit. We stand with you.
>
> @jenschke

> So glad to see the superbowl celebrating immigrants and diversity, that's what America is #Superbowl #lumber84
>
> @MicheelleeRubyy

Law and Order: America First

People whose interpretation of the commercial was negative relied on a frame that constructs the U.S. as a nation of law and order and whose success hinges on its ability to keep its citizens safe and free. While 84 Lumber's CEO was quickly identified as a supporter of Donald Trump, the commercial's narrative did not allow for an anti-immigration, pro-wall interpretation, giving people who support the current administration's rhetoric and policies no choice but to reject the commercial:

> @Workers4Trump @solmartpropert1 I will NEVER go to #84lumber AGAIN.
>
> @jlspokesjr

When constructing their rejection of the commercial and 84 Lumber, Twitter users define the company as clearly anti-American, and tied this assessment to the belief that the U.S. is founded on laws that any "real" American knows to respect:

> So that's the end of me setting up Lumber drops from 84 Lumber! #84lumber made their last drop on my sites! We like laws in the USA
>
> @icapturpix

> Watch the full ad Fox deemed too controversial. The will to break the law is always welcome here. #84Lumber
>
> @Patriotic_Punk

The belief that the U.S. is a law-abiding country is also reflected in tweets that discuss how the mother and daughter obviously entered the country illegally. Regardless of their plight, the tweets claim, they crossed without the proper documentation and broke the law.

Viewers also attacked 84 Lumber for excusing illegal immigration:

> #84lumber BOYCOTT 84 Lumber. 84 Lumber promotes illegal entry into the United States, provided assistance to felons, violation of our border
>
> @MerrisaSJC

> how dare you promote illegal immigration & try to make it acceptable by tugging on heartstrings. You're what's wrong in USA #Lumber84
>
> @dialygal

@MerrisaSJC's tweet that calls for a boycott is one of many to do so. Both of these tweets condemn 84 Lumber for advocating crime, but @dialygal sees the nation as a whole at risk. According to this Twitter user, people who reason based on emotions instead of the law are undermining the U.S. This tweet thus reproduces the myth of the "bleeding heart liberal." America, so this user argues, can only be set right if people adhere to the laws, an idea echoed by @sbpdl, whose tweets ties respect for the law to the notion of freedom:

> Is @lumber84 advocating violating the law as the new foundation of American freedom? #lumber84 Just evil, evil stuff

This focus on the importance of adherence to laws when it comes to undocumented immigrants is tied to a fear of what will happen to the country if people are allowed to enter without the proper paperwork.

Twitter users express concern about Mexican cartels, foreign criminals, and terrorists entering the country, directly linking illegal immigration to ISIS:

> #lumber84 good Ad—of course the little girl/mom are welcome—does rest of story address Mexican Cartel and the terrorists following them?
>
> @StanErwine

> Dear @ISIS. Your will to succeed in killing us is always welcome here #84Lumber.
>
> @BLK_ChuckNorris

Analysis also revealed Twitter users adhered to the belief that people who cross the border illegally enter the U.S. to engage in criminal activities, hurt US citizens' ability to be successful, and in general render the country less safe and successful:

> #84Lumber Coming here ILLEGALLY expecting 2 participate in the CONSENT OF THE GOVERNED undermines US CITIZEN SUCCESS (this tweet includes a link to a YouTube video entitled "Constitutional principles: Consent of the governed")
>
> @VeritasRanger

> #84Lumber HOW DARE YOU SNUB AMERICANS WHO BELIEVE IN LEGAL IMMIGRATION! We deserve to feel safe in our country "@AmyMek: Meanwhile in MIAMI, Florida . . . muslim terror group CAIR (aka HAMAS) openly threatens Jews and publicly vows to KILL Americans"
>
> @SmithHeddi

As exemplified by @SmithHeddi's tweet, viewers who relied on this law-and-order frame also expressed the view that 84 Lumber and their commercial were ignoring "real" Americans in favor of undocumented immigrants, forgetting about jobless Americans, veterans, and homeless people:

> @16_our_movement Where's #84Lumber compassion for the 500,000 #Veterans who are out of work & the 50,000 that are homeless? #BuildTheWall
>
> @10ATexan

> @84LumberNews In the sequel, can you hire American citizens from an unemployment office? That would be a tear-jerker, too. #84lumber
>
> @MakeSimelane

While the previous frame celebrates all forms of immigrations as adding to the diversity of the country, people who relied on this frame made a clear distinction between immigrants with the proper documentation and those without. "True" American immigrants are those who obeyed the law, while anyone else is seen as a criminal:

> #84lumber Spitting in the face of all immigrants who had to obey the law. Disgraceful and disgusting disregard for America and Americans.
>
> @wicked_infidel

> #lumber84 I'm sorry, why would I be okay with people illegally coming into the county? Come here legally&I I'll welcome you with open arms
>
> @crystalcorrdero

Only those people who understand that the foundation of this country is law and order are welcome to join, everyone else is showing disrespect for the nation.

Similar to the response to #RaceTogether, Twitter users also indicate discomfort with being confronted with views different from their own in a setting where they do not expect it. Many Twitter users explain their dislike of being "lectured" away by claiming that 84 Lumber is merely pandering to the liberals.

An Immigrant's Tale

The final frame centers on the immigrant experience, which allows for a positive as well as a negative interpretation of the commercial. This frame centers on the mother and the daughter as migrants, an interpretation that triggered a wide array of emotions among many of the viewers. The majority of the responses were positive; users linked the mother-daughter experience to their own immigration experiences, rendering the 84 Lumber brand part of their identity performance:

> Watched the beautiful ad for #84lumber moved to heavy ugly face tears grateful to my abuelito and my parents 4 having the will to succeed
>
> @SNCLmusic

> .@kristinamonllos #84lumber ad.is so wonderfully heartfelt; reminiscent of how much my great-grandparents wanted 2 be #Americans
>
> @shariannebrill

These tweets, and others like them, are reminiscent of the first frame; they present immigrants as desperate to succeed, and wanting nothing more than to be a part of this country. Some users list the values they see as paramount to being a successful immigrant, such as courage and sacrifice, ones they see reflected in the commercial:

> #Lumber84 is like my immigrant story- courage, resilience and love #NoBanNoWall #HereToStay #SB51
>
> @Karla_QP

> Our mothers cross borders to give us a better future! Thank u mom!#Lumber84 #HereToStay
>
> @LisMarieFL

On the other hand, some viewers, like users who rely on the law-and-order frame, question the commercial's apparent praise of people who cross the border illegally. They see the ease with which the mother and daughter cross the border as a slap in the face of people who did migrate legally, and find people's praise of the commercial insulting:

> People sneaking in here are noble? MY MOM was an immigrant!She learned English,took the test, raised her hand! THATS AN IMMIGRANT! #Lumber84
>
> @SoCalLynn

This user seems to realize the importance of immigrants to the country (in line with the American dream frame), but refuses to see undocumented immigrants on the same level as legal immigrants, and as a solution, argues that only people who follow the rules (per the law and order frame) are allowed to call themselves immigrants.

Finally, several viewers critique the ad for "romanticizing" illegal immigration:

> .@84LumberNews, warming commercial. However, you forgot the #HumanTrafficking, murder, rape, coyotes, etc. that many encounter. #84Lumber
>
> @Fidaddle

> Sadly, if it was factual, the mother and daughter would have been aasaulted by male illegals along the way. #84Lumber "@CharlieKirk11: I can't believe there was a super bowl glorifying illegal immigration. A terrible message to send. Horrible."
>
> @PurebredPolly

Many other tweets touch on the rape statistics among female border jumpers and critique 84 Lumber for selling the idea of illegal immigration without mentioning the biggest dangers for females crossing Central

America. This particular interpretation appeared to be apolitical, with viewers expressing disappointment in the company's narrow and idealistic view of a complex topic.

Reading "The Journey"

In short, 84 Lumber's commercial presents such an open narrative; it allows for multiple, contradictory interpretations. How people view the commercial depends on the frame they adopt, and only one of the three frames found through the analysis results in a positive brand image. In line with existing research into the impact of visually open advertisements (e.g., Ketelaar, van Gisbergen, & Beentjes, 2012), this case study confirms that a commercial whose meaning is not immediately clear does not lead to the reproduction of the company's intended narrative and does little for the brand in general.

#WeAccept: Discussing Diversity

The Airbnb commercial was first aired during the 2017 Super Bowl, and its intention was unequivocal: to increase acceptance of all people, but especially "those who have been displaced" (Airbnb, 2017). #WeAccept presented the narrative that acceptance, inclusion, and diversity make the world a better place. While the campaign never spoke about the Trump administration's stance on refugees and immigration, the meaning of the commercial is diametrically opposed to Trump's policies, thus opening itself up for a mixture of praise and pushback. So how did viewers respond to such a politically charged narrative? As was the case with the #RaceTo gether campaign, responses fell into two camps: supporters and opponents.

#UnityinDiversity: Reconstructing #WeAccept

A large number of tweets shared the company's news release verbatim, while others thanked the company for creating the commercial (e.g.,"Thanks @Airbnb for being a powerful force for good. #weaccept"—@sarahfoofoo79), and again others complimented the company on the sincerity of commercial, the beauty of the message, telling Airbnb they were "l-e-g-i-t" (@psiraise), and needed to "preach!" (@ninanochera). Twitter users reflected on the message of unity and diversity through a number of constructions. Some linked the campaign to other movements such as #GirlPower (@desislavaluna), while others applauded the inclusivity of the commercial, used hashtags such as #UnityinDiversity (@mandkalak) to capture the essence of the campaign, and imploring people to "love all, serve all, accept all" (@GotzCEO).

In their acceptance of Airbnb's narrative, Twitter users reproduced two value systems: Christianity and Americanism (i.e., patriotism and the acceptance of "typical" American ideals such as liberty and equality; cf. Hall, 2013). Some users, when retweeting the commercial or expressing their agreement with the campaign in other ways, used bible scriptures or other expressions of faith to explain their approval of #WeAccept, such as @She SeesFar, who retweeted the commercial using the hashtags #WeAccept as well as #NoBanNoWall and #Matthew25 (which contains three parables explaining the need for Christians to take care of those who have less). Others talk about how Christian values take precedence over any law:

> The law of God is bigger than the law of the land. #resist #weaccept #dump trump
>
> @Gee_sauce_

Other Twitter users rely on the patriotic values apparent in the "American dream" frame used for the 84 Lumber campaign described above to explain their support for #WeAccept. They equate acceptance and tolerance with what America truly is, connect #WeAccept to the pledge of allegiance, and use slogans that have been used since the American revolution to connect the notion of acceptance to an Americanist discourse:

> Because THIS is America! #weaccept
>
> @lguerrero24

> #weaccept #strongertogether Thank you @airbnb United we stand. Acceptance and diversity make us strong. One nation, indivisible.
>
> @AlbrightCheryl

People with a positive view of the commercial interpreted the narrative as a political stance against the current administration and its policies on immigration. Users lamented the current political climate, expressing dismay that in 2017 a campaign about "unity and racial harmony is controversial" (@orfgao), and retweeted news stories that labeled the campaign as a critique of Trump's immigration policies. Tweets included praising Airbnb and the other companies with political commercials during the Super Bowl for "leading the way in denouncing the Donnie Trump Hate message" (@TheBrownCube), while others used the hashtag to attack Donald Trump's perceived discrimination:

> #weaccept What we don'f accept is racism, sexism, homophobia or discrimination based on religious affiliation. It's simple Trump.
>
> @bethelliott63

Tweets also used hashtags that indicated a link to the online social movements that actively and openly campaign against the Trump administration, such as #Resist.

The positive reception of the narrative and its hashtag was reflected by the large number of companies that used the hashtag to show their support. Some nonprofits, especially those geared toward refugee and immigration issues, such as @miles4migrants and @UNHCRSerbia pledged support for Airbnb's campaign to house refugees, while others expressed general approval of the campaign.

Most people viewed the commercial as a liberal, anti-Trump narrative, and it was this aspect of the narrative that led to resistance to the campaign.

#BoycottAirbnb: Resisting #WeAccept

Compared to the discussions that occurred in response to #RaceTogether and 84 Lumber's commercial, there was less pushback to the #WeAccept campaign. This, however, does not necessarily mean that most people agreed with the commercial. It is much more likely that because the advertisement was not very open and did not allow for a great deal of oppositional or negotiated interpretations, most people who did not agree with the concept just ignored it. The themes that came out of the analysis were very similar to the ones found for the #RaceTogether campaign. Like the responses to that campaign, most of the tweets that critique #WeAccept appear to do so in line with the color-blind ideology. Users complain about having to accept people and things they are not willing to accept, and that they, as white people, feel left out and unaccepted by society:

> #weaccept a lot more than we should
> Multiculturalism & Diversity have been forced upon us
> It seems everyone's culture is respected but ours (this tweet is accompanied by a picture of the earth with the words "multiculturalism the death of the west")
>
> @Politikking

This idea of white people as victim of a society geared toward the acceptance of ethnic minorities reflects the color-blind beliefs discussed above. The color-blind narrative is extended to include Americanist values, too:

> Sorry but this is very anti White and pro angry looking people. #WeAccept only those who embrace America and American values.
>
> @TwoSpiritCamila

This tweet exemplifies how people who adhere to the color-blind ideology generally know it is not acceptable to express racist beliefs, but they will cloak racially charged ideas in sentiments unrelated to race, in this case, Americanism (e.g., Hehman, Gaertner, & Dovidio, 2011). Airbnb's request to accept everyone is deemed unacceptable because only those who support American ideals should be allowed to be a part of the U.S. This belief is further explicated by Twitter users who reference terrorist activities on U.S. soil as a reason to not accept everyone without question:

> #weaccept I would accept it if the World Trade Center, Boston marathon and the other thousands of events never happened.
>
> @Deplorable1234

While @Deplorable1234's tweet doesn't explicitly name the perpetrators of these crimes as non-white Americans, the implication that the people Airbnb is asking Americans to accept are those who commit crimes against them, is there. Other Twitter users were not so circumspect:

> #weaccept ??? FUCK YOU!!! 3200 AMERICANS killed on AMERICAN SOIL by MUSLIM TERRORIST since 1974!!! #WeDoNotAccept !!!!!!!!
>
> @LonestarCowboy7

The #WeAccept campaign thus triggered a fear of putting Americans' lives at risk. The belief that anything unknown could pose a threat to the safety of the country and its people runs deep and appears to drive the resistance to the commercial.

#WeAccept: Negotiating the Narrative

The Twitter users who engaged with #WeAccept appear to faithfully reproduce the narrative created by Airbnb. They extend the idea of acceptance and inclusion to incorporate religious beliefs and Americanism, and saw a clear rejection of the Trump administration and its policies in the campaign, even though the CEOs of the company never directly admitted to having any political purpose. While negative tweets were far fewer than with the other race-oriented campaigns, the themes from the tweets about #RaceTogether campaign resurfaced, indicating that when it comes to race, the color-blind ideology is very much the dominant framework for a large group of people.

CONCLUSION

Do consumers accept corporate narratives created through commercials and social media campaigns? This chapter attempted to provide exploratory insight into the answer to this question by analyzing a select number of campaigns focused on race and gender. Two campaigns focused on beauty products (#ChooseBeautiful and #WorthSaying) and three campaigns centered on race (#RaceTogether, 84 Lumber's "The Journey," and #WeAccept) were analyzed to uncover patterns in how people use Twitter to negotiate corporate narratives.

The analysis in this chapter showed that consumers have no qualms in reproducing the narratives created by campaigns for beauty products. Especially if the campaign has a narrow focus that can easily be incorporated into dominant postfeminist ideologies, as was the case with #ChooseBeautiful, tweets tend to reproduce the dominant narrative. Consumers appear comfortable using the brand's message as part of their identity performance, using it to enhance their own sense of empowerment. When it comes to race, the answer is a bit more diluted. The #RaceTogether campaign was especially problematic, with both sides rejecting the narrative, albeit for different reasons. The two other campaigns received more mixed responses though, probably because unlike #RaceTogether they did not represent concrete initiatives. However, #WeAccept and the 84 Lumber campaign met with both praise and resistance. While some supporters of the campaigns discussed in this chapter support the narrative, extending it with Christian and Americanist values, others outright reject the messages presented in their narratives, relying on claims of colorblindness and a law-and-order frame to do so. Again, as mentioned in previous chapters it appears that people on opposite sides of the political aisle don't just disagree on issues but have completely disparate views of what the country looks like and needs in terms of solving its racial issues. The staking of different claims about what "being American" entails (abiding the law? Inclusion?) shows that any dialogue between the groups is unlikely and bound to be unproductive. In fact, the tweets discussed in this chapter did not show any dialogue between people with opposing points of view. It appeared instead that people used Twitter as a platform to broadcast their opinions by connecting with those who thought like them, and ignoring or calling out those who did not.

8

I Tweet, You Tweet

Examining How Ethnic Minority Groups Use Social Media

> But that is really the power of Twitter, of social media, it really changes your perception of things (African American male)

Twitter users are the final piece of the puzzle when examining how Twitter is used to construct race and gender. Numerous studies have examined why people use social media in general (e.g., Whiting & Williams, 2013) and the role that particular aspects of Twitter usage play in people's lives (e.g., Marwick & Boyd, 2011a). In addition, much attention has been paid to the role that Twitter can play in altering public consciousness (e.g., Bonilla & Rosa, 2015). Ethnic minority groups, African Americans in particular, are commonly perceived to be at the heart of the counternarrative space that has been said to characterize Twitter (e.g., Anderson & Hitlin, 2016; Jackson & Foucault Welles, 2015). Furthermore, Black Twitter has been extensively investigated as a space for African Americans to connect and share cultural understandings (e.g., Brock, 2012; Sharma, 2013).

To date, however, no study has examined how members of ethnic minority groups use Twitter and what they think about Twitter as a platform for dialogue and resistance. With the claims reported elsewhere in this book that Twitter affords users from marginalized groups a space to contest dominant narratives, it seems especially relevant to examine how ethnic minority groups view this claim. Using results from focus groups, personal interviews, and an online survey, this chapter explores how social media users from ethnic minority groups utilize the platform and how they view the role that Twitter and other social media play in their lives and in society at large. I first discuss what is known about why people use social media, present research on the different affordances created by Twitter, and then use the findings from the interviews, surveys, and focus groups to explore the meaning of Twitter usage for members of ethnic minority groups.

EXPLAINING SOCIAL MEDIA USAGE

Numerous researchers have looked into why people turn to social media and identified uses such as socialization, entertainment, information seeking, self-promotion, sharing personal experiences, expressing one's opinion, and surveillance (e.g., García-Martín & García-Sánchez, 2015; Park, Kee, & Valenzuela, 2009; Pérez & Gómez, 2011; Whiting and Williams, 2013) What people use social media for also influences their behavior offline. Park et al. (2009) established that people who rely on Facebook groups for information and group participation are more likely to be engaged in civic and political activities, for instance.

The uses people have for Twitter are very similar: In an early study, Java, Song, Finin, and Tseng (2007) reported that people appear to use the platform to talk about their daily lives, to have conversations with others, share information, and report news. While Twitter is an inherently public, conversation-driven medium, many perceive and use it as a very private, intimate space, posting highly personal updates (e.g., Acar & Deguchi, 2013). Tweets are also used to strengthen social bonds and to build and maintain communities (Marwick & Boyd, 2011a). Because Twitter allows people to publicly affiliate with a group, thus cementing their belonging to a certain community, some research has found that Twitter users associate mainly with people like them (Java, et al., 2007; Brown, et al., 2015). Conversely, people also use Twitter to interact with people with whom they would not engage in the real world, such as politicians (Loader, et al., 2016).

As far as using Twitter for political purposes, scholars are generally optimistic about the platform's potential to provide a space for young people to engage with politics in a way that appeals to them. However, research has hinted at the possibility that while young people enjoy reading political discussions on social media, they are not very likely to participate out of fear of conflict, the risk of being deceived by seemingly trustworthy information, as well as the belief that anything they do on social media will not really have an impact (Loader, et al., 2016; Svenings-son, 2014).

Users' behavior on Twitter is also influenced by concerns about impression management (e.g., Cunningham, 2013). Users experience tension between the desire to be seen as authentic (and thus refusing to consider one's audience as a factor in one's tweets) and the desire to use Twitter to create a "personal brand," complete with a strategy for attracting certain audiences (Marwick & Boyd, 2011a, p. 119). The context collapse inherent to all social media, but in particular to Twitter, where tweets are public by default, further complicates the decision about one's online behavior (Marwick & Boyd, 2011b).

Another factor that plays a role in users' behavior is Twitter's speed and ability to share large volumes of information quickly. The use of hashtags and the retweet function allows people to easily find information from a variety of perspectives and involve outsiders in conversations, building communities around topics. Twitter can thus create the idea that users are "surrounded by a conversation" (Boyd, Golder, & Lotan, 2010, p. 1), as well as encourage a sense of belonging through retweets and mentions. But just because the medium affords high levels of user activity does not mean that all Twitter users are heavily engaged with the platform. Subsequently, participation on Twitter is characterized by a balancing act between reading and lurking, and sharing, creating, and interacting (e.g., Gleason, 2013; Gruzd, Wellman, & Takhteyev, 2011; Kist, Tollafield, & Dagistan, 2014).

This brief overview of how and why people use social media in general and Twitter in particular reveals some of the tensions present in the different activities Twitter users undertake. This chapter aims to shed light on how users from ethnic minority groups balance these tensions in their use of the platform.

EXPLORING ETHNIC MINORITIES' USE OF SOCIAL MEDIA

As discussed in previous chapters and surmised from the interpretive content analysis conducted so far, ethnic minorities active on Twitter use the platform to connect to others, construct and debate their racial identity, and negotiate how they are seen by the dominant culture. But how do these Twitter users view this activity themselves? What goals and expectations guide the creation of these narratives? In other words, how do members of ethnic minority groups use social media in general and Twitter in particular to express themselves and to engage in dialogue about issues related to race and gender?

To answer these questions and shed light on the process that goes into creating the narratives discussed in the rest of the book, I administered an online survey and carried out focus groups and personal interviews among African American, Latinx, and Asian Americans. Purposive and snowball sampling were used to recruit respondents. Announcements on social media and flyers posted at a medium-sized historically black institution in the southeastern United States were used to solicit participation. If respondents were interested in participating in a face-to-face interview, they were asked to invite two to four friends who were active on social media. If this was not feasible or desirable, they were asked to participate in a personal interview or fill out the online survey. The focus groups ranged in size from two to five participants. Five focus groups were held with African Americans, one was held with Latinx respondents. Two personal interviews were held with Asian Americans, and one was held with an African American. A total of 36 people completed the online open-ended questionnaire: 12 were Latinx; 17 were African American; five were Asian American/Pacific Islander; and three identified as biracial. People who completed the questionnaire and identified as Caucasian/White or who did not reveal their ethnic background were excluded from the analysis. In total, the responses from 58 participants were included in the analysis.

The focus groups, interviews, and surveys used open-ended questions to investigate participants' social media use, with a specific focus on Twitter. After providing consent, participants answered questions about why they used social media; with whom they connected and why; what they thought about the kinds of interactions they observed; how, when, and why they engaged in discussions; what they thought about these discussions; and what they thought about the trending topics covered in the previous chapters and some of the tweets discussed in these chapters. As theoretical saturation was apparent after two months of data collection and analysis, no further participants were recruited.

When conducting research that asks respondents to discuss what they do, there is always the risk of self-reporting bias due to social desirability. Even when questions are not deemed sensitive, it is possible that respondents provide socially desirable as opposed to truthful answers in order to impress others and avoid feeling bad about oneself (e.g., Miller, 2012; Moorman & Podsakoff, 1992). When asking social media users to talk about what they do online, this raises the question whether respondents are reporting on their actual behavior or performing for the interviewer. While this is always a concern, this particular study had several safeguards in place to prevent social desirable answers as much as possible. The questions, as mentioned above, were open-ended, for example, "What kind of people do you follow? Why?" or "What did you think about this meme/tweet/hashtag?" The online surveys were open-ended and anonymous, relieving respondents from as much pressure to perform as possible, and the focus groups were held among people who knew each other. This meant that the respondents didn't need much probing from the interviewer to carry on a conversation (and thus few clues about what a socially desirable answer would be). It also meant that respondents would call each other out if they felt a response was disingenuous. Finally, as the analysis below reveals, similar patterns were uncovered across the different modes of data collection and participants, implying that while it is possible that (some) respondents performed rather than participated, the impact of this performance was minor.

The data were analyzed using grounded theory analysis' constant comparative technique (Corbin & Strauss, 1990; Glaser, 1965). An initial close reading made it clear that the participants not only talked about what they did on Twitter and other social media, but also the rules or expectations that guided their behavior. A follow-up close reading of the interview and focus groups transcripts as well as the responses to the online survey was then used to extract codes to designate the behavior and perceived rules that determine people's behavior. A reiterative process was used to fine tune the different codes and with each new interview or completed survey, the codes were revised and adjusted when necessary. Once data collection was complete, the behaviors and expectations for those behaviors were grouped into three uses people had for social media: to be heard, to hold conversations, and to create connections.

VOICES: SPEAKING OUT ON SOCIAL MEDIA

Even though Twitter, like other social media, is hailed as a platform for people to connect and interact, at its heart, Twitter is about broadcasting individual expressions. When the social media site first started, the question people were prompted to answer when tweeting was "what are you doing." Although this was later replaced with "what's happening," the fundamental idea is the same. Participants mentioned the importance of social media in giving people a voice, and tied it to the marginalization that some of the respondents experienced. As one Asian American female pointed out:

> I think it's helpful because it's kind of a way to give voice to an issue that you would normally not have

This points to the ability of social media platforms to give marginalized groups the space to speak that they have been denied in the mainstream media, an idea echoed by an African American male:

> I think that's our way of degrading them. Because we can't come face to face and be like, you know what you did is wrong, so we gonna get at you through social media. I think it's positive because you know it's not positive to make fun of people, but somebody gotta say something and we the minority, so we not gonna get heard, so this is our way to get heard, and that's positive

This particular response is about how people on Twitter used memes to mock Donald Trump's statements about women captured on video and leaked to the media in October 2016. The participant pointed out that the memes mainly made fun of Donald Trump, making light of the sexual harassment he alludes to, and argued that while this is not constructive, this is the only way for a minority group to be heard. This raises the question about what people actually say on Twitter and to what extent "giving voice" translates into the constructive meaning making that the techno-optimists argue is made possible by Twitter.

What's Tweeting: Exploring What Social Media Users Say

The data also provided insight into what people say when they are on social media. When posting on platforms such as Twitter, respondents appeared concerned with the creation of a positive image. The intricacies of impression management have been well-documented elsewhere, with authors pointing to the delicate balance between authenticity and positivity (e.g., Ellison, Heino, & Gibbs, 2006), and it appears that participants, when considering what to tweet, definitely aimed to "look the part," i.e., to create a presentation that was positive and interesting (Rosenbaum, Johnson, Stepman, & Nuijten, 2013, p. 51):

> I like to post positive stuff, because you know people like your employers will look at your twitter and social media, so I don't try to post anything too reckless (African American female)

At the same time, respondents showed an awareness of the importance of having their tweets reflect who they were, even if that meant editing or deleting tweets:

> I probably delete something I tweet every day, I am not the person I was five minutes ago. Sometimes . . . because I use Twitter to express myself and my thoughts and how I'm feeling, so if I was in my feelings an hour ago but now I've had a nice long discussion with myself and God, then I don't feel this way no more so I delete it (African American female)

In some cases, participants indicated delaying posting or tweeting about something because they weren't certain how they felt about it yet:

> I want to give it time to find out how I feel about it before I subscribe to (Asian American female)

There is an awareness that posting on social media is a form of branding, a way to create a self-image that is both appealing and authentic (Liberman, 2013), and thus an act that requires some thought.

Tied to the tendency to create an authentic, yet positive presentation is the desire to use social media to inspire and uplift others:

> I like to post stuff like memes, but it be more so either educational, something that is influencing you to be better. . . . So if something is cute and catchy then I'll post that. It's like more so inspirational stuff, you know, go to school and get your education, check, and then it will say, get a good job, check. . . . Or maybe sometimes quotes from the bible (African American female)

Participants appeared to share thoughts, quotes, and beliefs important to them, but as the participant above pointed out, "cute and catchy" is a defining feature too, indicating that the use of Twitter to uplift others is another way to create a positive brand of self.

Besides using their social media expressions to create a positive, upbeat self-image, respondents also indicated that they tweeted to vent, or to "stay true" to who they are, the other side of the coin of impression management (Rosenbaum, et al., 2013, p. 51):

> If someone did something that made me upset, I will share that (Latina)

This use of Twitter was very common, with participants indicating that they used Twitter as opposed to other social media platforms to vent. Twitter functions as an "insight into your thoughts" (African American female), a modern-day high-speed stream of consciousness. The speed of the platform and the brevity of its messages makes it easy to use, to type up a quick observation about something going on and get those out to one's audience.

Using Twitter as a second screen, i.e., as a way to comment on shows and movies while watching them, was common for most participants, who indicated they often tweeted about shows or movies that they were watching. The kinds of updates or tweets that respondents talked about reflected two kinds of positions. On the one hand, some indicated to talk about the show in terms of their personal experience, i.e., did they like it, what did they think about certain narrative developments, what do they expect to happen in following episodes:

> I've seen fans (including myself) get upset about the possible death of Glenn on The Walking Dead (African American female)

These tweets then become part of the fan discourse about these shows, informing others' opinions and providing insight into how other people view the shows. One Twitter user described himself as a "self-appointed movie critic" (African American male), indicating the power ascribed to one's voice in informing people's opinions.

> On the other hand, some participants took a more critical approach:
> They talk about how empowering it was, or how stupid they made us look, or if they liked something else better, what they related to, what they didn't (African American female)

This critical use of the second screen was echoed by other respondents, who describe using Twitter to express their frustration about popular television shows, movies such as *Doctor Strange*, expectations about *Get Out* (which at the time of this focus group had not come out yet), and reality shows featuring African Americans. Their critique centered on the representation of minorities, and while the participants who mentioned making statements like that appear fairly adamant about their dislike of the poor media portrayal of their ethnic groups, they also described seeing large numbers of people on Twitter and other social media buying into the stereotypes. While the respondents recognized that shows like *Empire* are unrealistic, they see friends "eating it up" and "thriving off the wildness" (African American female), accepting the representation as unproblematic.

Some of the participants indicated that talking about politics on Twitter was second nature to them, and an important part of the persona they had created online:

> I did tweet about Kaepernick back when that was going on. . . . Of course, people didn't agree with it, but me being Black, and me understanding why he is doing it, you know mainly I was saying that other people don't understand why he kneels down. . . . When I'm on that kind of mindset, as far as like my, you know, my pro-Black mindset, that's usually when I get on Twitter and do a little spiel about you know, Black issues (African American male)

> Yes!!! I support Donald Trump and feel that as a Christian I am obligated to share why so that others might be encouraged to form their own opinions and see why and how I got to my conclusions (Latina)

As these examples demonstrate, Twitter's collapse of interpersonal communication and broadcasting (Honeycutt & Herring, 2009) affords people a space to take their personal convictions to a wider audience. Twitter is a place to share through performance ("do a little spiel"), and to influence public discourse on issues related to race and social justice. As the African American male quoted above indicated, "other people don't understand," i.e., they reproduce a white discourse on Kaepernick's actions, and Twitter provides him with the space to challenge that reproduction (cf. Carney, 2016). This belief was echoed by other participants, such as the Latina who indicated she used social media to educate people on "how society will be affected if immigrants are deported from this country."

Other participants, however, were very adamant that they avoided all political discussion on Twitter:

> I don't get into the controversial stuff. I don't know the last time that I posted something like (African American female)

> This is my first time voting, and I'm not tweeting on politics (African American male)

Respondents indicated they preferred to keep their political opinions to themselves, and that while they do not mind reading about politics, they don't like to express their own political viewpoints—that is not what they wanted their social media to be about. The "ownership" of the platform then is both a reason for social media users to express themselves freely or keep it clean of anything that could be seen as controversial.

Expressing political opinions is usually tied to having personal experience with a topic:

> The only subjects I say anything about are the ones I feel personally involved in, you know especially with the whole immigration, you know, I work with a lot of immigrant workers, and I do see it on a very personal level, how they are mistreated (Asian American male)

This respondent reflected the belief shared by others that social media allow them to reach an audience outside their own social circle and educate or persuade them. Participants also claimed ownership of Twitter ("it's my Twitter"—African American female), which gives them the right to express their political convictions. Of all the social media platforms they used, Twitter was the one used mainly for political expressions.

Controlling the Voice: Rules and Expectations

Besides addressing what they do on social media, participants also addressed the expectations or "unwritten rules" surrounding their social media expressions. These provide an interesting insight into the divergence between people who will "exude their Blackness" (African American male) and others who will not tweet on politics.

One of the unwritten rules that some appeared to adhere to was not venturing outside the social norms proposed by their online community:

> I try not to express my political viewpoint because I am a sociology major and my viewpoint does not usually fit the viewpoint of the general population (Latina)

> I try to stay away from the whole race thing because my view point is a lot different from everybody's else, being biracial. My mindset is just not as pro-Black like everybody else's (Biracial male)

Participants indicated a fear of standing out or of being different from their community of followers / friends as a reason to not speak out. What's interesting here is that respondents didn't mention a fear of being attacked; the mere fact of being labeled as different was enough to silence their voices. People don't want to offend anyone in their community of followers and will eschew politics if that is what it takes ("Just funny stuff that doesn't offend any party"—Latina). It appears that ensuring that one's opinions matches those of the people around you is an essential factor in determining what to tweet:

> Let me just say this, let me see where other people's heads are at with this thought that I have (African American male)

In addition, participants didn't just consider possible negative fallout from their updates; they also take into account how much positive feedback a specific opinion can get them:

> And another thing is if you think you can make a funny tweet about it and get a lot of retweets (African American female)

> If you have a good thought, you know, if you think, somebody else has got to be thinking this, somebody else gonna find this appealing (African American male)

Part of the attraction of social media is the ability to feel popular, or achieve a sense of "micro celebrity," i.e., utilizing social media like Twitter to create and maintain a faithful audience (Marwick & Boyd, 2011b, p. 140). This will subsequently inform how people use their voice.

In short, both the anticipation of social judgment, as well as the prediction of social approval informs whether or not people post political statements.

Interestingly, participants realized this too, and point to the resulting bandwagon effect that they have observed among their friends on social media:

> That is one of the cons about Twitter. Like people do stuff just to get a retweet, and they make everything a racial issue, and everything is not a racial issue (African American female)

The motives behind people's sociopolitical statements on Twitter are drawn into question by this participant, who accused her fellow Twitter users of using racial problems to gain a following. The next statement takes this idea a step further:

> because honestly, like everyone is saying F trump, but I promise you they couldn't tell you what Trumps for, where he stands on education, but because it's so popular to be anti-Trump, they're going to jump on the bandwagon. (African American female)

Here, the participant doesn't just question people's motives, but their actual understanding of an issue, claiming that people's desire to fit in will influence their political opinions. Others questioned people's motives for joining in protests organized by the Black Lives Matter movement. One participant talked about a Black Lives Matter march in Atlanta, stating that most people just went out there "to make a tweet to say I was there" (African American male). The participants in this study rejected those kinds of tweets as inauthentic, or not reflecting "your sense of your own voice" (African American female). At the same time, they recognized the importance of using a predesignated hashtag during a Black Lives Matter event to help create a trending topic, showing an awareness of the importance of creating a movement that transcends the physical realm into the virtual.

However, the importance of making a meaningful and authentic contribution and not one that is informed by popular opinion is underscored by another rule brought up by the respondents: the need for well thought-out, relevant statements. Besides wanting to make sure their statements would not upset any of their followers, participants also referred to the importance of sounding informed:

> I don't post about politics, I don't know that much and I don't want to look dumb (African American male)

It is interesting that on platforms where people share the most random thoughts, participants indicate insecurity when they anticipate social judgment. This theme returned quite often, with respondents reinforcing the idea that tweeting about politics without really knowing anything about it was simply unthinkable:

> When it's something I know a lot about. Like when I was on Twitter and was into doing the back and forth, but if I knew a lot about it, then I would, but if I didn't know a lot about it, then I would just stay out of it (African American female)

The expectation that one should only tweet about political topics when it's something one feels very passionate about was also reflected by numerous participants, such as the Asian American female who shared she had to feel "very, very passionate or moved" to share her opinion on a political issue. Talking about politics on social media is apparently not something that these users do on a whim.

Another factor that people consider when deciding what to say and what not to say was related to whether their statements would create a negative atmosphere on "their" Twitter or "their" page. Negativity was a recurring theme, with respondents claiming they would delete feedback that got too negative, as this was "their" platform, after all. When asked what prompted her to post about political issues, an African American female responded with "But because there are so many negative thinking people on social media I keep my posts to a minimum," indicating a fear of ensuing negatively framed discussions.

Participants eschewed any form of "drama," and an Asian American participant indicated she would unfollow people who treated social media like "an open diary." Others explained not responding to certain hashtags, even if they felt moved or annoyed by them because the issue they addressed was just too ridiculous:

> I do remember her saying that, I was like are you an idiot, you're rich, your Armani suits, you ain't . . . I didn't even entertain that. Like I know you're not my abuela. What is wrong . . . that is just foolish to me, so I didn't even entertain that (Latina on #Notmiabuela)

While others referenced the often-polarized nature of discussions on Twitter as a reason to not speak out:

> That's the thing. I have so much to say about it, but I just stay out of it because I can't fight with everybody on social media (African American female)

This statement is interesting, as recent research on the polarity on Twitter (Smith, Rainie, Shneiderman, & Himelboim, 2014) indicates that when it comes to controversial topics, Twitter conversations tend to take place in distinct groups, each with their own opinions, and with little to no connections to people with different views. It appears that even within these "deliberative enclaves" (Dahlberg, 2007, p. 828), there is discord and disagreement that renders users too uncomfortable to speak out. The notion of expected hostile interaction will be further explored in the next section on conversations.

CONVERSATIONS ON SOCIAL MEDIA

Conversations, or interactions with other users, are one of the main attractions of social media platforms. It's social media's ability to connect people and allow for the critical interaction between social actors that makes it a viable alternative to the traditional public sphere (Carney, 2016; Dahlberg, 2001). Conversation was the second group of behaviors that participants in this study talked about, and above everything else it was seen as the essence of Twitter (and other social media):

> It's always a discussion going on, it always keeps everyone aware because like I said it's like a chain reaction, one person sees it and then the next one and the next one, and now everyone is talking about it (African American female)

People actively seek out conversation, both in whom they follow ("there needs to be a guarantee for interaction"—African American female) and what they post ("I usually post a witty thought-provoking aphorism to get discussion going"—Asian American male).

Topics of Conversation

Participants identified several drivers of their interactions on social media. Anticipated entertainment was the main reason to join a conversation. Sharing or retweeting, an indirect way to create conversation (Boyd et al., 2010), was often motivated by how funny respondents thought the content of the hashtag was. Again, like with the decision whether or not to make political statements, conversation is in part informed by an assessment of one's audience, their likes and dislikes, and how to best appeal to those.

Participants also indicated that the dialogue that took place during live-tweeting was one of the most enjoyable aspects of using a second screen. As an African American female pointed out:

> It's like when you talk to the TV, it's like that. It's like having people in the room with you

Live-tweeting was mentioned mostly in conjunction with major television events such as award shows and sports events where large crowds of people would be watching, and social media could recreate the idea of co-viewing. Social media in general, but especially Twitter, was seen as the ideal platform to recreate those living room conversations. Live-tweeting was also popular during the 2016 presidential debates, with participants discussing how they would tweet throughout the debates:

> Like I'll hop in on the discussion, like when they're doing the debate . . . it's like a big discussion board, everyone is talking about it, everyone has their opinion, and sharing what they're seeing and what they feel personally about the presidential candidates (African American female)

When asked why the respondent liked participating in these discussions, her explanation was that she likes to feel included, again alluding to the desire to fit in with one's community.

Racial issues were one of the more popular topics of conversation according to the data collected for this study. Respondents indicated seeing and participating in discussions between people on both sides of the fence, and challenging people on their ideas:

> Topics involving race relations, sexism, discrimination, police brutality, LGBTQ rights, military issues. I usually challenge the OT to reexamine in their ideas and stereotypes (Biracial male)

Many of the respondents touched on #BlackLivesMatter and #AllLivesMatter, alluding to the ongoing debate between supporters of both movements:

> Of course, it's white people saying all lives matter, and the thing Black people have been trying to say and even the reason why this whole thing is a hashtag, a movement in the first place, is because we understand that all lives matter, but, with all lives, when you say all, you have to say all, so what we're saying is Black lives will matter, and all lives do matter as soon as Black lives matter (African American male)

This particular theme—all lives will truly only matter when Black lives do—was reiterated by numerous other participants, and reflects the struggle over signs that Carney (2016) found. Respondents indicated they viewed the All Lives Matter movement as an attempt to shift the discourse surrounding police brutality away from the issue of race and toward a post-racial discourse. Their statements included examples of how they engaged with #AllLivesMatter supporters in order to keep control of the discourse:

> This girl had shared a video of this white boy getting shot in front of the police, and she shared that video and she wrote on the caption, it's alright honey, Black Lives Matter got you. So somebody commented under that . . . like this dude, a white dude, he was like, are you sure about that? You need to go see what Black Lives Matter really about because I don't think they will have his back, and he posted two videos of two dudes saying white people don't matter, f white people and stuff like that, it's all about Black Lives Matter. And then that's when, I guess he made the conclusion that Black Lives Matter was a hate group, so . . . I see where he was going with that, like he perceived it in the wrong way, and that's when I commented under there, like, you know, Black Lives Matter is not about that. You need to go look up who started that and actually what they started it for (African American male)

While the respondent did not indicate whether the white man ever responded, his actions show that he understands that #BlackLivesMatter is a contested sign, and the only way to ensure the control of its meaning is to engage with those arguing the interpretation of the movement. As one African American female pointed out, social media is probably the best place to have these conversations, since if she had to face the people who were making these kinds of statements about African Americans, she would probably end up "hitting you."

Participants also indicated engaging in conversations to seek support from like-minded people. Finding affirmation for one's beliefs seems to be one of main reasons for engaging in online conversation:

> And it's nice to feel like other people hear you and can relate to you, it's nice to feel like that even though you're feeling some type of way about whatever is going on, you're not the only person that feels that way (African American female)

Respondents indicated they would often sit back and keep an eye on a specific hashtag to see what other people were saying, and if they saw people tweet ideas that they agreed with, they would join the conversation. The comfort that one experiences while interacting with people with similar ideas was seen as the most productive discussion environment as "you can be more open to new ideas or sharing" (African American female). While not all respondents agreed that consensus is important in instigating change, with some Latinx participants calling hashtags such as #HispanicGirlsUnited exclusive, they do recognize that:

> we need those groups, I'm just not part of . . . I don't like being part of those. But that statement, I think did more to give Hispanic girls confidence (Latina)

There is an understanding that an exclusive environment is important for building up marginalized groups, allowing them to create a sense of a collective identity through sharing (cf. F. Shaw, 2012).

Conversations about politics, specifically the election and the newly elected President Trump and his cabinet were commonplace, although respondents mainly talked to like-minded people:

> Lately a lot about the current president and his actions and policies. With President Trump trying to enforce this travel ban, a lot of my social friends have been chiming in on how wrong they think this ban is (African American male)

This raises the question whom people talk to on social media. One of the concerns raised by scholars is whether social media platforms encourage the cross-political dialogue that is necessary for a healthy democracy, or whether they create echo chambers, where people only engage with like-minded people. This question was addressed in chapter 6, where analysis of tweets show that people mainly engage with those who agree with their political opinions. What did social media users themselves have to say about that?

Conversation Partners

While most scholars acknowledge that social media mainly serve to keep people connected with their friends and family, some also express the belief (or hope) that people will connect with individuals outside their immediate social circle (e.g., Carlisle & Patton, 2013; Levenshus, 2010). The interaction between opposing points of view is a vital aspect of democracy (Dahlgren, 2005; Habermas, 1989; Mouffe, 1999), so knowing whom people talk to on social media is essential.

The "rules" that participants had for following or friending people provide good insight into the people with whom they are most likely to interact. A common thread here is the tendency to limit one's friends/followers to those already in their social circle. Additionally, respondents connected with people with whom they shared interests or hobbies, even if they had not met them in real life. Another factor that some participants consider is whether someone has interesting things to share, such as celebrities or successful entrepreneurs. There seems to be a clear expectation of reciprocity on Twitter, i.e., "If you follow me, then I may follow you" (African American male), and following decisions are guided by the likelihood of interaction. Even though scholars have long talked about the asymmetrical relationships that characterize Twitter, it appears that for these Twitter users, reciprocity is key.

Subsequently, many participants touched on how their social media audiences are made up of people like them, effectively turning their social media platforms into echo chambers, i.e., a space that "reinforces established perspectives and opinions" (Colleoni, et al., 2014, p. 317). As one African American male points out: "Your Twitter is a reflection of who you are around, in a sense."

While some respondents indicated that they used to follow people different from them, they also explained that this has changed since the 2016 election:

> Yes, I've been friends with a lot of the dumb people on my account because I thought being in the deep south, I thought I could use social media to promote facts on injustices and I realized that that doesn't matter. Because the people that I . . . they still voted who they voted for. Some people still didn't

> go out to vote. So it doesn't matter. Yeah, I saw a lot of that. I just unfriended . . . I unfollowed some that I just couldn't shake off of me, I love you so much I am just going to unfollow (Latina)

Recognizing the potential influence of social media and the subsequent importance of creating a platform that was more than just a reflection of her beliefs, this participant attempted to surround herself with people whose opinions diverged from hers. In fact, earlier in the focus group, this respondent mentioned how she tried to not participate in "exclusive groups" like #HispanicGirlsUnited and tried to follow as many different cultures as possible. However, the outcome of the 2016 presidential election led her to conclude that not only did her efforts not make a difference, she could no longer handle seeing updates from people on the other side of the political spectrum. Her decision to unfollow people is the equivalent of the silencing of conversations that Wells et al. (2017) observed in their survey of Wisconsin voters. When people become passionate, they talk more but are also less comfortable sharing their ideas with people who are likely to disagree. It appears that the 2016 election and all the events that surrounded it had a similar effect on participants in this study:

> In the past 8 years I have deleted friends that had differing views from myself. While I know this may be counterproductive, I've felt that I don't have share the same opinions with these people. These days when I posts political posts, I feel that people respond to me and agree (African American female)

While respondents used to have more of a heterogeneous following on social media, it appears that current political developments led them to create a more homophilic environment.

Many of the social media users who participated in this study appear to exist in a bubble where most conversations center on support. People are not looking to be persuaded; they are, in the words of an Asian American respondent, "looking for affirmation of what we believe in." As an African American female summarizes, "My Twitter is full of people like me, so there are no real disagreements."

At the same time, respondents appear to recognize the importance of having discussions with a diverse group of people:

> Even if I were to say that the majority of my followers are Black, we're a diverse people and we're open, we're not closed minded (African American female)

> A lot of my Hispanic friends, we're diverse (Latina)

Respondents thus argued that even though their following shared ethnic backgrounds, that did not mean that they did not differ in their social or political views. Statements such as these reflect the belief that conversations should expose people to different points of view.

Conversations: Rules and Expectations

What expectations or guidelines steer discussions toward or away from some of the topics mentioned above? Several themes, or "rules" were drawn from the data that provided insight into when people engage in conversation.

Again, like with their own status updates or tweets, participants wanted to be able to make sensible contributions to a conversation. They did not feel comfortable jumping into a discussion whose topic they could not relate to in some way. One African American respondent explained how she usually never participates in discussions on Twitter, except the one time that some of the people on her timeline were talking about light-skinned versus dark-skinned African American females, and she had to enter the conversation and add her opinion because "this is a topic that has hurt me personally." Being knowledgeable about a topic was also seen as a prerequisite to online conversations:

> I feel like people talk about trending topics to express their opinion but I don't feel like people actually do research about what is actually going on. People just jump in the conversation to state their viewpoint and that's about it (Latino)

The importance of being able to make a meaningful contribution appears to be one of the rules that participants adhere to in conversations.

Tied to this was the notion of only presenting arguments that one truly stands behind, i.e., being authentic and consistent. Respondents critiqued those people who would occasionally join a conversation using #BlackLivesMatter or other hashtags related to race and/or social justice (e.g., #HispanicGirlsUnited) but whose online behavior did not reflect a consistent focus on these kinds of issues:

> like we will protest for probably like two or three days and after that you don't hear about it no more. You know, somebody get killed and we will be outraged, and like a week or two later talking about something else, you know, you talking about Pokemon Go or something like that. We're not serious, and they're not going to take us serious if we don't show that we're serious (African American male)

Similarly, participants critiqued people for only paying online lip service to the goal of the movement, while their offline behavior did not reflect their online stance:

> On the internet, we're at home, we're Black Lives Matter all day. Behind that door on this computer, Black people this, Black people that, but we go out and we go around Black people and then we hate on each other and talk about each other and hurt each other, so . . . it's not strong enough (African American female)

Respondents also discussed the distinction between online and offline behavior as problematic, bringing up examples of people who make statements in discussions that they know they would never make in real life:

> I don't like arguing with people on social media because people have different agendas on social media, you can sit there and argue with someone all day. And that's not what they really thinking but on social media, they go about it a different way African American male)

The possibility of interacting with someone who wasn't really sincere in their claims was seen as a reason to not engage in discussions:

> I try not to (jump in on trending topics), because I know, psychologically, it's kind of like a group think kind of thing . . . I feel like people just kind of follow it because it's the most pertinent thing at the moment, but not necessarily an active reflection of what they believe in . . . it's the group think phenomenon, they're losing their individuality and they take on this group personality (Asian American female)

The need to be authentic and "real" appears to not only play a role in designing the image one presents to the online community (e.g., Rosenbaum, et al., 2013), but also a driving force in limiting interactions on social media. Interestingly, this issue is only raised in relation to discussions on race, politics, or social issues. People's authenticity is never brought up when participants talk about "fun" hashtags such as #UnansweredHipHopQuestions. It is possible that respondents feel more vulnerable or that they want to ensure that the other party is taking the conversation as seriously as they are and not just using them for entertainment. The belief that a conversation could possibly not engender any change in the participants appears to be a reason to not have the conversation at all.

Another expectation for interaction was that discussions on politics and race were only relevant if they were held among a diverse group of people whom one might impact with the discussion. When one's followers on social media are all of the same mind, participants indicated they did not think engaging in political discussion was worth it:

> We're all on the same page on my timeline so I don't feel the need to tweet, unless somebody says something off the wall (African American female)

When discussing hashtags such as #HispanicGirlsUnited, respondents questioned the usefulness of the conversations this sparked:

> You're preaching to the choir. They already know that not all Hispanic girls get pregnant. They already know that . . . I don't think white women in the deep south who think all Hispanics are illegal were listening to those comments (Latina)

Implicit in these statements is that conversations need to lead to more than a feeling of support if they are to be seen as useful. As one respondent pointed out, simply sharing emotions with like-minded people doesn't lead to any change, again underscoring the belief that discussions about social issues should somehow cause a change. There appears to be a desire to interact with their opponents, as suggested by Mouffe (1999) in her work on agonistic pluralism, even if this means having people make racist statements on one's timeline and then "attacking them" (African American female).

Good conversations should thus leave one or more parties more informed, more aware, and preferably with a changed mind. People indicate to enjoy constructive discussions between opposite sides (the Habermasian dialogic pluralism):

> I like discussions, "Oh, I see your viewpoint, but maybe I can give you another side of it, and then we can discuss and talk about it" (Asian American male)

Besides enjoying these discussions, participants also reported that these kinds of discussions can lead to change:

> If they (the tweets) reach certain people who will become aware, then the problem will be solved sooner (African American male)

> The fact that upper middle class deep Southern young adults are even starting to embrace the Black Lives Matter movement lets me know that people are learning. I think it may eventually change their minds but for now, it's changing attitudes we have towards things or people we don't like understand (African American female)

Respondents recognized that exposure to opposing points of view could only lead to a constructive conversation and/or a change in perspective if a person was open to change, or not yet fully convinced by any particular opinion:

> but something on the side that I'm a little neutral about and it's out there often enough I will read more about it and that's probably where persuasion could happen on social media. But for something you feel so strongly about, I don't think it's gonna help (Asian American female)

> People who don't really know, who are like in the middle (African American male on whose minds Twitter could change)

When engaging with people from the opposite end of the spectrum, participants pointed to the importance of respect in their interactions:

> Usually it's (*the responses the participant receives*) is very sensible. I guess when I do put it up, I'm very considerate, I just tell them my personal experience about it and it's not really a confrontation, an argument, I just give them my personal experience, and after that people just start discussing about it, like, oh yeah, you're right, and it mellows down a bit (Asian American male)

The respondents talked about what constitutes a constructive conversation at length, coming to the conclusion that many of the discussions that take place on social media platforms do not adhere to the two basic tenets of constructive dialogue: the ability to listen and respect the other side.

One of the tenets of constructive conversation was identified as the ability to listen. All of the respondents agreed that listening "for understanding," as one respondent put it, was essential to having a useful discussion:

> I don't know if they are useful because no one listens for understanding anymore. People listen to respond without any regard for the opposite side's view (African American female)

The participants seemed to agree with the user above. They described a social media environment where people seek out a position they can side with, and then stand by that side without any consideration for the arguments:

> When posting on Facebook, people miss out on subtleties, and they go from one extreme to another, and sometimes when you read it, it's like a shouting match . . . it's mostly you're wrong and I'm right, and people . . . they quickly form sides (Asian American female)

Subsequently, discussions have become about being heard over all the other voices on social media:

> I'm not trying to get you to agree with me I'm more so calling you out on your name and telling you why you don't matter (African American female)

Respondents described discussions on social media as "rapid fire" (Asian American male), where people merely use social media to get their own (strong) opinions out there, or to voice their disapproval of someone else's opinion. Participants described how they post things on social media just to indicate strong agreement or disagreement, without any intention to listen to different perspectives. Subsequently, conversations only serve to strengthen existing opinions:

> Most people have already made up their minds. Those who are hardcore believers don't change positions. Usually I see allies of the same cause walk away with better understanding of an issue (Biracial male)

One respondent mentioned how in discussions, people "stick to *their* facts" (African American female, italics mine), which is an especially interesting statement, since the increased polarization of society has led to a situation where people regard anything that does not support their point of view as "fake news" or "alternative facts":

> once you have that opinion instilled in you, you believe it, no matter what's going on, no matter what else you see, because that's what you've been taught, so that's all that you know, and so I really don't think that the conversations . . . I think the conversations keep people aware, but I don't think it's gonna change anything or anyone's mind (African American female)

The power of conversations then, does not lie in the ability to bring people closer together—the aim of the Habermasian dialogue. Instead, it appears that conversations on social media are more like the agonistic dialogue that Mouffe (1999) described, where people attack their opponents for their diverging views.

A second tenet of constructive conversation distilled from the various interviews and questionnaires is respect. As these respondents pointed out when asked if discussions could be useful:

> It is important to hear dissenting opinions. Though, sometimes they get out of hand with crude language (African American female)

> I think that it is useful if both people are willing to have an educational discussion and not name call or cross the line at all (Latina)

Respondents appear to share the view that conversations on social media can be useful and make a difference, but only if they are carried out in a respectful manner.

When discussing why so many of them do not engage in political conversations on social media, the vast majority of participants brought up the hostility and personal attacks that characterized many of the interactions on social media, indicating that they believe that conversations should be marked by mutual respect and civility. Many respondents lamented how disagreements between people quickly escalated into personal attacks, with users unfollowing each other and calling each other names. Subsequently, several respondents question if it is at all possible to have good conversation on social media:

> It could if done with the right tone, but I seem to only pick up on combative exchanges (African American male)

> Most people are not able to have a discussion without it ending in both of them getting mad at each other (Latina)

Others indicate that the hostility is why they avoid any and all conversations entirely:

> That's the thing. I have so much to say about it, but I just stay out of it because I can't fight with everybody on social media (African American female)

> There aren't enough people looking to learn from one another. I see too many mean-spirited attacks (African American male)

This hostility can be attributed to anonymity that social media affords its users. Participants bring up the fact that a lot of people approach dialogue on social media very differently from how they approach interactions in real life. Similarly, the fact that the conversation takes place across a technological platform could blind people to the humanity of the other users:

> People forget there is a person behind the comment, or when you're arguing with the other person, I don't think you notice that there's a person . . . so they say things that are kind of hurtful I think, the language they use and the way they demonize the other person's point of view. It can get pretty extreme (Asian American female)

When Mouffe (1999) described her views on contemporary political dialogue, she acknowledged the existence of a nonproductive form of interaction: antagonistic dialogue. This kind of interaction is marked by a refusal to acknowledge the other side as an equal partner who deserves respect, and a subsequent desire to annihilate the opposition through hateful dialogue (see also Bouvier, 2015). It appears that respondents see a great deal of this kind of dialogue on their social media and not only perceive it as detrimental to good conversations, but also are less likely to engage with others because of it.

But not all heated debate is bad. Besides arguing that antagonistic dialogue does not contribute to democracy, Mouffe also made the argument that the passionate, heated debate that characterized so much of today's political interaction is in fact necessary to maintain a healthy democracy. Even though respondents made it clear that in their eyes a lot of the conversations on social media violate unspoken rules about civility, they also discussed the potential of these, at times heated, interactions to change people's attitudes or opinions. Respondents recognized that even though people would often "tweet outlandish things every day and people would egg them on" (African American female), this could lead to a constructive conversation. Some participants gave examples of "going back and forth" (biracial male) with someone and, as a result of that debate, looking up new information, and changing their position, indicating that a heated debate is not always the unproductive violation of social rules discussed above.

In short, while the participants in this study do engage in conversations on social media and see these conversations as an effective way to engender change under certain conditions, they also claim to limit their participation due to the perceived or real violation of the rules they see as guiding these interactions. When it comes to using social media to engender change, the participants agreed that the most effective way to do this was by creating connections.

CREATING CONNECTIONS

The original social media platforms, Facebook and MySpace, were created for the sole purpose of connecting people. Today, the use of hashtags allows users to connect to people and information outside their own circle of followers. Connecting with people and ideas was identified as the third activity that people engage in on social media. Respondents indicated to see the ability to connect outside one's normal circle of friends as the single most empowering aspect of social media use.

Connecting People

When discussing the hashtags analyzed in previous chapters, it became clear that the ability of these hashtags to connect people who shared similar ideas but were otherwise perfect strangers was seen as one of the main ways to engender social change:

> And it (#BlackLivesMatter) connected different parts of different places where Black people reside. It connected us to different spots (African American male)

> It started a movement (African American male)

Even though participants themselves indicated they usually only followed like-minded people, they recognized that public platforms such as Twitter allow people to use hashtags to connect with people outside their own social circle, and created a space for different kinds of people to co-exist and connect. Respondents understood this connectivity was not limited to #BlackLivesMatter. In fact, when discussing the countermovement, #AllLivesMatter, participants were quick to point out that the only reason it gained traction was because of social media's ability to connect people through the hashtag. In line with Carney's (2016) findings, respondents viewed #AllLivesMatter as a method of undermining the power of the #BlackLivesMatter movement by drawing attention away from its cause and in a way, "taking away its thunder" (African American female):

> Even though the majority of white people do use #AllLivesMatter, I think it's just an attention stunt . . . I think they're not getting the attention that they're so used to having, and I feel like #AllLivesMAtter is a power thing, like they look at #BlackLivesMatter and how it gives us, you know, that strength and courage, and it gives us something to believe in so we feel like we have power, and then they have #AllLivesMatter and it's a reminder like, no, you don't have any power (African American female)

While participants discussed the power of Twitter and, to a lesser extent, Facebook, to create a grassroots movement made up of people from diverse communities with shared beliefs, they also realized that politicians could use this same power to their advantage:

> They've always been there, I don't think they've changed their mind, they're just, oooh! He (Trump) found them, it was like, let me find all the supporters, and he found them through social media, . . . they all came out and that's how he found them and united them and, voila (Latina)

Interestingly, while #BlackLivesMatter was generally discussed in a positive light—uniting people, spreading awareness, and building a platform for physical demonstrations—some respondents were not as optimistic about other race-based hashtags:

> I think those types of things only cause more of a divide because it creates an us and them. I think they are counterproductive. I have not seen many people in those discussions reach out and create bridges (Latina—discussing #NotMiAbuela and #HispanicGirlsUnited)

While this respondent recognized that hashtags like #NotMiAbuela can connect like-minded people, she also pointed out that these were exclusive and focused on creating parallel but nonintersecting narratives.

Connecting Ideas

A second dimension of connections that respondents touched on was the ability to be made aware of ideas and information that one would not have run across without social media. Many participants used social media to stay informed on what was going on outside of their own social circle:

> I use it to read the news, observe trends, to see what I'm missing out, what social movements I'm not aware outside of my small inner circle (Asian American female)

Social media are generally seen as a good source of information about the world:

> But that is really the power of Twitter, of social media, it really changes your perception of things. Because first of all, without Twitter I would not have probably known about that movie (*Get Out*), half the things about the election (African American male)

Some respondents indicated a belief that social media offer a viable alternative to the information provided by the mainstream media:

> The mainstream news are always showing only events that are in favor to the dominant society (Latina)

In addition, respondents talk about seeing posts and hashtags that didn't make sense to them and then researching what was going on to better understand their social media timeline:

> Like when I first saw the hashtag, I was like what? I was like grab her what?! What is wrong with you guys? And then I click on it and I was like, y'all telling me this is the person we want to be our next president (African American female speaking on #PussyGrabsBack)

This belief is reflected in the discussion surrounding #BlackLivesMatter as well. Participants acknowledged that social media have really helped to spread awareness of ongoing police brutality against African Americans. Even though recording police brutality was seen as nothing new (some brought up Rodney King as an example of how recordings of police violence have been around much longer than social media), respondents agreed that, thanks to social media, news about police brutality could be spread a lot more quickly and among a much wider population. This in turn has made minority populations aware that the world painted in the mainstream media is perhaps not very realistic:

> Twitter helps spread the message that the world isn't as great as we have been told, we're not as free as we thought (African American female)

Participants also indicated to actively use social media to find out different opinions and challenge their own world views. When touching on the idea of connecting people to new information and ideas, respondents always returned to the belief that exposure to different ideas is an important first step in one's ability to grow, learn, and eventually change:

> Being able to engage or read differing opinions is important so that you can grow intellectually. Also, it teaches people empathy to learn through someone else's perspective (Asian American female)

Somehow, social media use, and specifically the engagement with information outside of one's own perspective, was commonly viewed through the lens of how it could bring about change and close the gap between people with divergent political views. Respondents discuss sharing stories and ideas with the belief that they could change people's minds:

> Many of my friends actually just work in corporate . . . it's a totally different world, and . . . I'm more like a blue collar worker, . . . and so my stories are new to a lot of people. Most people . . . will say I have never seen this side before. I work behind the scenes, and most people can only see what's in front of them, and I give them the backstory of it, and they listen about it, and they are usually pretty shocked by it, oh wow, we never thought about it that way (Asian American male)

This particular respondent talked about sharing his experience in working with legal immigrants with an eye to changing the minds of his followers about immigration policies. Participants argued that exposure to new information could "light a flame" (African American male), i.e., spark interest in a topic, and eventually, change someone's mind.

CONCLUSION

This study presented findings from focus groups, personal interviews, and online questionnaires with African American, Asian American, and Latinx social media users. A qualitative, explorative analysis provided insight into how the participants use this platform to connect and interact with others to collaboratively construct meaning.

Results showed that participants use social media in general to be heard, engage in conversations, and connect with new people and information. People use social media to create a positive sense of self, to inspire others, and to vent; and while some use these platforms for political expressions, the results show that participants only engaged in such expressions if the topic was particularly salient to them. Respondents were hesitant to speak out on controversial issues because it clashed with their view of social media as places to have fun, because of a desire to fit in with their online community and not alienate any followers, because they are not certain they can make a sensible contribution, and to avoid any form of drama.

When looking at the kinds of conversations taking place on Twitter, it is clear that the entertainment aspect of Twitter dominates most conversations. Some indicated to participate in social or political discussions when an issue was particularly pertinent or personally relevant. Conversations also centered on seeking (and finding) affirmation and support. Respondents reported to mainly talk to people who were like them and that if they had in the past tried to create a more diverse community of followers, they had given up on this after the 2016 election. When looking at the expectations that guided (and in some cases limited) conversations, it became apparent that participants only engage in conversations if they felt they could relate to the topic at hand and were able to make a meaningful contribution. In addition, respect and listening ranked very high as a prerequisite for any conversation; many respondents indicate they did not participate in interactions on social media because of the high degree of hostility in such conversations. Interestingly, respondents also indicated they saw no point in sharing their opinions if their audience was going to agree with them. They preferred talking with people who had different opinions. In spite of respondents' recognition that most conversations on social media were agonistic at best and antagonistic at worst, they indicated that discussions on these platforms could change people's minds about issues if these people were open to change.

Finally, it appears that participants attached the most value to social media's ability to connect users with people and ideas that they might have otherwise not run across. Respondents discuss how social media inform them about current events they otherwise would not have heard about and how they enjoy engaging in conversations with people they would not encounter in their daily lives through the use of shared hashtags. Although the participants choose to follow people with whom they share (some) similarities, thanks to Twitter's public nature and technological affordances such as the hashtag and the retweet, people are still able to search for expressions by and conversations among diverse groups of people and join in. In other words, while people may prefer to see updates from people like them and adjust their social media following accordingly, they also believe in reaching outside that circle and exposing themselves to other people and ideas.

Conclusion

The stories told through Twitter provide a rich tapestry of meanings that reflect every imaginable perspective on race and gender in American culture. People use Twitter to share, lament, celebrate, reject, and mock the mainstream understandings on race and gender, demonstrating how Twitter serves as a space to negotiate existing cultures. Their use of Twitter to connect and interact reveals the extent and limitations of the platform's potential for inclusive participation and deliberation.

In the introduction, I asked how the meanings created by Twitter users reflect or counter mainstream cultural interpretations, what this reveals about the potential of Twitter to serve a virtual public sphere, and the nature of the digital culture produced by the interactions in that sphere. The interpretive content analysis of tweets and interviews with Twitter users presented in the past seven chapters have provided insight into how people use Twitter to (re)negotiate cultural beliefs and the kinds of dialogue that are involved in this construction of meaning. This chapter will reflect on the findings and discuss what they imply about Twitter as a virtual public sphere and a site for the construction of digital cultures.

CONSTRUCTING GENDER AND RACE ON TWITTER

In the past seven chapters, I have provided a qualitative exploration of howlTwitter users (re)negotiate cultural understandings of race and gender. The analysis looked at specific arenas of discussion often seen on Twitter, from entertainment and popular culture, to politics, social justice issues, and advertising. In addition, I examined how social media users from an ethnic minority background made sense of their use of the various social networking platforms.

Reconstructing Gender and Race in Entertainment

The first section addressed how people used Twitter to construct their understanding of race and gender when discussing popular culture, i.e., when responding to trending hashtags and television shows that centered on African Americans, Asian Americans, and Latinx.

When examining the discourses that are produced on Twitter, it appears that the stereotypes surrounding women are contested most frequently. African American and Latinx female Twitter users, for instance, have embraced the anger and temper that is part of the stereotypes surrounding them as a source of pride instead of a negative characteristic. Women across the three ethnic groups reject the idea of being submissive and uneducated and take to Twitter to express their resistance to the physical standards society has placed on them. At the same time, however, Twitter users comfortably reproduce the notion of the tough, strong woman, whether she is the African American strict mother or the Asian American tiger mom. While this is a reproduction of an existing stereotype, it fits with the earlier rejection of women as submissive and the acceptance of the angry, hot-tempered trope. In addition, the notion that women are expected to sacrifice everything for their family also goes uncontested, with only Latinx daughters questioning their place in the family.

Men's stereotypes appear to be contested less frequently. Twitter users embrace the mainstream media's portrayal of African American and Latinx men as tough and violent, yet with respect for their elders, and have no issues with the representation of Asian American men as effeminate and geeky. But there are limitations to the acceptance of these stereotypes, often caused by intertextual references the users themselves pick up on, or the actor's sexuality. Findings reveal that typecasting is an important factor in whether or not a character's stereotypical portrayal is accepted. In addition, while viewers have no qualms accepting homosexual characters, their behavior is expected to follow certain patterns. In addition, the fact that many Twitter users take to the platform to express their view of these men as "eye candy," subjecting these men to a female gaze, shows that viewers can use Twitter to undermine dominant discourses surrounding male sexuality.

A final theme that came out of the analysis was the use of Twitter to debate what success meant to different ethnic minority groups. While all three chapters showed that people celebrated the success of ethnic minority groups, tweets showed a negotiation of dominant tropes surrounding success. Some of the stereotypical ideas were rejected (e.g., the notion that all Asian Americans are good at math), while others (success takes sacrifice from the family, the Asian American as a model minority, African Americans always come up from the bottom) were reproduced and remained unchallenged. In short, Twitter users appropriate and modify the meaning of selected mediated cultural expressions, creating an understanding of the world around them that is in part oppositional, in part accepting, and above all, helps the user better make sense of their reality (cf. Deuze, 2006).

The analysis for these three chapters clearly points to the role Twitter plays in providing a space for marginalized groups to form networked counterpublics. Twitter affords them the ability to connect and create their own narratives in response, or as a counterpoint, to mainstream understandings (cf. Fraser, 1992; Papacharissi, 2002). These counterpublics allowed users to share and collaborate with others on how they view their racial identity. Analysis revealed that users' collaboration resulted in a clear rejection of society's tendency to construct narratives about ethnic heritage and subsequent belonging based on looks. In addition, Latinx and Asian American users turned to Twitter to share their frustration of being labeled perpetual foreigners by mainstream society and collaborated to create a counternarrative of belonging.

When looking at the digital culture produced by people's use of Twitter, it appears that the interpretations created hinge to some degree on the semiotic space offered by the hashtag. Findings showed that hashtags provided a semiotic frame for the tweets that used it, shaping the expressions produced in that thread. A hashtag such as #BeingABlackGirlIsLit, for instance, was more likely to lead to empowering interpretations that reject stereotypical views than #GrowingUpHispanic, which centered on providing entertainment by tweeting experiences that others were likely to recognize and find funny. Similarly, #BeingAsian led to a more stereotypical interpretation of the Asian American identity than #NotYourAsianTigerMom. Interestingly, this finding did not carry over in the media texts individuals discussed on Twitter. The semiotic space provided by media texts (e.g., over-the-top costume design or outlandish accents) was not always used by viewers to create alternative interpretations, who would still reproduce the dominant stereotypes associated with the characters under discussion.

Above everything else, these three chapters revealed the importance of Twitter in creating a space for people to participate in the creation of personalized meanings and connect over issues related to ethnic minorities. The social media platform affords its users the space to construct individualized understandings that reflect the remediation and bricolage central to digital cultures (cf. Deuze, 2006). In addition, Twitter creates a networked public where users can share frustration and inside jokes, tease out their own racial identity, and seek support for the issues they face.

Twitter, Politics, and Social Justice

The two chapters in this section examined how people used Twitter to broadcast and interact about politics and social justice, allowing a direct look into if and how Twitter functions as a virtual public sphere. These two chapters took a close look at the values and dialogue that underpinned different virtual movements and political campaigns geared toward race and gender.

One of the more interesting findings from this section is that people appear to take to Twitter when they feel marginalized by the mainstream media. Twitter users from a variety of political and social backgrounds express the idea that their voices are ignored in society at large, and Twitter is a platform that allows them to be heard. This points to the importance people attach to having a presence in public space. It also underlines the value that people see in gaining visibility on Twitter; somehow gaining a voice on Twitter can make up for not being heard elsewhere in mainstream society. People's tendency to take to Twitter when marginalized shows that Twitter is perceived as a suitable space for the formation of networked counterpublics and influencing public consciousness. This could be attributed to the public nature of the medium, affording people a global reach and possible influence, or users' ability to find like-minded individuals who can provide the affirmation the users cannot find elsewhere.

The same technological affordances that give marginalized groups the opportunity to unite and broadcast their ideas are available to all other groups as well, providing a voice to both marginalized groups and those groups who support dominant discourses. As demonstrated in chapter 5, this means that for almost every single one of the virtual movements analyzed in this chapter (e.g., #MasculinitySoFragile, #BlackLivesMatter) there is a countermovement that protests everything the original movements stands for (e.g., #FemininitySoFragile, #AllLivesMatter). Twitter has effectively created a public online space that allows for the existence of multiple, parallel networked (counter)publics (Papacharissi, 2002).

A closer examination of the tweets associated with the different campaigns and movements revealed that proponents held diametrically opposed views of the problems facing the nation, further providing evidence for the idea of parallel (counter)publics. People in support of social justice movements like #YesAllWoman and #SayHerName believe that racial and gender inequality lie at the root of many of the problems facing society. Countermovements created in response to these virtual movements, however, propagate beliefs that are firmly rooted in a post-feminist and post-racial discourse. They view any claims of inequality or discrimination as an attack on basic American values such as liberty and equality. This focus on Americanism is also reflected in tweets that supported the Trump campaign, while tweets from Clinton supporters shifted from a belief in gender equality and empowerment preelection to a concern for the future of the country and its values postelection. The values and beliefs upheld by the various movements and campaigns are vastly different, indicating that people on different sides of the aisle rely on different discourses to understand the problems facing society, creating completely separate spheres of discussion and understanding.

This is reflected in the interactions analyzed for these chapters as well. Analysis showed that users mainly take to Twitter to augment their bonding social capital. They reach out to like-minded people and create networked publics, i.e., communities of people like them. Cross-ideological dialogue does, however, take place. When users interact with the "other," they usually do so by hijacking the opposite side's hashtag and making inflammatory statements aimed at alienating the opponent. This kind of dialogue is a far cry from the deliberative interaction that Habermas had in mind when he coined the public sphere. However, not all of the dialogue results in the antagonistic dialogue, or mud-slinging described by some scholars. Some of it also resembled Mouffe's (1999) agonistic dialogue. This kind of dialogue, whereby opponents engage in heated interactions aimed at proving a point rather than seeking a compromise, does not fit in with the ideal of the public sphere. It does, however, fit Mouffe's agonistic pluralism, whereby interactions are characterized by passion and conflict, and which she views as the essence of democracy, which requires the "vibrant clash of democratic political positions" (Mouffe, 2000, p. 16, 1999; Papacharissi, 2009).

Who Tells the Story: Analyzing Twitter Users

The final section in the book explored how Twitter is used. Chapter 7 examined how Twitter users interact with corporate narratives created as part of marketing campaigns, while chapter 8 investigated how African Americans, Asian Americans, and Latinx use Twitter to express themselves and connect and interact with others to create cultural understandings.

When examining how Twitter users made sense of Dove's #Choose Beautiful, L'Oréal's #WorthSaying, Starbucks' #RaceTogether, Airbnb's #WeAccept, and 84 Lumber's "The Journey," it became apparent that consumers easily reproduced the narratives that fit a postfeminist ideology, using them as part of their online identity performance. Race-related campaigns met with a more mixed response. The #RaceTogether campaign encountered mostly resistance, as documented in similar work on the campaign (Logan, 2016). The findings presented in this chapter showed that this resistance was the result of either a color-blind ideology that denied the existence of racial issues or the belief that the campaign itself embodies the post-racial discourse that fails to acknowledge institutional racism. This same ideology returned in people's responses to "The Journey" and #WeAccept, with supporters accepting the narrative using a mainly Americanist ideology and opponents rejecting the narratives based on the same color-blind ideology mentioned above as well as a law-and-order frame. The analysis showed that Twitter users, even when resisting mainstream narratives, rely on interpretations from the mainstream culture, and only rarely use Twitter to express ideas and values outside the hegemonic mainstream. An exception to this was the immigrant experience frame used in interpreting "The Journey," a discourse usually not acknowledged in mainstream culture unless accompanied by an Americanist perspective. Like in the previous section, little evidence was found for cross-political dialogue, with most Twitter users merely engaging with like-minded people to strengthen their bonds.

The final chapter addressed how African Americans, Asian Americans, and Latinx view their usage of social media platforms in general and Twitter in particular. Findings indicated that users balanced the belief that social media's value lies in its ability to expose and connect them to different ideas and people with the reality that most of them associate with people like them. Social media users indicated to rely on social media to just have fun, not make any statements that would upset their friends/followers, or make them sound uneducated. Speaking out on political issues was especially common if the issue was particularly salient and the participant felt well-informed. In addition, interactions were limited by the fact that respondents indicated that while respect and listening were paramount to having a successful conversation, many of them were characterized by hostility. In spite of this, respondents agreed that discussions on these platforms could, under the right circumstances, engender individual and social change. Furthermore, Twitter's public nature meant that while users may prefer to be surrounded by people like them, choosing only to follow like-minded users, they could easily, through the use of hashtags and retweets, find and connect with those not in their social circle. Social media use could expose people to new information or connect them to people outside their own circle. In short, while participants were more likely to interact with like-minded users, the technological affordances of Twitter allow individuals to expose themselves to people and ideas outside of their comfort zone.

TWITTER, THE PUBLIC SPHERE, AND DIGITAL CULTURE

Findings point to the complexity of drawing a single conclusion about the role that Twitter plays in facilitating a virtual public sphere and allowing for the creation of an inclusive, counterhegemonic digital culture. In the remainder of this chapter I address four main points that arose from the analysis. These include the kinds of voices involved in the construction of meaning on Twitter, the nature of the narratives created by Twitter users, the use of Twitter for the creation of networked (counter)publics, and the kind of dialogue observed on the platform.

Voices on Twitter

One of the questions addressed in this book centers on who participates on Twitter and which voices are heard. While the techno-optimists discussed in the introduction argue that Twitter's democratizing potential can be attributed to the inclusion of a more diverse group of platform users, critics posit that the effects of the digital divide as well as the dominance of for-profit corporations reduces the voices actively heard on social media to the same middle class and corporations that dominate the mainstream media.

The research presented in this book showed that participation on Twitter appears to be extremely diverse, allowing for a variety of voices to contribute to the ideas circulating on the platform. Findings show that, contrary to mainstream media, Twitter is inclusive and participatory, affording anyone who wishes to speak out the opportunity to contribute to the ideas that flow across and out of the platform. The participation of such a varied group of people means that Twitter conversations produce a rich collection of ideas and beliefs that are not necessarily represented in mainstream culture.

The creation of a shared culture, even among participants with the same values and beliefs, is often a contested process (e.g., Reed, 2014). The findings from the present research shows how Twitter renders this process more open and inclusive, granting space to voices that varied both in terms of geographical origin as well as cultural beliefs. Analysis showed how Twitter can connect people across geographical boundaries, with ideas coming in from every imaginable corner of the country. The analysis of tweets demonstrated how users share a wide variety of experiences to create a shared culture (e.g., auditioning in New York and being bullied by a PE teacher in #MyYellowFaceStory). Interviews with Twitter users revealed how this broader inclusion was seen as one of the most valuable affordances of social media, as many indicated to learn the most from those outside of their social circle. While inclusion does not equate attention or prominence, as it is very much possible to sideline or ignore users, Twitter's public nature means that the outright exclusion of voices from a conversation is next to impossible. As a result, discussions about cultural identities and meanings on Twitter are more inclusive but also more contested. Take the hashtag #BeingABlackGirl IsLit as an example. It was specifically meant for African American women to celebrate their identities, yet it also revealed the struggle over some of the dimensions of the Black female cultural identity. One example was the notion of the strong African American woman, with some Twitter users embracing this trope and others rejecting it because it did not allow them to show their vulnerabilities. Twitter rendered this struggle public, as it did with the struggle over the identity of Asian Americans as captured by the #BeingAsian hashtag.

Twitter's public nature does open hashtags and the cultures associated with them up to comments and critique from outsiders. This was witnessed through the hijacking of hashtags to contest the meanings propagated by the hashtag, individual Twitter exchanges between supporters and detractors, and the creation of counter-hashtags (e.g., #NotAll Men and #AllLivesMatter). Hashtags like these or tweets that contest a hashtag could be said to detract from the hashtag's original message, and take away from the group's ability to safely form counterhegemonic discourses (e.g. F. Shaw, 2012). While these are valid concerns, the research shows (as I will discuss in more detail below), that in spite of these detractors, people are still able to use Twitter to form counternarratives. The argument could be made that these kinds of interjections contribute to a more diverse and democratic exchange of ideas, and that the engagement with "the other" leads to the formation of a stronger group identity. Ultimately then, the cultural beliefs to come out of Twitter discussions reflect ideas from a wider group of people than was possible with more exclusive pre-Web 2.0 activist and consciousness-raising groups.

The fierce debate that ensued about certain topics and within specific hashtags revealed the importance that Twitter users attach to their voices being heard and the ability to contribute to the perceived consensus to come out of Twitter discussions. Twitter users appear to share the perception that the consensus created on Twitter is an important indicator of the cultural values that dominate a society. While this is merely a belief seemingly held by the active users, as participation on Twitter is not universal within societies, this does in part explain why some ideas (e.g., #BlackLivesMatter, #RaceTogether) are so contested. Another possible explanation could be the sense of ownership expressed by the users interviewed in chapter 8, who often talked about "my Twitter." Twitter is seen as a personalized, safe space, where users feel their ideas and beliefs should be heard and recognized by others, especially if these run counter to the ideas presented in the mainstream media. This makes sense when one considers that the default subject position in mainstream culture is that of a white, straight, middle-class male (cf. Reed, 2014). Twitter is one of the online cultural spaces that, because of the absence of an owner-driven narrative, allows for the presence and creation of alternative subject positions which can then inform its digital culture. Inclusion in Twitter's digital cultures is paramount for groups whose subject position is not naturally recognized by mainstream culture.

The major culture industries also appear to recognize the power of being heard on Twitter, as evidenced by their attempts to be one of the voices on Twitter. Consumer engagement with a brand is an essential element of a company's success; therefore, corporations will use social media marketing campaigns, and television companies will rely on actors live-tweeting to gain a voice and hopefully become a part of the creation of Twitter's digital culture. In this sense, the concern voiced by some, that the Internet in general, and Twitter in particular, are susceptive to commercial interests, are not unfounded (cf. Creeber & Martin, 2014; Jenkins, 2006; Papacharissi, 2010; Reed, 2014).

The visibility that one can gain on Twitter does not end with this platform alone. Many of the case studies presented in this book gained such a following they drew the attention of the mainstream media, Dahlgren's "second tier" of the public sphere (2013). The kind of media coverage given to these Twitter-driven movements (e.g., #OscarsSoWhite) generally consists of sharing a selection of tweets accompanied by an editorial viewpoint and a summary of the dominant sentiment. While the decision to rely on Twitter as a source of news is often the result of the ease and efficiency with which information and audience feedback can be obtained (e.g., Broersma & Graham, 2012), the fact that the tweets, and voices implicit in them, are broadcast without editing means the mainstream media further legitimize the importance of being heard on Twitter

Twitter provides users with a space where they can be heard and participate in the negotiation of cultural meanings. The analyses presented in this book showed that Twitter allows for the inclusion of a wide variety of voices, but that the space is also utilized by commercial interests to gain a following. This leads to a richer, more contested, but also somewhat commodified debate about cultural identities and meanings.

The Nature of the Narratives

Twitter has commonly been heralded as a space for marginalized groups to create and present narratives that run counter to the hegemonic ideas presented in the mainstream media (e.g., Bonilla & Rosa, 2015). Earlier work on Twitter and the creation of counternarratives found that while

Twitter provided marginalized groups with a space to construct meanings that ran counter to dominant interpretations of events and issues, the platform was also often used to reproduce hegemonic narratives (e.g., Carney, 2016; Chaudhry, 2016; Cisneros & Nakayam, 2015; Jackson & Foucault Welles, 2015; Maragh, 2016). The research presented in the previous chapters echoes these findings, with tweets both resisting and subscribing to dominant narratives about race and gender.

On the one hand, hashtags that were created specifically to resist dominant interpretations of specific groups or events (e.g., #OscarsSo White, #BlackPowerIsForBlackMen, #BlackLivesMatter, #Resist) created counterhegemonic narratives. Trending topics such as these addressed racial and gender inequality, countered the post-racial and postfeminist discourse that informs American culture, and demanded acceptance from mainstream society. Many of the responses to popular cultural expressions, such as some of the television shows analyzed in the first section of the book, resisted dominant cultural understandings as well.

This does not mean, however, that these counterhegemonic narratives function completely outside of dominant cultural norms and values. In many cases, oppositional narratives use concepts from the dominant culture as stepping stones or starting points for contestation. As a result, the narratives created on Twitter show a genuine negotiation with the mainstream culture, whereby ideas from this culture are altered to better reflect users' cultural position. This is evidenced in hashtags like #SayHerName, #MyYellowFaceStory, and #NotMiAbuela where people, whose stories are usually excluded from the mainstream media, use Twitter to negotiate a narrative that accommodates their cultural position while simultaneously acknowledging the dominant narrative.

On the other hand, the research presented in the previous chapters also found that many Twitter users recreated hegemonic narratives. Hashtags such as #AllLivesMatter, #BackTheBlue, and #FemininitySoFragile are but a few examples of the trending topics that resisted the subversive narratives created on Twitter. In addition, findings showed that the hegemonic narratives reflected in the mainstream media still have a large impact on the meanings that Twitter users produce. This is not unexpected, as not all Twitter users belong to a marginalized group and thus may not feel the need to resist dominant narratives. I will discss this in more detail in the next section.

What was interesting, however, was that the reproduction of dominant narratives also occurred when members of marginalized groups could be expected to be among the participants in the Twitter conversation. When analyzing the responses to shows like *Fresh Off the Boat, Empire,* and *Devious Maids,* or marketing campaigns like the ones organized by Dove, the narratives created on Twitter revealed at least a partial acceptance of dominant norms and values. Twitter users reproduced dominant cultural understandings as well as stereotypes without much resistance, even when one can assume that at least some of them belonged to the groups harmed by these stereotypes. Even hashtags that were created to empower or at least provide entertainment for ethnic minority groups often reproduced the dominant narratives about these groups (e.g., #Thanks givingWithBlackFamilies, #GrowingUpHispanic). It appears that while Twitter may provide the space for the creation of counternarratives and is, at times, used to do so, the dominance of mainstream interpretations in people's sense-making is not erased by the technological affordances offered by the platform. At the end of the day, individual users create the meanings that circulate on Twitter, and these users are still a part of the dominant culture, even if that culture subordinates them.

Culture industries clearly still play a central role in the construction of meaning on Twitter as well (cf. Reed, 2014). While Twitter increases people's ability to participate in the process of meaning making, this is no reason to discard the "models of media power" (Hills, 2009, p. 114), as analyses reveal that many people still accept dominant discourses at face value. The extent to which people contest the offered narratives appears to hinge on how much semiotic excess (Fiske, 1987; Jasinksi, 2001) is offered by a television storyline or a hashtag. Some hashtags like #MyYellowFaceStory offer Twitter users a considerable amount of room to create their own narratives, as does a humorous storyline on someone's Colombian accent, or an open advertisement like 84 Lumber's "The Journey." Analysis shows that when offered the space, people can, and some do, take it to construct their own, often counterhegemonic, narratives. However, when presented with a narrative that makes sense and provides the most enjoyment when accepted as is (e.g., Luscious in *Empire* as the "Black Brute") people are not very likely to take to Twitter to contest it, even if this narrative contains stereotypical views. Commercial interests thus are able to influence the narratives created by Twitter users.

The only times when Twitter users appear to reject closed and enjoyable hegemonic narratives is when they clash with beliefs that are highly salient. As indicated by the interviews discussed in chapter 8, many social media users are reluctant to speak up on issues they deem controversial unless they are personally relevant. The content analysis revealed the same pattern, with people only contesting hegemonic narratives if they touched on a personal issue. An excellent example of this is the #NotMiAbuela hashtag created in response to the Clinton advertisement. As evidenced by the analysis, the sacrificial role played by mothers in Latinx families is deemed a pivotal part of the culture. The attempt by a white politician to reappropriate that trope for her own gain is seen as not only unacceptable but an affront to something both important and personal. The same applies to discussions among African American and Asian American women about unrealistic beauty standards. They challenge these on Twitter because they view this as a highly personal topic. When they do, Twitter allows for the magnification of their ideas, permitting a single person's resistance to be picked up by others and become a shared narrative.

Twitter as a Networked (Counter)Public

The research presented in this book also confirms Twitter functioning as a networked (counter)public. Numerous investigations have pointed at how marginalized groups use Twitter and other social media platforms to deliberate and create oppositional interpretations, i.e., as networked counterpublics (e.g., Bonilla & Rosa, 2015; Carney, 2016; Jackson & Foucault Welles, 2015; Guo & Harlow, 2014; Harris, 2008; Keller, 2012). The analyses presented in the previous chapters clearly back up these claims. Many of the cases examined included members of ethnic minorities or otherwise marginalized groups using Twitter to share experiences (e.g., #ThanksgivingWithBlackFamilies, #HispanicGirlsUnited, #YesAllWomen), connect with others, empower each other, magnify their voices, and, at times, use the platform to rail against the mainstream representation of their group. In the case of the latter, Twitter functions as a subaltern counterpublic, wherein members of these marginalized groups create counternarratives in an attempt to better define themselves and their culture (cf. Fraser, 1992).

Twitter bestows an unprecedented visibility on these networked counterpublics. In the past, counterpublics were created away from the public eye and only made it into public spaces whenever the members were ready to take their ideas into the mainstream. But if the hashtag utilized by a networked counterpublic gains enough tweets, it will make it into the top trending lists, gaining visibility, power, and the attention from detractors. As evidenced by the many countermovements created in response to hashtags that support networked counterpublics (e.g., #AllLivesMatter, #FemininitySoFragile) detractors are concerned about the potential of Twitter to magnify these oppositional voices and bring them to public attention. Twitter thus functions both as a site for rival counterpublics to battle over competing interests and as a platform where supporters and opponents of dominant ideas struggle over the construction of meaning.

In addition to confirming existing research on Twitter as networked counterpublics, the research presented in this book also showed that the perception of marginalization, not the actual marginalization itself, prompts people to take to Twitter in search of a community of like-minded people. This became apparent when analyzing the tweets generated by Trump supporters. While research (discussed in chapter 6) showed that both 2016 presidential candidates received an almost equal amount of negative press coverage prior to the election, only tweets by Trump supporters showed a feeling of exclusion from the mainstream public sphere. This reflects the tenor of the Trump campaign, which capitalized on the feelings of economic stagnation and exclusion from the American dream shared by many working-class white Americans (Garriott, 2017). While Trump voters may not have been any more marginalized than Clinton supporters, they, due to a combination of factors, including their own perceived lack of socioeconomic mobility, the campaign's focus on their status as outsiders to American society, and the media's negative coverage of their candidate, constructed themselves as a subordinate group ignored and misrepresented by the dominant culture. Hashtags like #WomenWhoVoteTrump and other pro-Trump hashtags (analyzed in chapter 6) reflected this sentiment. They produced tweets that showed a sense of exclusion from the mainstream discourse as reflected in the media, with some signaling that their participation on Twitter was the direct result of that feeling of marginalization. Twitter users who participated in these hashtags indicated taking to Twitter to find and unite with like-minded people, i.e., to form a networked subaltern counterpublic.

This raises questions about our understanding of networked counterpublics as well as the public sphere against which they are juxtaposed. Counterpublics, according to Fraser (1992), are created to give a space and a voice to people who have neither in any other public space and who are denied the privileges associated with access to the public sphere. The purpose of counterpublics is to offset the advantages experienced by those who do have access to the mainstream public sphere. While the Trump supporters who used Twitter to express their dissatisfaction may have felt marginalized, whether they truly were, is questionable. Trump supporters are less likely to have completed a college education than people who supported Clinton (Tyson & Maniam, 2016) and more likely to belong to the working or middle class (Kotkin, 2016), but these are not specifically markers of marginalization. Literally adhering to Fraser's definition would mean rejecting these tweets as part of a counterpublic and placing them within the mainstream public sphere. Yet the language utilized by these people indicated a belief that their voices were unrecognized and rejected by that same public sphere and that Twitter was one of the few places where they were heard. This raises the question about what counts more when labeling something a networked counterpublic or just a networked public: How much the specific group is technically marginalized, or how much they feel marginalized?

The fact that this question has even come up underscores the fragmented nature of the mainstream media that make up today's public sphere. The days when everyone obtained their news from the same networks and/or major newspapers are long gone (e.g., Mitchell, Gottfried, Barthel, & Shearer, 2016). Not only that, but as discussed in chapter 6, people with different political preferences obtain their news from different sources (e.g., Mitchell, et al., 2014). Different news outlets can paint vastly different pictures of the state of the world, creating different conceptions about how much any one particular group is heard or ignored, which discourses dominate the public sphere, and which are considered outsiders. Subsequently, groups can be made to feel marginalized depending on their choice of news source. The finding that these groups view Twitter as a viable space to express their unhappiness at this marginalization, connect with others in similar positions, and influence public opinion underscores the value of Twitter as a space to counter the ideas circulating in the mainstream public sphere.

While Twitter is a suitable space for the creation of networked counterpublics, the previous chapters show it is important to not underestimate the pushback these counterpublics receive from hegemonic publics. These publics use the same technological affordances to create a countermovement and draw attention to their ideals. Twitter is not just a counterpublic, then, it is best described as a space that is filled with parallel and opposing networked publics, each vying for attention and aiming for their ideas to make it into the public eye. Furthermore, the creation of multiple, intersecting, and at times conflicting networked (counter)publics on Twitter underscores the idea of the virtual public sphere consisting of "culturally fragmented cyberspheres" (Papacharissi, 2002, p. 23). The existence of parallel publics in the same space alone, however, is not enough to argue that Twitter could function as a virtual public sphere. This hinges on the actual participation and interaction between the different publics, i.e., the dialogue (cf. Papacharissi, 2010).

Dialogue on Twitter

Twitter is mainly used as a broadcasting platform, i.e., a space people use to express themselves and share beliefs and experiences important to them. Research presented in this book shows that when Twitter users interact with others, it is often with people like them. These kinds of interactions serve to augment social bonding capital and have been seen as important to building understanding, group identity, and creating social movements. However, many scholars discussed elsewhere in this book have touched on the importance of conversations between diverse groups of people, i.e., people who many not be on the same side of the aisle (e.g., Conroy, et al., 2012). Does the existence of multiple, parallel networked (counter)publics mean that the techno-optimists were wrong and Twitter is unable to create a single, unified, inclusive public sphere (e.g., Kellner, 2000; Papacharissi, 2002)? More than likely, the answer here is no. As discussed in chapter 8, Twitter users show a clear awareness of the "other," i.e., the publics (or hashtags) diametrically opposed to theirs. Moreover, findings show that Twitter users do interact with people on the other side of an issue, in spite of the concern voiced by scholars who questioned whether people in counterpublics would be able to reach out to beyond their own community (e.g., Fraser, 1992; Jaggar, 1999).

The nature of the dialogue on Twitter is an important element in the debate about whether or not Twitter can serve as a virtual public sphere (e.g., Papacharissi, 2010). Scholars such as Dahlberg (2001) have laid out clear expectations for online dialogue if those interactions are to make up a public sphere, including the ability to interact rationally, step into another's shoes, reflexivity, and sincerity. While some of these were observed among the interactions discussed in this book, others are a little more difficult to pinpoint (how does one know if a Twitter user is being honest about their intentions, for instance). The issue with relying on a list of requirements to decide whether a social media platform qualifies as a public sphere is that it fails to acknowledge the reality of (online) political conversations. Interactions in a democratic society are, as Mouffe (1999, 2000) argued, more likely to be agonistic than rational and deliberative, hardly the rational interaction that marks the Habermasian public sphere, but no less important in voicing political opinions and building democracy (see also Burroughs, 2013; Papacharissi, 2009, 2010; Van Zoonen, et al., 2011).

When looking at the kind of cross-political dialogue that takes place on Twitter, it quickly became apparent that this is not the reflexive, collaborative dialogue that scholars such as Habermas (e.g., 1989, 2006) and Dahlberg (e.g., 2001) talked about when discussing the public sphere. Dialogue on Twitter, as discussed in earlier chapters, is often messy and filled with emotions. Hence, the interactions observed between Twitter users is more in line with Mouffe's (1999, 2000) work on agonistic pluralism, an alternative to the ideals of deliberative democracy that underpin Habermas's work. Interactions are contentious yet respectful (or agonistic) at best and hostile and destructive (or antagonist) at worst. Twitter users do not often engage with the other in an attempt to create shared understanding or reach a compromise, the hallmark of deliberative dialogue, but they will interact agonistically, i.e., engage in conversation in order to convince someone their ideas are wrong, a conversation style that, according to Mouffe (1999, 2000) is the essence of today's democratic societies.

Not only that, but the interactions about social issues do not always revolve around politics and instead will include references to mass media content (e.g., commercials and television shows), or topics that are usually considered part of the private sphere. The findings in this book thus underline the notion that social media such as Twitter have rendered the distinction between private (the not widely accessible space) and public (the space used for public citizenship) obsolete (cf. Papacharissi, 2002, 2010). With the disappearance of this distinction and the fact that social discussions are increasingly centered on "identity politics" (Bennett, 2012, p. 37), this kind of dialogue can be argued to be a part of the political as well (e.g., Papacharissi, 2010). Reducing the public sphere to conversations that center on politics only does not recognize the fact that for many people, politics are intertwined into their daily lives as citizens, consumers, and private persons, and their conversations reflect that (e.g., McGugian, 2005; Papacharissi, 2009).

Twitter thus clearly shows democratizing potential. As such then, it is more than just a public space; its ability to enhance democracy means the platform could be perceived as a possible virtual public sphere (Papacharissi, 2010). Whether or not one can accept Twitter as such hinges on a willingness to rethink the premises that underpin the Habermasian public sphere. In particular, one would need to acknowledge that contemporary democracies are more likely to be characterized by agonistic interactions than rational deliberation and accept that the conversations that drive a democracy encompass more than just politics.

#ANDTHATSHOWITENDED

Back in 1973, would #IAmNotACrook have made it to Twitter's top-trending list? I think the answer is a solid yes. The hashtag would contain sarcastic comments and whimsical memes to indicate users' suspicions of President Nixon's words, and people would have used it to challenge a variety of his policies. Hashtags such as #IStandWithNixon would have started trending shortly afterward too, with users clamoring to extol Nixon's virtues, calling out those who dared to mock the president for failing to respect the nation, and relying on personal anecdotes of minor wrongdoings to explain that everyone makes mistakes. The battle would have reignited a year later with Nixon's resignation.

Although neither #IAmNotACrook nor #IStandWithNixon obviously never trended back in 1973, this imaginary anecdote captures the role Twitter plays in people's sense-making of current events described in this book. The research presented in the previous chapters shows how Twitter gives individuals a space to respond to events in real time, connect with others like them, and, if the individuals are so inclined, simultaneously expose themselves to and interact with people and ideas far outside their usual social circle to construct meaning. The findings provide insight into how people use Twitter to construct collaborative understandings of race and gender, and in doing so, reveal Twitter's potential role in strengthening and maintaining democracy.

Constructing Digital Cultures has shown that Twitter provides a pluralistic space that allows for the participation of a multitude of voices. The platform consists of multiple, parallel publics, or mini-public spheres, that give groups, who might have otherwise gone unheard, a space to connect, deliberate, and above all, find their voice. Even if there are struggles within a group about cultural meanings, Twitter provides them with a space to have these disagreements. These voices create a diverse set of participatory cultures that reject, negotiate, and accept the mainstream culture, showing that Twitter may not be the fully countercultural space that some scholars had envisioned, but that it does allow for the creation of a diverse set of meanings. The platform does more than just offer a safe, exclusive space for different networked publics, though. It also allows users to connect with groups outside their own, and through agonistic dialogue, strengthen democracy. While these kinds of interactions may not occur as often as some might have hoped, they do show that Twitter has the potential to serve as a virtual public sphere, if the individuals active on the platform are willing to engage.

Notes

1. This book uses term "Latinx" in place of the term "Latino/a." Latinx is a gender-neutral term and is seen as a more inclusive way to denote mixed-gendered groups than Latino/as or Hispanic (see, e.g., deOnís [2017] for a more in-depth discussion). The terms "Latina" and "Latino" are used to refer to single-gendered groups. See also chapter 3.

2. An earlier version of this chapter was presented at the 2016 PCA/ACA convention in Seattle, WA.

References

Acar, A., & Deguchi, A. (2013). Culture and social media usage: Analysis of Japanese Twitter users. *International Journal of Electronic Commerce Studies, 4*(1), 21–32. doi: 10.7903/ijecs.989.

Acosta, D.M. (2014). Tweet up? Examining Twitter's impact on social capital and digital citizenship in higher education. *About Campus, 18*(16), 10–17. doi: 10.1002/abc.21139.

African American Policy Forum (2015). *Say her name: Resisting police brutality against Black women.* Center for Intersectionality and Social Policy Studies. Retrieved from http://static1.squarespace.com/static/53f20d90e4b0b80451158d8c/t/55a810d7e4b058f342f55873/1437077719984/AAPF_SMN_Brief_full_singles.compressed.pdf.

Ahuvia, A. (2001). Traditional, interpretive, and reception based content analysis: Improving the ability of content analysis to address issues of pragmatic and theoretical concern. *Social Indicators Research, 54*, 139–172.

Ahluwalia, P., & Miller, T. (2014). The prosumer. *Social Identities, 20*(4–5), 259–261. doi: 10.1080/13504630.2015.1004830.

Airbnb (2017, February 5). #WeAccept. Retrieved from https://www.airbnb.com/weaccept.

Al-Tahmazi, T.H. (2015). The pursuit of power in Iraqi political discourse: Unpacking the construction of sociopolitical communities on Facbeook. *Journal of Multicultural Discourses, 10*(2), 163–179. doi: 10.1080/17447143.2015.1042383.

Altheide, D.L. (1987). Ethnographic content analysis. *Qualitative Sociology, 10*(1), 65–76.

Anderson, E. (2012). Reflections on the Black-White achievement gap. *Journal of School Psychology, 50*(5), 593–597. doi: 10.1016/j.jsp.2012.08.007.

Anderson, M., & Hitlin, P. (2016, August 15). Social media conversations about race. *Pew Research Cente*r. Retrieved from http://www.pewinternet.org/2016/08/15/social-media-conversations-about-race/

Andrews, W., & Kaplan, T. (2015, December 15). Where the candidates stand on 2016's biggest issues. *New York Times.* Retrieved from https://www.nytimes.com/interactive/2016/us/elections/candidates-on-the-issues.html

Aparicio, F.R. (2003). Jennifer as Selena: Rethinking Latinidad in media and popular culture. *Latino Studies, 1,* 90–105.

Ashley, C., & Tuten, T. (2015). Creative strategies in social media marketing: An exploratory study of branded social content and consumer engagement. *Psychology and Marketing, 32*(1), 15–27. doi: 10.1002/mar.20761.

Avila-Saavreda, G. (2010). A fish out of water: New articulations of US-Latino identity on *Ugly Betty. Communication Quarterly, 58*(2), 133–147.

Báez, J. (2015). Television for *All* women? Watching Lifetime's *Devious Maids.* In E. Levine (Ed.), *Cupcakes, pinterest, and ladyporn. Feminized popular culture in the early twenty-first century* (pp. 51–70). Urbana, IL: University of Illinois Press.

Bahadur, N. (2014). Dove "real beauty" campaign turns 10: How a brand tried to change the conversation about female beauty. *The Huffington Post.* Retrieved from http://www.huffingtonpost.com/2014/01/21/dove-real-beauty-campaign-turns-10_n_4575940.html

Baird, C.H., & Parasnis, G. (2011). From social media to social customer relationship management. *Strategy and Leadership, 39*(5), 30–37. doi: 10.1108/10878571111161507.

Balance, C.B.B. (2012). How it feels to be viral me: Affective labor and Asian American YouTube performance. *Women Studies Quarterly, 40*(1&2), 138–152.

Barker-Plummer, B., & Barker-Plummer, D. (2017). Hashtag feminism: digital media, and new dynamics of social change: A case study of #YesAllWomen. In G.W. Richardson (Ed.), *Social Media and Politics: A new way to participate in the political process, Vol. 2* (pp. 79–97). Santa Barbara, CA: Praeger.

Barksdale, A. (2015, December 10). 18 times Black Twitter broke the internet in 2015. *The Huffington Post.* Retrieved from http://www.huffingtonpost.com/entry/18-times-black-twitter-broke-the-internet-in-2015_us_56686a65e4b0f290e5217d78.

Bastos, M.T., Raimundo, R.L.G., & Travitzki, R. (2013). Gatekeeping Twitter: message diffusion in political hashtags. *Media, Culture, & Society, 35*(2), 260–270. doi: 10.1177/0163443712467594.

Beltran, M. (2004). Mas Macha: The new Latina action hero. In Y. Tasker (Ed.), *Action and Adventure Cinema* (pp. 186–200). London, UK: Routledge.

Benner, K. (2017, February 5). In Airbnb's Super Bowl ad, implied criticism of Trump's travel ban. *The New York Times.* Retrieved from https://www.nytimes.com/2017/02/05/technology/airbnb-super-bowl-ad-trump-travel-ban.html

Bennett, W.L. (2005). Social movement beyond borders: Organization, communication, and political capacity in two eras of transnational activism. In D. della Porta & S.G. Tarlow (Eds.), *Transnational protest and global activism* (pp. 203–226). Lanham, MD: Rowman & Littlefield.

Bennett, W.L. (2012). The personalization of politics: Political identity, social media, and changing patterns of participation. *American Academy of Political and Social Science, 644,* 20–39. doi: 10.1177/0002716212451428.

Berry, J.W. (1997). Immigration, acculturation, and acceptance. *Applied Psychology: An International Review, 46*(1), 5–68.

Bessant, J. (2014). The political in the age of the digital: Propositions for empirical investigation. *Politics, 34*(1), 33–44. doi: 10.1111/1467–9256.12015.

Bissell, K., & Rask, A. (2010). Real women on real beauty: Self-discrepancy, internalization of the thin ideal, and perceptions of attractiveness and thinness in Dove's campaign for real beauty. *International Journal of Advertising, 29*(4), 643–688. doi: 10.2501/S026S048710201385.

Blades, L.A. (2013, August 15). A Black man's view on #BlackPowerIsForBlackMen. *Uptown*. Retrieved from http://www.uptownmagazine.com/2013/08/a-black-mans-view-on-blackpowerisforblackmen/

Blow, C.M. (2016, September 12). About the "basket of deplorables." *New York Times*. Retrieved from https://www.nytimes.com/2016/09/12/opinion/about-the-basket-of-deplorables.html

Bogle, D. (2007). *Toms, Coons, Mulattoes, Mammies, & Bucks: An interpretive history of Blacks in American films*. New York, NY: Continuum.

Bolt, D. (2014). An advertising aesthetic: Real beauty and visual impairment. *The British Journal of Visual Impairment, 32*(1), 25–32. doi: 10.1177/0264619613512619.

Bonilla-Silva, E. (2013). *Racism without racists: Color blind racism and the persistence of racial inequality in the United States*. Lanham, MD: Rowman & Littlefield.

Bonilla, Y., & Rosa, J. (2015). #Ferguson: Digital protest, hashtag ethnography, and the racial politics of social media in the United States. *American Ethnologist, 42*(1), 4–17. doi: 10.1111/amet.12112.

Boulianne, S. (2016). Campaigns and conflict on social media: A literature snapshot. *Online Information Review, 40*(5), 566–579. http://dx.doi.org/10.1108/OIR-03–2016–0086.

Bouvier, G. (2015). What is a discourse approach to Twitter, Facebook, Youtube, and other social media: Connecting with other academic fields? *Journal of Multicultural Discourses, 10*(2), 149–162. doi: 10.1080/17447143.2015.1042381.

Bowen, G.A. (2006). Grounded theory and sensitizing concepts. *Interntional Journal of Qualitative Methods, 5*(3), 12–23.

Boyd, D. (2011). Social Network Sites as Networked Publics: Affordances, Dynamics, and Implications. In Z. Papacharissi (Ed.), *Networked Self: Identity, Community, and Culture on Social Network Sites* (pp. 39–58). New York, NY: Routledge.

Boyd, D., Golder, S., & Lotan, G. (2010). Tweet, Tweet, Retweet: Conversational aspects of retweeting on Twitter. *HCISS '10 Proceedings of the 2010 43rd Hawaii International Conference on System Science* (pp. 1–10). Washington, DC: IEEE Computer Society.

Boynton, G.R., Cook, J., Daniels, K., Dawkins, M., Kopish, J., Makar, M. McDavid, W., Murphy, M., Osmundson, J., Steenblock, T., Sudarmawan, A., Wiese, P., & Zora, A. (2014). The political domain goes to Twitter: Hashtags, retweets and URLs. *Open Journal of Political Science, 4*(1), 8–15.

Briceño, N. (2016, June 29). 31 Tweets about Growing up "Hispanic" that are way too real. *Buzzfeed*. Retrieved from https://www.buzzfeed.com/norbertobriceno/growinguphispanic?utm_term=.uszgVKD8V#.hxkEKMaRK

Brickner, R.K. (2016). Tweeting care: Educators' dissent through social media in US and Canada. *Labour/Le Travail, 77*, 11–36.

Bridges, J. (2014, June 2). #NotAllMen don't get it. *Time*. Retrieved from http://time.com/2809276/notallmen-dont-get-it/

Brittain, A.S. (2012). Understanding African American adolescents' identity development: A relational developmental systems perspective. *Journal of Black Psychology, 38*(2), 172–200. doi: 10.1177/0095798411414570.

Brock, A. (2012). From the Blackhand side: Twitter as a cultural conversation. *Journal of Broadcasting and Electronic Media, 56*(4), 529–549. doi: 10.1080/08838151.2012.732147.

Broder Van Dyke, M. (2014, January 14). "How I met your mother" puts a character in yellowface. *Buzzfeed*. Retrieved from https://www.buzzfeed.com/mbvd/32-powerful-tweets-that-takedown-yellowface-on-how-i-met-you?utm_term=.wgKMQbEgQ#.ogMerwEyr.

Broersma, M., & Graham T. (2012). Social media as beat: Tweets as news source during the 2010 British and Dutch elections. *Journalism Practice, 6*(3), 403–419.

Brothers Writing to Live (2013, August 15). #BlackPowerIsForBlackMen: Letters from Brothers writing to live. *The Feminist Wire*. Retrieved from http://www.thefeministwire.com/2013/08/blackpowerisforblackmen/

Brown, C., Hendrickson, E., & Littau, J. (2014). New opportunities for diversity: Twitter, journalists, and traditionally underserved communities. *Journal of Social Media Studies, 1*(1), 1–16. doi: 10.15340/2147336611760.

Brown, C., Willis, E., Havard, C., & Irwin, R.L. (2015). From tailgating to Twitter: Fans' use of social media at a Gridiorn matchup between two historically Black colleges. *Journal of Applied Sport Management, 7*(3), 1–18.

Bruns, A., & Burgess, J.E. (2011). #Ausvotes: How Twitter covered the 2010 Australian federal election. *Communication, Politics, and Culture, 44*(2), 37–56.

Bruns A., & Burgess, J.E. (2012). Researching news discussions on Twitter: New methodologies. *Journalism Studies, 13*, 1–13. doi: 10.1080/1461670X.2012.664428.

Bruns, A., & Highfield, T. (2013). Political networks on Twitter. *Information, Communication, & Society, 16*(5), 667–691. doi: 10.1080/1369118X.2013.782328.

Bruns, A., & Moe, H. (2014). Structural layers of communication on Twitter. In K. Weller, A. Bruns, J. Burgess, M. Mahrt, & C. Puschmann (Eds.), *Twitter and Society* (pp. 15–28). New York, NY: Peter Lang.

Burch, L.M., Frederick, E.L., & Pegoraro, A. (2015). Kissing in the carnage: An examination of framing on Twitter during the Vancouver riots. *Journal of Broadcasting and Electronic Media, 59*(3), 339–415. doi: 10.1080/08838151.2015.1054999.

Burgess, J., Foth, M., & Klaebe, H. (2006). *Everyday creativity as civic engagement: A cultural citizenship view of new media*. Paper presented at the Communication Policy & Research Forum, September 25–26, Sydney, Australia.

Burroughs, B. (2013). Obama trolling: Memes, salutes and an agonistic politics in the 2012 Presidential Election. *The Fibreculture Journal, 22*, 258–276.

Cabosky, J. (2106). Social media opinion sharing: Beyond volume. *Journal of Consumer Marketing, 33*(3), 172–181. doi: 10.1108/JCM-02–2015–1323.

Cabrera, S.A., & Williams, C.L. (2014). Consuming for the social good: Marketing, consumer citizenship, and the possibilities of ethical consumption. *Critical Sociology, 40*(3), 349–367. doi: 10.1177/0896920512458599.

Capachi, C. (2013, December 17). Suey Park: Asian American women are #NotYourAsianSidekick. *The Washington Post*. Retrieved from https://www.washingtonpost.com/blogs/she-the-people/wp/2013/12/17/suey-park-asian-american-women-are-notyourasiansidekick/

Carlisle, J.E., & Patton, R.C. (2013). Is social media changing how we understand political engagement? An analysis of Facebook and the 2008 presidential election. *Political Research Quarterly, 66*(4), 883–895. doi: 10.1177/1065912913482758.

Carney, N. (2016). All lives matter but so does race: Black lives matter and the evolving role of social media. *Humanity & Society, 40*(2), 180–199. doi: 10.1177/0160597616643868.

Carroll, W.K., & Hackett, R.A. (2006). Democratic media activism through the lens of social movement theory. *Media, Culture, & Society, 28*(1), 83–104. doi: 10.1177/0163443706059289.

Casaló, L.V., Flavían, C., & Giunalíu, M. (2008). Promoting consumer's participation in virtual brand communities: A new paradigm in branding strategy. *Journal of Marketing Communications, 14*(1), 19–36. doi: 10.1080/13527260701535236.

Castells, M. (2015). *Networks of outrage and hope: Social movements in the internet age* (2nd ed.). Cambridge, UK: Polity Press.

Chang, R.S. (1996). Reverse racism! Affirmative action, family and the dream that is America. *Hastings Constitutional Law Quarterly, 23*, 1115–1134.

Chaudhry, I. (2016). "Not so black and white": Discussions of race on Twitter in the aftermath of #Ferguson and the shooting of Michael Brown. *Cultural Studies—Critical Methodologies, 16*(3), 296–304. doi: 10.1177/1532708616634814.

Cheng, S. (2016, May 4). Inside the hashtag protest of Hollywood's Asian-American problem. *Buzzfeed*. Retrieved from https://www.buzzfeed.com/susancheng/whitewashedout?utm_term=.mijay3oKy#.pkoV9xGg9.

Cherry, E., Ellis, C., & DeSoucey, M. (2011). Food for thought, thought for food: Consumption, identity, and ethnography. *Journal of Contemporary Ethnography, 40*(2), 231–258. doi: 10.1177/0891241610379122.

Cheryan, S., & Monin, B. (2005). "Where are you *really* from?": Asian Americans and identity denial. *Journal of Personality and Social Psychology, 89*(5), 717–740. doi: 10.1037/0022–3514.89.5.717.

Chow, K. (2015, March 26). Why it's so hard for us to agree about Dong from the "Unbreakable Kimmy Schmidt." *NPR: Code Switch*. Retrieved from http://www.npr.org/sections/codeswitch/2015/03/26/395127808/why-its-so-hard-for-us-to-agree-about-dong-from-the-unbreakable-kimmy-schmidt

Chu, T., & Kwan, V.S.Y. (2007). Effect of collectivistic cultural imperatives on Asian American meta-stereotypes. *Asian Journal of Social Psychology, 10*, 270–276. doi: 10.1111/j.1467–839X.2007.00236.x.

Chumsky, A. (2015, April 15). Why Dove's "choose beautiful" campaign sparked a backlash. *Fortune*. Retrieved from http://fortune.com/2015/04/15/why-doves-choose-beautiful-campaign-sparked-a-backlash/

Chun, E.W. (2013). Ironic Blackness as masculine cool: Asian American language and authenticity on YouTube. *Applied Linguistics, 34*(5), 592–612. doi: 10.1093/applin/amt023.

Cicchirillo, V. (2015). Priming stereotypical associations: Violent video games and African American depictions. *Communication Research Reports, 32*(2), 122–131. doi: 10.1080/08824096.2015.1016148.

Cisneros, J.D., & Nakayam, T.K. (2015). New Media, old racisms: Twitter, Miss America, and cultural logics of race. *Journal of International and Intercultural Communication, 8*(2), 108–127. doi: 10.1080/17513057.2015.1025328.

Clark, R. (2014). #NotBuyingIt: Hashtag feminists expand the commercial media conversation. *Feminist Media Studies, 14*(6), 1108–1110. doi: 10.1080/14680777.2014.975473.

Cloete, A.L. (2015). Living in a digital culture: The need for theological reflection. *HTS Teologiese Studies/Theological Studies, 71*(2), 1–7.

Cohen, R.J. (2014). Brand personification: Introduction and overview. *Psychology and Marketing, 31*(1), 1–30. doi: 10.1002/mar.20671.

Colleoni, E., Rozza, A., & Arvidsson, A. (2014). Echo chamber or public sphere? Predicting political orientation and measuring political homophily in Twitter using big data. *Journal of Communication, 64*, 317–332. doi: 10.1111/jcom.12084.

Company (2015, March 16). What "race together" means for Starbucks customers. *Starbucks Newsroom*. Retrieved from https://news.starbucks.com/news/what-race-together-means-for-starbucks-partners-and-customers.

Conley, T.L. (2014). From #RenishaMcBride to #RememberRenisha: Locating our stories and finding out justice. *Feminist Media Studies, 14*(6), 1111–1113. doi: 10.1080/14680777.2014.975474.

Conover, M.D., Ratkiewicz, J., Gonçalves, B., Flammini, A., & Menczer, F. (2011). Political polarization on Twitter. *Proceedings of the Fifth International AAAI Conference on Weblogs and Social Media.*

Conroy, M., Feezell, J.T., & Guerrero, M. (2012). Facebook and political engagement: A study of online political group membership and offline political engagement. *Computers in Human Behavior, 28*, 1535–1546. doi: 10.1016/j.chb.2012.03.012.

Conway, B.A., Kenski, K., & Wang, D. (2013). Twitter use by presidential candidates during the 2012 campaign. *American Behavioral Scientist, 57*(11), 1596–1610. doi: 10.1177/0002764213489014.

Coppa, F. (2014). Pop culture, fans and social media. In J. Hunsinger & T. Senft (Eds.), *The Social Media Handbook* (pp. 76–93). New York, NY: Taylor & Francis.

Corbin, J., & Strauss, A. (1990). Grounded theory research: Procedures, canons, and evaluative criteria. *Zeitschrift für Soziologie, 19*(6), 418–427.

Corcoran, M., Newman, K., & Devasagayam, P.R. (2016). Consumer perception of corporate activism: Strategic implications for marketing. *International Journal of Academic Research in Business and Social Sciences, 6*(10), 52–60.

Cottle, S. (2011). Media and the Arab uprisings of 2011: Research notes. *Journalism, 12*(5), 647–659. doi: 10.1177/1464884911410017.

Creeber, G., & Martin, R. (2009). Introduction. In G. Creeber & R. Martin (Eds.), *Digital cultures: Understanding new media* (pp. 1–11). Maidenhead, UK: Open University Press.

Creswell, J.W. (2003). *Research design. Qualitative, quantitative, and mixed methods approaches* (2nd ed.). Thousand Oaks, CA: Sage.

Cross, M. (2011). *Bloggerati, Twitterati. How Blogs and Twitter are transforming popular culture*. Santa Barbara, CA: Praeger.

Cummings, K., & Gotshall, C. (2014). Citizenship and consumption: Media theory in the age of Twitter. In R.S. Fortner, & P.M. Fackler (Eds.), *The Handbook of Media and Mass Communication Theory* (1st ed., pp. 612–628). Hoboken, NJ: Wiley. doi: 10.1002/9781118591178.ch33.

Cunningham, C. (Ed.). (2013). *Social Networking and Impression Management: Self-Presentation in the Digital Age*. Lanham, MD: Lexington Books.

Dahlberg, L. (2001). Computer-mediated communication and the public sphere: A critical analysis. *Journal of Computer-Mediated Communication, 7*(1). doi: 10.1111/j.1083–6101.2001.tb0013.

Dahlberg, L. (2005). The corporate colonization of online attention and the marginalization of critical communication? *Journal of Communication Inquiry, 29*(2), 160–180. doi: 10.1177/0196859904272745.

Dahlberg, L. (2007). Rethinking the fragmentation of the cyberpublic: From consensus to contestation. *New Media & Society, 9*(5), 827–847. doi: 10.1177/1461444807081228.

Dahlgren, P. (2005). The Internet, public spheres, and political communication: Dispersion and deliberation. *Political Communication, 22*(2), 147–162. doi: 10.1080/10584600590933160.

Dahlgren, P. (2013). *The political web. Media, participation, and alternative democracy.* Basingstoke: Palgrave Macmillan.

David, J.H., Sanger, D.E., & Haberman, M. (2017, January 24). Trump to order Mexican wall and curtail immigration. *New York Times*. Retrieved from https://www.nytimes.com/2017/01/24/us/politics/wall-border-trump.html

Dávila, A. (2000). Talking back: Hispanic media and US Latinidad. *Centro Journal, XII*(1), 37–47.

Davis, J. (2016, September 27). What's driving corporate activism? *New Republic.* Retrieved from https://newrepublic.com/article/137252/whats-driving-corporate-activism

Davis, R. (2016, August 12). The very best of #BeingABlackGirlIsLit hashtag. *Essence.* Retrieved from http://www.essence.com/2016/08/12/beingablackgirlislit-trending-twitter-again

Davis, W. (2017 January 27). It's not just the park service: "Rogue" federal Twitter accounts multiply. *National Public Radio.* Retrieved from http://www.npr.org/sections/alltechconsidered/2017/01/27/512007632/its-not-just-the-park-service-rogue-federal-twitter-accounts-multiply.

Davis, G.F., & White, C.J. (2015). The new face of corporate activism. *Stanford Social Innovation Review, Fall.* Retrieved from https://ssir.org/articles/entry/the_new_face_of_corporate_activism.

Davis, R., Piven, I., & Breazeale, M. (2014). Conceptualizing the brand in social media community: The five sources model. *Journal of Retailing and Consumer Services, 21*, 468–481.

De Zúñiga, G., Puig-i-Abril, E., & Rojas, H. (2009). Weblogs, traditional sources online and political participation: An assessment of how the Internet is changing the political environment. *New Media & Society, 11*(4), 553–574. doi: 10.1177/1461444809102960.

Dean, J. (2010). *Blog theory. Feedback and capture in the circuits of drive.* Cambridge: Polity Press.

DeOnís, C. (2017). What's in an "x"? An exchange about the politics of "Latinx." *Chiricú Journal: Latina/o Literatures, Arts, and Cultures, 1*(2), 78–91. doi: 10.2979/chiricu.1.2.07.

Deuze, M. (2006). Participation, remediation, bricolage: Considering principal components of a digital culture. *The Information Society, 22*, 63–75. doi: 10.1080/01972240600567170.

Devos, T., & Banaji, M.R. (2005). American = white? *Journal of Personality and Social Psychology, 88*(3), 447–466. doi: 10.1037/0022-3514.88.3.447.

DeVries, N.J., & Carlson, J. (2014). Examining the drivers and brand performance implications of customer engagement with brands in the social media environment. *Journal of Brand Management, 21*(6), 495–515. doi: 10.1057/bm.2014.18.

Dimitrova, D.V., & Bystrom, D. (2013). The effects of social media on political participation and candidate image evaluations in the 2012 Iowa caucuses. *American Behavioral Scientist, 57*(11), 1568–1583. doi: 10.1177/0002764213489011.

Dimitrova, D.V., Shehata, A., Strömbäck, J., & Nord, L.W. (2014). The effects of digital media on political knowledge and participation in election campaigns: Evidence from panel data. *Communication Research, 41*(1), 95–118. doi: 10.1177/0093650211426004.

Dixon, J.C., & Rosenbaum, M.S. (2004). Nice to know you? Testing contact, cultural, and group theories of anti-Black and anti-Hispanic stereotypes. *Social Science Quarterly, 85*(2), 257–280.

Dong, Q., & Murrillo, A.P. (2007). The impact of television viewing on young adults' stereotypes towards Hispanic Americans. *Human Communication, 10*(1), 33–44.

Doane, A. (2007). The changing politics of color-blind racism. In R. Coates & R. Dennis (Eds.), *Research in race and ethnic relations, vol. 14: The new Black: alternative paradigms and strategies for the 21st century* (pp. 159–174). Amsterdam, Netherlands: Elsevier.

Dragiewicz, M., & Burgess, J. (2016). Domestic violence on #qanda: The "man" question in live Twitter discussion on the Australian Broadcasting Corporation's Q & A. *Canadian Journal of Women and The Law, 28*(1), 211–229. doi: 10.3138/cjwl.28.1.211.

duBrowa, C. (2015, March 17). Why I deleted my Twitter account and why I'm back. *Medium.* Retrieved from https://medium.com/@coreydu/why-i-deleted-my-twitter-account-and-why-i-m-back-ad91b5133d84#.fleebxp5y.

Duggan, M., Ellison, N.B., Lampe, C., Lenhart, A., & Madden, M. (2015, January 9). *Demographics of key social networking platforms.* Retrieved from http://www.pewinternet.org/2015/01/09/demographics-of-key-social-networking-platforms-2/

Duggan, M., & Smith, A. (2016, October 25). The political environment on social media. *Pew Research Center.* Retrieved from http://www.pewinternet.org/2016/10/25/the-political-environment-on-social-media/

Edelman, M. (2001). Social movements: Changing paradigms and forms of politics. *Annual Review of Anthropology, 30*, 285–317.

Ellison, N., Heino, R., & Gibbs, J. (2006). Managing impressions online: Self-presentation processes in the online dating environment. *Journal of Computer-Mediated Communication, 11*, 415–441. doi: 10.1111/j.1083-6101.2006.00020.x.

Eriksson, M. (2016). Managing collective social trauma on social media: The role of Twitter after the 2011 Norway attacks. *Media, Culture, and Society, 38*(3), 365–380. doi: 10.1177/0163443715608259.

Esco, K.M. (2011). Understanding "Black Twitter": A look at the increasingly diverse internet population. *Public Relations Tactics, 18*(10), 15.

Evans, C. (2014). Twitter for teaching: Can social media be used to enhance the process of learning? *British Journal of Educational Technology, 45*(5), 902–915.

Facebook IQ (2015, March 5). *Digital diversity: A closer look at Asian Americans in the US*. Retrieved from https://insights.fb.com/2015/03/05/closer-look-asian-americans-us/

Falicov, C.J. (2010). Changing constructions of machismo for Latino men in therapy: "The devil never sleeps." *Family Process, 49*(3), 309–329.

Farrell, H. (2012). The consequences of the internet for politics. *Annual Review of Political Science, 15*, 35–52. doi: 10.1146/annurev-polisci-030810–110815.

Feng, Y. (2016). Are you connected? Evaluating information cascade in online discussion about the #RaceTogether campaign. *Computers in Human Behavior, 54*, 43–53. doi: 10.1016/j.chb.2015.07.052.

Finlay, L. (2011). *Phenomenology for therapists: Researching the lived world*. Chicester, UK: Wiley-Blackwell.

Finley, T. (2015, July 15). Black Twitter nailed what it was like #Growing UpBlack. *The Huffington Post*. Retrieved from http://www.huffingtonpost.com/entry/growingupblack-takes-black-twitter-down-memory-lane_us_55a675dae4b0896514cfe581.

Fiske, J. (1987). *Television Culture*. London: Routledge.

Florini, S. (2014). Tweets, tweeps, and signifyin': Communication and cultural performance on "Black Twitter." *Television & New Media, 15*(3), 223–237. doi: 10.1177/1527476413480247.

Fraser, N. (1992). Rethinking the public sphere: A contribution to the critique of actually existing democracy. In C. Calhoun (Ed.), *Habermas and the public sphere* (pp. 109–142). Cambridge, MA: MIT Press.

Freelon, D., McIlwain, C.D., & Clark, M.D. (2016). *Beyond the hashtag: #Ferguson, #BlackLivesMatter and the online struggle for offline justice*. Washington, DC: Center for Media and Social Impact.

Fregoso, R.L. (1995). Homegirls, Cholas, and Pachucas in Cinema: Taking over the public sphere. *California History 74*(3), 316–327.

Fordham, S. (1993). "Those loud Black girls": (Black) women, silence, and gender "passing" in the academy. *Anthropology and Education Quarterly, 24*(1), 2–32.

Fuchs, C. (2012). Some reflections on Manuel Castells' book networks of outrage and hope. Social movements in the internet age. *Triple C: Communication, Capitalism & Critique, 10*(2), 775–797.

Fuchs, C. (2014). Social media and the public sphere. *TripleC, 12*(1), 57–101.

Gadkari, P. (2013, November 7). How does Twitter make money? *BBC News*. Retrieved from http://www.bbc.com/news/business-24397472.

Gallardo-Camacho, J., Lavín, E., & Fernańdez-Garcia, P. (2016). Analysis of the most discussed television programs on Twitter and their relationship with the traditional audience in Spain. *Palabra Clave, 19*(1), 185–201. doi: 10.5294/pacla.2016.19.1.8

Ganesh, S., & Zoller, H.M. (2012). Dialogue, activism, and democratic social change. *Communication Theory, 22*(1), 66–91. doi: 10.1111/j.1468–2885.2011.01396.x.

García-Martín, J., & García-Sánchez, J-N. (2015). Uses of Facebook, Tuenti, Twitter, and MySpace among Spanish young people. *Behavior and Information Technology, 34*(7), 685–703. doi: 10.1080/0144929X.2014.993428.

Garriott, P.A. (2017). Race Trumps class? Whiteness, social class, and the 2016 election. *American Psychological Association*. Retrieved from http://www.org/pi/ses/resources/indicator/2017/01/race-class.aspx

Garza, A. (2014, October 7). A Herstory of the #BlackLivesMatter movement by Alicia Garza. *The Feminist Wire*. Retrieved from http://www.thefeministwire.com/2014/10/blacklivesmatter-2/

Gaver, W.W. (1991). Technological affordances. *CHI '91 Proceedings of the SIGCHI conference on Human Factors in Computing Systems*, New Orleans, LA, April 27–May 2, 1991, 79–84. doi: 10.1145/108844.108856.

Geier, B. (2015, March 19). Why this Starbucks' PR exec deleted his Twitter account. *Fortune*. Retrieved from http://fortune.com/2015/03/19/starbucks-vp-twitter-delete/

Gensler, S., Völckner, F., Liu-Thompkins, Y., & Wiertz, C. (2013). Managing brands in the social media environment. *Journal of Interactive Marketing, 27*, 242–256. doi: 10.1016/j.intmar.2013.09.004.

Georgakopoulou, A. (2014). Small stories transportation and social media: A micro-perspective on the "Greek crisis." *Discourse & Society, 25*(4), 519–539. doi: 10.1177/0957926514536963.

Gerbaudo, P. (2012). *Tweets and the streets: Social media and contemporary activism*. London, UK: Pluto Press.

Gere, C. (2008). *Digital Culture* (expanded 2nd ed.). London, UK: Reaktion Books.

Gerodimos, R., & Ward, J. (2007). Rethinking online youth civic engagement. Reflections on web content analysis. In B. Loader (Ed.), *Young citizens in the digital age: Political engagement, young people, and new media* (pp. 114–126). London, UK: Routledge.

Gil de Zúñiga, H., Copeland, L., & Bimber, B. (2013). Political consumerism: Civic engagement and the social media connection. *New Media & Society, 16*(3), 488–506. doi: 10.1177/1461444813487960.

Gilens, M. (1996). Race and poverty in America: Public misperceptions and the American news media. *The Public Opinion Quarterly, 60*(4), 515–541.

Glaser, B.G. (1965). The constant comparative method of qualitative analysis. *Social Problems, 12*(4), 436–445.

Gleason, B. (2013). #Occupy Wall Street: Exploring informal learning about a social movement on Twitter. *American Behavioral Scientist, 57*(7), 966–982. doi: 10.1177/0002764213479372.

Goldstein, J. (2017, January 19). The surprising history of "snowflake" as a political insult. *ThinkProgress*. Retrieved from https://thinkprogress.org/all-the-special-snowflakes-aaf1a922f37b#.31ox1qeh0

Goodwin, M. (2016, November 11). *New York Times*: We blew it up on Trump. *New York Post*. Retrieved from http://nypost.com/2016/11/11/new-york-times-we-blew-it-on-trump/

Gotanda, N. (1996). Failure of the color-blind vision: Race, ethnicity, and the California Civil Rights Initiative. *Hastings Constitutional Law Quarterly, 23*, 1135–1151.

Gottfried, J., & Shearer, E. (2016, May 26). News use across social media platforms 2016. *Pew Research Center: Journalism & Media.* Retrieved from http://www.journalism.org/2016/05/26/news-use-across-social-media-platforms-2016/

Graham, J. (2017, February 5). Airbnb aims #WeAccept Super Bowl ad at immigrants, refugees. *USA Today.* Retrieved from http://www.usatoday.com/story/tech/talkingtech/2017/02/05/airbnb-aims-weaccept-super-bowl-ad-refugees-immigrants/97533188/

Grant, E. (2015, July 7). College student Jada Mosley wanted to foster community among Black women online, so she created the hashtag #HowItFeelsToBeABlackGirl. *Buzzfeed.* Retrieved from https://www.buzzfeed.com/essencegant/howitfeelstobeablackgirl-captures-what-its-really-like-to-be?utm_term=.bpZmZ1e0Z#.meZ2ezVme.

Grant, W.J., Moon, B., & Grant. B. (2010). Digital dialogue? Australian politicians' use of the social network tool Twitter. *Australian Journal of Political Science, 45*(4), 579–604. doi: 10.1080/10361146.2010.517176.

Gray, E. (2016, October 21). How "nasty woman" became a viral call for solidarity. *The Huffington Post.* Retrieved from http://www.huffingtonpost.com/entry/nasty-woman-became-a-call-of-solidarity-for-women-voters_us_5808f6a8e4b02444efa20c92.

Gray, H. (1989). Television, Black Americans, and the American dream. *Critical Studies in Mass Communication, 6,* 376–386.

Greenwood, S., Perrin, A., & Duggan, M. (2016, November 11). Social media update 2016. *Pew Research Center: Internet, science, and tech.* Retrieved from http://www.pewinternet.org/2016/11/11/social-media-update-2016/

Groshek, J., & Al-Rawi, A. (2013). Public sentiment and critical framing in social media content during the 2012 US presidential campaign. *Social Science Computer Review, 31,* 563–576. doi: 10.1177/0894439313490401.

Gruzd, A., Wellman, B., & Takhteyev, Y. (2011). Imagining Twitter as an imagined community. *American Behavioral Scientist, 55*(10), 1294–1318. doi: 10.1177/0002764211409378.

Guilamo-Ramos, V., Dittus, P., Jascard, J., Johansson, M., Bouris, A., & Acosta, N. (2007). Parenting practices among Dominican and Puerto Rican mothers. *Social Work, 52*(1), 17–30.

Guo, L., & Harlow, S. (2014). User-generated racism: An analysis of stereotypes of African Americans, Latinos, and Asians in YouTube videos. *Howard Journal of Communications, 25,* 281–302. doi: 10.1080/10646175.2014.925413.

Guo, L., & Lee, L. (2013). The critique of YouTube-based vernacular discourse: A case study of YouTube's Asian Community. *Critical Studies in Media Communication, 30*(5), 391–406. doi: 10.1080/15295036.2012.755048.

Guzman, I.M. (2006). Mediating Frida: Negotiating discourses of Latina/o authenticity in global media representations of ethnic identity. *Critical Studies in Media Communication, 23*(3), 232–251. doi: 10.1080/07393180600800841.

Habermas, J. (1989). *The structural transformation of the public sphere. An inquiry into the category of bourgeois society.* Cambridge, UK: Polity Press.

Habermas, J. (2006). Political communication in media society: Does democracy still enjoy an epistemic dimension? The impact of normative theory on research. *Communication Theory, 16,* 411–426.

Hackman, M. (2015, October 1). The price of free: How Apple, Facebook, Microsoft and Google sell you to advertisers. *PC World*. Retrieved from http://www.pcworld.com/article/2986988/privacy/the-price-of-free-how-apple-facebook-microsoft-and-google-sell-you-to-advertisers.html

Halavais, A. (2014). Structure of Twitter: Social and technical. In K. Weller, A. Bruns, J. Burgess, M. Mahrt, & C. Puschmann, (Eds.), *Twitter and Society* (pp. 29–41). New York, NY: Peter Lang.

Hall, S. (2013). Americanism, Un-Americanism, and the gay rights movement. *Journal of American Studies, 47*, 1109–1130.

Halpern, D., & Gibbs, J. (2013). Social media as catalyst for online deliberation. Exploring the affordances of Facebook and YouTube for political expression. *Computers in Human Behavior, 29*, 1159–1168. doi: 1016/j.chb.2012.10.008.

Hamdy, N., & Gomaa, E.H. (2012). Framing the Egyptian uprising in Arabic language newspapers and social media. *Journal of Communication, 62*, 195–211. doi:10.1111/j.1460–2466.2012.01637.x

Hamedy, S. (2015, September 24). How did "Empire" fans react to the show's return on Twitter? *Los Angeles Times*. Retrieved from http://www.latimes.com/entertainment/tv/showtracker/la-et-st-empire-season-two-episode-1-twitter-20150924-htmlstory.html.

Hanna, R., Rohm, A., & Crittenden, V.L. (2011). Were all connected: The power of the social media ecosystem. *Business Horizons, 54*(3), 265–273. doi:10.1016/j.bushor.2011.01.007.

Hardaker, C. (2010). Trolling in asynchronous computer-mediated communication: From user discussions to academic definitions. *Journal of Politeness Research, 6*(2), 215–242. doi: 10.1515/JPLR.2010.011.

Hardt, M., & Negri, A. (2011, October 11). The fight for "real democracy" at the heart of Occupy Wall Street. *Foreign Affairs*. Retrieved from https://www.foreignaffairs.com/articles/north-america/2011–10–11/fight-real-democracy-heart-occupy-wall-street.

Hargittai, E. (2002). Second-level digital divide: Differences in people's online skills. *First Monday, 7*(4). Retrieved from http://firstmonday.org/ojs/index.php/fm/article/view/942/864.

Harrington, S., Highfield, T., & Bruns, A. (2013). More than a backchannel: Twitter and television. *Participations, 10*(1), 405–409.

Harris, A. (2008). Young women, late modernity politics, and the participatory possibilities of online cultures. *Journal of Youth Studies, 11*(5), 481–495. doi: 10.1080/13676260802282950.

Hattery, A.L., & Smith, E. (2012). *African American families today: Myths and realities*. Lanham, MD: Rowman & Littlefield.

Hautman, N. (2016, December 6). Twitter reveals top trending topics and retweets of 2016: Rio Olympic, Pokemon Go and More! *US Magazine*. Retrieved from http://www.usmagazine.com/entertainment/news/twitter-reveals-top-trending-topics-retweets-of-2016-w454091.

Heath, T. (2017, February 6). 84 Lumber and the big Super Bowl ad to nowhere. *The Washington Post*. Retrieved from https://www.washingtonpost.com/news/business/wp/2017/02/06/84-lumber-and-the-big-budget-super-bowl-ad-to-nowhere/

Hehman, E., Gaertner, S.L., & Dovidio, J.F. (2011). Evaluations of presidential performance: Race, prejudice, and perceptions of Americanism. *Journal of Experimental Psychology, 47,* 430–435. doi: 10.1016/j.jesp.2010.11.011.

Hermes, J., & Stello, C. (2000). Cultural citizenship and crime fiction. Politics and the interpretive community. *European Journal of Cultural Studies, 3*(2), 215–232.

Hess, A. (2016, May 25). Asian American actors are fighting for visibility. They will not be ignored. *The New York Times*. Retrieved from http://www.nytimes.com/2016/05/29/movies/asian-american-actors-are-fighting-for-visibility-they-will-not-be-ignored.html

Hijmans, E. (1996). The logic of qualitative media content analysis: A typology. *Communications, 21*(1), 93–108.

Hill Collins, P. (2004). *Black sexual politics: African Americans, gender, and the new racism*. New York, NY: Taylor and Francis.

Hills, M. (2009). Participatory culture: Mobility, interactivity, and identity. In G. Creeber & R. Martin (Eds.), *Digital cultures: Understanding new media.* (pp. 107 116). Maidenhead, UK: McGraw-Hill.

Honeycutt, C., & Herring, S.C. (2009). Beyond microblogging: Conversation and collaboration via Twitter. *Proceedings of the 42nd Hawaii International Conference on System Sciences.*

Hong, J. (2006, February 9). *Family Ties.* University of Southern California Asia Pacific Arts. Retrieved from http://asiapacificarts.usc.edu/w_apa/showarticle.aspx?articleID=9628&AspxAutoDetectCookieSupport=1

hooks, b. (2004). *Feminist theory: From margin to center* (2nd ed.). Cambridge: South End Press.

Hoon Park, J., Gabbadon, N.G., & Chernin, A.R. (2006). Naturalizing racial differences through comedy: Asian, Black, and white views on racial stereotypes in *Rush Hour 2*. *Journal of Communication, 56,* 157–177. doi: 10.1111/j.1460-2466.2006.00008.x.

Horeck, T. (2014). #AskThicke: "Blurred lines," rape culture, and the feminist hashtag takeover. *Feminist Media Studies, 14*(6), 1105–1107. doi: 10.1080/14680777.2014.975450.

Hoskins, G.T. (2013). Meet the Habermasses: Charting the emergence of a social media-enabled public sphere in new democracies. *The International Journal of Technology, Knowledge, and Society, 9,* 25–39.

Howard, J.A. (2000). Social psychology of identities. *Annual Review of Sociology, 26,* 367–393.

Howard, P.N., & Hussain, M.H. (2011). The upheavals in Egypt and Tunisia: The role of the digital media. *Journal of Democracy, 22*(3), 35–48.

Howe, A. (2014). Not your average Mexican: *Breaking Bad* and the destruction of Latino stereotypes. In D.P. Pierson (Ed.), *Breaking Bad. Critical essays on the contexts, politics, style, and reception of the television series* (pp. 87–102). Lanham, MD: Lexington Books.

Hsu, H. (2009, April 27). The name's Du Xiao Hua, but call me Steve: What's up with Chinese people having English names? *Slate*. Retrieved from http://www.slate.com/articles/arts/culturebox/2009/04/the_names_du_xiao_hua_but_call_me_steve.html

Huang, H.H., & Mitchell, V.-W. (2014). The role of imagination and brand personification in brand relationships. *Psychology and Marketing, 31*(1), 38–47. doi: 10.1002/mar.20673.

Huang, P.H. (2012). From tiger mom to panda parent. *UCLA Asian Pacific Law Journal, 17*, 40–44.

Huckfeldt, R., & Mendez, J.M. (2008). Moths, flames, and political engagement. *The Journal of Politics, 70*(1), 83–96. doi:10.1017/S0022381607080073.

Hughes, J. (2014, November 13). "How to get away with murder" fans take over Twitter asking #whokilledsam? *The Wrap*. Retrieved from http://www.thewrap.com/how-to-get-away-with-murder-fans-take-over-twitter-asking-whokilledsam/

Humes, K.R., Jones, N.A., & Ramirez, R.R. (2011). Overview of Race and Hispanic Origin: 2010. *2010 Census Briefs*. Retrieved from http://www.census.gov/prod/cen2010/briefs/c2010br-02.pdf

Huntemann, N. (2015). No more excuses: Using Twitter to challenge the symbolic annihilation of women in games. *Feminist Media Studies, 15*(1), 164–167, doi: 10.1080/14680777.2015.987432.

Iosifidis, P., & Wheeler, M. (2015). The public sphere and network democracy: Social movements and political change? *Global Media Journal, 13*(25). Retrieved from http://www.globalmediajournal.com/open-access/the-public-sphere-and-network-democracy-social-movements-and-political-change.php?aid=64445

Isaac, M., & Ember, S. (2016, November 8). For Election Day influence, Twitter ruled social media. *The New York Times*. Retrieved from https://www.nytimes.com/2016/11/09/technology/for-election-day-chatter-twitter-ruled-social-media.html?_r=0

Jackson, S.J., & Foucault Welles, B. (2015). Hijacking #MyNYPD: Social media dissent and networked counterpublics. *Journal of Communication, 65*, 932–952. doi: 10.1111/jcom.12185.

Jaffe, S. (2016, April 25). Feminism for sale. We need collective action, not "marketplace feminism." *New Republic*. Retrieved from https://newrepublic.com/article/132991/feminism-sale

Jaggar, A.M. (1999). Multicultural democracy. *Journal of Political Philosophy, 7*(3), 308–329.

Jansen, B.J., Zhang, M., Sobel, K., & Chowdury, A. (2009). Twitter power: Tweets as electronic word of mouth. *Journal of the American Society for Information Science and Technology, 60*(11), 2169–2188.

Jasinski, J. (2001). *Sourcebook on Rhetoric*. London, UK: Sage.

Java, A., Song, X., Finin, T., & Tseng, B. (2007). Why we Twitter: Understanding microblogging usage and communities. *Proceedings of the Joint 9th WEBKDD and 1st NSA-KDD workshop 2007*.

Jenkins, H. (2006). *Convergence culture: Where old and new media collide*. New York, NY: New York University Press.

Jhally, S., & Lewis, J. (1992). *Enlightened racism: The Cosby Show, audiences, and the myth of the American Dream*. Boulder, CO: Westview Press.

Jin, D.Y., & Feenberg, A. (2015). Commodity and community in social networking: Marx and the monetization of user-generated content. *The Information Society, 31*, 52–60. doi: 10.1080/01972243.2015.977635.

Johnson, M.A. (1999). Pre-television stereotypes: Mexicans in US newsreels, 1919–1932. *Critical Studies in Mass Communication, 16*, 417–435.

Johnston, J., & Taylor, J. (2008). Feminist consumerism and fat activists: A comparative study of grassroots activism and the Dove real beauty campaign. *Signs, 33*(4), 941–966.

Juang, L.P., Qin, D.B., & Park, I.J.K. (2013). Deconstructing the myth of the "tiger mother": An introduction to the special issue on tiger parenting, Asian-heritage families, and child / adolescent well-being. *Asian American Journal of Psychology, 4*(1), 1–6. doi: 10.1037 / a0032136.

Jungherr, A. (2014). The logic of political coverage on Twitter: Temporal dynamics and content. *Journal of Communication, 64*, 239–259. doi:10.1111 / jcom.12087.

Jungherr, A. (2016). Twitter use in election campaigns: A systematic literature review. *Journal of Information Technology, 13*(1), 72–91. doi:10.1080 / 19331681.2015.1132401.

Jurgensen, J. (2014, June 2). "Breaking Bad" and "The Walking Dead" top Twitter ratings, Nielsen says. *The Wall Street Journal*. Retrieved from https: / / blogs.wsj.com / speakeasy / 2014 / 06 / 02 / breaking-bad-and-the-walking-dead-top-twitter-ratings-nielsen-says /

Juris, J.S. (2012). Reflections on #Occupy everywhere. Social media, public space, and emerging logics of aggregation. *American Ethnologist, 39*(2), 259–279. doi: 10.1111 / j.1548–1425.2012.01362.x.

Kalsnes, B., Krumsvik, A.H., & Storsul, T. (2014). Social media as a political backchannel Twitter use during televised election debates in Norway. *Aslib Journal of Information Management, 66*(3), 313–328. doi: 10.1108 / AJIM-09–2013–0093.

Kavanaugh, A.L., Reese, D.D., Carroll, J.M., & Rosson, M.B. (2005). Weak ties in networked communities. *The Information Society, 21*, 119–131. doi: 10.1080 / 01972240590925320.

Kawai, Y. (2005). Stereotyping Asian Americans: The dialectic of the model minority and the Yellow Peril. *Howard Journal of Communications, 16*(2), 109–130. doi: 10.1080 / 10646170590948974.

Keller, J. (2012). Virtual feminisms: Girls' blogging communities, feminist activism, and participatory politics. *Information, Communication & Society, 15*(2), 429–447. doi: 10.1080 / 1369118X.2011.642890.

Kellner, D. (2000). Habermas, the public sphere, and democracy: A critical intervention. In L.E. Hahn (Ed.), *Perspectives on Habermas* (pp. 259–287). New York, NY: Open Court.

Kelleher, T. (2009). Conversational voice, communicated commitment, and Public Relations outcomes in interactive online communication. *Journal of Communication, 59*, 172–188. doi: 10.1111 / j.1460–2466.2008.01410.x.

Kendall, M. (2013, August 14). #SolidarityIsForWhiteWomen: Women of color's issues with digital feminism. *The Guardian*. Retrieved from https: / / www.theguardian.com / commentisfree / 2013 / aug / 14 / solidarityisforwhitewomen-hashtag-feminism

Kennedy, T.L.M. (2007). The personal is political: feminist blogging and virtual consciousness-raising. *Scholar & Feminism Online, 5*(2). Retrieved from http: / / sfonline.barnard.edu / blogs / kennedy_01.htm

Ketelaar, P., van Gisbergen, M., & Beentjes, J. (2012). Interpretation of highly visual "open" advertisements in Dutch magazines. *Journal of Visual Literacy, 31*(1), 23–52.

Keum, B.T., Wong, S.N., & DeBlaere, C. (2014). Body image and Asian American men: Examination of the drive for muscularity scale. *Psychology of Men and Masculinity, 16*(3), 284–293. doi: 10.1037/a0038180.

Kietzman, J.H., Hermkens, K., McCarthy, I.P., & Silvestre, B.S. (2011). Social media? Get serious! Understanding the functional building blocks of social media. *Business Horizons, 54,* 241–251. doi: 10.1016/j.bushor.2011.01.005.

Kim, C.J. (1999). The racial triangulation of Asian Americans. *Politics Society, 27,* 105–138. doi: 10.1177/0032329299027001005.

Kim, M., & Chung, A.Y. (2005). Consuming orientialism: Images of Asian/American Women in Multicultural advertising. *Qualitative Sociology, 28*(1), 67–91. doi: 10.1007/s11133-005-2631-1.

King, G. (2002). *Film Comedy.* London, UK: Wallflower Press.

King Collier, A. (2015, September 24). "Empire" season premiere proves online watch parties are back. *NBC News.* Retrieved March 14, 2016 from http://www.nbcnews.com/news/nbcblk/black-viewers-htgawm-empire-scandal-connect-online-n432491.

Kissell, R. (2015, February 26). "Empire's" growth spurt fueled by young women, urban markets. *Variety.* Retrieved March 14, 2016 from http://variety.com/2015/tv/news/empire-ratings-growth-women-urban-markets-1201442207/

Kist, W., Tollafield, K.A., & Dagistan, M. (2014). Leading ourselves (tweets optional). An analysis of selected Twitter users. *Journal of Adolescent and Adult Literacy, 58*(4), 317–326. doi: 10.1002/jaal.362.

Knobloch-Westerwick, S., & Meng, J. (2009). Looking the other way: Selective exposure to attitude-consistent and counterattitudinal political information. *Communication Research, 36*(3), 426–448. doi: 10.1177/0093650209333030.

Kohlbacher, F. (2006). The use of qualitative content analysis in case study research. *Forum: Qualitative Social Research, 7*(1).

Kos (2016, May 6). The Taco Bowl tweet was the most racist "Olive branch" of the year. *Daily Kos.* Retrieved from http://www.dailykos.com/stories/2016/5/6/1523909/-The-Taco-Bowl-tweet-was-the-most-racist-olive-branch-of-the-year.

Kotkin, J. (2016, November 9). The improbably demographics behind Donald Trump's shocking presidential victory. *Forbes.* Retrieved from https://www.forbes.com/sites/joelkotkin/2016/11/09/donald-trumps-presidenti-victory-demographics/#36d7ab5d3b96.

Kreiss, D. (2016). Seizing the moment: The presidential campaigns' use of Twitter during the 2012 electoral cycle. *New Media & Society, 18*(8), 1473–1490. doi: 10.1177/1461444814562445.

Krippendorf, K. (2004). *Content analysis: An introduction to its methodology* (2nd ed.). Thousand Oaks, CA: Sage.

Kukreja, C., & Green, M. (2016, August 22). The big issues of the 2016 election: Where Trump and Clinton stand (with lesson plan). *KQED News.* Retrieved from: https://ww2.kqed.org/lowdown/2016/08/22/election-2016-where-clinton-and-trump-stand-on-the-major-issues-interactive/

Kushin, M.J., & Yamamoto, M. (2010). Did social media really matter? College students' use of online media and political decision making in the 2008 election. *Mass Communication and Society, 13*, 608–630. doi: 10.1080/15205436.2010.516863.

Kwon, H.J. (2016, February, 29). Asian students talk about how they got their "English names." *The Tab*. Retrieved from http://thetab.com/us/emory/2016/02/29/asian-students-english-names-1166.

Lachenal, J. (2015, September 23). #MasculinitySoFragile highlights toxic masculinity's weak points. *The Mary Sue*. Retreived from http://www.themarysue.com/masculinity-so-fragile-hashtag/

Langlois, G. (2011). Meaning, semiotechnologies, and participartory media. *Culture Machine, 12*, 1–27.

Larsson, A.O., & Moe, H. (2011). Studying political microblogging: Twitter users in the 2010 Swedish election campaign. *New Media & Society, 14*(5), 729–747. doi: 10.1177/1461444811422894.

Lartey, J. (2017, January 25). Trump bans agencies from 'providing updates on social media or to reporters.' *The Guardian*. Retrieved from https://www.theguardian.com/us-news/2017/jan/24/epa-department-agriculture-social-media-gag-order-trump.

Lau, A.S.M., Lum, S.M., Chronister, K.M., & Forrest, L. (2006). Asian American college women body image: A pilot study. *Cultural Diversity and Ethnic Minority Psychology, 12*(2), 259–274. doi: 10.1037/1099–9809.12.2.259.

Lee, T.G. (2015, February 5). "Today, we've arrived": Fresh off the boat makes TV history. *NBC News*. Retrieved from http://www.nbcnews.com/news/asian-america/today-we-ve-arrived-fresh-boat-makes-tv-history-n300676.

Lee, T.G. (2016, June 28). #BeingAsian continues "necessary" conversation among Asian Americans. *NBC News*. Retrieved from http://www.nbcnews.com/news/asian-america/beingasian-continues-necessary-conversation-among-asian-americans-n600811.

Lee, L.F., Hutton, A.P., & Shu, S. (2015). The role of social media in the capital market: Evidence from consumer product recalls. *Journal of Accounting Research, 53*(2), 367–404. doi: 10.1111/1475–679X.12074.

Leong, F.T., & Hayes, T.J. (1990). Occupational stereotyping of Asian Americans. *The Career Development Quarterly, 39*, 143–154.

Leong, K.J. (2005). *The China mystique: Pearl S. Buck, Anna May Wong, Mayling Soon and the transformation of American orientalism*. Berkeley, CA: University of California Press.

Levenshus, A. (2010). Online relationship management in a presidential campaign: A case study of the Obama's campaign management of its internet-integrated grassroots effort. *Journal of Public Relations Research, 22*(3), 313–335. doi: 10.1080/10627261003614419.

Lewis, S., Pea, R., & Rosen, J. (2010). Beyond participation to co-creation of meaning: Mobile social media in generative learning communities. *Social Science Information, 49*(3), 351–369. doi: 10.1177/0539018410370726.

Liberman, C.J. (2013). Branding as social discourse: Identity construction using online social and professional networks. In C. Cunningham (Ed.), *Social Networking and Impression Management: Self-Presentation in the Digital Age* (pp. 107–128). Lanham, MD: Lexington Books.

Lin, R., Levordashka, A., & Utz, S. (2016). Ambient intimacy on Twitter. *Cyberpsychology: Journal of Psychosocial Research on Cypberspace, 10*(1), article 6. doi: 10.5817/CP2016–1-6.

Lin, Y.-R., Keegan, B., Margolin, D., & Lazer, D. (2014). Rising tides or rising stars? Dynamics of shared attention on Twitter during media events. *PLoS ONE, 9*(5), e94093. doi: 10.1371/journal.pone.0094093.

Lindgren, S. (2011). YouTube gunmen? Mapping participatory discourse on school shooting videos. *Media, Culture, & Society, 33*(1), 123–126. doi: 10.1177/0163443710386527.

Lindgren, S., & Lundström, R. (2011). Pirate Culture and Hacktivist Mobilization: The cultural and social protocols of #WikiLeaks on Twitter. *New Media and Society, 13*(6), 999–1018. doi: 10.1177/1461444811414833.

Lindlof, T.R. (1991). The qualitative study of media audiences. *Journal of Broadcasting and Electronic Media, 35*(1), 23–42. doi: 10.1080/08838159109364100.

Linthicum, K. (2016, May 5). Latino Twitter to Donald Trump: A taco bowl is not the way to our heart. *Los Angeles Times*. Retrieved from http://www.latimes.com/politics/la-na-trailguide-05052016-latino-twitter-to-donald-trump-a-taco-bowl-is-not-1462488203-htmlstory.html

Lim, M. (2012). Clicks, cabs, and coffee houses: Social media and oppositional movements in Egypt, 2004–2011. *Journal of Communication, 62*, 231–248. doi: 10.1111/j.1460–2466.2012.01628.x.

Little, A. (2013, August 16). Social media minds the intersectional gap. *Ms*. Retrieved from http://msmagazine.com/blog/2013/08/16/social-media-minds-the-intersectional-gap/

Loader, B.D., & Mercea, D. (2011). Networking democracy? Social media innovations in participatory politics. *Information, Communication and Society, 14*(6), 757–769. doi: 10.1080/1369118X.2011.592648.

Loader, B.D., Vromen, A., & Xenos, M.A. (2016). Performing for the young networked citizen? Celebrity politics, social networking, and the political engagement of young people. *Media, Culture, & Society, 38*(3), 400–419. doi: 10.1177/0163443715608261.

Logan, N. (2016). The Starbucks Race Together initiative: Analyzing a public relations campaign with critical race theory. *Public Relations Inquiry, 5*(1), 93–113. doi: 10.1177/2046147X15626969.

Lorentzen, D.G. (2014). Polarisation in political Twitter conversations. *Aslib Journal of Information Management, 66*(3), 329–341. doi: 10.1108/AJIM-09–2013–0086.

Loza, S. (2013). Hashtag feminism, #SolidarityIsForWhiteWomen, and the other #femfuture. *Ada: A journal of Gender, New Media, & Technology, 5*. Retrieved from http://adanewmedia.org/2014/07/issue5-loza/

Maragh, R.S. (2016). "Our struggles are unequal": Black women's affective labor between television and Twitter. *Journal of Communication Inquiry, 40*(4), 351–369. doi: 10.1177/0196859916664082.

Markham, A., & Buchanan, E. (2012). Ethical decision-making and internet research: Recommendations from the AoIR ethics working committee (version 2.0). Retrieved from http://aoir.org/reports/ethics2.pdf.

Martynuska, M. (2016). The exotic other: Representations of Latina tropicalism in US popular culture. *Journal of Language and Cultural Education, 4*(2), 73–81. doi: 10.1515/jolace-2016–0017.

Marwick, A., & Boyd, D. (2011a). I tweet honestly, I tweet passionately: Twitter users, the context collapse, and the imagined audience. *New Media & Society, 13*(1), 114–133. doi: 10.1177/1461444810365313.

Marwick, A., & Boyd, D. (2011b). To see and be seen: Celebrity practice on Twitter. *Convergence: The International Journal of Research into New Media Technologies, 17*(2), 139–158. doi: 10.1177/1354856510394539.

Mastro, D.E., & Behm-Morawitz, E. (2005). Latino representation on prime-time television. *Journalism and Mass Communication Quarterly, 82*(1), 110–130.

Mastro, D., Behm-Morawitz, E., & Ortiz, M. (2007). The cultivation of social perceptions of Latinos: A mental models approach. *Media Psychology, 9*, 347–365.

Mastro, D.E., & Tropp, L.R. (2004). The effects of interracial contact, attitudes, and stereotypical portrayals of evaluations on Black television sitcom characters. *Communication Research Reports, 21*(2), 119–129.

Mastro, D., & Tukachinsky, R. (2011). The influence of exemplar versus prototype-based media primes on racial/ethnic evaluations. *Journal of Communication, 61*, 916–937. doi: 10.1111/j.1460-2466.2011.01587.x.

Masunaga, S. (2015, March 18). Starbucks brews up controversy with "Race Together" campaign. *Los Angeles Times*. Retrieved from http://www.latimes.com/business/la-fi-starbucks-race-20150318-story.html.

Mazali, T. (2011). Social media as a new public sphere. *Leonardo, 44*(3), 290–291. doi: 10.1162/LEON_a_00195.

McElroy, K. (2015). Gold medals, Black Twitter, and not-so-good hair: Framing the Gabby Douglas controversy. *#ISOJ, 5*(1), 5–24.

McGrown-Levy, A. (2016, July 11). #ImWithHer demonstrates how pop culture (hash)tags its candidates. *AV Club*. Retrieved from http://www.avclub.com/article/imwithher-demonstrates-how-pop-culture-hashtags-it-238037.

McGugian, J. (2005). The cultural public sphere. *European Journal of Cultural Studies, 8*(4), 427–443. doi: 10.1177/1367549405057827.

McRobbie, A. (2004). Post-feminism and popular culture. *Feminist Media Studies, 4*(3), 255–264. doi: 10.1080/1468077042000309937.

McRobbie, A. (2009). *The aftermath of feminism: Gender, culture, and social change.* Thousand Oaks, CA: Sage.

MediaKix Team. (2016, August 31). 10 examples of the most successful media campaigns. *MediaKix*. Retrieved from http://mediakix.com/2016/08/most-successful-social-media-campaigns-2016/

Merry, M. (2016). Making friends and enemies on social media: The case of gun policy organizations. *Online Information Review, 40*(5), 624–642.

Merskin, D. (2007). Three faces of Eva: Perpetuation of the hot-Latina stereotype in *Desperate Housewives. The Howards Journal of Communications, 18*, 133–151.

Mihailidis, P., Fincham, K., & Cohen, J.N. (2014). Toward a media literate model for civic engagement in digital culture: Exploring the civic habits and dispositions of college students on Facebook. *Atlantic Journal of Communication, 22*, 293–309. doi: 10.1080/15456870.2014.961400.

Milestones. (2016). Retrieved from https://about.twitter.com/company/press/milestones.

Millard, J. (2009). Performing beauty: Dove's "real beauty" campaign. *Symbolic Interaction, 32*(2), 146–168. doi: 10.1525/si.2009.32.2.146.

Miller, A. (2012). Investigating social desirability bias in student self-report surveys. *Educational Research Quarterly, 36*(1), 30–47.

Millington, A. (2015, May 7). Top ten Youtube ads in April. *Marketing Week.* Retrieved from https://www.marketingweek.com/2015/05/07/top-ten-youtube-ads-in-april/

Miranda, A.O., Bilot, J.M., Peluso, P.R., Berman, K., & Van Meek, L.G. (2006). Latino families: The relevance of connection among acculturation, family dynamics, and health for family counseling, research, and practice. *The Family Journal: Counseling and Therapy for Couples and Families, 14*(3), 268–273. doi: 10.1177/1066480706287805.

Mitchell, A., Gottfried, J., Kiley, J., & Matsa, K.E. (2014, October 21). Political polarization and media habits. *Pew Research Center.* Retrieved from http://www.journalism.org/2014/10/21/political-polarization-media-habits/

Mitchell, A., Gottfried, J., Barthel, M., & Shearer, E. (2016, July 7). Pathways to news. *Pew Research Center: Journalism & Media.* Retrieved from http://www.journalism.org/2016/07/07/pathways-to-news/

Molina Guzmán, I., & Valdivia, A.N. (2004). Brain, brow, and booty: Latina iconicity in US popular culture. *The Communication Review, 7,* 205–221. doi: 10.1080/10714420490448723.

Monilos, K. (2016, January 6). L'Oréal's Golden Globes campaign aims to get women talking about more than just beauty. *Adweek.* Retrieved from http://www.adweek.com/brand-marketing/lor-als-golden-globes-campaign-aims-get-women-talking-about-more-just-beauty-168840/

Monk-Turner, E., Heiserman, M., Johnson, C., Cotton, V., & Jackson, M. (2010). The portrayal of racial minorities on prime-time television: A replication of the Mastro and Greenberg study a decade later. *Studies in Popular Culture, 32*(2), 101–114.

Morozov, E. (2009, May 19). The brave new world of slacktivism. Retrieved from http://neteffect.foreignpolicy.com/posts/2009/05/19/the_brave_new_world_of_slacktivism.

Morozov, E. (2013). *To save everything, click here. The folly of technological solutionism.* New York, NY: PublicAffairs.

Morrison, K. (2015, March 25). What went wrong with the Starbucks #RaceTogether campaign? *Adweek.* Retrieved from http://www.adweek.com/digital/starbucks-race-together-campaign/

Moorman, R.H., & Podsakoff, P.M. (1992). A meta-analytic review and empirical test of the potential confounding effects of social desirability response sets in organizational behavior research. *Journal of Occupational and Organizational Psychology, 65,* 131–149.

Mouffe, C. (1999). Deliberative democracy or agonistic pluralism? *Social Research, 66*(3), 745–758.

Mouffe, C. (2000). Deliberative democracy or agonistic pluralism? *Political Science Series, 72,* 1–17.

Mowatt, R.A., French, B.H., & Malebranche, D.A. (2013). Black/Female/Body *Hypervisibility* and *invisibility.* A Black feminist augmentation of feminist leisure research. *Journal of Leisure Research, 45*(5), 644–660.

Murthy, D. (2012). Towards a sociological understanding of social media: Theorizing Twitter. *Sociology, 46*(6), 1059–1073. doi: 10.1177/0038038511422553.

Nakamura, L. (2008). *Digitizing race: Visual cultures of the internet.* Minneapolis, MN: University of Minnesota Press.

Neuendorf, K.A., & Kumar, A. (2015). Content analysis. In G. Mazzoleni (Ed.), *The International Encycopledia of Political Communication* (1st ed., pp. 1–10). Hoboken, NJ: Wiley.

Nielsen. (2013, March 20). New study confirms correlation between Twitter and TV ratings. Retrieved August 27, 2016 from http://www.nielsen.com/us/en/insights/news/2013/new-study-confirms-correlation-between-twitter-and-tv-ratings.html

Nielsen. (2014, August 4). Living social: How second screens are helping TV make fans. Retrieved August 27, 2016 from http://www.nielsensocial.com/living-social-how-second-screens-are-helping-tv-make-fans/

Nielsen. (2015a). *Asian Americans: Culturally connected and forging the future.* Retrieved September 4, 2016 from http://www.nielsencommunity.com/report_files/nielsen-asian-american-report-june-2015.pdf

Nielsen. (2015b, June 11). *Meet the fastest-growing multicultural segment in the US: Asian Americans.* Retrieved http://www.nielsen.com/us/en/insights/news/2015/meet-the-fastest-growing-multicultural-segment-in-the-us-asian-americans.html

Nishime, L. (2014). *Undercover Asian. Multiracial Asian Americans in visual culture.* Champaign, IL: University of Illinois Press.

Obar, J.A., Zube, P., & Lampe, C. (2012). Advocacy 2.0: An analysis of how advocacy groups in the United States perceive and use social media as tools for facilitating civic engagement and collective action. *Journal of Information Policy, 2,* 1–25.

Ono, K.A., & Pham, V.N. (2009). *Asian Americans and the media.* Malden, MA: Polity Press.

Ohlheiser, A. (2016, November 7). Inside the huge "secret" Facebook group for Hilary Clinton's biggest fans. *The Washington Post.* Retrieved from https://www.washingtonpost.com/news/the-intersect/wp/2016/11/07/inside-the-huge-secret-facebook-group-for-hillary-clintons-biggest-fans/

O'Reilly, L. (2017, February 5). The 84 Lumber Super Bowl ad's creative director explains the thinking behind the Mexican immigration-themed spot. *Business Insider.* Retrieved from http://www.businessinsider.com/84-lumber-super-bowl-ad-explained-2017–2.

Ortega, M. (2006). Being lovingly, knowingly ignorant: White feminism and women of color. *Hypatia, 21*(3), 56–74.

Oysterman, D., Gant, L., & Ager, J. (1995). A socially contextualized model of African American identity: Possible selves and school persistence. *Journal of Personaility and Social Psychology, 69*(6), 1216–1232.

Oysterman, D., & Sakamoto, I. (1997). Being Asian American: Identity, cultural constructs, and stereotype perception. *Journal of Applied Behavioral Science, 33*(4), 435–453.

Pachal, P. (2014, May 26). How the #YesAllWomen hashtag began. *Mashable.* Retrieved from http://mashable.com/2014/05/26/yesallwomen-hashtag/#B7Xd4dMmVaq9.

Palazzo, C. (2017, February 6). Airbnb says #WeAccept as Super Bowl LI ads get political. *The Telegraph.* Retrieved from http://www.telegraph.co.uk/technology/2017/02/06/airbnb-says-weaccept-super-bowl-li-ad/

Pantsuit Nation (n.d.). *Pantsuit Nation: Our Manifesto.* Retrieved from http://www.pantsuitnation.org/

Papacharissi, Z. (2002). The virtual sphere: The Internet as a public sphere. *New Media & Society, 4*(1), 9–27.

Papacharissi, Z. (2009). The virtual sphere 2.0: The Internet, the public sphere, and beyond. In A. Chadwick & P.N. Howard (Eds.), *Routledge Handbook of Internet Politics* (pp. 230–245). New York, NY: Routledge.

Papacharissi, Z. (2010). *A private sphere: Democracy in a digital age.* Cambridge: Polity Press.

Park, N., Kee, K.F., & Valenzuela, S. (2009). Being immersed in the social networking environment: Facebook groups, uses, and gratifications, and social outcomes. *Cyberpsychology and Behavior, 12*(6), 729–733. doi: 10.1089=cpb.2009.0003.

Parmalee, J.H., & Bichard, S.L. (2011). *Politics and the Twitter Revolution: How Tweets Influence the Relationship between Political Leaders and the Public.* Lanham, MD: Lexington Books.

Patterson, T.E. (2016a, June 13). Pre-primary news coverage of the 2016 presidential race: Trump's rise, Sanders' emergence, Clinton's struggle. *Shorenstein Center on Media, Politics, and Public Policy.* Retrieved from https://shorensteincenter.org/pre-primary-news-coverage-2016-trump-clinton-sanders/

Patterson, T.E. (2016b, July 11). News coverage of the 2016 presidential primaries: Horse race reporting has its consequences. *Shorenstein Center on Media, Politics, and Public Policy.* Retrieved from https://shorensteincenter.org/news-coverage-2016-presidential-primaries/

Patterson, T.E. (2016c, December 7). News coverage of the 2016 election: How the press failed the voters. *Shorenstein Center on Media, Politics, and Public Policy.* Retrieved from https://shorensteincenter.org/news-coverage-2016-general-election/

Payne, M. (February 7, 2017). 84 Lumber CEO: Super Bowl ad showing Trump's wall wasn't intended to be political. *The Washington Post.* Retrieved from https://www.washingtonpost.com/news/early-lead/wp/2017/02/04/company-re-tools-rejected-super-bowl-ad-but-you-can-still-see-the-original/

Perez, B.E. (2013). Woman-warrior meets mail-order bride: Finding an Asian American voice in the women's movement. *Berkeley Journal of Gender, Law, and Justice, 18*(1), 211–236. doi: 10.15779/Z384M9192S

Pérez, M., & Gómez, J.M. (2011). Why do people use social networks? *Communications of the IIMA, 11*(2), 41–49.

Pilon, A. (2016, December 26). These were the best viral campaigns of 2016. *Small business trends.* Retrieved from https://smallbiztrends.com/2016/12/best-viral-campaigns-of-2016.html.

Pittman, T. (2015, June 30). #HispanicGirlsUnited gives an honest look at what it's like to be Latina. *The Huffington Post.* Retrieved from http://www.huffingtonpost.com/2015/06/30/hispanic-girls-united-twitter-hashtag_n_7690610.html.

Poell, T. (2009). Conceptualizing forums and blogs as public spheres. In M.V.T Van den Boomen, S. Lammes, A.-S. Lehmann, J. Raessens, & M.T. Schäfer (Eds.). *Digital Material* (pp. 239–251). Amsterdam, Netherlands: Amsterdam University Press.

Poran, M.A. (2006). The politics of protection: Body image, social pressures, and the misrepresentation of young Black women. *Sex Roles, 55*, 739–755. doi: 10.1007/s11199–006–9129–5.

Presi, C., Maehle, N., & Kleppe, I.A. (2016). Brand selfies: Consumer experiences and marketplace conversations. *European Journal of Marketing, 50*(9/10), 1814–1834. doi: 10.1108/EJM-07–2015–0492.

Prince, R. (2014, January 9). What it means that *Scandal* is sizzling hot among Black women. *The Root*. Retrieved from http://www.theroot.com/blogs/journalisms/2014/01/abc_drama_scandal_is_popular_among_black_women.html.

Putnam, D. (2000). *Bowling alone. The collapse and revival of the American community*. New York, NY: Simon & Schuster.

Rainie, L., Smith, A., Schlozman, K.L., Brady, H., & Verba, S. (2012, October 19). Social media and political engagement. *Pew Research Center*. Retrieved from http://www.pewinternet.org/2012/10/19/social-media-and-political-engagement/

Ramirez Berg, C. (1990). Stereotyping in films in general and of the Hispanic in general. *Howard Journal of Communications*, 2(3), 286–300. doi: 10.1080/10646179009359721.

Ramirez Berg, C. (2002). *Latino images in film: Stereotypes, subversion, resistance*. Austin, TX: University of Texas Press.

Rayworth, M. (2014). 10 years after Dove's "real beauty" campaign, more brands fight for real women. *TakePart*. Retrieved from http://www.takepart.com/article/2014/01/30/10-years-after-doves-real-beauty-campaign-brands-are-fighting-female-form/

Reed, T.V. (2014). *Digitized Lives. Culture, power, and social change in the internet era*. New York, NY: Routledge.

Repanshek, K. (2017, January 25). UPDATED: "Unofficial" National Park Service Twitter accounts challenge Trump administration. *National Parks Traveler*. Retrieved from http://www.nationalparkstraveler.com/2017/01/updated-unofficial-national-park-service-twitter-accounts-challenge-trump-administration.

Richardson, B.L., Macon, T.A., Mustafaa, F.N., Bogan, E.D., Cole-Lewis, Y., & Chavous, T.M. (2015). Associations of racial discrimination and parental discrimination coping messages with African American adolescent racial identity. *Journal of Youth and Adolescence, 44*(6), 1301–1317. doi:10.1007/s10964–014–0196–6.

Rightler-McDaniels, J.L., & Hendrickson, E.M. (2014). Hoes and hashtags: Constructions of gender and race in trending topics. *Social Semiotics, 24*(2), 175–190. doi: 10.1080/10350330.2013.859355.

Ritzer, G., & Jurgenson, N. (2010). Production, consumption, presumption. The nature of capitalism in the age of the digital "prosumer." *Journal of Consumer Culture, 10*(1), 13–36. doi: 10.1177/1469540509354673.

Robinson, M. (2013, August 15). Spike Lee slams Russell Simmons for producing mock Harriet Tubman sex tape. *Business Insider*. Retrieved from http://www.businessinsider.com/spike-lee-slams-russell-simmons-for-producing-mock-harriet-tubman-sex-tape-2013–8.

Rogers, K. (2016, May 10). John Cho, starring in every movie ever made? A diversity hashtag is born. *The New York Times*. Retrieved from https://www.nytimes.com/2016/05/11/movies/john-cho-starring-in-every-movie-ever-made-a-diversity-hashtag-is-born.html.

Rogers, R. (2014). Debanalising Twitter: The transformation of an object of study. In K. Weller, A. Bruns, J. Burgess, Mahrt, M., & Puschmann, C. (Eds.), *Twitter and Society* (pp. ix–xxvi). New York, NY: Peter Lang.

Rokka, J., & Canniford, R. (2016). Heterotopian selfies: How social media destabilizes brand assemblages. *European Journal of Marketing, 50*(9/10), 1789–1813. doi: http://dx.doi.org/10.1108/EJM-08-2015-0517.

Romano, A. (2015, September 24). Some people sadly missed the point about #MasculinitySoFragile. *Mashable*. Retrieved from http://mashable.com/2015/09/24/masculinity-so-fragile/#ewy5_5tWVuqP.

Rosenbaum, J.E., Johnson, B.K., Stepman, P.A., & Nuijten, K.C.M. (2013). "Looking the part" and "staying true": Balancing impression management on Facebook. In C. Cunningham (Ed.), *Social Networking and Impression Management: Self-Presentation in the Digital Age* (pp. 35–61). Lanham, MD: Lexington Books.

Rossi, L., & Giglietto, F. (2016). Twitter use during TV: A full-season analysis of #serviziopubblico hashtag. *Journal of Broadcasting and Electronic Media, 60*(2), 331–346. doi: 10.1080/08838151.2016.1164162.

Rushton, C. (2016, October 14). #WomenWhoVoteTrump explain their choice on Twitter. *LA Times*. Retrieved from http://www.latimes.com/nation/politics/trailguide/la-na-trailguide-updates-womenwhovotetrump-explain-their-vote-1476449034-htmlstory.html.

Ryan, P. (2016, February 2). #OscarsSoWhite controversy: What you need to know. *USA Today*. Retrieved from https://www.usatoday.com/story/life/movies/2016/02/02/oscars-academy-award-nominations-diversity/79645542/

Said, E. (1978). *Orientalism*. London, UK: Routledge.

Samuel, N. (2016, June 10). It's already June?! Top Black Twitter moments of 2016 so far. *Madame Noir*. Retrieved from http://madamenoire.com/700776/black-twitter-moments-hashtags/16/

Sanders, S. (2015, March 22). Starbucks will stop putting the words "race together" on cups. *National Public Radio*. Retrieved from http://www.npr.org/sections/thetwo-way/2015/03/22/394710277/starbucks-will-stop-writing-race-together-on-coffee-cups.

Sanders, S. (2016, March 28). #B.erniemademewhite: No, Bernie Sanders isn't just winning with white people. *National Public Radio*. Retrieved from http://www.npr.org/2016/03/28/472160616/-berniemademewhite-no-bernie-sanders-isnt-just-winning-with-white-people.

Sanneh, K. (2001). Black in the box: In defense of African American television. *Transition, 10*(4), 38–65.

Sajuria, J., VanHeerde-Hudson, J., Hudson, D., Dasandi, N., & Theocharis, Y. (2015). Tweeting alone? An analysis of bridging and bonding social capital in online networks. *American Politics Research, 43*(4), 708–738. doi: 10.1177/1532673X14557942.

Sciachitano, M. (2000). "MOBS" on the net: Critiquing the gaze of the "cyber" bride industry. *Race, Gender, and Class, 7*(1), 57–69.

Scott, J-A., & Cloud, N. (2008). Rea*ffirm*ing the ideal: A focus groups analysis of the campaign for real beauty. *Advertising and Society Review, 9*(4). doi: 10.1353/asr.0.0012.

Schmitt, B. (2012). The consumer psychology of brands. *Journal of Consumer Pyschology, 22*, 7–17. doi: 10.1016/j.jcps.2011.09.005.

Schmidt, J.-H. (2014). Twitter and the rise of personal publics. In K. Weller, A. Bruns, J. Burgess, M. Mahrt, & C. Puschmann, (Eds.), *Twitter and Society* (pp. 3–15). New York, NY: Peter Lang.

Schradie, J. (2011). The digitial production gap: The digital divide and Web 2.0 collide. *Poetics, 39*, 145–168. doi: 10.1016/j.poetic.2011.02.003.

Seethaler, I. (2013). "Big Bad Chinese Mama": How Internet humor subverts stereotypes about Asian American women. *Studies in American Humor, 3*(27), 117–138.

Sharma, S. (2013). Black Twitter: Racial hashtags, networks, and contagion. *New Formations: A Journal of Culture/Theory/Politics, 78*(46), 46–64. doi: 10.3898/NEWF.78.02.2013.

Shaw, F. (2012). The politics of blogs: Theories of discursive activism online. *Media International Australia, 142*(1), 41–49.

Shaw, P. (2014). The public sphere and the Telangana movement. *Media International Australia, 152*, 143–157.

Shen, F.C., Wang, Y.-W., & Swanson, J.L. (2011). Development and initial validation of the internalization of Asian American stereotypes scale. *Cultural Diversity and Ethnic Minority Psychology, 17*(3), 283–294. doi: 10.1037/a0024727.

Shifman, L. (2014). *Memes in digital culture*. Cambridge, MA: Massachusetts Institute of Technology.

Shin, M., & Wong, Y.J. (2013). Beyond the tiger mom: Asian American parenting and parent-child relationships. In P. Barberis & S. Petrakis (Eds.), *Parenting. Challenges, practices, and cultural influences* (pp. 103–123). New York, NY: Nova Science.

Shrauger, J.S., & Schoeneman, T.J. (1979). Symbolic interactionist view of the self-concept: Through the looking glass darkly. *Psychological Bulletin, 86*(3), 549–573.

Small, T. A. (2014). The not-so social network: The use of Twitter by Canada's party leaders. In A. Marland, T. Giasson, & T.A. Small (Eds.), *Political Communication in Canada: Meet the press and Tweet the rest* (p. 92–111). Vancouver, Canada: University of British Columbia Press.

Smith, A. (2014, January 6). African Americans and technology use: A demographic portrait. *Pew Research Center. Internet, Science, & Tech*. Retrieved from http://www.pewinternet.org/2014/01/06/african-americans-and-technology-use/

Smith, M.A., Rainie, L., Shneiderman, B., & Himelboim, I. (2014, February 20). Mapping Twitter topic networks: From polarized crowds to community clusters. *Pew Research Center*. Retrieved from http://www.pewinternet.org/2014/02/20/mapping-twitter-topic-networks-from-polarized-crowds-to-community-clusters/

Springer, K. (2007). Divas, Black bitches, and bitter Black women: African American women in postfeminist and post-civil rights popular culture. In L. Spigel (Ed.), *Interrogating postfeminism* (pp. 249–276). Durham, NC: Duke University Press.

Stein, G.L., Gonzalez, L.M., Cupito, A.M., Kiang, L., & Supple, A.J. (2013). The protective role of familism in the lives of Latino adolescents. *Journal of Family Issues, 36*(10), 1255–1273. doi: 10.1177/0192513X13502480.

Sue, D.W., Bucceri, J., Lin, A.I., Nadal, K.L., & Torino, G.C. (2007). Racial microaggressions and the Asian American experience. *Cultural Diversity and Ethnic Minority Psychology, 13*(1), 72–81. doi: 10.1037/1099-9809.13.1.72.

Suhay, E., Blackwell, A., Roche, C., & Bruggeman, L. (2015). Forging bonds and burning bridges: Polarization and incivility in blog discussions about Occupy Wall Street. *American Politics Research, 43*(4), 643–679. doi: 10.1177/1532673X14553834.

Sun, W., & Starosta, W.J. (2006). Perceptions of minority invisibility among Asian American professionals. *Howard Journal of Communications, 17*, 119–142. doi: 10.1080/10646170600656870.

Sveningsson, M. (2014). "I don't like it and I think it's useless," people discussing politics on "Facebook": Young Swedes' understanding of social media use for political discussion. *Cyberpsychology: Journal of Psychosocial Research on Cyberspace, 8*(3), article 8. doi: 10.5817/CP2014-3-8.

Sylwester, K., & Purver, M. (2015). Twitter language use reflects psychological differences between Democrats and Republicans, *PLoS ONE, 10*(9), e0137422. doi:10.1371/journal.pone.0137422.

Taibbi, M. (2016, March 25). Donald Trump claims authorship of legendary Reagan slogan; has never heard of Google. *Rolling Stone*. Retrieved from http://www.rollingstone.com/politics/news/donald-trump-is-americas-stupidest-person-has-never-heard-of-google-20150325.

Tait, A. (2017, January 27). The myth of generation snowflake. How did "sensitive" become a dirty word? *The New Statesman*. Retrieved from http://www.newstatesman.com/politics/uk/2017/01/myth-generation-snowflake-how-did-sensitive-become-dirty-word.

Taylor, J., Johnston, J., & Whitehead, K. (2016). A corporation in feminist clothing? Young women discuss the Dove "Real Beauty" campaign. *Critical Sociology, 42*(1), 123–144. doi: 10.1177/0896920513501355.

Thrift, S.C. (2014). #YesAllWomen as feminist meme event. *Feminist Media Studies, 14*(6), 1090–1092.

Thomas, A.J., Witherspoon, K.M., & Speight, S. (2004). Towards the development of the stereotypic roles for Black women scale. *Journal of Black Psychology, 30*(3), 426–442. doi: 10.1177/0095798404266061.

Tsukayama, H. (2012, February 2). Facebook IPO: How does Facebook make its money? *The Washington Post*. Retrieved from https://www.washingtonpost.com/business/technology/facebook-ipo-how-does-facebook-make-its-money/2012/02/01/gIQAL03yiQ_story.html.

Tudoroiu, T. (2014). Social media and revolutionary waves: The case of the Arab spring. *New Political Science, 36*(3), 346–365. doi: 10.1080/07393148.2014.913841.

Tufekci, Z. (2017). *Twitter and tear gas: The power and fragility of networked protest* New Haven, CT: Yale University Press.

Tumasjan, A., Sprenger, T.O., Sandner, P.G., & Welpe, W.M. (2010). Predicting elections with Twitter: What 140 characters reveal about public sentiment. *Proceedings of the Fourth International AAAI Conference on Weblogs and Social Media*.

Twitter (2016, June 30). *Company facts*. Retrieved from https://about.twitter.com/company.

Tyson, A., & Maniam, S. (2016, November 9). Behind Trump's victory: Divisions by race, gender, education. *Pew Research Center*. Retrieved from http://www.pewresearch.org/fact-tank/2016/11/09/behind-trumps-victory-divisions-by-race-gender-education/

Vaglanos, A. (2015, April, 7). Dove's "choose beautiful" campaign says women are so much more than average. *The Huffington Post*. Retrieved from http://www.huffingtonpost.com/2015/04/07/dove-beauty-choose-beautiful-campaign-video_n_7010178.html.

Valdivia, A.N. (1998). Stereotype or transgression? Rosie Perez in Hollywood Film. *The Sociological Quarterly, 39*(3), 393–408.

Valenzuela, S., Park, N., Kee, K.F. (2009). Is there social capital in a social network site? Facebook use and college students' life satisfaction, trust, and participation. *Journal of Computer-Mediated Communication, 14*, 875–901.

Van Deursen, A.J.A.M., & Van Dijk, J.A.G.M. (2014). The digital divide shifts to differences in usage. *New Media & Society, 16*(3), 507–526. doi: 10.1177/1461444813487959.

Van Dijck, J. (2009). Users like you? Theorizing agency in user-generated content. *Media, Culture, & Society, 31*(1), 41–58. doi: 10.1177/0163443708098245.

Van Zoonen, L., Vis, F., & Mihelj, S. (2011). YouTube interactions between agonism, antagonism, and dialogue: Video responses to the anti-Islam film *Fitna*. *New Media & Society, 13*(8), 1283–1300. doi: 10.1177/1461444811405020.

Vargo, C.J., & Hopp, T. (2017). Socioeconomic status, social capital, and partisan polarity as predictors of political incivility on Twitter: A congressional district-level analysis. *Social Science Computer Review, 35*(1), 10–32. doi: 10.1177/0894439315602858.

Vega, T. (2014, August 12). Shooting spurs hashtag effect on stereotypes. *New York Times.* Retrieved from https://www.nytimes.com/2014/08/13/us/if-they-gunned-me-down-protest-on-twitter.html.

Viagas, R. (2016, May 3). Asian actors tell stories of prejudice in #MyYellowFace Story project. *Playbill.* Retrieved from http://www.playbill.com/article/asian-actors-tell-stories-of-prejudice-in-myyellowfacestory-project.

Vitak, J., Zube, P., Smock, A., Carr, C.T., Ellison, N., & Lampe, C. (2011). It's complicated: Facebook users' political participation in the 2008 election. *Cyberpsychology, Behavior, and Social Networking, 14*(3), 107–114. doi: 10.1089/cyber.2009.0226.

Wang, G. (2010). A shot at half-exposure. Asian Americans in reality TV shows. *Television & New Media, 11*(5), 404–427. doi: 10.1177/1527476410363482.

Walker, T. (2015, June 15). #AskRachel: How a hashtag became Black America's family reunion. *Huffington Post.* Retreived from http://www.huffingtonpost.com/torraine-walker/askrachel-twitter-hashtag_b_7585620.html.

Ward, L.M. (2004). Wading through the stereotypes: Positive and negative associations between media use and Black adolescents' conceptions of self. *Developmental Psychology, 40*(2), 284–294. doi: 10.1037/0012–1649.40.2.284.

Warren, C.S., & Rios, R.M. (2013). The relationships among acculturation, acculturative stress, endorsement of Western media, social comparison, and body image in Hispanic male college students. *Psychology of Men and Masculinity, 14*(2), 192–201.

Warshow, R. (1962). The gangster as a tragic hero. In R. Warshow (Ed.), *The immediate experience: Movies, comics, theatre, and other aspects of popular culture* (pp. 97–103). Garden City, NY: Doubleday.

Way, L.C.S. (2015). YouTube as a site of debate through populist politics: The case of a Turkish protest pop video. *Journal of Multicultural Discourses, 10*(2), 180–196. doi: 10.1080/17447143.2015.1041965.

Wei, L., & Hindman, D.B. (2011). Does the digital divide matter more? Comparing the effects of new media and old media use on the education-based knowledge gap. *Mass Communication and Society, 14*, 216–235. doi: 10.1080/15205431003642707.

Weiss, S. (2014, May 26). The power of #YesAllWomen. *The New Yorker.* Retrieved from http://www.newyorker.com/culture/culture-desk/the-power-of-yesallwomen.

Wells, C., Cramer, K.J., Wagner, M.W., Alvarez, G., Friedland, L.A., Shah, D.V., Bode, L., Edgerly, S., Gabay, I., & Franklin, C. (2017). When we stop talking politics: The maintenance and closing of conversation in contentious times. *Journal of Communication, 67*, 131–157. doi: 10.1111/jcom.12280.

West, C.M. (1995). Mammy, sapphire and jezebel: Historical images of Black women and their implications for psychotherapy. *Psychotherapy, 32*(3), 458–466.

Wester, F., Pleijter, A., & Renckstorf, K. (2004). Exploring newspapers' portrayals: A logic for interpretive content analysis. *Communications, 29*, 495–513.

White, M. (2010, August 12). Clicktivism is ruining leftist activism. *The Guardian*. Retrieved from https://www.theguardian.com/commentisfree/2010/aug/12/clicktivism-ruining-leftist-activism.

White, M.D., & Marsh, E.E. (2006). Content analysis: A flexible methodology. *Library Trends, 55*(1), 22–45.

Whiting, A., & Williams, D. (2013). Why people use social media: A uses and gratifications approach. *Qualitative Marketing Research, 16*(4), 362–369.

Williams, S. (2015). Digital defense: Black feminists resist violence with hashtag activism. *Feminist Media Studies, 15*(2), 341–343. doi: 10.1080/14680777.2015.1008744.

Wilson, C.C., & Gutierrez, F. (1995). *Race, multiculturalism, and the media*. Thousand Oaks, CA: Sage.

Wong, Y.J., Owen, J., Tran, K.K., Collins, D.L., & Higgins, C.E. (2012). Asian American male college students' perceptions of people's stereotypes about Asian American men. *Psychology of Men and Masculinity, 13*(1), 75–88. doi: 10.1037/a0022800.

Woodard, J.B., & Mastin, T. (2005). Black womanhood: *Essence* and its treatment of stereotypical images of Black women. *Journal of Black Studies, 36*(2), 264–281. doi: 10.1177/0021934704273152.

Woolley, J.K., Limperos, A.M., & Oliver, M.B. (2010). The 2008 presidential election, 2.0: A content analysis of user-generated political Facebook groups. *Mass Communication and Society, 13*(5), 631–652. doi: 10.1080/15205436.2010.516864.

Wortham, J. (2016). Black Tweets matter. *Smithsonian Magazine*. Retrieved from http://www.smithsonianmag.com/arts-culture/black-tweets-matter-180960117/

Wu, E.D. (2014, January 14). #NotYourAsianTigermom: The backstory. *History News Network*. Retrieved from http://historynewsnetwork.org/article/154439.

Wynn, J. (2016, March 16). Masculinity so fragile. *Everyday Socology*. Retrieved from http://www.everydaysociologyblog.com/2016/03/masculinity-so-fragile.html.

Yardi, S., & Boyd, D. (2010). Dynamic debates: An analysis of group polarization over time on Twitter. *Bulletin of Science, Technology, and Society, 30*(5), 316–327. doi: 10.1177/0270467610380011.

Yeh, C.J., Inman, A.G., Kim, A.B., & Okubo Y. (2006). Asian American families' collectivistic coping strategies in response to 9/11. *Cultural Diversity and Ethnic Minority Psychology, 12*(1), 134–148. doi: 10.1037/1099-9809.12.1.134.

Zamora Medina, R., & Zurutuza Munõz, C. (2014). Campaigning on Twitter: Towards the personal style campaign to activate the political engagement during the 2011 Spanish general elections. *Communication & Society, 27*(1), 83–106.

Zentella, A.C. (2007). "Dime con quien hablas, y te dire quien eres": Linguistic (in)security and Latina(o) unity. In J. Flores & R. Rosalod (Eds.), *A companion to Latino/a studies* (pp. 25–38). Malden, MA: Blackwell.

Zimmer, M., & Proferes, N. (2014). Privacy on Twitter, Twitter on privacy. In K. Weller, A. Bruns, J. Burgess, M. Mahrt, & C. Puschmann, (Eds.), *Twitter and Society* (pp. 169–181). New York, NY: Peter Lang.

Zimmerman, J. (2014, April 28). Not all men: A brief history of every dude's favorite argument. *Time*. Retrieved from http://time.com/79357/not-all-men-a-brief-history-of-every-dudes-favorite-argument/

Index

2016 presidential election, 19, 143, 153, 154, 155, 177, 178, 179, 180, 183, 184, 185, 188, 196, 197, 200, 201, 206, 207, 263, 264, 265, 276, 281, 285, 289
2016 US presidential campaign, 66, 91, 173–74, 177, 178, 179, 180, 182, 183, 184, 188, 190, 191, 194, 199, 206, 280, 281, 289
84 Lumber, 217, 227, 228, 236–43, 244, 245, 247, 281, 287
#84Lumber. *See* 84 Lumber

activism, 138–40, 141, 146, 152, 171; corporate, 227; discursive, 140, 141, 143, 146; hashtag, 30, 151
activists, 149, 172, 189, 284
affordances, 4, 5, 10, 14, 96, 137, 139, 174–75, 176, 191, 200, 207, 250, 276, 280, 282, 283, 287, 290
African Americans: culture, 19, 28, 30, 31–32, 42, 49, 54, 61; family, 52–56, 61; femininity, 28, 31, 32–44, 284; identity, 27, 29, 41, 44, 48–52, 54–57, 61, 62, 284; masculinity, 28, 31–32, 44–48; parenting, 35, 51, 53–54; representation, 18, 28–29; Twitter, 18, 29–31. *See also* community, African American
African American men: stereotypes, 28, 268, 278; sexuality, 28, 45–47, 52, 55, 56–58
African American women: angry, 28, 32, 34–37, 38–39, 278; education, 39, 43, 58; mothers, 32, 34–37, 42, 46, 52, 61, 278; physical features, 41, 42, 50; sexuality, 28, 32, 35–36, 39, 40–42, 52, 56–59, 61
agonistic pluralism, 186–87, 281, 291
Airbnb, 213, 217, 227–28, 243–46, 281
All-American Girl, 100
#AllLivesMatter, 137, 138, 141, 142, 143, 152, 153, 156–60, 163–65, 180, 262, 273, 280, 284, 288
Americanism, 159, 160, 180–81, 184, 188–89, 202, 236–37, 244–45, 247, 281–82
American values. *See* Americanism
Arab Spring, 2, 137, 141
Asian Americans: accent, 121–22, 279; citizenship and immigration, 115, 123; culture, 100–104, 113, 116, 117, 125, 132, 133; family, 102, 127, 133,

279; identity, 100, 102, 104, 113–16, 121, 133, 134, 279, 284; invisibility of, 99, 100, 113, 115, 117–18, 120, 125; model minority, 100–102, 106, 107, 121, 122–26, 133, 279; perpetual foreigner, 111, 116, 121, 133, 279; representation, 18, 99–102; Twitter, 18–19, 103. *See also* community, Asian American
Asian American men: effeminate, 101, 108–10, 133; as sex symbol, 110–12
Asian American women: Dragon Lady, 101, 106, 124; Lotus Blossom, 101, 104, 107, 108; lack of emotions, 131; Madam Butterfly, 101, 102, 108, 133; physical features, 119–21; sexuality, 102, 108; tiger mom, 102, 106, 108, 125–27, 129, 130, 131–33, 278
#AsianPrivilege, 145, 151, 156, 160
#AsianProblems, 103, 113, 115, 119, 129
#AskRachel, 19, 29, 31, 32, 42, 48, 49

#BackTheBlue, 138, 142, 143, 152, 157, 159, 180, 286
#BadHombres, 178, 190, 191, 192, 194, 195, 205
beauty: as a choice, 219–22, 224; ideals, 50, 151, 217, 218, 221, 226, 288; self-worth, 219
#BeautyBias, 17
#BeingABlackGirlIsLit, 27, 32, 33, 36, 41, 48, 49, 50–52, 56, 62, 279
#BeingAsian, 99, 103, 104, 105, 107, 108, 112–17, 119, 122, 125, 126, 129, 131–33, 279, 284
#BeingLatino, 66, 72, 84, 92, 93
belonging. *See* community
#BernieMadeMeWhite, 32, 173, 174, 178, 191, 193, 194, 198, 199
Better Call Saul, 66, 75, 77, 81
Black-ish, 6, 17, 27, 31, 34, 37, 40, 43, 44, 46, 47, 53, 54, 56
#BlackGirls, 30, 36
the Black Bitch, 28, 35–39, 42, 43, 45, 71, 166
the Black Lady, 28, 40, 58, 59, 60, 61, 64
Black Lives Matter, 159, 259, 267, 268. *See also* #BlackLivesMatter
#BlackLivesMatter, 2, 10, 30, 32, 137, 138, 139, 141, 142, 143, 147, 151, 152, 153, 157, 158, 160, 163, 164, 165, 167, 168, 262, 263, 266, 272, 273, 280, 284, 286, 288
the Black Superwoman, 32, 33, 60
#BlackPowerIsForBlackMen, 137, 142, 144, 150, 151, 165, 166, 286
#BlueLivesMatter, 137, 143, 157, 158
Bonilla, Yarimar, 14, 30
Bouvier, Gwen, 11
Boyd, Danah, 187
Bow. *See* Johnson, Bow
Breaking Bad, 19, 63, 65, 66, 75–78, 80, 81
the brute, 28, 45, 46, 47, 287

Carney, Nikita, 153, 157, 158, 262, 273
#ChooseBeautiful, 217–22, 224, 226, 227, 247
citizenship and consumerism, 215, 216, 292
civic narcissism, 183, 203, 204
clicktivism, 137, 139, 140, 171
Clinton, Hillary, 17, 66, 89, 91, 92, 143, 154, 155, 174, 178, 180–92, 196, 197, 199, 226, 281, 287, 289
collaboration, 5, 9–10, 29, 146, 165, 168, 170–72, 186, 200, 201, 213; to construct meaning, 1, 2, 13, 18, 20, 27, 28, 31, 54, 140, 178, 207, 215, 275, 279, 293
color-blind ideology, 16, 142, 143, 153, 156, 157, 160, 180, 190, 199, 229–35, 245–47, 282
community, 4, 9, 140, 149, 151, 152, 157, 192, 193, 196, 202–04, 250, 257, 258, 262, 267, 276, 288, 291; African American, 14, 29, 33, 49, 55, 56, 62–64; Asian American, 113, 130, 133; Latinx, 63, 64, 72, 78, 81, 82, 87, 88, 91, 96
content analysis, 287; hermeneutic, 20, 21, 23; ethnographic, 21;

interpretive, 20, 21, 23, 229, 251, 277; iterative process, 23, 253; sampling, 21, 22, 142, 25; sensitizing concepts, 23; theoretical saturation, 22, 23, 252
content injection, 164, 165, 183, 188, 198
context collapse, 5, 251
consumer engagement, 211–16, 285
consumerism, 17, 18, 217, 218, 221; political expression, 215, 216, 292
consumerist capitalism. *See* consumerism
consumerist ideology. *See* consumerism
#Cookie, 27, 31, 33, 38
Cosby Show, 27, 53
countermovement, 143–45, 151, 152, 155–57, 160, 161, 163, 165, 273, 280, 281, 288
counterpublics, 2, 8, 13, 143, 288–91; networked, 14, 70, 87, 93, 97, 119, 134, 142, 145, 197, 206, 279, 280, 281, 288, 289; subaltern, 8, 14, 19, 142, 154, 288, 289. *See also* publics
cultural citizenship, 8, 16–18, 292
culture, 5, 7, 13, 14, 18, 85, 97, 117, 125, 156, 223, 231, 245, 265, 277, 283, 284, 286–288; mainstream, 9, 10, 13, 73, 88, 96, 97, 100, 101, 133, 154, 230, 251, 282, 283, 285, 286, 287, 289, 293; participatory, 9, 10, 13, 14, 18, 16, 216, 293; popular, 10, 12, 16, 18, 31, 49, 65, 87, 102, 103, 277, 278, 286; renegotiation, 132–33, 134, 277. *See also* digital culture
culture industries, 8, 15, 285, 287
cyberbalkanization, 200

Dahlberg, Lincoln, 291
Dahlgren, Peter, 7, 9, 162
Dean, Jodi, 12, 15
debate, 3, 7, 11, 12, 17–19, 27, 40, 145, 146, 167, 228, 236, 251, 262, 271, 272, 278, 284; political, 200; about potential social media, 7, 8, 13, 24, 139, 174, 291; presidential, 19, 191, 192, 194, 261; scholarly, 52, 216, 217. *See also* dialogue
deliberative democracy, 186, 207, 291
deliberative enclaves, 260
#Deplorables, 10, 178, 190, 191
Devious Maids, 63, 65–68, 70–75, 79, 87, 93, 94, 286
dialogic pluralism, 186, 200, 268
dialogue, 14, 18, 138, 141–46, 166, 212, 236, 247, 249, 251, 261, 277, 280, 283; agonistic, 12, 166, 168, 170–72, 177, 186–88, 200, 201, 204–7, 270, 276, 281, 291–93; antagonistic, 12, 169–71, 177, 186, 191, 198, 200, 201, 205, 206, 271, 276, 281, 293; co-optive, 143, 165, 171; collaborative, 146, 147, 165, 168, 170, 171, 186, 201, 291; constructive, 11, 12, 165, 186, 254, 268–70, 272; cross-political, 175–77, 185–89, 198, 207, 264, 273, 281, 282, 291; deliberative, 20, 169, 173, 177, 186, 188, 204, 205, 206, 207, 270, 281, 291; inflammatory, 11, 12, 177, 271, 272, 281; lack thereof, 183, 270; political, 16, 17, 174, 175, 186, 215, 271; rules, 266–72; about race, 230–33
digital culture, 2, 3, 7, 10, 12, 15, 18–21, 23, 24, 31, 137, 277, 283, 285, 293; bricolage, 62, 97, 133, 279; remediation, 62, 279
digital divide, 13, 283
discourse, 6, 34, 35, 41, 55, 62, 96, 97, 105, 111, 137, 138, 141, 167, 168, 178, 188, 201, 204, 222, 229, 230, 236, 255, 256, 262, 278, 290; consumerist, 17; counterhegemonic, 7, 54, 70, 103, 146, 284; co-opting, 143; dominant, 15, 19, 93, 102, 143, 152, 155, 177, 226, 280, 287; feminist, 144, 145, 146; hegemonic, 13, 14, 16, 30, 102, 105; mainstream, 12, 14, 151, 152, 289; oppositional, 143; political, 11, 206, 237, 238; populist, 16; post-racial, 157, 158, 161, 180, 231, 234, 262, 281, 282, 286; racist, 16; resist, 102; vernacular, 13, 14, 30; virtual, 30. *See also* Americanism; postfeminism

discrimination, 51, 120, 141, 144, 149, 150, 151, 155, 156, 166, 171, 193, 194, 232, 244, 262, 281
Dove, 17, 217–22, 281, 286
Dr. Ken, 99, 103, 106, 108, 110, 112–14, 115–17, 123, 127, 128

echo chamber, 10–11, 175, 176, 187, 264
Empire, 19, 27, 31, 33, 34, 38, 39, 44–48, 53–55, 57–60, 256
Escobar, Pablo, 74–81, 78–81, 86
exchanges, 37, 38, 60, 76, 91, 112, 113, 186, 187, 271, 284. *See also* dialogue

Facebook, 3, 11, 16, 71, 99, 102, 143, 177, 197, 211, 215, 250, 269, 272, 273
feminism, 30, 42, 140, 141, 143–46, 148–50, 157, 161, 169–71, 217, 218, 222, 226. *See also* hashtag feminism; postfeminism
#FemininitySoFragile, 144–45, 156, 160, 162, 280, 286, 288
feminist consumerism, 217–18
#Ferguson, 10
Fraser, Nancy, 289
#FreshOffTheBoat. *See Fresh Off the Boat*
Fresh Off the Boat, 6, 19, 99, 103, 112, 117, 118, 121, 123, 126, 128, 129, 132, 286
Fring, Gustavo, 76, 80, 81
Fuchs, Christian, 14

Gerbaudo, Paolo, 10, 166–67
grounded theory, 20, 23, 253
#GrowingUpBlack, 32, 48, 51
Guo, Lei, 30, 65

Habermas, Jurgen 7, 8, 11, 12, 16, 165, 169, 186, 200, 207, 268, 291
Habermasian. *See* dialogue, deliberative
the harlot, 64, 71, 72, 73
hashtag: counter, 143, 145, 146, 284; creating community, 29, 49, 54, 120, 134, 162, 191–93, 203, 204, 263, 272, 276, 288, 289; feminism, 140; facilitator of conversation, 4, 10, 163–65, 172, 176, 185, 191, 198, 205, 206, 226, 276, 282; hijacking of, 50, 165, 183, 188, 198, 204, 226, 281, 284; semiotic frame, 4, 105, 224, 227, 279, 287. *See also* activism
hashtag activism. *See* activism
Hawaii Five-O, 103, 106, 111, 118, 121
Hill Collins, Patricia, 39, 40, 42, 47–50, 55, 57
Hispanic. *See* Latinx
#HispanicGirlsUnited, 66, 70, 72–74, 83–89, 95, 263, 265, 266, 268, 273, 288
the hombre, 81, 97
#HowIMetYourRacism, 103, 118
#HowItFeelsToBeABlackGirl, 32, 33, 36, 42, 43, 51, 52, 55, 59, 61
How to Get Away with Murder (HTGAWM). *See* #HTGAWM
homophily, 175, 176, 265
#HTGAWM, 31, 35, 38, 44, 46

identity, 3, 15, 23, 152, 163, 166, 221, 222, 254, 258; brand, 213, 214; collective, 146, 162, 163, 167, 171, 263, 284, 290; denial, 115; ethnic, 14, 17, 19, 22, 251, 279, 280; gender, 19, 144–45; micro celebrity, 258; national, 180, 181, 189; and the political, 148, 292, 292. *See also* African American, identity; Asian American, identity; Latinx, identity; performativity
#IfTheyGunnedMeDown, 10, 30
#IAmANastyWomanBecause, 178, 190, 191, 195, 196
immigration, 174, 191, 202, 228, 236–44, 257, 275; undocumented, 88, 191, 205, 236, 239–42, 268. *See also* Latinx, immigration
impression management, 254, 255
#ImWithHer, 154, 174, 178, 179, 181–85, 188–90, 192, 196
intertextuality, 46–47, 75

Jaggar, Alison M., 206
Jane the Virgin, 63, 65, 75, 79, 81

Jenkins, Henry, 9, 12
the Jezebel, 28, 42
Johnson, Bow, 32, 37, 40, 43, 56

Keating, Annalise, 32, 35, 36, 38, 41, 46

Latinidad, 82, 83, 97
Latinx: accent, 64, 68, 69, 83, 84, 86, 96; culture, 19, 63–65, 82–85, 88, 92, 94, 96, 97; family, 66, 75, 81, 82, 85, 88–95, 97; femininity, 64, 65, 66–74; identity, 17, 64, 82–86, 96, 97; immigration, 66, 87, 88, 92, 97; language, 64, 67, 68, 72, 73, 82–86; masculinity, 64, 65, 74–81, 95, 96; representation, 18, 63, 64; Twitter, 17, 18. *See also* community, Latinx
Latinx men: criminal, 64, 75–79; comic relief, 64; fathers, 96; sexuality, 75, 79, 80
Latinx women: clown, 64, 66, 67, 69, 71, 75; sexuality, 64, 72–73; temper, 71–72, 96
#LetLizSpeak, 178, 203
#LightGirls, 30
Loader, Brian D., 177
L'Oreal, 217, 218, 225, 225, 226, 281
#Lumber84. *See* 84 Lumber
Lyons, Cookie, 27, 31–35, 38, 39, 54, 55, 57, 59, 60

machismo, 74, 75, 89
#MAGA, 157, 174, 177–84, 186–89, 192, 204, 205
mammy, 28, 35, 36, 43, 54, 60
Maragh, Raven S., 216
marginalization: construction of meaning, 12, 13, 17, 146, 154, 249, 280, 285, 286, 188; formation of community 263, 279, 280, 188; lack of equality, 144, 155; perception of, 196, 199, 200, 207, 280, 288–90; use of social media, 2, 8, 18, 140, 141, 143, 191, 193–95, 201, 216, 253, 286, 288–90; voices and/or opinions, 12, 13, 14
marianismo, 89, 93–95
#MasculinitySoFragile, 142, 144, 145, 147, 148, 162, 169, 170, 280
McRobbie, Angela, 224
meme, 1, 17, 38, 39, 46, 48, 58, 92, 154, 192, 252, 254, 255, 292
mentions (@), 4, 128, 170, 176, 184, 185, 195, 251
Modern Family, 63, 66–74, 90, 91
Morozov, Evgeny, 139, 174
Mouffe, Chantal, 11–12, 170, 172, 186, 187, 206, 268, 270, 271, 281, 291
#MyYellowFaceStory, 103, 120, 122, 127, 283, 286, 287

Narcos, 63, 65, 70, 73–81, 86
narratives: corporate, 20, 212, 222, 227, 243, 281; creation of counter narratives, 14, 15, 30–31, 37, 44, 53, 62, 70, 87, 104, 111, 133–34, 140, 142, 143, 145, 146, 155, 166, 172, 192, 197, 212, 214, 218, 249, 251, 273, 279, 284–88; creation of, 31, 142, 167; dominant, 19, 62, 74, 75, 93, 100, 104, 130, 131, 138, 172, 178; hegemonic, 7, 12, 29–30, 134, 145, 221, 287; interpretation of, 20, 33, 44, 80, 212, 214, 227, 229, 235, 236, 238, 243–45; negotiation of, 18, 20, 46, 69, 70, 80, 141, 168, 188, 212, 215, 217, 227, 229, 232, 234, 236, 238, 243, 282; reproduction of dominant narrative, 16, 30, 62, 106, 157, 172, 180, 222, 224–26, 244, 246, 247, 281, 286, 287; resisting dominant narratives, 7, 29, 30, 44, 53, 65, 73, 78, 106, 123, 140, 141, 146, 166, 178, 193, 201, 230, 245
#NastyWoman, 174, 178, 190–93, 195, 198, 205
National Park Service, 201
neoliberalism, 90, 143, 190, 221, 222, 226
#NoBanNoWall, 178, 200, 201, 205, 237, 244
#NotAllMen, 142, 145, 146, 156, 161, 163
#NotMiAbuela, 19, 63, 65, 66, 91–93, 260, 273, 286, 287

#NotYourAsianFetish, 104, 105
#NotYourAsianSideKick, 103–5, 107, 115, 118, 142, 145, 147–51, 155
#NotYourAsianTigerDad, 103, 127, 129
#NotYourAsianTigerMom, 103, 108, 125–27, 129–32

#Occupy, 137, 139, 141
Occupy Wall Street, 2. *See also* #Occupy
Ono, Vincent N., 101
Orientalism, 114, 120, 121
#OscarsSoWhite, 31, 103, 285

Pachuca-chola-homegirl, 73, 74, 96
Pantsuit Nation. *See* #PantSuitNation
#PantSuitNation, 138, 141–43, 147, 153–55
Papacharissi, Zizi, 7, 8, 11, 15, 17, 140, 174–76, 183, 203, 215, 216, 279, 280, 285, 290, 291, 292
participation, 3–5, 7, 9, 10, 12–15, 18, 21, 31, 59, 139–41, 162, 174, 175, 183, 213, 215, 216, 240, 250–53, 262, 265, 266, 272, 276, 277, 279, 283, 284, 287, 289, 290, 293
participatory culture. *See* culture; participatory
perfomative excess, 65, 66, 70, 109
performativity, 5, 17, 65, 148, 155, 162, 213, 214, 221–22, 224, 227, 241, 247, 252, 256, 282
Pham, Vincent N., 101
political: campaigns, 66, 91, 173, 174, 177–80, 182–84, 188, 190, 191, 194, 199, 206, 280–82, 289; polarization, 175–77, 181, 187, 199, 260, 270
Pope, Olivia, 32, 40, 42, 43, 56, 59
postfeminism, 33, 34, 221, 222, 224, 226, 247, 281, 282, 286
presidential candidates, 19, 66, 91, 173, 173, 177, 191, 261, 289
prosumer, 216
publics: networked, 4, 19, 54, 62, 97, 140–42, 280, 281, 283, 290, 291, 293; personal, 5, 13
public sphere, 1, 2, 7–14, 16–18, 20, 21, 24 137, 142, 162, 169, 172, 173, 175, 177, 183, 186, 197, 200, 207, 261, 277, 280, 281, 283, 285, 289–93; pseudo, 13

Quantico, 31, 99, 103, 16, 121

#RaceTogether, 2, 217, 227–35
racism, 16, 17, 36, 50, 51, 56, 72, 84, 103, 110, 117, 120, 121, 131, 141, 143, 145, 150, 153, 156, 157, 160, 164, 165, 171, 194, 205, 229–32, 234, 235, 244, 245, 268, 282
Ramirez Berg, Charles, 64, 66, 70–71, 77–78
reciprocity, 4, 9, 11, 176, 213, 264
#TheResistance, 178, 201–5
Respeto, 92, 94, 95
retweet, 5, 10, 70, 72, 96, 110–13, 117, 169, 176, 182, 187, 188, 220, 222, 223, 244, 251, 261, 276, 282
Robot Asian, 112, 113
Rock, Chris, 46
Rosa, Jonathan, 14, 30

Salamanca, Tuco, 63, 75, 77, 81, 93
Sanders, Bernie, 191, 198
Sapphire, 28, 36, 166
#SayHerName, 32, 138, 141, 142, 144, 147, 148, 152, 155, 280
Scandal, 18, 19, 27, 31, 32, 34, 38, 40, 42–44, 54, 56, 60
self-expansion theory, 213–14
sexism, 36, 47, 144–46, 151, 153, 154, 161, 162, 181, 199, 205, 244, 262
Shaw, Frances, 154
#ShePersisted, 178, 203
signifyin', 29
the sissy, 28, 47
social capital, 213; bonding, 197, 198, 200, 202–04, 207, 281, 290; bridging, 198, 200, 202, 207
social media, 201; alternative source of information, 6, 274–75, 282; anticipated response, 257–60, 261,

282; brand consumption, 212–16; collaboration, 5–7; connectivity, 4, 5, 137; corporate ownership of, 14; political involvement, 16–18, 138–40, 146, 174–77; interactivity, 8–12; marketing, 20, 211–16, 246; meaning making, 1, 12–15, 20, 23, 29, 30, 65, 102; ownership of, 260; uses of, 2, 3, 4, 6, 9–11, 148, 249–61, 263–65, 267–75, 282
social movements, 2, 10, 19, 137–41, 163, 164, 167, 171, 274, 290
social justice, 19, 97, 137–39, 141, 142, 146, 149, 161, 171, 172, 189, 220, 225, 256, 266, 277, 280
#SolidarityIsForWhiteWomen, 142, 144, 148, 149, 150
slacktivism, 137, 139
snowflake, 205. *See also* #Snowflake
#Snowflake, 178, 200, 204
the spitfire, 66, 67, 70
Starbucks, 155, 212, 227, 229–34, 281
#StarringJohnCho, 19, 99, 103, 111
stereotype reversal, 70–71
stereotypes: contesting, 74, 76, 80, 86, 94, 95, 105, 106, 112, 120, 130, 144, 145, 194, 195, 213, 262, 278, 279; negotiation of, 19, 36, 47, 61, 62, 66–71, 77, 85, 96, 97, 109–11, 131–33, 287; racial, 15, 23, 28, 29, 31, 39, 63–65, 75, 99–101, 121, 128; reproduction of, 16, 30, 35, 37, 42, 45, 53, 54, 59, 60, 65, 71, 72, 81, 102, 107, 125–27, 256, 278, 79
subpolitics, 140, 141
symbolic annihilation, 235
symbolic interactionism, 162, 163

#TacoGate, 66, 178, 191, 194
techno-optimism, 8, 9, 11, 13, 62, 174, 175, 254, 283, 290
techno-skeptics, 10, 139, 171, 174
#ThanksgivingWithBlackFamilies, 32, 53, 54
the tragic mulatto, 28, 32, 39–41
trending topics, 1, 4, 17–19, 21, 22, 27, 33, 63, 82, 103, 142, 162, 201, 252, 259, 266, 267, 286, 288
trolling, 145, 165
tropicalism, 73, 85, 97
Trump, Donald, 66, 153, 157, 168, 174, 178–206, 236–38, 243–46, 254, 256, 259, 263, 273, 281, 289
Twitter: Black Twitter, 2, 14, 29–31; collapse of private and public, 5, 13, 17, 67, 97, 105, 147, 179–81, 203–4, 251, 256, 282, 291, 292; as a community, 4, 9, 14, 140, 152, 162, 192, 193, 203, 250, 251, 257, 258, 262, 267, 276, 288; corporate ownership, 14, 17, 18; history of, 3; popularity of, 3; *See also* African Americans, Twitter; Asian Americans, Twitter; Latinx, Twitter
Twitter use: to celebrate identity, 134, 241; creating group identity, 14, 62, 133, 134, 162, 163, 166–67, 171, 250–51, 263, 279, 280, 284, 290; creating personal identity, 221, 222, 227, 241, 247, 250–51, 254–55; causing change, 140, 141, 171, 268, 272, 282; empowerment, 29, 104, 105, 219–26, 263, 281; to engage with political opponents, 165, 171, 185, 186, 198, 200, 207, 262, 270, 281, 282; engaging with politics, 250, 256–59, 261–62, 280, 282; to gain recognition, 5, 7, 12, 30, 88, 105, 140, 147, 149, 151, 152, 199, 254, 280, 284, 289; to give voice to marginalization, 8, 14, 140, 141, 165, 191, 193, 201, 206, 216, 253, 254, 275, 276, 280; power to shape public discourse, 6–7, 13, 62, 97, 137, 141, 146, 201, 256, 280; power to shape opinions, 173, 255, 256; reframe events, 6, 97, 131, 132, 147–49, 155–62; second screen, 6, 17, 31, 37, 133, 216, 228, 255, 256,

261; site of resistance, 7, 29, 30, 41, 53, 65, 85, 95, 102, 105, 118, 122, 146, 201, 238–40, 244–46, 256; support, 119, 120, 133, 147, 223, 255, 263, 268, 280

Ugly Betty, 64, 66, 67, 87, 89, 90
The Unbreakable Kimmy Schmidt, 103, 109, 110, 121

Van Dijck, José, 201, 224
Vergara, Sofia, 67, 68, 71
virality, 12, 15, 58, 218, 227, 228
virtual movements, 138–43, 146, 147, 153, 155, 156, 162–64, 171, 206, 280, 281

#WeAccept, 213, 217, 227, 228, 243–47, 281, 282
Weeds, 66, 72, 75, 81, 92
#WhiteWashedOut, 103, 110, 115, 118, 138, 141, 142, 164
#WomenWhoVoteTrump, 178, 191–93, 196–99, 289
#WorthSaying, 211, 218, 219, 223–27, 247, 281

yellow face, 100, 103, 118
Yellow Peril, 100, 101, 108, 131
#YesAllWomen, 137, 142, 145–47, 155, 156, 161, 163, 280, 288
YouTube, 11, 14, 15, 16, 30, 65, 99, 102, 103, 211, 215, 216, 240

About the Author

Judith E. Rosenbaum (PhD, Radboud University Nijmegen) is an Assistant Professor of Communication and Journalism at the University of Maine. She previously worked at Albany State University in Georgia as a faculty member in the Mass Communication program. Her interest in social media was first piqued in 1995 when she joined a digital bulletin board system. She quickly discovered this was a great way to stay in touch with old friends, make new ones, and procrastinate. As she progressed through her academic career, her interest in social media became more professional. Rosenbaum's research examines how people interact with the media and what factors drive this interaction. Moreover, she is interested in how people's media use can become a tool to engender individual and social change. Her research projects rely on a variety of methods, including quantitative, qualitative, and mixed method techniques. She has published in a variety of journals and edited volumes, including *Media Psychology, Communication Research, Psychology of Popular Media Culture, Participations,* and *Communication Yearbook*. Her research has also involved community-based research projects, including an NIMHD-funded program aimed at reducing health disparities in Southwest Georgia, and a crime reduction and prevention program funded by the Department of Justice via the Byrne Innovation Program. Even though her bulletin board–days are behind her, Rosenbaum still likes to spend time on various social media platforms. On Twitter, she can be found under @JudithRBaum.

CPSIA information can be obtained
at www.ICGtesting.com
Printed in the USA
BVOW08*0322231017
498274BV00002B/4/P

9 781498 546904